POLYMATHS OF ISLAM

POLYMATHS OF ISLAM

POWER AND NETWORKS OF KNOWLEDGE IN CENTRAL ASIA

JAMES PICKETT

CORNELL UNIVERSITY PRESS
Ithaca and London

Publication of this book was made possible, in part, by a grant from the First Book Subvention Program of the Association for Slavic, East European, and Eurasian Studies.

First published 2020 by Cornell University Press

Printed in the United States of America

Library of Congress Cataloging-in-Publication Data
Names: Pickett, James, 1983– author.
Title: Polymaths of Islam : Power and Networks of Knowledge in Central Asia / James Pickett.
Description: Ithaca, New York : Cornell University Press, 2020. | Includes bibliographical references and index.
Identifiers: LCCN 2020000455 (print) | LCCN 2020000456 (ebook) | ISBN 9781501750243 (cloth) | ISBN 9781501750250 (epub) | ISBN 9781501750830 (pdf)
Subjects: LCSH: Ulama—Uzbekistan—Bukhoro Region—19th century. | Ulama—Political aspects—Uzbekistan—Bukhoro Region. | Bukhoro Region (Uzbekistan) —History—19th century. | Asia, Central—Civilization—Islamic influences.
Classification: LCC DS328.2. P48 2020 (print) | LCC DS328.2 (ebook) | DDC 958.7—dc23
LC record available at https://lccn.loc.gov/2020000455
LC ebook record available at https://lccn.loc.gov/2020000456

For Herb Pickett (1943–2018), a polymath in his own right

Contents

Acknowledgments *ix*

List of Abbreviations *xiii*

Technical Note *xv*

Introduction: Islamic Scholars and the Central Asian Backdrop 1

1. Defamiliarizing the Familiar: Conceptualizing Religion and Culture in Turko-Persia 18

2. Centering Bukhara: The Reconstruction and Mythologization of an Abode of Knowledge 42

3. Bukhara Center: Islamic Scholars as a Network of Human Exchange 73

4. Patricians of Bukhara: Turkic Nobility, Persianate Pedagogy, and Islamic Society 98

5. High Persianate Intellectuals: The Many, Many Guises of the Ulama 127

6. Between Sharia and the Beloved: Culture and Contradiction in Persianate Sunnism 161

7. Opportunity from Upheaval: Scholarly Dynasties between Nadir Shah and the Bolshevik Revolution 196

8. The Sovereign and the Sage: The Precarious, Paradoxical Relationship between the Ulama and Temporal Power 218

Conclusion: United in Eclecticism 243

Epilogue: Efflorescence before the Eclipse 248

Bibliography 257

Index 291

Acknowledgments

This book has been in the works for over a decade—almost exactly the amount of time students typically spent in a madrasa. I have had a tremendous amount of help along the way, accumulating more debts than I can possibly acknowledge here.

This research was made possible by funding from the Mellon Foundation, Princeton's Porter Ogden Jacobus Fellowship program, IREX, Fulbright-Hays/Institute of International Education, and American Councils of Learned Societies. The Social Science Research Council's InterAsia Program, in particular, was instrumental not only in providing vital financial support but also as a forum for intellectual exchange.

I began this research at Princeton University, and I am profoundly grateful for the unparalleled mentorship of Stephen Kotkin, who dared me to push boundaries and taught me to think like a historian. Michael Cook and Jo-Ann Gross were closely involved in my research from the start and imparted indispensable technical depth and regional expertise. At Princeton I am also indebted to the guidance of Amineh Mahallati, Ekaterina Pravilova, Bhavani Raman, Michael Reynolds, Cyrus Schayegh, and Dan Sheffield; and for the support of colleagues in my program, including Hannah-Louise Clark, Simon Fuchs, Zack Kagan-Guthrie, Radha Kumar, Christian Sahner, and Seiji Shirane.

I would never have set out to study Central Asia in the first place were it not for the undergraduate tutelage of Adeeb Khalid, who has been an active presence ever since then. Eric McGlinchey provided early encouragement to embark on this path, and Scott Levi generously helped me land on my feet in Uzbekistan. My early trajectory was also shaped by superb Georgetown University scholars—James Millward, Richard Stites, and John Voll.

I am fortunate to have found an institutional home away from home at the Institute of Iranian Studies of the Austrian Academy of Sciences. The scholars there have fundamentally shaped this research: Ulfat Abdurasulov, Justine Landau, Christine Nölle-Karimi, and Florian Schwarz. I am especially grateful to Paolo Sartori and Thomas Welsford for honest and detailed feedback at every stage of this project.

I am deeply indebted to Devin DeWeese, who journeyed to Pittsburgh to workshop the draft manuscript in its entirety. I am similarly grateful to my colleagues at the University of Pittsburgh who contributed to the workshop (Raja Adal, Reid Andrews, Bill Chase, Niklas Frykman, Michel Gobat, Diego Holstein, Holger Hoock, Ruth Mostern, Carla Nappi, Lara Putnam, Marcus Rediker, Pernille Røge, Amir Syed, Gregor Thum, Molly Warsh, Mari Webel, and many others), as well as to the Humanities Center for a helpful colloquium on one of the chapters (especially discussants Jeanette Jouili and Neil Doshi). Also at Pitt, Ryan Horne provided constant guidance on map design. I benefited tremendously from my InterAsia postdoctoral fellowship at Yale, and the feedback provided by Tiraana Bains, Rohit De, Shivi Kalyanakrishnan, Peter Perdue, Ayesha Ramachandran, Helen Siu, and Julie Stephens.

Ulfat Abdurasulov, Akmal Bazarbaev, Daniel Beben, Alfrid Bustanov, Devin DeWeese, Jeff Eden, Nargiza Ismatova, Christine Nölle-Karimi, Paolo Sartori, Amin Venjara, Andreas Wilde, Waleed Ziad—all generously shared invaluable leads and sources with me, in addition to providing helpful feedback on content. I am indebted to Owen Cornwall and Matthew Melvin-Koushki for suggesting appropriately literary translations (any errors are, of course, my own). I am grateful for chapter feedback from Nick Abbott, Christopher Baker (and others at a 2014 workshop in Bishkek), Chris Fort, Nile Green (and others at his Persianate conference series), Sam Hodgkin, Artemy Kalinovsky, Mana Kia, Heather Lanthorn, Bruce Lawrence, Robert McChesney, Tara Mendola, Alexander Morrison, Douglas Northrop (and others at the University of Michigan *kruzhok*), Beatrice Penati, Patryk Reid, Ron Sela, Urmy Shukla, Eric Tagliacozzo (and others at the 2017 "Asia Inside Out" workshop in Hanoi), Rian Thum, Kevin Van Bledel, and Andreas Wilde.

This book would be much impoverished absent the incredible support of Ambassador George Krol, who will in my mind forever be a shining example of how diplomacy can advance cultural exchange. I am grateful to my host families: Timur, Kamila, Rustam, and Gulnara; Tatiana and Diana; Boris and Lidya. From the scholarly community in Uzbekistan, I benefitted tremendously from colleagues—Babur Aminov, Akmal Bazarbaev, Aftandil Erkinov, Saidolimkhon Gaziev, Sanjar Gulamov, Nasriddin Mirzaev, Saidakbar Mukhammadaminov, and especially Bakhtiyar Babajanov—whose erudition and generosity was an inspiration. In Russia, I thank Nuriya Akhatovna, Milana Azarkina, Elena Firsova, Aleksei Khismatullin, Ilias Mustaqimov, Olga Yastrebova; and Najaf Haider, Chander Shekar, and Ustad Muhammad Suleman Siddiqi in India. I am grateful to the many archive and library administrators—too many to name—who translated my research questions into call numbers and put the archival wheels into motion. The project would not have been possible without Bakhrom Abdukhalimov of the Uzbek Academy of Sciences and his support of international academic collaboration.

Roger Haydon's superb oversight as an editor ensured that the final product rose to the very high bar he sets, as did the tireless efforts of CUP's editing team—Karen Hwa, Irina Burns, and Sarah Noell. The book was also improved tremendously by the peer reviewers, as well as by the reviewers of the two sections of chapter 7, originally published in "Nadir Shah's Peculiar Central Asian Legacy," published in the *International Journal of Middle East Studies* 48, no. 3 (July 2016): 491–510.

This project rests on the support network provided by my family: Herb and Nancy; Jen and Chad; Tim and Mary; Melanie, Clayton, Claire, and Luke; Chuck, Martha, Michael, and Sarah. Jessica always encouraged me to dive in headfirst—and then showed me how to do it better. She is an emotional touchstone and invaluable partner in crime.

Abbreviations

AV IVR RAN	Archive of the Orientalists of the Russian Academy of Sciences (Arkhiv vostokovedov Instituta vostochnykh rukopisei RAN), Saint Petersburg
AVPRI	Archive of Foreign Policy of the Russian Empire (Arkhiv vneshnei politiki Rossiiskoi Imperii), Moscow
BL	British Library, London
IIaLI AN RT	G. Ibragimov Institute of Language, Literature, and Art: Tatarstan Academy of Sciences (Institut iazyka, literatury i iskusstva imeni G. Ibragimova Akademii nauk Respubliki Tatarstan), Kazan
IVANTaj	Rudaki Institute of Institute of Language, Literature, Oriental and Written Heritage, Academy of Sciences of the Republic of Tajikistan (Institut iazyka, literatury, vostokovedeniia i pis'mennogo naslediia imeni Rudaki Akademii nauk Tadzhikistana), Dushanbe
IVANUz	Al-Biruni Institute of Oriental Studies, Academy of Sciences of the Republic of Uzbekistan (Institut vostokovedeniia imeni Abu Raikhana Beruni Akademii nauk Respubliki Uzbekistana), Tashkent
IVR RAN	Institute of Oriental Manuscripts of the Russian Academy of Sciences (Sankt-Peterburgskii filial Instituta vostokovedenii, Rossiiskoi Akademii Nauk: Institut vostochnykh rukopisei), Saint Petersburg
NAI	National Archive of India, Delhi
NBKGU	Manuscripts and Rare Books section of Kazan State University (Nauchnoi biblioteki imeni N.I. Lobachevskogo Kazanskogo gosudarstvennogo universiteta, Otdel rukopisei i redkikh knig), Kazan
NBSPGU	Oriental Department of the Scientific Library of Saint Petersburg State University (Vostochnyi otdel nauchnoi biblioteki imeni Gor'kogo SPbGU), Saint Petersburg

NBT	National Library of Tajikistan (Natsional'naia biblioteka Tadzhikistana), Dushanbe
OR RNB	Rare Books Collection of the National Library of Russia (Otdel redkikh knig Rossiiskoi natsional'noi bilbioteka), Saint Petersburg
RGADA	Russian State Archive of Early Acts (Rossiiskii gosudarstvennyi arkhiv drevnikh aktov), Moscow
RGVIA	Russian State Military-Historical Archive (Rossiiskii gosudarstvennyi voenno-istoricheskii archiv), Moscow
RGIA	Russian State Historical Archive (Rossiiskii gosudarstvennyi istoricheskii arkhiv), Saint Petersburg
TsGARUz	The State Archive of Uzbekistan (Tsentral'nyi archiv Respubliki Uzbekistana), Tashkent

Technical Note

For the sake of readability, I have elected to employ diacriticals in the notes but omit them from the main text (following Robert McChesney's lead in *Waqf in Central Asia*). I adhere to the *International Journal of Middle East Studies* (*IJMES*) Persian transliteration schema for both Persian- and Arabic-origin words to avoid separate transliterations of the same term (e.g., *maẕhab* instead of *madhhab*, regardless of the dominant language of the source). I transliterate the final "ha" in Persian words as *a* rather than *ih*, and observe *majhūl* voweling (i.e., ē, ō), to match eastern pronunciation, both of which constitute minor deviations from the *IJMES* schema. With a few exceptions, I transliterate only the Arabic singular rather than irregular plural to avoid confusion on the part of nonspecialists, even when it results in an English plural of an Arabic word. Words from modern Tajik and Uzbek (i.e., written in modified Cyrillic or Latin alphabets) are normalized to match their equivalents as written in the Arabic alphabet.

For Turkic-origin words, I follow the field convention of transcribing rather than transliterating in order to approximate the original pronunciation. I rely on the schema in András Bodrogligeti's *A Grammar of Chagatay* combined with elements of *IJMES* to better streamline with Arabic and Persian conventions (e.g., *ch* rather than *ç* or *č*, *gh* rather than *ǧ* or *ġ*, *ng* for the nasal Turkic *ŋ*). For many proper nouns (e.g., tribal designations) of Turkic origin, I have followed the lead of Yuri Bregel (especially in *Firdaws al-Iqbāl: History of Khorezm*) wherever possible.

Russian transliteration follows the simplified Library of Congress conventions, dropping connecting diacritical marks. For the few words of South Asian origin, I follow a schema developed by Pasha Mohamad Khan to better align with conventional Islamicate renderings.

I have converted hijri dates to the Common Era equivalent. For place names, I use the modern spelling for well-known locales (e.g., Khorezm) but transliterate the less commonly known ones.

POLYMATHS OF ISLAM

Introduction
Islamic Scholars and the Central Asian Backdrop

This book is about the Islamic scholars of Bukhara during the long nineteenth century. Much like an image in a rear-view mirror, every element of that description is more extensive than it appears. "Islamic" brings to mind scripture and mosque, but the agents in this book considered poetry, occult sciences, and medicine to be encompassed by the term as well. "Scholars" conjures the image of stodgy professors confined to the university, but the English translation scarcely does justice to the Arabic term "ulama." The ulama taught in Islamic colleges (madrasas); they also carried out the administrative functions of the state, led mystical orders, and coordinated merchant networks. "Bukhara" refers narrowly to a museum-city now located in Uzbekistan, but I focus on the site as the pivot of a much grander network of social-cultural exchange. Finally, "long nineteenth century" is a European historical term referring to the period from the French Revolution in 1789 to the start of World War I in 1914. But I have in mind an even longer nineteenth century stretching from the collapse of Nadir Shah Afshar's empire in 1747 to the Bolshevik Revolution in 1917. This period encompasses the zenith of the Persianate high cultural world and its twilight.

Islamic scholars were among the most influential individuals in their society, and that power rested on their mastery of diverse forms of knowledge rather than birthright. Instead of imagining those varied competencies and practices as embodied by separate professions, this book conceptualizes them as distinct practices and disciplines mastered by a single milieu. Instead of imagining stratified castes of "ulama" as against "sufis" as against "poets," we have a unified social group of multitalented polymaths selectively performing sharia, asceticism, and poetry as circumstances dictated. These polymaths of Islam were the custodians of the only form of institutionalized high culture on offer in Central Asia. Their authoritative command over many different forms of knowledge—from medicine to law to epistolography and beyond—allowed them to accumulate substantial power and to establish enduring family dynasties. The Turkic military elite relied on these scholars to administer the state, but the ulama possessed an independent source of authority rooted in learning, which created tension between these two elite groups with profound ramifications for the region's history.

Most of the Islamic scholars in this book were enmeshed in the cultural institutions of the city-state-cum-Russian-protectorate of Bukhara. Bukhara served as their educational foundation, and those same individuals mythologized the city into a timeless cultural-religious pole, an epicenter of Turko-Perso-Islamic high culture. In this dialectic, the ulama both shaped and were shaped by the city of Bukhara, both as an idea and an institution. The specific intellectual competencies underwritten by the city's vast educational system allowed Bukhara to serve as the center of a transregional educational network that stretched far beyond its political boundaries. The more the specific array of knowledge forms cultivated in Bukhara resonated in adjacent regions, the more students from those areas flocked to its madrasas. Bukhara's centrality was the product of a sustained mythologization project that kicked into high gear in the early modern period, continued into the era of Russian imperial expansion, and rested on centuries of cultural production, both physical and textual. Indeed, the relatively recent resurgence of Bukhara—dating to the sixteenth century and reaching a crescendo in the nineteenth—was a testament to the creative power of the ulama and their patrons.

The chapters that follow revolve around these intersecting themes: knowledge, culture, religion, and the ways by which Islamic scholars marshaled all three to wield power. Imagine for a moment that you were born in Central Asia during the long nineteenth century and were lucky enough to be sent to one of Bukhara's prestigious madrasas. You spend at least a decade learning highly intricate, often otherworldly disciplines written in what was effectively a foreign language. What would you do with such a skill set? What happened when one of your social roles came into conflict with another, an inevitable side effect of such dramatic eclecticism? How did memorizing an

Arabic grammar manual word-for-word or reading astrological signs sustain family dynasties that outlasted the rule of kings? There are no easy answers to these questions, but that is exactly what the ulama managed to accomplish. Throughout the pages to come, Muslim polymaths will raise cities to mythological heights and challenge the dominance of the most fearsome of rulers.

Situating Central Asia, Locating Bukhara

For many, the term "Central Asia" conjures an exotic picture of caravansaries dotting vast deserts, trackless steppe, and towering peaks. This imagery is not entirely off base. In terms of terrain, many a think piece has emphasized the confluence of mountains, desert oases, and arid plains as defining features of the region.[1] As far as mountains are concerned, the Altai, Pamir, and Tian Shan ranges loom large. With regard to steppe, it is conventionally the Qipchaq (in modern-day Kazakhstan) and Mongolian grasslands that scholars have in mind. And the "Central Asian" deserts are generally the Qizil Qum, Qara Qum, and Takla Makan. These territories are not bound by any single objective criterion, and the edges bleed into areas more often considered to be the Middle East, Siberia, South Asia, and Inner/East Asia.[2]

Like most area studies, "Central Asia" is an artificial construct, and is used in this book casually rather than analytically—and also promiscuously, alongside other terms such as Eurasia, the Islamic world, and Turko-Persia, depending on the context.[3] Now boasting sophisticated historiography,

1. Adshead, "World History and Central Asia," 7; Christian, "Inner Eurasia as a Unit of World History," 175.

2. Nile Green writes that "models of geographical space . . . are cultural constructions born of particular moments in time." "Rethinking the 'Middle East' after the Oceanic Turn," 556.

3. No single emic term used in Islamic texts perfectly coterminous with the space implied by "Central Asia." Some studies use *Mā warā ʾ al-nahr* (lit. "that which is beyond the [Amu/Oxus] river"), but I have elected not to because it refers to a more limited territory separate from Khorezm and Khurasan. The Greek version of the same concept—"Transoxania" (also used in some studies instead of "Central Asia")—is just as unfamiliar and awkward as *Mā warā ʾ al-nahr*. The modern valence of "Central Asia" has not prevented some scholars from projecting the category backward in time, as though it has intrinsic analytical value. Starr, *Lost Enlightenment*. Yuri Bregel's superb historical atlas of Central Asia covers over 2,000 years of history. Yet the coordinates depicted are constant throughout, hovering over the five Soviet republics that make up Central Asia. *An Historical Atlas of Central Asia*.

Moreover, the idea of a continent of "Asia" had no currency in precolonial sources; *āsiyā* first appears as a concept in Central Eurasian Persian sources in European-influenced publications, such as Bukhara's first Persian-language newspaper, *Bukhāra-yi sharīf* (1911). Previously, world geography had been organized according to the "seven climes" (*haft kishwar/iqlīm*), a concept absorbed into the Islamic tradition from pre-Islamic Iran. Meanwhile, Eurasia includes, but is not limited to, Central

Central Asia is a convenient construct, and one that gestures at that ill-defined space on the map between the Caspian Sea and the Tian Shan mountain range—but with several important caveats. The first is that my research is Bukhara-centric, even though it ranges far beyond the political boundaries of the city-state of Bukhara. This means that readers will more frequently be envisioning deserts and oases than mountains and steppes. It also means that the nomadic culture that is commonly emblematic of Central Asia often remains in the background. The second caveat is that other terms used in this book—especially Islamic and Persianate, which are more thoroughly conceptualized in the next chapter—were organically meaningful in the time and place in question and are used more analytically.

With those qualifications in mind, let us take a tour of Central Asia, radiating outward from Bukhara. The city's population around the turn of the nineteenth century was just under 100,000: sizable by the region's standards, but modest in comparison with Muslim metropoles such as Istanbul or Delhi.[4] The city boasted substantial religious and educational infrastructure, with madrasas (Islamic colleges) and mosques on virtually every block and cupolas dotting the skyline.[5] Local Bukharans spoke a mix of Persian (now called Tajik) and Turkic (today's Uzbek), or—if current speech is any guide—a dialect that combined elements of both.[6] Yet the many other tongues that could be heard at the city's seventy-odd bazaars are suggestive of its cosmopolitanism. Russian merchants haggled with Indian traders in the city streets, and in the barracks Cossack soldiers drilled Iranian artillerists.[7] The vast majority of residents were Sunni Muslims, but they lived alongside a sizable Jewish, Shi'i, and (by the end of the nineteenth century) Russian Orthodox minority.

Asia. In practice, it tends to gesture at Russian borderlands (France is equally Eurasian in a geographical sense, but is rarely what people have in mind), just as "Inner Asia" tends to point at China's Central Asian borderlands. See Kotkin, "Mongol Commonwealth?."

4. Based on a detailed comparison of available sources, O. A. Sukhareva puts the population of the late nineteenth century through the early Soviet period at around 75,000. Sukhareva, *Bukhara XIX–nachalo XX v.*, 97–103. A Bukharan author writing in 1910 put the population at 180,000. Gulshanī, *Tārīkh-i humāyūn*, f. 3a. Tashkent, Khoqand, and Kashgar all had similar populations. Sukhareva, *Bukhara XIX–nachalo XX v.*, 83; Levi, *The Rise and Fall of Khoqand*, 154; Thum, *The Sacred Routes of Uyghur History*, 114. Other cities in the region were less populated. Meanwhile, Delhi's population was already 150,000 in the mid-nineteenth century, passing 200,000 by 1900. Gupta, *Delhi between Two Empires, 1803–1931*, 4, 47. Istanbul's population was comparable to that of Saint Petersburg, likely passing a million souls by 1900. Karpat, *Ottoman Population, 1830–1914*, 103.

5. On the history of the city's infrastructure, see chapter 2.

6. Kerimova, *Govor tadzhikov Bukhary*; Pickett, "Categorically Misleading, Dialectically Misconceived."

7. RGVIA F 1141 O 1 D 102.

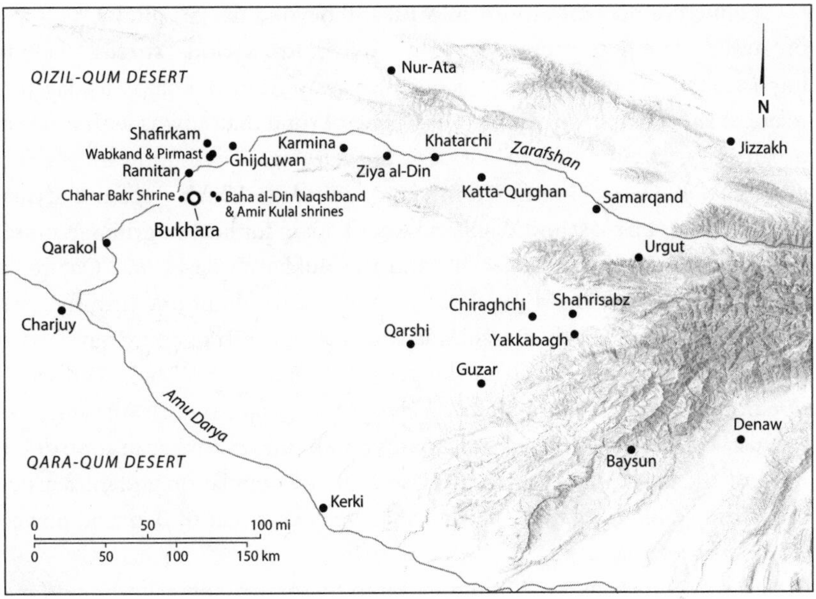

FIGURE 1. Map of Bukharan Oasis

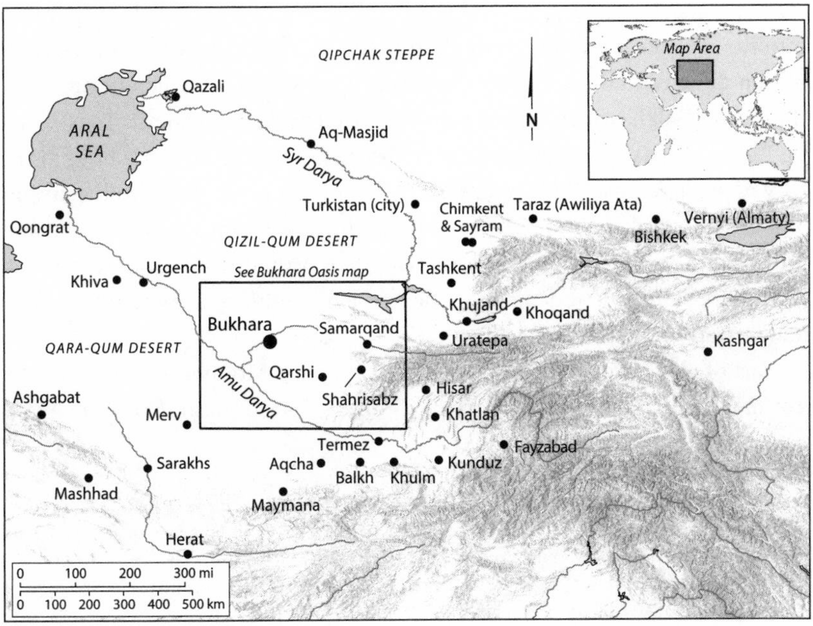

FIGURE 2. Map of Central Asia

The picture becomes more colorful still beyond the city limits. Villages of Arabs were interspersed among nomads of various stripes, including Kazakhs and Turkmen.[8] A few miles away from Bukhara city lay the major shrine complex of Chahar Bakr, and beyond that, towns with modest urban infrastructure dotted the oasis as well. Nearby Ghijduwan boasted a madrasa built by Timur's (Tamerlane) grandson Ulugh Beg, and settlements such as Pirmast and Wabkand were known for holy pilgrimage sites.[9] Several days travel southwest, beyond the Bukharan oasis, was Qarshi, a town renovated by the Mongols with a population about one-fifth the size of Bukhara. Significantly, Qarshi was one of the only cities consistently controlled by Bukhara throughout the period covered in this book—a distinction not shared by the more famous city of Samarqand, which was annexed by Russia in 1868. Nevertheless, Samarqand was under Bukharan control for most of the precolonial period and was a city of population and infrastructure comparable to that of Bukhara, having been a seat of Timurid power for several centuries.

Several subregions were integrated into Bukhara's cultural orbit and are frequently mentioned in this book. To the northwest, across the Qizil Qum desert, was the oasis of Khorezm, the dominant polity of which is generally known by the name of its main city, Khiva.[10] To the south of Bukhara lay territory that is now northern Afghanistan, but referred to here as Khurasan (or more specifically eastern Khurasan), since it was decisively incorporated into the Afghan state only in the latter half of the nineteenth century. This region directly to the south of the Amu River was dominated culturally by the city of Balkh, which is now overshadowed by Mazar-i Sharif. To the east of Bukhara, past Samarqand and Shahrisabz, was the mountainous territory of what is now Tajikistan, referred to in this book as the Kuhistan (lit. "mountainous place"). Northeast of Samarqand were the cities of Jizakh and Tashkent, both preceding the fertile Farghana Valley, which was dominated by the city-state of Khoqand from the mid-eighteenth century to the Russian annexation of 1876.

East of the Farghana Valley, over the Tian Shan Mountains, one finds the Tarim Basin, which was part of the Chinese Qing Empire from the 1750s

8. One Bukharan author wrote that these Central Asian Arabs still spoke Arabic, a claim backed by later scholarship. Gulshanī, *Tārīkh-i humāyūn*, f. 8a; Tsereteli, "The Influence of the Tajik Language on the Vocalism of Central Asian Arabic Dialects."

9. Many of these shrine-towns of the Bukharan oasis were knitted together into a pilgrimage circuit called the "Seven Saints" (*haft pīr/yetti pīr*).

10. Historical authors also sometimes used the name of Khiva's sister-city, Urgench, to refer to the polity as a whole metonymically. Khorezm is the modern spelling of Khwārazm.

until 1865, and then again from the late 1870s until 1911 (with a period of Muslim city-state rule under Ya'kub Beg during the interregnum). Although somewhat separate in the academic literature, the urban oases of the Tarim Basin were arguably closer in terms of culture to the territories of Khorezm, Bukhara, and the Farghana Valley than any of them were to the nomadic steppe belt to the north.

Central Asia was encircled by the remnants of the early modern "Gunpowder Empires" and emergent colonial powers. Of the latter, the borders of the Russian empire were close at hand already by the eighteenth century, and by the 1860s–80s enveloped Central Asia entirely. China—both a victim and purveyor of colonialism—was also just a stone's throw away to the east for the entire period covered by this book, having conquered the Tarim Basin already in the mid-eighteenth century. The Afghan Durrani Empire briefly extended its power into Khurasan (northeastern Iran) in the late eighteenth century, but Kabul did not consolidate its hold over regions bordering Bukhara for another hundred years. The presence of other prominent powers of the era, particularly the Qajars, Ottomans, and what was left of the Mughals (the British deposed the last emperor in 1857), was less palpable.

Periodization and the Geopolitical Backdrop

Two political events frame the time period discussed in this book: the collapse of Nadir Shah's empire in 1747 and the Bolshevik Revolution in 1917 (enveloping Bukhara with the advance of the Red Army in 1920). However, many of the book's thematic arcs are not specific to that timeframe, and experience substantial continuity with Eurasia's early modern era, stretching back into the sixteenth century—and even earlier along some vectors. This book liberally embraces "multiple temporalities" depending on the question at hand. A premodern-modern dichotomy is invoked in some instances, a "high Persiananate" continuity in others, and (more rarely) a precolonial-colonial split in still others. All have their virtues and pitfalls.[11]

Because political history is not a central concern, the chapters are organized thematically rather than chronologically. One of the remarkable characteristics of the ulama as a social group was their ability to move between territories with little regard for changing state boundaries. The scholarly elite

---

11. On the "high Persianate" as an era, see Melvin-Koushki and Pickett, "Mobilizing Magic," 233. On the pitfalls of defining one period as "*pre*ceding" another, see Smail and Andrew, "History and the 'Pre'History and the 'Pre.'"

depended on the Turkic nobility for patronage and livelihood.[12] However, many potential sponsors allowed the ulama to move between polities and weather regime changes with impunity. Nevertheless, some basic historical narrative is necessary to offer a sense of the profound geopolitical transformations that unfolded during the time period discussed.

Until the colonial period, the story of Central Asia had been one of the rise and fall of successive empires of the steppe: sprawling polities established based on (literal) horse power.[13] Scythians, Seljuks, Mongols, Timurids, to name a few—these dynasties came from pastoral-nomadic backgrounds and ruled vast Eurasian empires that encompassed both grasslands and sedentary zones. As Ibn Khaldun observed centuries ago, these dynasties often began as rugged conquest regimes, only to embrace the urban culture of newly incorporated territories and retire to their palaces within a few generations.[14] This repeated process of synthesis between Turko-nomadic traditions and urban Persianate culture has led to the coining of the term "Turko-Persia" to encompass the region as a whole.[15] The Shibanids (1500–1599), along with their Ashtarkhanid successors (1599–1747), might be considered the final exemplars of this pattern, in the sense that they managed to establish some degree of imperial control over much of Central Asia, and toeholds beyond.[16]

The Turko-Persian conqueror Nadir Shah Afshar played a catalyzing role in upending this pattern. Marshaling a military that married tradi-

---

12. I have opted for an emic designation for the ulama (which might have been termed "clergy"), but an etic term for the Turkic nobility (which might have been termed *'umarā'*, Arabic plural of *amīr*): ulama as a term has been much more readily adopted into academic English usage. As used here, the term "amir" refers specifically to the Manghit monarch of Bukhara. "Nobility" as a metaphor comes with some trepidation. On the dangers of Eurocentric terminology, see Chamberlain, *Knowledge and Social Practice in Medieval Damascus, 1190–1350*, 21. These issues are explored further in chapters 4 and 8.

13. The phrase "empires of the steppe" was coined in the classic study Grousset, *The Empire of the Steppes*.

14. Ibn Khaldun, *The Muqaddimah*.

15. Canfield, "Introduction: The Turko-Persian Tradition." This pattern began even before the nomads were predominantly Turko-Mongol (the Scythians of antiquity were Indo-European).

16. Dynastic nomenclature for early modern Central Asia is a confusing mess. I use "Shibanid" and "Ashtarkhanid" because those are terms nineteenth-century sources tend to use. However, "Abu'l-Khayrid" is increasingly replacing "Shibanid" because it is more faithful to Chinggisid dynastic logic. Bregel, "Abu'l-Khayrids"; Dickson, "Uzbek Dynastic Theory in the Sixteenth Century," 209. "Toqay-Timurid" (sometimes "Tuqay-Timurid") is similarly faithful to appenage politics and is equivalent to both "Janid" and "Ashtarkhanid." McChesney, "The 'Reforms' of Bāqī Muḥammad Khān," n. 6. "Ashtarkhanid" is incongruent with the other dynastic names because it refers to the place of origin of the dynasty—Astrakhan—rather than a tribal branch. McChesney, "The Chinggisid Restoration in Central Asia: 1500–1785"; Welsford, *Four Types of Loyalty in Early Modern Central Asia*. Yet "Toqay-Timurid" runs the risk of suggesting a connection with the Timurid dynasty of the fourteenth–early sixteenth centuries, to which it was unrelated.

tional cavalry with superior firearm technology, Nadir Shah soundly defeated the Ashtarkhanid monarch of Bukhara in 1740—a one-sided victory that presaged Russian military dominance a century later.[17] This ushered in an era of fragmented city-states and complex, overlapping forms of sovereignty. Much of the literature hews to a "three khanates" model, taking for granted that Bukhara, Khiva, and Khoqand were the dominant political units even before those polities became Russian protectorates in the mid-nineteenth century.[18] Similarly, Afghanistan is assumed as a cohesive state before Kabul extended durable political control over its hinterlands in the same general timeframe as the Russian conquest. However, before the Russian conquest, the "three khanates" model obscures an era of competing, culturally contiguous city-states, satrapies, and aspiring empires.

Within this complex geopolitical environment, the dynasty that appears the most frequently in this book is that of the Manghits (a branch of the Uzbek tribe), which ruled the city-state of Bukhara from 1747 to 1920.[19] The earliest Manghits began their careers as deputies of the last Ashtarkhanid khans, with a local power base in Qarshi, and often serving as the real power behind the throne. The Ashtarkhanid defeat at the hands of Nadir Shah Afshar was empowering for the Manghits, as their founder, Rahim Biy, served in the Afsharid military, and was eventually complicit in executing the final Bukharan ruler descended from Genghis Khan.[20]

Early Manghit rulers made some headway in expanding the city-state's boundaries beyond the Bukharan oasis. Shah-Murad (r. 1785–1800) conquered Merv in 1788/89, though he did not permanently incorporate it into Bukhara's domain. He also contested the Durrani monarch Timur Shah of Kabul for control over eastern Khurasan (especially the greater Balkh region), a conflict that ended in a stalemate. Nevertheless, Shah-Murad's rule was a period of modest state-building, especially compared to the disastrous final decades of the preceding Ashtarkhanid dynasty.[21] The reign of his son and

---

17. Axworthy, "The Awkwardness of Nader Shah"; Wilde, *What Is Beyond the River?*, 322–47. Nadir Shah was riding high from a victory over the much more powerful Mughal Empire, which similarly presaged British dominance in India.

18. Pickett, "Written into Submission."

19. The best concise overview of the Manghit dynasty is Bregel, "The New Uzbek States: Bukhara, Khiva and Khoqand c. 1750–1886." On the prehistory of the Manghits/Noghay, see Trepavlov, *The Formation and Early History of the Manghït Yurt*. On the emergence of the idea of an O'zbeg (Uzbek) tribal confederation/ulus in the fifteenth and sixteenth centuries, see Bregel, "Uzbeks, Qazaqs and Turkmens," 228–29; Lee, *Qazaqlïq*.

20. Pickett, "Nadir Shah's Peculiar Central Asian Legacy," 494–95.

21. Sela, *The Legendary Biographies of Tamerlane*, chap. 6.

successor, Amir Haydar (r. 1800–1826), was less auspicious. Under Haydar, Bukhara suffered damaging invasions at the hands of Khiva, lost to Khoqand any lingering influence over Tashkent and the Syr Darya region, and suffered numerous tribal rebellions.[22] During this period, the city-state of Bukhara was largely limited to the oasis itself, plus Samarqand—although even control over Samarqand was not entirely consistent.[23]

During the last decades before the Russian conquest, Manghit Bukhara stood as one of the last examples of "early modern" state expansion in the region, alongside similar examples in Khorezm, Khoqand, Qajar Iran, and Afghanistan.[24] The military victories of these states were based on cavalry units, comparable even to the steppe empires of antiquity, but also on the adoption of new gunpowder technology, just like the gunpowder empires immediately preceding them. Much more so than the Ashtarkhanids, Nasrallah Manghit (r. 1827–60) aggressively incorporated Russian- and Iranian-trained artillery into his military. He leveraged it both to counterbalance the tribal cavalry units under his command and get the upper hand against rival city-states.[25] Often but a fine line existed between cajoling unruly tribal units and subduing rival polities.

Thus, one cannot draw a straight line of political-military decline from Nadir Shah to the Russian conquests: Nasrallah had his triumphs. Yet the scale of Bukharan expansion during the immediate precolonial period should not be overstated. The Manghit state was nowhere near the size of its Ashtarkhanid predecessor, nor was it equal to contemporary aspiring empires, such as Qajar Iran or Afghanistan. Even under an aggressive ruler such as Nasrallah, Bukhara's expansionary days were in the past.

The age of semiautonomous city-states ended with the Russian conquest, alongside the military advances of the Afghan ruler Abd al-Rahman (r. 1880–1901). In Russian Turkestan, a few "lucky" city-states were preserved as protectorates (namely, the three khanates of Bukhara, Khiva, and—until 1876—Khoqand), but the nature of the state was radically transformed under

22. Even Ḥaydar had some successes, apparently extending some limited influence over the city-states of eastern Khurasan (such as Balkh, Maymana, and Kunduz), even though they remained largely autonomous. Bregel, "The New Uzbek States," 397.

23. For instance, in 1823/24 the Khaṭāy-Qipchaq tribe drove out Ḥaydar's governor and plundered Samarqand Muḥammad Ḥakīm Khan, *Muntakhab al-tawārīkh*, vol. 1, 407–8.

24. Abdurasulov, "Ot Arabshakhidov k Kungradam"; Levi, *The Rise and Fall of Khoqand*; Ashraf, "From Khan to Shah"; Lee, *The "Ancient Supremacy."* Further south, one might also add the Maratha and Sikh states to this roster.

25. Holzwarth, "Bukharan Armies and Uzbek Military Power, 1670–1870."

Russian "protection."[26] With Russian troops guaranteeing territorial integrity, protectorate rulers extended their control over areas that had previously been independent or at least semiautonomous and leveraged new technologies to extract resources. In the Bukharan case, this meant that the protectorate's control extended over Shahrisabz and the Kuhistan (which became "east Bukhara"), while territories absorbed into Russian Turkestan—most notably Samarqand—slipped permanently beyond its grasp.

During the colonial period, the ulama ranged throughout the protectorates into directly ruled Russian Turkestan and beyond.[27] The differences between direct and indirect rule were quite important, particularly from the perspective of Islamic scholars. Russia wiped out the Turkic nobility, which means that the patronage dynamics underlying many of the chapters do not apply to the directly ruled territories after 1865 (i.e., the conquest of Tashkent and the subsequent establishment of the governor-generalship). The Russians implemented a dual legal system in Turkestan, which meant that many ulama retained positions such as *qazi* (albeit under another name—*narodnye sudy* or "Popular Judges"—after 1885), but owed their positions to local elections.[28] The ulama adapted to these changes, and the colonial system did not impede their movement; and in some ways—such as the construction of railroads—even facilitated it. But the traverse from Bukhara to Samarqand, for instance, was a much different sort of undertaking in 1865 than it was in 1875.

This book is therefore also about the Russian Empire, or at least its subjects. The Russian imperial presence indirectly opened up new resources for the Turkic military elite, which they invested in new religious infrastructure and patronage of Persianate literary culture. The ulama of Turkestan and the protectorates were not integrated into the Orenburg Spiritual Assembly, as were their peers of the Volga-Urals, and they remained aloof from the new world pounding at the gates.[29]

---

26. In contrast with other semicolonial scenarios, the Central Asian "khanates" (with khanate being a term used in Russian sources, but not in Bukharan ones) were not *legally* protectorates. Bukhara was formally an independent country, with internal powers gradually eroded by a series of unequal treaties in the decades following its defeat of 1868.

27. As a military governor-generalship, even the direct rule areas of Russian Turkestan were still more indirectly ruled than the rest of the Russian Empire.

28. Morrison, *Russian Rule in Samarkand, 1868–1910*, chap. 7; Sartori, *Visions of Justice*.

29. Crews, *For Prophet and Tsar*; Tuna, *Imperial Russia's Muslims*; Frank, *Muslim Religious Institutions in Imperial Russia*. The Orenburg Spiritual Assembly was a bureaucratic institution intended to administer Russia's Muslim population, modeled on the Orthodox Church.

The Fragmented Historiographical Landscape

Bukhara and its environs are something of an orphan in the historiographical landscape. Academic conversations tend to take place within siloed area studies and research positions within history departments, and Bukhara does not fit neatly into any of them. This book engages with different historiographies: most notably, those of Central Asia, the Russian Empire, South Asia, and Islamic studies.

The merits of such an expansive approach are both practical and intellectual. Although scholarship on both precolonial Central Asia and Russian Turkestan has grown by leaps and bounds since the opening of Soviet archives in 1991, it is not by itself large enough to sustain rigorous internal dialogue—a state of affairs unlikely to change in the near future. Until now, there has been no monograph-length treatment of the Central Asian ulama during any time period, despite their pivotal influence as a social group across time and space. By contrast, the respective political histories of the Manghit dynasty of Bukhara, Ming Dynasty of Khoqand, and Qonghrat dynasty of Khiva have been the subjects of important recent studies.[30] Meanwhile, the literature on Central Asian sufism in this period has been developed to the point where it should be of interest to scholars of other fields, as has the history of the Russian Empire in the periphery.[31]

Despite these scholarly developments, literature about Central Asia is sparse relative to other fields. Fortunately, no particular reason exists to privilege "Central Asia" as the dominant territorial category for a much larger cultural ecumene. Turko-Persia was colonized by at least three separate empires—Russia, Britain, and China—and South Asian studies, in particular, offers a robust body of literature with which to engage.[32] The texts, forms of knowledge, and cultural symbols that permeated Afghanistan and the Mughal

30. Von Kügelgen, *Legitimatsiia sredneaziatskoi dinastii Mangitov*; Wilde, *What Is beyond the River?*; Solov'eva, *Liki vlasti blagorodnoi Bukhary*; Babadzhanov, *Kokandskoe khanstvo*; Levi, *The Rise and Fall of Khoqand*; Abdurasulov, "Ot Arabshakhidov k Kungradam"; Sartori, "Seeing Like a Khanate."

31. On Central Asian sufism, see, for instance, DeWeese, *Islamization and Native Religion in the Golden Horde*; Aḥrār, *The Letters of Khwāja ʿUbayd Allāh Aḥrār and His Associates*; Babadzhanov, "On the History of the Naqshbandiya Mujaddidiya in Central Mawaraʾnnahr in the Late 18th and Early 19th Centuries"; von Kügelgen, "Rastsvet Nakshbandiia-Mudzhaddidiia v Srednei Transoksanii s XVIII–do nachala XIX vv.: Opyt detektivnogo rassledovaniia." On colonial Turkestan, see, for instance: Brower, *Turkestan and the Fate of the Russian Empire*; Sahadeo, *Russian Colonial Society in Tashkent*; Morrison, *Russian Rule in Samarkand, 1868–1910*.

32. Examples of the rich scholarship on Islam and Persianate culture in South Asia include Alam, *The Languages of Political Islam*; Subrahmanyam, *Courtly Encounters: Translating Courtliness and Violence in Early Modern Eurasia*; Green, *Bombay Islam*; Eaton, *The Rise of Islam and the Bengal Frontier*.

Empire, and the insights produced by the corresponding scholarship are often valid in the Central Asian case as well.

It may seem less of a stretch to situate this book within literature from the broader sweep of Islamic (and even pre-Islamic) history. But because of the continuity implied by "Islamic history," an explanation is necessary. This book considers the Bukharan ulama in the context of their predecessors in medieval Nishapur or Damascus, just as in other places it compares the city-states of the long nineteenth century to those of ancient Sogdiana.[33] The continuity-change debate is a hallmark of most historical subfields, but the longue durée approach has been particularly controversial in Islamic studies, and with good reason. In the past such arguments have been used to justify an "essence" of Islam and Islamic society, constant across time and space.[34] Despite this danger, the notion that the demise of Sogdian high culture might tell us something about the Persianate world or Nizami's innovative take on Alexander's universal Persian kingship could help us understand the nineteenth-century Bukharan chronicles is part of what makes this history so captivating. Therefore, I highlight historical change while acknowledging, in line with the self-understanding of the ulama, that there is enough cultural continuity over the longer sweep of history to justify engaging that historiography.

The Russian conquest was only one of many twists and turns in that long-term history, but one that situates my research in scholarship about Eurasian imperial borderlands. The "imperial turn" taken by the historiography has productively shifted the attention toward the borderlands and away from the "nation" as an enduring unit of analysis.[35] The antidote to the previous focus on imperial centers has often been increased attention on orientalist views of the "other," or challenges of provincial administration.[36]

What remains lacking is an engagement with the so-called borderlands on their terms. Territories that seemed peripheral to Moscow or London were someone else's borderlands as well, or even centers in their own right. This book takes the profound changes wrought by colonialism seriously, and its agents can be considered perhaps the least integrated subjects of the Russian Empire (and, less frequently, Chinese and British empires). But they were not only that, and there ought to be a place in the new imperial history for

33. Bulliet, *The Patricians of Nishapur*; Lapidus, *Muslim Cities in the Later Middle Ages*.

34. For an examination of how chronology, especially longue durée chronology, leads to implicit assumptions about the essence of Islam in even the most sophisticated studies, see Bashir, "On Islamic Time."

35. Burton, *After the Imperial Turn*.

36. For instance, Burbank, Von Hagen, and Remnev, *Russian Empire: Space, People, Power, 1700–1930*; Schimmelpenninck van der Oye, *Russian Orientalism*.

recovering the worlds experienced by provincial and colonial subjects without privileging the outlook of their colonial sovereigns.

Archives and Libraries, Manuscripts and Documents

None of the polities discussed in this book survive today, nor is there any successor state encompassing all of the Turko-Persian cultural space. Consequently, records are scattered across Eurasia between numerous countries and repositories. Research was conducted primarily in archives and manuscript libraries in Uzbekistan, Russia, Tajikistan, and India. Particularly in the post-Soviet space, practical documents produced by state bureaucracies are kept in "archives," whereas "books" (often in manuscript form) intended for long-term preservation tend to reside in "libraries."[37] Manuscripts in Persian, Arabic, and Turkic, as well as archival documents produced both within the Bukharan amirate-cum-protectorate and by the Russian Empire, inform the picture presented in the pages to come. The majority of these sources are unpublished and have rarely, if ever, been used for historical research, particularly in English.[38]

Just as critical as language and repository is the issue of textual genre. A core argument of this book is that the ulama were consummate polymaths, and different genres illuminate different facets of their world.[39] Bukhara produced several biographical dictionaries (*tazkira*) specifically cataloging the great poets of the realm. They consisted of anywhere from a hundred to several thousand individual entries, usually amounting to only a few hundred words each. Most biographical dictionaries specifically targeted one discipline in particular, and nearly all of those composed in Bukhara during the late nineteenth and early twentieth century cataloged poets.[40] Like studies of ulama that have come before, this book makes extensive use of *tazkira* sources of various stripes.[41]

Sufi hagiographies have received particular attention in studies of Central Asia. The form of these sources ranges from a variation on the

---

37. The reality is much messier than this rule of thumb, but it is nevertheless a useful heuristic: Messick, *Sharīʿa Scripts*, 21–25; Pickett and Sartori, "From the Archetypical Archive to Cultures of Documentation."

38. Whereas most sources on medieval Europe or classical antiquity have been edited and published for over a hundred years, in the Central Asian case even major dynastic chronicles are still accessible only in manuscript form.

39. Genre, and how it shapes the way we understand the ulama and their world, is a problem tackled in much greater detail in chapter 6.

40. To be clear, even though poetry was the organizing principle, none of these individuals were only poets. On the virtues and challenges of poetical *taẕkiras*, see Losensky, *Welcoming Fighānī*, 18–19.

41. Chapter 4 contains a more detailed discussion of the place of "ulamology" in the historiography.

biographical dictionary genre, often exclusive to a specific sufi spiritual lineage (*silsila*), to narratives of the miraculous life of one particularly exalted holy person. Meanwhile, chronicles tend to focus on the deeds of the Turkic nobility, but Islamic scholars constantly appear in supporting roles, and this historical genre helps round out the picture presented in other sources.[42]

To get at the juridical personae of the ulama, I turn to a genre that has received scant attention even from regional specialists. Central Asian manuscript collections contain dozens of exemplars of practical notebooks known as *jung*.[43] The majority of *jung* were predominantly legal, but there were also medical and literary *jung*, and most of them were marked by the polymathy of their authors.[44] The legally oriented *jung* were often transcriptions of legal opinions, assembled into a single place for future reference, and represented an intermediary point in the jurisprudential lifecycle. The documents on which these notebooks were based (e.g., fatwas)[45] represent another source base on which I relied during my research.[46]

Still many other sources are sui generis, defying easy generalizations. Some scholars wrote accounts of their lives, but these vary in content and style so much that they can hardly be said to constitute a genre of writing.[47] Others wrote pilgrimage guides, and one Bukharan scholar even wrote a geography of the amirate.[48] Islamic scholars writing about Bukhara from the

42. For a discussion of Bukharan chronicles, see von Kügelgen, "Bukhara Viii. Historiography of the Khanate, 1500–1920."

43. This genre of writing had become so widespread by the nineteenth century that some were even lithographed. For instance, *Jūng-i fatāwā wa maḥżarāt 1325*. According to Dehkhoda's *Lughat-nāma*, this word may be a calque from the Chinese word for ship (*junk*), translated directly from the Arabic word for ship (*safīna*) used in Iran for *ghazal* collections. The term appears both with long (*jūng*) and short vowels (*jung*).

44. These texts are diverse to the point that it is only with some trepidation that I follow the lead of catalogers and describe texts as *jung* in which the term itself does not appear. However, it was indeed an emic concept, and *jung* notebooks are occasionally reference in non-*jung* texts; e.g., Żīyāʾ, *Tazkirat al-khaṭṭāṭīn*, f. 167b.

45. Fatwas were often referred to as *riwāyats* in the Central Asian context, though there was also a technical distinction at times between the draft opinion (a *riwāyat*, lit. "report") written by a clerk, which became a fatwa when endorsed by the *muftī*. Sartori, *Visions of Justice*, 263. I generally refer to both by the more generic term "fatwa."

46. Although the genre's general lack of proper nouns means that the contents of *jungs* and fatwas are difficult to tie to a specific time and place, they nevertheless offer a general picture of social issues considered to be of pressing concern.

47. For instance, Muḥammad ḥiṣārī wrote a memoir (*Yāddāsht-hā*) in elevated, rhyming prose, whereas the teenage reminiscences of ʿAbd al-Ghafūr Turkistānī (*Bayān-i dāstān*) are an idiosyncratic blend of humorous stories and spiritual reflections, all punctuated by colloquial dialect.

48. Muḥammad Gulshanī, *Tārīkh-i humāyūn*. See chapter 2 for a discussion of sources that focus on Bukhara as a place.

outside often included details and insights absent in the local sources.[49] And Russian sources are characterized by concerns fundamentally different from all of these, and provide crucial insights not present in local writing.

Core Arguments

The chapters that follow are organized thematically rather than chronologically. The book begins with the rise and mythologization of Bukhara and then examines the ulama as a social group in terms of their cultural role and relationship with the military elite.

The first chapter offers a conceptual discussion of Islam in Turko-Persia, providing a model for thinking about the ecologies of elite culture before the nation. It explains how Turkic culture related to the Persianate, and how Persian high culture, in turn, related to Islam.

Chapters 2 and 3 historicize the rise of Bukhara as a sacred center of Islam. By the colonial period Islamic scholars had successfully mythologized Bukhara into a timeless religious and cultural center by endowing the city's geography with symbolic significance derived from sacred Islamic history and Persian literature. The third chapter also traces the extent of this appeal by assessing how far the social currency of a Bukharan education traveled, arguing for "little Persianate spheres" radiating outward from the city.

If early chapters question where an Islamic scholar might deploy the skills and knowledge he acquired in Bukhara, subsequent sections examine what he could do with those forms of knowledge. These chapters aggregate data from biographical dictionaries to argue for the rise of the "high Persianate intellectual" in Central Asia.[50] In prior centuries the roles of sufi, jurist, poet, calligrapher, or occultist often implied distinct social groups. However, by the nineteenth century one individual would frequently master all of these skills. There was near-total overlap between these personas, challenging conventional differentiations between sufis and ulama as separate communities.

Chapters 7 and 8 interrogate the relationship between the ulama and political-military power. The conquests of Nadir Shah Afshar catapulted not only new Turkic military dynasties into power but scholarly ones as well. Beneficiaries of this dramatic political upheaval bequeathed a remarkably

---

49. On the Tatar view of Bukhara, see Frank, *Bukhara and the Muslims of Russia*. From the other direction, many published Arabic sources written by Central Asian émigrés to the Middle East also inform my research.

50. In practice, "ulama," "Islamic scholars," "high Perisanate intellectuals," and "polymaths of Islam" are all used synonymously in this book, with the latter two emphasizing the social group's eclecticism.

stable power dynamic to their heirs, who formed the core of a Persianate elite, which buttressed Central Asian society until the Bolshevik conquest. Even as Islamic scholars depended on the Turkic military elite for patronage, they imagined their moral universe to be separate and superior. By the late nineteenth century, the Turkic nobility had strengthened its control over the ulama, and in some instances the ulama even began to undermine their own moral autonomy and prerogative to independently interpret religion. Nevertheless, the disconnect between ideology and practice meant that Islamic scholars often undermined and even challenged the very power on which they relied for material resources.

The ulama of Bukhara embodied a social-cultural orientation fundamentally different from ours today. The geopolitical landscape of the long nineteenth century in Central Asia contained many shape-shifting actors and networks that defy easy categorization. Rather than turning to political boundaries or national categories for an organizing rubric, this book focuses on cosmopolitan Perso-Islamic culture and the scholars who lived and breathed it. Modernist concerns such as identity and ethnicity throw us off the scent of an older social logic rooted in the mastery of elite texts and patterns of sociability. Even after this broader cultural world was split between colonial empires, cosmopolitan Persianate culture not only survived, but thrived: after all, it had never been reducible to, or uniformly dependent on, any single state for its existence.

The following pages chart the contours of a transregional, cosmopolitan social group, and examine the cultural efflorescence they produced on the eve of military defeat and colonial subjugation. This writing was on the wall only in retrospect, and the ulama did not perceive a serious threat to the social order until 1920, when Bolshevik munitions started raining down on Bukhara the Noble, the Abode of Knowledge. This is the story of the last historical moment of an enduring cultural tableau and the actors that performed it, both of which had roots stretching back over a millennium, but neither of which was compatible with the -isms—nationalism, socialism, atheism, Islamism, and modernism—of the twentieth century.

CHAPTER 1

Defamiliarizing the Familiar

Conceptualizing Religion and Culture in Turko-Persia

Understanding the Islamic scholars of Bukhara requires that we set aside assumptions about culture and religion and build some new scaffolding to cover the void. Nation, ethnicity, identity—these are all concepts that have been thoroughly theorized for the modern period, but when superimposed on earlier centuries they are unhelpful at best and actively misleading at worst. Religion has received more evenhanded conceptual attention, but anachronism is present in that literature as well. This chapter integrates different conceptual tools for understanding social and cultural dynamics in the premodern world to render the familiar unfamiliar and vice versa.

The invention of tradition is a well-established concept, as is the notion that many national identities are of recent provenance.[1] Much of what we might consider timeless or "traditional" was only recently objectified as such within the last century or two. Similarly, numerous studies have established the historical contingency of "secular" culture as separable and distinct from religion. Persian poetry understood as a "cultural" foil to "religious" Arabic texts is burdened by a dichotomy that would not have been appreciated by the original authors. But where does that leave us before the innovation of

1. Hobsbawm and Ranger, *The Invention of Tradition.*

the modern categories that shape our thinking? If Persian culture was not the same as Iranian national culture, then what was it? If we are to decenter Islam from the Arabian Peninsula, then why did Arabic texts remain core to any educated person's repertoire—even into the early twentieth century? And what of the "Turko" part of the term Turko-Persia featuring in the title of this chapter?[2]

The questions of how Persian high culture relates to Islam, or what it meant to write in Turkic, are exactly the issues that make this book more than a narrow consideration of elite that happened to live in what we now consider Central Asia. Islamic scholars of Bukhara were in different ways representative of a broader constituency of literati whose members were to be also found in western China, Iran, India, and even North Africa. However, because reconceptualizations of culture and religion in the preindustrial era are still in their infancy and often scattered across disparate literatures, this chapter builds on them, combines them, and in some cases critiques or repurposes them.[3]

Chasing the Cosmopolis

To understand how culture and power and religion interacted in long nineteenth-century Central Asia, it is critical to first appreciate that premodern culture and society were organized by dynamics fundamentally distinct from those of the present-day world.[4] Even though the vast majority of the world's population was uneducated, and despite treacherous expanses separating urban centers, many of the cultures enacted by elite strata were astonishingly uniform.[5] These continua of transregional acculturation constituted the environment within which Islamic scholars imagined their world, just as they created it. This world was the cosmopolis.

This cultural dynamic persisted—and even flourished—against the backdrop of the industrializing Russian Empire from the 1860s on. Colonial empire brought with it profound changes to cultural and religious organization in Central Asia, reshaping understandings of ethnicity and orthodoxy,

2. Canfield, "Introduction: The Turko-Persian Tradition."

3. By contrast, terms discussed in the introduction (e.g., "Central Asia," "early modern") are mostly used casually rather than analytically.

4. Crone, *Pre-Industrial Societies*. This is not to propose a simple premodern versus modern dichotomy for all subjects and questions. Instead, it is to observe that change in many areas *accelerated* as a consequence of industrialization.

5. The "elite" modifier is a critical one: elite high cultures uniform across vast distances coexisted and interacted with local cultures that differed from one another even across minimal distances.

and sowing the seeds that would eventually displace the cosmopolis. Yet the endurance of those older forms—too often waved away as unchanging "tradition"—has remained a blind spot in the literature.[6] Positing the cosmopolis as a quintessentially premodern cultural complex places the inexorable transition to colonial modernity in its proper context and complicates its hegemony.

Insights from the literature that theorizes cosmopolitan high culture in the preindustrial world allow us to move beyond anachronistically imposing modern categories into arenas in which they had no salience.[7] This scholarship is scattered and has predominantly been applied to other regions, so it is essential to recapitulate its most important facets and synthesize them in relation to high culture and religion in Eurasia specifically. This is doubly important since the few previous efforts to apply conceptual literature on cosmopolitan high culture to the Persianate world have been misleading in several key respects, particularly with regard to religion.

The cosmopolis has been most extensively theorized by Sheldon Pollock, who elegantly defines it as the study "of how and why people may have been induced to adopt languages or life ways or modes of political belonging that affiliated them with the distant rather than the near, the unfamiliar rather than the customary."[8] This model provides conceptual vocabulary for understanding earlier cultural dynamics on their terms. It provides tools for explaining why elite in Sri Lanka and Afghanistan interacted with the *Mahabharata* (a Sanskrit epic), why Irish monks well outside the territories of the former Roman Empire were known for their enviable Latin, why Vietnamese Buddhist monks living in Hanoi authored new works in classical Chinese, and—relevant for our purposes—why Islamic scholars of Bukhara parsed many of the same Persian texts as their colleagues in Sarajevo. This model helps us to distance ourselves from modern categories of ethnicity and explain why the Persian cosmopolis was no more the patrimony of Tajiks or Iranians than Latin was the exclusive birthright of Italians. And it clarifies why Persian borrowed so much from the Arabic language and

6. As Sheldon Pollock points out, it is remarkable how dependent theories about colonialism are on the period that came before it, given how little we know about the earlier eras (particularly in Asia). Pollock, "Introduction," 1, 4.

7. Substantial literature viewed the pre-Soviet period through the prism of Soviet-created nations. This pattern was established by Soviet scholarship, and echoed in Western studies; e.g., Allworth, *The Modern Uzbeks*.

8. Pollock, *The Language of the Gods in the World of Men*, 10. Although Pollock's focus is the Sanskrit cosmopolis, other scholars—notably Alexander Beecroft—have expanded his model to place it in a broader continuum of literary systems, from oral cultures to specifically modern forms: *An Ecology of World Literature*, 19–20.

its literary forms but Arabic took so little from Persian—just as Tamil derived concepts from the Sanskrit cosmopolis but not vice versa.[9]

The cosmopolis paradigm has much to offer, but it also comes with cumbersome baggage. On the one hand, Pollock's concept of the premodern cosmopolis is superficially connected to much more extensive literature on modern cosmopolitan*ism*; on the other hand, it is disconnected from scholarship using different terminology to describe cultural and social phenomena that are conceptually related.[10] The literature on cosmopolitanism conflates studies of cosmopolitanism as a philosophical position (à la Kant, counterposed to currents of Romantic nationalism) with examinations of deracinated communities of elite actors moving between discrete empires and states.[11] This first literature does not inform my research despite the connection implied by the shared etymology, and despite the overlap asserted in parts of the secondary literature.

Meanwhile, seemingly unrelated scholarship substantially enhances our understanding of the cosmopolis. The idea of elite, transregional high culture may initially bring to mind recreation and pleasure, but the cosmopolis was hardly divorced from power. The genesis of a given cosmopolis was often intimately bound up in the projection of imperial authority, and imperial networks lingered on even after the collapse of the empire itself.[12] Empires facilitated exchange between vast territories, spreading exactly the sorts of high cultural forms encapsulated by the Persian cosmopolis.[13] Bolstered by imperial power, those cultures were embraced beyond the reach of the state and persisted after the state disintegrated.[14] Thus the (post)imperial "commonwealth" as an

9. This refers to the highest register of language interaction, that is the written and literary. The directionality of exchange suggested by the cosmopolis-vernacular model does not necessarily apply at the colloquial level. This is not to say that there were no borrowings in the other direction at all; see Taffazoli, "Arabic Language II. Iranian Loanwords." However, the difference is a scale of magnitude.

10. Pollock's notion of the cosmopolis is intellectually indebted to literature on cosmopolitanism, as he himself emphasizes: "Cosmopolitanisms." However, this shared intellectual genealogy is not sufficient to make one an epiphenomenon of the other. Meanwhile, Dimitri Obolensky's notion of a Byzantine "commonwealth" seems much more reminiscent of Pollock's cosmopolis than transimperial cosmopolitans moving between European colonies. Obolensky, *The Byzantine Commonwealth*.

11. In important respects, cosmopolitanism is the exact opposite of the cosmopolitan*ism* as conceptualized by Pollock, in which the educated elite moved within a single high cultural sphere rather than between them. For a survey of this literature in the Middle Eastern context, see Hanley, "Grieving Cosmopolitanism in Middle East Studies." Recent examples include Alavi, *Muslim Cosmopolitanism in the Age of Empire*; Meyer, *Turks Across Empires*.

12. This is true of the Persian cosmopolis as well, though not quite in the way it is often assumed. See box on "The Mysterious Formation of the Persian Cosmopolis."

13. The Mongol Empire serves as a striking example of the spread of Persian high culture being facilitated by the imperial exchange. Allsen, *Culture and Conquest in Mongol Eurasia*.

14. Fowden, *Empire to Commonwealth*, chap. 6.

analytical framework overlaps considerably with the idea of the cosmopolis, and both are arguably different ways of engaging the same phenomenon.[15]

The cosmopolis is often conceived of as a world literary high culture, and the ulama of Bukhara, who are at the heart of this nonliterary book, lived in an exceedingly literary world.[16] It should not be forgotten that literature is often produced by scholars trained in institutions—institutions established through the investment of resources, resources extracted through coercive force.[17] Thus we must expand our horizons to include the interaction between literary texts (arguably all texts in the Persianate case) and the social forces that produced them.[18]

Contesting the Persianate, Reconciling the Islamic

How does this conceptual groundwork help make sense of the cultural soup that filled territories across Eurasia and beyond? I take the idea of the Persian cosmopolis (with the adjective "Persianate" describing the same phenomenon) to refer to a canon of literature and the outcome of interactions with that canon.[19] Although this canon was not reducible to the *Shah-nama* (the Persian epic

---

15. Obolensky, *The Byzantine Commonwealth*; Kotkin, "Mongol Commonwealth?" The fact that Greek Byzantine textual production spawned "vernacular" literary spheres (such as Church Slavonic, referent to Byzantine genres and terms) stands as further evidence that Obolensky and Pollock are dealing with the same phenomenon. Lenhoff, "Toward a Theory of Protogenres in Medieval Russian Letters," 32. "Islamic Republic of Letters" stands as a similar framework for making sense of premodern, trans-regional culture. Binbaş, *Intellectual Networks in Timurid Iran*; al-Musawi, *The Medieval Islamic Republic of Letters*; Casanova, *The World Republic of Letters*.

16. Sanskrit has an internally theorized concept of "literature" (*kāvya*), which helps Pollock narrow his inquiry (even though his notion of the cosmopolis is not limited to literature per se). *The Language of the Gods in the World of Men*, 3. Beecroft offers a universal definition: "all self-consciously aesthetic use of language." *An Ecology of World Literature*, 14.

17. There is little doubt that empire played a role in Beecroft's two primary cases of interest: classical Chinese and *koiné* Greek: Beecroft, *Authorship and Cultural Identity in Early Greece and China*. By contrast, Pollock considers the absence of empire as a defining feature of the Sanskrit cosmopolis, since it was "constituted by no imperial state or church"; he also notes that this state of affairs to be "peculiar." Pollock, *The Language of the Gods in the World of Men*, 18–19.

18. Persian did not explicitly theorize what was "in" and what was "out" with regard to "literature" in the precolonial period (unlike Sanskrit, for instance). The idea of *adabiyāt*, separating the "classical literary" section of the canon from other kinds of texts, was developed by nineteenth-century Iranian modernists in dialogue with European ideas. Utas, "'Genres' in Persian Literature 900–1900," 199–200.

19. This interaction between texts, discourse, and practice is articulated nicely by legal scholars in a very different context: "some of the most important forms of canonicity have less to do with the choice of materials than with the tools of understanding that people use to think about the law . . . These elements of 'deep canonicity' include characteristic forms of legal argument, characteristic approaches to problems, underlying narrative structures, unconscious forms of categorization, and the use of canonical examples." Balkin and Levinson, "Legal Canons: An Introduction," 5. For a use-

of kings), the cosmopolitan space overlapped closely with areas that embraced that text and other core entries in the canon (e.g., Sa'di's *Gulistan*).[20] The ulama of Bukhara lived and breathed the much the same Persian literature as their peers in India, Iran, and in the Ottoman Empire—a textual canon a thousand years in the making.[21]

Those same intellectuals read Arabic texts as well, and explaining the relationship of Persianate language and culture to Arabic has plagued applications of the cosmopolis framework to the Persian case. Most scholars have dealt with this challenge by eliminating Islam from the equation, characterizing the Persian cosmopolis as a "secular" overlay on top of the Islamic world but without any particular connection to religion.[22] Leaving aside the fact that understanding the Persian cosmopolis as essentially "secular" begs the basic question of why its reach never extended much further than the Islamic world,[23] it also fails to appreciate Talal Asad's historicization of the emergence of the secular as a category separate from religion.[24]

---

ful taxonomy of different sorts of canons (all of which were active in the Persian cosmopolis), see Halbertal, *People of the Book*, 3 passim.

20. This canon also produced a "cosmopolis" in the more literal sense of the world—a world-city, a sacred geography. The spatial dimension of the cosmopolis is a major focus of Pollock's work and has been discussed in reference to the Persian case as well. Pollock, *The Language of the Gods in the World of Men*, chap. 5; Cornwall, "Alexander and the Persian Cosmopolis, 1000–1500"; Eaton and Wagoner, *Power, Memory, Architecture*, 23–24.

21. Scholars of classical antiquity and early modern Europe, in particular, have illustrated how pedagogy emphasizing a specific set of texts (or "canon") implicitly shaped elite worldviews and trained subjects. Too, "Introduction." See also Brown, *The Canonization of Al-Bukhārī and Muslim*, chap. 2.

22. Hamid Dabashi characterizes the religious nature in the princely mirror genre as "occasional gestures of piety" and a "retrieval of pre-Islamic, Sassanid theories of kingship." *The World of Persian Literary Humanism*, 75. This is the same genre used by Muzaffar Alam to show that "*sharīʿa* here is redefined, in part to signify a kind of protest against an overly legalistic approach." Alam, *The Languages of Political Islam*, 12–13. Rigid separation between secular culture and religion is also a hallmark of Soviet historiography, which until recently framed much of the scholarship on Central Asia. See Rempel', *Dalekoe i blizkoe*, 68–70. New conceptual treatment of the Persianate concept has sought to decouple it from Iran (an aim shared by this book) and also from religion (an aim not shared by this book). Green, "Introduction: The Frontiers of the Persianate World (ca. 800–1900)," 7–8; Amanat, "Pathways to the Persianate," n. 20; Eaton, "The Persian Cosmopolis (900–1900) and the Sanskrit Cosmopolis (400–1400)," 64–65; Eaton and Wagoner, *Power, Memory, Architecture*, 21–26; Perry, "New Persian: Expansion, Standardization, and Inclusivity," 74. There is room for multiple working definitions of "Persianate," and the "big tent" conceptualized by Green and Amanat, respectively, is appropriate for anchoring a growing field of study, whereas fusing the term with Pollock's narrower cosmopolis framework can be more fruitful for analysis.

23. Eaton and Wagoner explore a number of interesting exceptions to this tendency, in which Persianate architectural forms seemed to extend into territories under "Hindu" rule in the Deccan plateau. Eaton and Wagoner, *Power, Memory, Architecture*, 26. When Persian did appear in outside of the Islamic world, it was employed for narrower diplomatic purposes in state chanceries or in migrant communities. Ford, "The Uses of Persian in Imperial China"; Subrahmanyam, "Iranians Abroad."

24. Asad, *Genealogies of Religion*. Following Clifford Geertz, many researchers find it useful to posit culture and religion as intertwined, but distinct, phenomena, though I do not attempt to dis-

Ferdowsi and Ibn Balkhi: Secular Iranian Proto-Nationalists? A Zoroastrian Third Column?

How should we understand Ferdowsi's masterpiece, the *Shah-nama*, in relation to Islam and the Arabic cosmopolis? This is a critical question since the Arab literary theorist Ali ibn al-Athir (d. 1233) characterized it as "the Qur'an of the Persians," a notion embraced by some modern authors as well.[25] Other scholars have described that same epic as Zoroastrian in outlook or "fundamentally secular," a label that has also been applied to Ibn Balkhi's twelfth-century *Fars-nama*.[26]

In 930 CE, Mardawij ibn Ziyar rose against the Abbasid Caliphate (then protected by the Buyid dynasty), possibly with the intention of reestablishing a Zoroastrian, Persian empire.[27] His murder at the hands of his Turkic slaves in 935 marked the last attempt of any kind to explicitly reestablish the pre-Islamic paradigm, rather than synthesize something new.[28] However much continuity we observe in traditions

entangle them. There were exceptions to Persianate culture's containment within the Islamic world: Eaton and Wagoner show that Persianate architectural forms seemed to extend into territories under "Hindu" rule in the Deccan plateau. Eaton and Wagoner, *Power, Memory, Architecture*, 26. Persian was also employed for narrow diplomatic purposes in state chanceries or in migrant communities in China and southeast Asia. Ford, "The Uses of Persian in Imperial China"; Subrahmanyam, "Iranians Abroad."

25. Phrased as *Qurʾān al-qawm*. Quoted in Cornwall, "Alexander and the Persian Cosmopolis, 1000–1500," 60. Chamanara, *Kitāb-i muqaddas-i Ērānīyān*. See also discussion in Tavakoli-Targhi, *Refashioning Iran*, chap. 6.

26. Perry, "New Persian: Expansion, Standardization, and Inclusivity," 74; Eaton and Wagoner, *Power, Memory, Architecture*, 25.

27. Extant sources on Mardāwīj are suggestive rather than conclusive in this regard. Al-Masʿūdī (d. 956) emphasizes that Mardāwīj had a throne and crown modeled on that of Anushirvan (r. 531–579), a famous Sasanian monarch, and that he propagated prophecies to the effect that he was destined for world domination. Masʿūdī, *Murūj al-ẕahab wa-maʿādin al-jawhar*, 270, par. 3600. C. E. Bosworth argues that his goal was "reconstituting the ancient Persian empire and faith." Bosworth, "Ziyarids." As Mitra Mehrabadi points out, the evidence is far from clear, and Patricia Crone notes that Mardāwīj also claimed that the spirit of Solomon—an Abrahamic figure commanding respect from Muslims—dwelt within him. Mehrabadi, *Tārīkh-i silsila-i Ziyārī (History of the Ziyarid Dynasty)*, 53; Crone, *The Nativist Prophets of Early Islamic Iran*, 251, 269. Ibn Isfandiyār's history of Tabaristan makes no mention of any particularly Zoroastrian-leanings on the part of Mardāwīj—even though the same text includes a translation of a Sasanian-era Zoroastrian polemic (the "Letter of Tansar). Isfandiyār, *Tārīkh-i Ṭabaristān*. In other words, Mardāwīj was just as likely of the same mold as other figures in Crone's study; that is, embracing facets of pre-Islamic Persian culture but without explicitly challenging the dominant paradigm of Islam.

28. Mardāwīj's successors in the Ziyārid dynasty hung on to power locally for another century, but as Islamic rulers without any revanchist ambitions. Whatever their personal religious beliefs, they performed Islamic culture: subsequent rulers minted coins with engraved with praises to Allah (in Arabic script), and one dynast—Kaykāwus—wrote the famous princely mirror *Qābūs-nāma*. Simi-

held over from pre-Islamic Iran—and there was a great deal—all of it was reformulated as Islamic.[29]

It was this new, Islamic dispensation within which Ferdowsi and Ibn Balkhi wrote their magisterial works. Both productions wear pre-Islamic cosmology and Zoroastrian imagery on their sleeve, but they are presented as fully compatible with Islam.[30] The prophet celebrated within the first hundred lines of the *Shah-nama* is Muhammad, not Zoroaster. And even though much of the *Fars-nama* glorifies pre-Islamic Persian rulers, when the armies of Islam eventually march into Fars province, Ibn Balkhi describes resistors there as "infidels" (*kuffar*) who violate their agreement to pay the poll tax (*jizya*) required of nonbelievers.[31]

It is possible that the Islamic language deployed by the likes of Ferdowsi and Ibn Balkhi was subordinate to deeper motives subversive to Islam.[32] But such arguments rest on conjecture, since we have no historical tools to assess sincerity, and anyway miss the point: characterizing Persianate culture as somehow less meaningfully "Islamic" advances a scripturalist understanding of religion that has been largely repudiated in other historiographic contexts.[33]

Where, then, does religion fit into the Persianate model? To put it pithily, the relationship between the Persian cosmopolis and Islam is precisely that

lar to other texts, the *Qābūs-nāma* drew from pre-Islamic genres and traditions, but was explicitly articulated within an Islamic worldview. Kaykāwus ibn Iskandar ibn Qābūs, *Kitāb-i naṣhīḥat-nāma: Qābūs-nāma*, 134.

29. Crone, *The Nativist Prophets of Early Islamic Iran*; Morony, *Iraq after the Muslim Conquest*.

30. Davis, "Religion in the Shahnameh," 342.

31. Ibn Balkhī, *Fārs-nāma*, 112–17. Ibn Balkhi writes that after the people of Fars province learned of the brutal repression of a rebellion in Istakhr (a major Sasanian city, and sometimes capital), "they remained pure and loyal, and every day [the influence of] Islam spread until they became Muslims." Ibn Balkhī, 117.

32. Even if the case, the sincerity of these authors does not change the epistemic impact of Islamic Persian (i.e., New Persian) on the expression of religion. Alan Williams argues that the tenets of Zoroastrianism came through even in the syntactical structure of Middle Persian writing. "The Continuum of 'Sacred Language' from High to Low Speech in the Middle Iranian (Pahlavi) Zoroastrian Tradition," 135. This style of writing was radically transformed in New Persian, and along with it the content.

33. Devin DeWeese demonstrates that the Islamization of distinctively Turkic traditions did not make those Turks any less "Islamic." In converting to Islam, Turks also nativized religion, just as did Ferdowsi and Ibn Balkhi vis-à-vis Sasanian culture. DeWeese, *Islamization and Native Religion in the Golden Horde*. Similarly, scholars situated in South Asian studies have chafed against the idea of "syncretism" for implying one "real" form of the religion as against the mixed or hybrid form. Ernst and Stewart, "Syncretism." Shahab Ahmed marshals a similar critique against differentiating the "Islamicate" from the Islamic: *What Is Islam?*, 159–72.

of the Arabic cosmopolis and Islam.[34] This is where Pollock's specific usage of the term "vernacular" comes into play.[35] When used in relation to the cosmopolis, the vernacular does not carry the conventional definition referring to a local, colloquial dialect of a language. Instead, vernaculars in this more technical sense are languages and associated cultures that emerge from a larger one but cater to a narrower, more regional audience.[36] Just like cosmopolitan languages, vernaculars were sophisticated instruments of literature and high culture, and did not necessarily require any less education and training to attain.[37] The vernacular cultural complex derives vocabulary, genres, symbols, and other cultural forms from the cosmopolitan culture, but the cosmopolitan analog takes comparatively little in return.[38]

By this logic, New Persian emerged as a vernacular of Arabic, even though it developed into a cosmopolis in its own right.[39] It is difficult to overemphasize the importance of Arabic to the Persian cosmopolis. New Persian would not exist without Arabic loan words, and most Persianate authors (including Ferdowsi, who is sometimes remembered as a "language nationalist") liberally sprinkled Arabic quotations and references throughout ostensibly

---

34. The figure of Alexander the Great serves as an instructive example of the formative role of Islam in the Persian cosmopolis. Under Sasanian culture, he is a cursed figure (*gizistag* in Middle Persian), reviled for the distant memory of his conquest of Iran. Under Islamic influence, Alexander was transformed into the Persianate king par excellence and a Muslim avant la lettre, both in Arabic and Persian writing—a story fully explored in Cornwall, "Alexander and the Persian Cosmopolis, 1000–1500." For a Sasanian text which held that Alexander desecrated a fire temple in Samarqand and destroyed its sacred books, see Daryaee, *Šahrestānīhā ī Ērānšahr*, 19.

35. The same goes for Turkic vis-à-vis Persian; as Ferenc Péter Csirkés argues, the development of Turkic as a literary language was connected to Islamization: "Chaghatay Oration, Ottoman Eloquence, Qizilbash Rhetoric," 53.

36. This phenomenon is evident far beyond Central Asia. For instance, what Fallou Ngom refers to as the "ʿAjamization of Islam"—that is, the process of rendering local African languages in Arabic script—is identical to the vernacularization of Persian from Arabic and Turkic from Persian, respectively. Ngom, *Muslims beyond the Arab World*, 19.

37. Texts written in eastern Turki ("Chaghatay") range from the complex poetry of Alisher Navoi, saturated with Arabic and Persian terminology, to linguistically simpler texts intended to be read out loud at a sufi shrine to a popular audience. Thum, *The Sacred Routes of Uyghur History*, 131 passim.

38. Pollock, *The Language of the Gods in the World of Men*, 20–28; Beecroft, *An Ecology of World Literature*, chap. 4.

39. Note that both Pollock and Beecroft respectively and independently consider Persian and Arabic to both be cosmopolitan languages. Beecroft, *An Ecology of World Literature*, 109. On the Arabic cosmopolis, see also Ricci, *Islam Translated*. As Pollock notes, all cosmopolitan languages "began their careers as vernaculars." Pollock, *The Language of the Gods in the World of Men*, 20. Pollock specifically mentions Arabic as "superimposed"—in terms of "lexicon and versification to figures, genres, and themes"—on top of Persian. Pollock, 286, 322. "New Persian" refers to the language that reemerged in Arabic script from the tenth century, and as differentiated from Middle Persian (Pahlavi), which was written in a modified Aramaic script.

Persian works.[40] After all, an educated person throughout much of Islamic Eurasia was expected to know both languages, and Arabic works were core to the Persianate curriculum, even though Persian works were not essential canon in Arab lands.[41]

Put simply, the Persian cosmopolis was definitionally part of the Arabic one, by virtue of its origins as an Arabic vernacular—and few would characterize the Arabic cosmopolis as bearing no relationship to Islam.[42] We can speak of practices and artifacts that seem to us more and less religious, even during the premodern period, but separating out religion is notoriously tricky business in any context. Moreover, it is unnecessary for answering many historical questions and attempting to do so in the Persianate case has led to misleading anachronism. It is unfortunate that the term "Persianate" appears to privilege a separable Persian high culture over the Arabic complex to which it was referent, but—with proper groundwork—it is a concept worth preserving.[43]

I conceive the Persian cosmopolis to be inclusive of the Islamic, which allows terminology to be customized according to the question at hand.[44] Thinking in terms of the Islamic world—or Arabic cosmopolis, which I consider synonymous—helps us to understand why Bukharan scholars would travel so far for the Hajj. But the Persianate dimension is necessary for clarifying why those same Islamic scholars wrote Bukhara into both the sacred geography provided by core Arabic texts as well as Persian epics. Similarly, more localized frameworks are necessary for still other questions, which brings us to Turkic culture and the even thornier issues of ethnicity and identity.

---

40. Perry, "Šāh-nāma v. Arabic Words."

41. For Marshall Hodgson, who coined the term "Persianate," Persianate was a subset of the Islamic world more broadly. Hodgson, *The Venture of Islam*, 2:293. By contrast, Said Arjomand argues that Persian culture also subsumed the Islamicate: "if Persian was thus Islamicized, Islam was at the same time Persianized." Arjomand, "The Salience of Political Ethic in the Spread of Persianate Islam," 7. Certainly, permeation existed between these high cultures; after all, the cosmopolis paradigm was developed in part in response to the more rigid category of "civilizations." According to the conceptualization used in this book, however, the Persian cosmopolis did not fully encompass the Arabic one. The *Shāh-nāma* was not particularly popular in fourteenth-century Yemen, and ulama in Marrakesh were not quoting Hafez. Cairo stood as an interesting border zone, where Persian had some purchase but was not indispensable or expected for any educated person.

42. This understanding stands in some tension with characterizations of the relationship between Arabic and vernacular literatures as one of competition and antagonism. al-Musawi, *The Medieval Islamic Republic of Letters*, 27, 47 passim.

43. This predominant characterization of the Persian cosmopolis as "secular" and separate from Islam has led Shahab Ahmad to reject the Persianate concept entirely, since the underlying phenomenon stands as "a major historical paradigm that is most meaningfully conceptualized not in terms of the Persianate, Turkic, or Perso-Turkic, but of Islam." Ahmed, *What Is Islam?*, 85. Instead, Ahmed prefers the term "Balkans-to-Bengal complex."

44. "Different spatial models suit different questions and methodologies, not to mention different periods." Green, "Rethinking the 'Middle East' after the Oceanic Turn," 557.

The Mysterious Formation of the Persian Cosmopolis: Iranian Civilization or Sasanian-Abbasid Commonwealth?

Where did this Persian cosmopolis come from?[45] Already in the tenth century we have foundational Persian writing, such as Ferdowsi's *Shah-nama* and Rudaki's poetry, complete with forms and language fully legible a full millennium later. A robust literary language and culture had seemingly blinked into existence almost overnight.

Most longue durée histories of Iran, as well as many introductions to the Persianate concept, posit fundamental continuity with pre-Islamic Persian empires.[46] By this dominant narrative, Persian*ate* high culture is essentially the persistence of an Iranian civilization traceable back to the Sasanian (224–650 CE), Arsacid (c. 250 BC–226 CE), and ultimately Achaemenid periods (550–330 BC).

There are serious problems with the Persianate-as-Iranian-civilization paradigm. It simultaneously glosses over discontinuities between the courtly cultures presided over by the aforementioned dynasties over more than a millennium and overlooks the cultural influence of Elamite, Aramaic, and Greek literary cultures. More important, it underemphasizes the profoundly Islamic and imperial character of the rise and initial spread of New Persian. New Persian language and culture traveled to regions never controlled by the Sasanians, and it did so initially along with the military advance of the first two Islamic dynasties (the Umayyads and Abbasids), eventually producing synthetic artifacts such as the *Fars-nama*. Prior to Islamization, Central Asia was the epicenter of Sogdian language and culture. Yet the Sogdian influence on New Persian is vanishingly slight.

Evidence is sparse, but it seems that merchants, soldiers, and Khurasani elite found opportunity in upheaval during the Islamic advance, and projected elements of Sasanian high culture eastward. (This was not a state policy of the caliphate but was enabled by the empire.) What emerged from the rubble of the Sasanian Empire, under the banner of Islam, was something altogether novel. Thus, even the rise of the Persian cosmopolis is inseparable from the rise

45. Much of the extant literature engaging this question is technically fragmented between disciplines (especially philology and archaeology). For a more extensive review and discussion, see Pickett, "The Persianate Sphere during the Age of Empires," chap. 1.

46. For instance, Spooner, "Epilogue: The Persianate Millennium."

of Islam: the two are not any more or less divisible than Islam and Arabic as a literary-cultural formation. Rather than the persistence of Iranian culture—a residual Achaemenid commonwealth—we have the spread of an emergent Persian vernacular high culture, nested within the imperial language of Arabic, and with a cosmopolitan destiny of its own.

Local Culture, Vernacular Literature, and the Problem of "Ethnicity"

A brief anecdote recounted in a mid-nineteenth century Central Asian chronicle captures the challenges of grafting modern categories onto preindustrial societies. One day a Turkic prince was visiting the bazar when he noticed that a commoner had just purchased a curiously multi-colored cow. "What is the name of your cow?" asked the prince in Persian. The hapless Uzbek peasant was justifiably confused by the bizarre question posed in the high language—a question that the prince had apparently botched in execution, such that the peasant did not understand the meaning. When the perplexed farmer failed to answer, the prince flew into a fury and began whipping the peasant, who in turn began to run to and fro screaming in Turkic, "My ox's name is 'Ox'! Its color is piebald!" Before the situation could deteriorate any further, one of the prince's servants stepped in and quietly explained to the cow's owner that the prince was merely inquiring about the beast's price.[47]

In this story we encounter a Turkic prince barking orders in bungled Persian to an Uzbek peasant who replies in Turkic dialect, the intended upshot of which the prince likewise fails to comprehend.[48] The history in which the anecdote appears is written in Persian, but the dialogue with the peasant is quoted in the original Turkic. The peasant in the story is described as "Uzbek," but the Turkic prince addressing him is instead identified by his specific tribe (Keneges, a branch of the Uzbek tribe), and the Turkic language uttered by the peasant is designated as Turki. It is unclear whether the Turkic-speaking peasant might have understood the Persian-speaking noble had the sentiment been coherently expressed. What is clear, however, is that

47. Ḥakīm Khan, *Muntakhab al-tawārīkh*, 1:404.

48. The Timurid prince Babur (founder of the Mughal Empire) wrote in his memoir that even bazaar merchants spoke and comprehended the literary language of Alisher Navoi. It is difficult to know what to make of this curious claim, especially given that the *Bābur-nāma* is written in much simpler Turkic than anything penned by Navoi. Bābur, *Bābur-nāma*, 5.

any relationship between ethnicity, language, and culture is elusive for the time and place considered in this book.[49]

For all the preceding discussion of cosmopolises of various stripes, many of the individuals performing those cultures were Turkic in some cultural or ethnic sense.[50] This fact prompts the question: What did terms such as "Uzbek" or "Afghan"—still predominant as analytic categories in the secondary literature today—signify during this time period? And what did it mean when a Turk wrote in Persian, and why might he have opted for Turkic written culture in other contexts?[51] Rather than grasping for a definition of ethnicity apropos for premodern Eurasia, I deploy the term "Turkic" to refer separately to a social structure, on the one hand, and a manifestation of high culture within the cosmopolis model, on the other.[52] Conceiving of the Turkic nobility as a power group is the more common usage of this term in the pages to come, but it is worth first exploring Turkic as a literary culture in relation to Persian and Arabic.

Marshall Hodgson articulated it first and best when he effectively described Turkic as a vernacular of Persian.[53] Nested Russian matrioshka dolls serve as a productive metaphor: Turkic language and culture incorporated the Persian cosmopolis, which in turn took the literature and symbols of the Arabic one for granted.[54] Turkic written culture was Persianate, and through the

---

49. The residue from this prenational world influences dialectical continuums in Central Asia to the present day, which has distorted received categories in modern language textbooks. Pickett, "Categorically Misleading, Dialectically Misconceived."

50. The term "Turk" was most frequently invoked in premodern sources as a foil to "Tajik" (i.e., the sedentary population), and—perhaps counterintuitively—as a means of associating dynasties with the Mongol Empire. Lee, "The Historical Meaning of the Term Turk and the Nature of the Turkic Identity of the Chinggisid and Timurid Elites in Post-Mongol Central Asia."

51. Central Asian Turkic is often referred to as "Chaghatay," but this term does not appear in reference to a language in any of the sources I used for my research, which invariably use the term *Turkī*. I prefer the more general term "Turkic" to gesture at the linguistic diversity in Turkic writing, which was significantly less standardized across time and space than Persian and Arabic. For a genealogy of the term "Chaghatay," see Péri, "Notes on the Literary-Linguistic Term 'Čaġatay.'"

52. For a careful consideration of how ethnicity as a category might be fruitfully applied to preindustrial contexts, see Elliott, *The Manchu Way*, 4 passim; James, "Uses and Values of the Term Kurd in Arabic Medieval Literary Sources"; Kia, *Persianate Selves*, chap. 5.

53. Hodgson's work predated the cosmopolis-vernacular model, and he did not use the specific term "vernacular." But in describing Turkish as a "Persianate" language referent to Persian literature for model and inspiration, his conceptualization is remarkably similar to that of Pollock and Beecroft. Hodgson, *The Venture of Islam*, 2:293.

54. Pollock's model effectively treats the vernacular-cosmopolitan spectrum as a binary, which has prompted Owen Cornwall to characterize Arabic as a "shadow cosmopolis." "Alexander and the Persian Cosmopolis, 1000–1500," 62–63. Arabic is all the more shadowy, and Persian all the more cosmopolitan, because Persian was not referent to Arabic high culture to sustain the form of epic literature (such as the *Shāh-nāma*)—a genre absent (or at least formally unrelated) in Arabic literature. Cornwall, "Alexander and the Persian Cosmopolis," 17–18. However, Arabic writing drew raw

mediation of Persian also Islamicate.[55] The residue of Perso-Islamic language and culture is palpable in many of the earliest Turkic documents, even in those not written in Arabic script.[56] In other words, Turkic vernacular high culture competed with the Persian cosmopolis, but not by rejecting the dominant paradigm on which both were premised.[57]

Thus an individual could elect to participate in the vernacular high culture or the cosmopolitan one—and many did both at the same time.[58] Alisher Navoi, for example, wrote poetry in both Turkic and Persian, just as Mirza Asadallah Beg "Ghalib" fashioned verses in both Urdu and Persian.[59] The Turkic literary productions of Islamic scholars were routinely touted in Persian-medium literary anthologies.[60] It is important to note that either choice of literary culture demanded a great deal of education, no matter what background one was coming from. This point, as well as broader questions of identity and ethnicity, are put into relief by the example of two scholars—Jum'a-quli "Khumuli" and Mirza Baba Hisari.

In his memoir, Khumuli is explicit that he came from a rural, and specifically Turkic background. By contrast, Hisari was most likely from an urban environment and a native speaker of a Persian dialect, but his memoir does not specify his native language. Yet both individuals wrote in literary Persian, a cosmopolitan language accessible to both of them only through sustained madrasa study. Hisari noted that he had to spend six months studying the

---

material from Persian sources, the same as it did from Greek ones, to formulate universal histories in the first few centuries of Islam. Humphreys, *Islamic History*, 129–30; Pourshariati, *Decline and Fall of the Sasanian Empire*, 10 passim.

55. Robert Canfield describes this phenomenon as "Turko-Persia" or, more specifically, "Turko-Persian Islamicate culture." "Introduction: The Turko-Persian Tradition," 1.

56. Legal documents written in Uyghur script (a modified Aramaic alphabet borrowed from Sogdian, and then later in turn borrowed for Mongolian) from the eleventh century not only incorporate legal loan words from Arabic (via Persian); they impose Arabic short vowels. Erdal, "The Turkish Yarkand Documents," 260, 262, 265. Even Mamluk Turkic literature from the more thoroughly Arabic-dominant context of Egypt had a decidedly Persianate character. Eckman, "The Mamluk-Kipchak Literature," 304; Bodrogligeti, "Notes on the Turkish Literature at the Mameluke Court," 273. This assertion does not pertain to the scattered fragments and inscriptions of Old Turkic, some of which predated Islam. Erdal, *A Grammar of Old Turkic*, chap. 1.

57. "Dominant paradigm" is used here in Wael Hallaq's sense, though with reference to Islamic religion and high culture more broadly, rather than exclusively the Sharia. *The Impossible State*, 9–10.

58. For instance, the Ashtarkhanid ruler Subḥān-qulī Khan (r. 1680–1702) wrote medical treatises in both Persian and Turkic. *A Turkic Medical Treatise from Islamic Central Asia*, 7–8.

59. Even the Jadid Sadriddin Ayni—patron saint of the SSR-cum-nation-state of Tajikistan—wrote in both Persian and Turkic: ʿAynī, *Bukhārā inqilābīning tāʾrīkhī*. Navoi wrote in Persian despite his defense of Turkic as the "more articulate and eloquent" language. Nawāʾī, *Muḥākamat al-lughatayn*, 5.

60. Similarly, the earliest biographical dictionaries dedicated to Urdu poets in India were written in Persian. Hermansen and Lawrence, "Indo-Persian Tazkiras as Memorative Communications," 156.

formal, written language of Persian before even being considered ready to begin his formal education.[61] Knowledge of a spoken Persian dialect may have helped somewhat with mastering the formal language, but Persian was an acquired skill irrespective of "ethnic" background, and the broader Persianate cultural skill set even more so.[62] Similarly, composing Turkic poetry might have been somewhat easier for Khumuli (who wrote a divan containing both Turkic and Persian poetry), but he too would have required training to engage the vernacular Turkic (but still Persianate) literary milieu of Alisher Navoi.[63]

At first glance, Khumuli would seem to have some notion of ethnicity or "Turkicness" in mind. Yet Khumuli's remarks on his Turkic background were explicitly designed to make a religious point. In pointing to his Turkic origins, Khumuli was emphasizing the nomadic status of his kin and their disconnectedness from more refined forms of Islam. He criticized his native tribe for its negligence in Islamic observance, citing a Qur'anic passage to compare those of his clan to early bedouin who were similarly weak in religion.[64] Thus Khumuli's apparent discussion of ethnicity was intended as a metaphor for his religious journey into textual, learned Islam.[65]

Though Khumuli and Hisari hailed from different backgrounds, both ultimately came to engage and enact the same Persianate high culture (with at least Khumuli accessing the vernacular Turkic register as well). In no case was the choice between cosmopolitan and vernacular spheres a choice between national or secular culture and the religious.

Despite the omnipresence of "identity" in the secondary literature, questions of ethnicity and community are not an area of central concern for this

---

61. Ḥiṣārī referred to the written Persian language as *kitābat-i zabān-i faṣāhat*. Ḥiṣārī, *Yāddāsht-hā*, f. 12b–13a. For an explanation of why Ḥiṣārī would have had to study literary Persian in order to access the Arabic-centric madrasa curriculum, see chapter 4.

62. "Tajik" was not used to describe a language or dialect before the twentieth century; Persian was known as *Fārsī*. For a discussion of regional dialects in the Persianate world, which required even native speakers of colloquial Iranian languages to learn the literary language, see Dudney, "A Desire for Meaning: Ḳhān-i Ārzū's Philology and the Place of India in the Eighteenth-Century Persianate World," 104–10.

63. *Dīwān-i Khumūlī*, ms. IVANUz no. 345.

64. Khumūlī wrote in the first lines of his memoir that through religious learning (*ta ʿlīm-i ʿilm ū īmān*) and the Grace of God he abandoned the Bedouin tribes "most stubborn in unbelief (*kufr*) and hypocrisy" (Q 9:97) and joined those that "believe in God and the Last Day" (Q 9:99). Khumūlī, *Tarjuma-i ḥāl*, f. 1b.

65. In Khumūlī's view, Islam "sat lightly" on the shoulders of his extended family. Allen Frank writes that the ulama would often travel into rural, nomadic territories to educate such communities in "proper" Islam. "A Month among the Qazaqs in the Emirate of Bukhara." Devin DeWeese criticized the tendency in scholarship to uncritically accept views such as that of Khumūlī as representing "authentic" Islam. *Islamization and Native Religion in the Golden Horde*, 9.

book.[66] The Persian cosmopolis is here understood as a process of acculturation and performance, not identity.[67] Turkicness probably meant something to Khumuli, but sources shed light on what that might have been only fleetingly and indirectly.[68] Texts often referenced "Uzbeks/Turks and Tajiks" to refer metonymically to all the denizens of the particular realm rather than to distinguish a single individual.[69] Certainly, these terms referred to some kind of collective identity, but what that entailed is difficult to pin down, and certainly was quite distinct from modern national identities.[70]

Some premodern authors indeed grappled with questions of identity and ethnic loyalty, but most were not terribly concerned with such distinctions.[71] Reformist intellectuals ("Jadids") of the late colonial period were keenly interested in questions of identity and nation, but the categories they used were quite novel in Central Asia (hence their designation as "modernists"). During previous periods, tribal designations were far more important to group identification than the few markers that eventually emerged as Soviet Socialist Republics-cum-nation-states.[72] Sources speak of Tajiks, Uzbeks, and Turkmen, but they also reference Keneges, Sarts, Qalmyqs, Ghalchas, and many other scraps left on the Soviet cutting room floor.[73]

---

66. Thomas Welsford observes: "Notable is the fact that, in recent years, the concept of 'identity' has been blunted by the ubiquity of the term's invocation, becoming in some instances less a spur to analytical thought than a figleaf for its absence: a totem to which one doffs one's cap before getting down to telling one's chosen story." Welsford, *Four Types of Loyalty in Early Modern Central Asia*, 15.

67. This not to say that questions of group feeling in the pre-industrial period are infeasible or inherently uninteresting. For a sophisticated approach to premodern senses of belonging in the Persianate world, see Kia, *Persianate Selves*.

68. For the treatment of ethnicity in the premodern world, see Cook, "Pharaonic History in Medieval Egypt"; Crone, "The Significance of Wooden Weapons in Al-Mukhtār's Revolt and the 'Abbasid Revolution"; Cooperson, " 'Arabs' and 'Iranians."

69. See also Subtelny, "The Symbiosis of Turk and Tajik"; Bregel, "Uzbeks, Qazaqs and Turkmens."

70. For instance, rhyming conventions seem to be the primary concern in the following quote: "Every group (*firqa*) and every tribe (*ṭā'ifa*), from far and wide, Turk and Tajik." Żiyā', *Tazkirat al-khaṭṭāṭīn*, f. 72b. Even when ethnic categories referred to an individual, such as the poet Jāmī's famous couplet about his friendship with Alisher Navoi, it is difficult to discern the exact meaning of ostensible ethnonyms: "Though he was a Turk, and I am Tajik; We were happy with each other" (fifteenth century). Jāmī was from Herat and his ancestors from Isfahan, so it is clear that he did not have in mind the modern ethnic category of "Tajik."

71. Examples of premodern authors who explicitly wrote about ethnicity include Maḥmūd al-Kashgarī on the Turks or al-Beruni on the Indians/Hindus. On the former, see Dankoff, "Kāšġarī on the Beliefs and Superstitions of the Turks."

72. Khalid, *The Politics of Muslim Cultural Reform*, 188–90.

73. The ethnonym "Uyghur" provides an instructive parallel case. As with "Uzbek" and "Tajik," "Uyghur" did not consistently refer to the Turkic population of western China as a distinct ethnic group until the late nineteenth century. The difference is that "Uyghur" had fallen out of use in the sixteenth century. Brophy, "Taranchis, Kashgaris, and the 'Uyghur Question' in Soviet Central Asia,"

Conceiving of Turkic as the product of a specific canon and associated pedagogy referent to both the Persianate and Islamic offers something tangible to replace modern categories of ethnicity.[74] The Turkic vernacular cultural complex was inherently Persianate and Islamic, nested within the Persian cosmopolis and Arabic shadow cosmopolis, respectively. Because Turkic vernacular culture is not a major focus here, "Turkic" is more frequently used in a social-institutional sense, drawing a conceptual distinction between the "Turkic nobility" (sometimes "Turkic military elite") and the "Persianate ulama" or "high Persianate intellectuals" as personifying discrete rubrics of power. In some respects, this is a problematic model. On its face it would seem to adhere to Soviet/nationalist narratives, suggesting a stereotype of cultured Tajik intellectuals holding down the civilizational fort against Turko-nomadic hordes.[75] My intention is precisely the opposite: these terms refer to distinct kinds of social and political authority that overlapped in practice and were not reducible to ethnic background or language.

Thus terms with seemingly ethnic connotations come into play throughout but are endowed with different meanings. It is difficult to speak of an "Uzbek" ethnicity before the twentieth century, but we might point to a vague Turkic descent group known as "Uzbeks" defined by kinship-based loyalty. Similarly, the ulama could engage in the Turkic vernacular sphere, but that did not make them part of the military elite. It is important to differentiate between social strata and the act of participation in a cultural complex. Multiple sources of power were active in Central Asia during the long nineteenth century, and there was authority inherent in the word as well as the sword.

"Speaking Persianate"? Power in Performance

The Persianate cultural complex was not merely a recreational pastime for the privileged classes: the cosmopolis was also a contest with political stakes.

169–70. As a result, there has been less temptation for historians to draw direct continuity between the modern nationality and terms found in premodern sources in the Uyghur case.

74. The heuristic posited here is not to suggest that it was impossible to convey Turkic cultural concepts in Persian-medium texts or engage Persian literature in Arabic. For instance, Ron Sela's main source in exploring the Turko-nomadic roots of a royal inauguration ceremony is a Persian text: *Ritual and Authority in Central Asia*. Rather, the point is that those symbols, terms, and practices (a Turkic cultural canon) were not assumed in most Persian texts in the same way the Persian canon was present in Turkic texts.

75. Yuri Bregel offers a more sophisticated version of this schema, but one I would still prefer to distance from the ethnic implications. Bregel, "The Role of Central Asia in the History of the Muslim East," 5.

Studies of "culture" and "intellectuals" are prone to gloss over this fact, flattening hierarchies all too real for the historical actors themselves. This is how writing with religious imagery becomes neutral and "secular," and how vernacular alternatives become "ethnic" and primordial.

It is true that Jews, Zoroastrians, Hindus, and Christians all participated in the Persianate, and often without any purpose that could be characterized as "Islamic." But when they did, they reproduced and reinforced a cosmopolis that intrinsically embraced a larger, Islamic "shadow" cosmopolis. Participating in the cosmopolis did not require them to convert to the religion of Islam, but it mostly precluded the fluid articulation of features from separate cultural complexes, cosmopolitan or otherwise.[76] Non-Islamic concepts expressed in Arabic, Persian, and Turkic are often expressed in Islamic terms, illustrating a centripetal pull toward symbols legible within the dominant paradigm.[77]

Thus Jewish poets could be included in the ranks of high Persianate intellectuals despite their Jewish faith, but their poetry was indistinguishable from that of their Muslim peers (see box on "Zabiha's Poetry"). Even Persian poetry in Hebrew script followed rules of Persian poetry derived from Arabic prosody, and was saturated with Perso-Islamic imagery.[78] Similarly, Hindu poets writing in Persian in South Asia expressed Indic religious concepts predominantly through Islamic terms and imagery deemed equivalent.[79] Zoroastrian writing in New Persian, such as *The Ballad of Sanjan*, explicitly repudiated Islam, but did so through language saturated with intertextual Qur'anic references.[80] Identity and belief were not prerequisites for participation in

76. "Paradoxically, Muslim philosophers and mystics have been most ready to confer universalistic recognition on the Indian religions to the extent that Indian doctrines and practices could be assimilated to Islamic categories." Ernst, "The Limits of Universalism in Islamic Thought," 2.

77. A sizable body of Christian writing in Arabic did not emerge until the eighth century, after the rise of Islam. Moreover, even translations of the Bible were suffused with Qur'anic terminology, which some scholars have described as a "Muslim cast" to the language. Griffith, *The Bible in Arabic*, 136–37; Sahner, "From Augustine to Islam," 926–27.

78. Poetical excepts were occasionally included in the first dedicated Persian-language newspaper in Central Asia, which was in fact a Judeo-Persian newspaper, published in Farghana in 1910. *Raḥamīm* no. 2 (May 21, 1910), 2. The paper drew on some elements of specifically Jewish tradition as well (e.g., use of the *anno mundi* Jewish calendar the title page), but the language of the text itself is fully Persian (e.g., the Russian word for "university," *universitet*, is glossed as "madrasa").

79. Pelló, "Drowned in the Sea of Mercy," 143; Ernst, "The Limits of Universalism in Islamic Thought." The few exceptions to this rule reinforce the broader point. Some Sanskrit-Persian translation projects in the Mughal court opted to simply transliterate key Indic terms into Persian, which proved so incommensurable with the Persian cosmopolis that later scribes were forced to gloss the text with Nagari script. Truschke, *Culture of Encounters*. More often Indic concepts were rearticulated in Perso-Islamic terms, thereby reshaping and expanding the cosmopolis. See, for instance, Zutshi, *Kashmir's Contested Pasts*; Gandhi, "Mughal Self-Fashioning, Indic Self-Realization."

80. Williams, *The Zoroastrian Myth of Migration from Iran and Settlement in the Indian Diaspora*, 144–51. The *Qissa-i Sanjān* is a curious text, as it contains references to the Gathas, and a Middle

these high cultural spheres, but the cosmopolis was nevertheless partisan toward a specific set of symbols and religious structures.[81]

An unusual entry in a poetical anthology underscores these points. The individuals included in biographical dictionaries were overwhelmingly Muslim, but a Jewish poet of late-eighteenth-century Samarqand, identified only by his pen name (*takhallus*) "Zabiha," was also included in one such volume.[82] His poetry was praised as "beautiful," and he was described as especially learned in interreligious debates.[83] Zabiha was able to capitalize on the areas of overlap between his Jewish background and the cosmopolis in which he was engaging—for instance by drawing on his expertise in the Torah (accepted within Islam as an imperfect, supplementary source of revelation), and prominently featuring Moses in his poetry (who after all was an Islamic prophet as well).[84] By articulating his world through the Arabic-scripted Persian (as opposed to Hebrew-scripted Persian), by mastering the dominant paradigm, Zabiha acquired power and connections.[85]

Zabiha's Poetry: Mystical, Islamicate, Persianate, Jewish

What treasure is this that the world is completely destroyed by Him?;
And what candle is this, that everyone's heart is His moth?
Within the bounds of the world, all become drunk from your cup;
Oh God, oh God, what sort of wine is this in your goblet?

Persian invocation in the British Library manuscript. Williams, *The Zoroastrian Myth of Migration*, 143, 152.

81. In sixteenth-century Peru, native intermediaries learned to articulate Incan religion within Christian categories almost immediately after the conquest; that act of translation had a transformative impact on native religion. In the Andean case as well there was room to equate indigenous practices with Christian categories, but the power differential was far starker. Fuchs, *Del paganismo a la santidad*, 110, 235 passim. On the Mayan case, see Hanks, *Converting Words*, 4 passim.

82. More specifically, Ẕabīḥā was active during the reign of Shāh-Murād Manghit (r. 1785–1800) (identified by his sobriquet "Amīr Kabīr"). Wāżiḥ, *Tuḥfat al-aḥbāb*, f. 89. Throughout this book, pen names (*takhalluṣ*) will be designated with quotation marks.

83. "In religious debates (held between) mixed groups he [Ẕabīḥā] studied the holy books (*kutub-i samāwī*)." Wāżiḥ, *Tuḥfat al-aḥbāb*, f. 89.

84. Note that "holy books" (*al-kutub al-samāwiyya*) in this sense normally includes the Torah, Gospels, Psalms, as well as the Qur'an. Allen Frank writes that in at least one case a Tatar madrasa student received instruction specifically in the Torah from a Jewish scholar. Frank, *Bukhara and the Muslims of Russia*, 107.

85. What came to be classified as "Judeo-Persian" (or "Judeo-Arabic") was merely "Persian" written in Hebrew characters, with dialects differing far more by region than by ethnicity. Lazard, "The Dialectology of Judeo-Persian," 39–46; Shohat, "The Invention of Judeo-Arabic," 174–78.

There is a wine-bearer (*saqi*) in this flagon-full feast—the man of the Word, Moses!; All eyes are [on] the goblet [of promise?] in his hand
A scholar is a lover of religion, a marvel such that all are his friend; Everyone who has fallen into error is his Beloved (*janana*)
The poetic verse spun by Zabiha this very evening; Will be heard by all the denizens of the world
Although creeds come in many different colors; They are all songs from the instrument of oneness.[86]

Although he successfully capitalized on the conceptual overlap between his two worlds, Zabiha could never hope to achieve the powerful post of *qazi* (Islamic judge), a barrier that Shi'a living in Central Asia also encountered.[87] Nor was he likely to rise through the ranks of a sufi order.[88] In these respects Zabiha had much in common with the other "sometimes ulama," trapped between worlds, confined to the liminal margins of the cosmopolis. He also shared many of the same barriers faced by individuals versed in sophisticated local forms of religion—still Sunni, still Muslim, but lacking formal education and removed from the cosmopolis.

Yet Zabiha played a role, however modest, in constituting the dominant Perso-Islamic paradigm, and shaping it. Despite astonishing continuities over the longue durée of Persianate history, the cosmopolis was an intrinsically dynamic process, with new ingredients added—and, far more frequently, old ones reasserted—on a constant basis. This meant that, in principle, new ingredients could be absorbed into the Persianate (and thereby Islamic) canon, and then circulated widely. Indeed, the very origins of the Persian cosmopolis trace to exactly such a process, whereby pre-Islamic Sasanian culture and religion were Islamized. Yet, by the early modern period, the Persian cosmopolis was also a conservative edifice, stabilized through centuries of very gradual accretions.[89]

86. Wāżiḥ, *Tuḥfat al-aḥbāb*, ff. 89–90.

87. In the last line of the poem, Ẕabīḥā alludes to Ibn Arabi's concept of the oneness of being (*waḥdat al-wujūd*), a mystical principle that had been widespread since the thirteenth century.

88. By contrast, this was not necessarily a barrier in the case of India, where confessional lines blurred to an astonishing degree. Amin, *Conquest and Community*; Bayly, "The Limits of Islamic Expansion in South India." There is little evidence of this level of syncretism in Central Asia.

89. Despite the astonishing, protracted efforts to absorb elements of Indic thought into the Persian cosmopolis (which has deservedly received a great deal of attention in recent scholarship), few of the products of that translation project traveled beyond India. Meanwhile, other Indian innovations more easily legible within a Perso-Islamic rubric (such as Bedil's poetry, or the Naqshbandiyya-

This is why participants such as Zabiha were more likely to reproduce existing structures than to change Persianate discourse. Although simultaneously exhibiting admiration for his literary prowess, Zabiha's biographer introduced him as a "stubborn Jew," reminding readers of his unwillingness to convert, and rhyming the phrase using terms established in the literary canon.[90] Zabiha's poetry may have featured Moses, but it did so through a metaphor drawn directly from Islamic scripture.[91] Even the pen name "Zabiha" was an allusion to the Qur'anic story of Abraham's sacrifice.[92] Expressing his world through Persian cosmopolitan discourse was empowering for Zabiha on an individual basis, even though it played a small part in reinforcing the cultural configuration that ensured his marginalized status within the hierarchy.[93]

To varying degrees, Zabiha's challenges were shared by anyone wishing to access the cosmopolis—even Muslims. Rearticulating Judaism through Perso-Islamic constructs was not so different from Khumuli framing his Turkic heritage with an analogy from the early history of Islam in the Qur'an. In both cases a certain epistemic violence was present in this subordination of the local to the cosmopolitan, the particular to the universal.[94] Local traditions are often sanitized from cosmopolitan texts, as are symbols and concepts from competing universalist cultures.[95] For others (notably women)

Mujaddidiyya) took off like wildfire in Central Asia, successfully absorbed into the Persianate canon during the exact same time period.

90. *Ẕabīḥā az ṭāʾifa-i yahūd-i ʿanūd*: the last two words are also rhymed in ghazal no. 914 of Jalal al-Din Rumi's famous *Dīwān-i shams*.

91. Moses is referred to as the "spokesman of God" (*Kalīm Allāh*) in reference to a Qur'anic passage emphasizing that God spoke to him directly (Q 4:164), as explicated in Hadith (e.g., *Ṣaḥīḥ al-Bukhārī* 7510), which was a metaphor deployed throughout Persian literature.

92. "Ẕabīḥā" almost certainly refers to al-ẕabīḥ, "The Sacrificed One," referring to Abraham's willingness to sacrifice his son. Although the Qur'an leaves the identity of the son ambiguous, later Muslim scholars settled on Ishmael rather than Isaac as the canonical interpretation.

93. This assertion stands in some tension with the recent wave of scholarship emphasizing tolerance and diversity in the Mughal Empire. By necessity the Mughal state allowed for the advancement of non-Muslims on a scale beyond anything visible in Central Asia, and the interconfessional diversity on display in the Mughal court is far beyond that of contemporary courts in early modern Europe. Yet, as Finbarr Barry Flood remarks, studies of cosmopolitanism are sometimes guilty of "casting premodern societies as the inverse of our own anticosmopolitan dystopias." *Objects of Translation*, 4.

94. "Translation is the forcible replacement of the linguistic and cultural difference of the foreign text with a text that will be intelligible to the target language reader . . . Whatever difference the translation conveys is now imprinted by the target-language culture, assimilated to its positions of intelligibility, its canons and taboos, its codes and ideologies." Venuti, *The Translator's Invisibility*, 18. This contention runs counter to recent scholarship from South Asian studies, which argues against an implicit power differential in translating Hindu concepts into Islamic terminology. Nair, "Sufism as Medium and Method of Translation," 401–2.

95. The twin poles of "high" versus "local" culture ought to be conceived of as two ends of a spectrum in constant interaction with one another. Locally specific vocabulary, traditions, and

permutations of those same challenges (especially access to advanced education and the public sphere) were highly restrictive.[96] Performing the cosmopolis was possible only after extensive training, and success in an arena that usually activated Islamic discourse. Putting the power of knowledge front and center is not meant to resurrect the specter of Muslim rulers oppressing minority religions. Unlike his Shi'i colleagues, Zabiha simultaneously engaged the Hebrew/Judeo-Persian literary sphere, and so at least had the option of ignoring the Persian cosmopolis altogether.[97] Something is lost in any act of translation, and the gravitational pull of the cosmopolis was strong.

Putting power back into the equation allows us to better understand why the cosmopolis allowed for a remarkably diverse constituency in some contexts and inclined toward conformity in others. Conceptualizing the cosmopolis in terms of high cultural mastery rather than ethnicity or confession helps us toward the former; the understanding that it was an Islamic edifice helps us toward the latter. The extent to which Zabiha was considered a full participant was the extent to which the ulama—resting their claim to power on mastery of an Islamic canon—were unnecessary. Similarly, new texts incorporated into the canon directly shaped what constituted knowledge, and therefore who was accepted as fully "knowledgeable" (the very definition of the term "ulama"). It mattered a great deal that mystical philosophy, occultism, and myriad other forms of knowledge had been absorbed into the Persian cosmopolis. It also mattered that Jewish theology or local nomadic forms of Islam—sometimes dismissed as "shamanism," but locally understood as Islamic—were not. None of this negates Persian as a medium of cross-confessional interaction, nor denies the reality of non-Muslim Persianate actors. Rather, it reminds us that the Persianate curriculum was permeated with Islamic terminology, and those symbols mattered.

---

worldviews tend to be more visible in colonial ethnographic writing than in Central Asian sources; exceptions do exist such as treatises on handicrafts and shrine narratives meant to be read aloud to an audience. Dağyeli, *Gott liebt das Handwerk*; Thum, *The Sacred Routes of Uyghur History*. See also discussion in Messick, "Islamic Texts: The Anthropologist as Reader," 32–35. As Michael Cook argues, there are limits to the notion of "infinite entropy," and "more metropolitan forms of Islam have always had the potential to trump local differentiation." *Ancient Religions, Modern Politics*, xvii.

96. According to Nurten Kılıç-Schubel, there were networks of female ulama in Central Asia: "Writing Women." But they were mostly excluded from the majority of textual production, in a process not so different from the sanitization of local heterodoxies.

97. Ẕabīḥā's biographer explicitly stated that he composed poetry in both Persian and Hebrew (*manẓūmāt-i mulīḥa bi-zabān-i ʿibrī wa fārsī namūda*). Wāżiḥ, *Tuḥfat al-aḥbāb*, f. 89. It is possible that the biographer had Hebrew-medium poetry in mind, but he also could have meant Judeo-Persian written in Hebrew script. For a brief overview of Judeo-Persian literary culture, see Ḥakham, *The Musā-Nāma of R. Shimʾon Ḥakham*.

Much of this discussion engages the dialectic produced by individuals contesting, shaping, and reconstituting their dominant high cultural paradigm. The ulama of Bukhara were masters of "speaking Persianate," which meant articulating their world through a symbolic discourse that monopolized the available trajectories of social and political advancement, at least until the colonial period.[98] The rules of the game were largely predetermined by a thousand years of broad consensus, shifting incrementally through repeated interaction. Individuals could certainly choose to ignore the Persianate entirely, but that choice also confined them to a local community (such as Zabiha's colleagues who elected to engage exclusively through Judeo-Persian, or Khumuli's nomadic kin).[99] Engagement entailed rendering one's lived experience within the dominant paradigm, one not equally permeable to all experiences or backgrounds.

The ulama of Bukhara "spoke Persianate" to shape the cosmopolis and refract their lived experience through its lens. In doing so, they spoke for religion, defined the good life, and drew the boundaries that defined their world—at least until the cosmopolis came crashing down.

A Sprawling Cultural Edifice

Not every chapter in this book draws on each of these conceptual tools equally. Yet even where the specter of the cosmopolis is less palpable, it is worth keeping in mind that in Bukhara and its environs a high Persianate cultural complex endured even into the early twentieth century. The ulama wove Bukhara into a transregional cultural continuum, a world of Turkic vernacular texts in dialogue with Persian cosmopolitan ones, which were enmeshed in an even larger Islamic world. This elite curriculum was by no means the only form of culture, nor necessarily the most sophisticated, even if the ulama strove to sanitize and universalize the locally particular. The ability to render the multifarious society around them in terms valued across time and geography was precisely what made the ulama so powerful.

98. "Speaking Persianate" reworks Stephen Kotkin's metaphor ("speaking Bolshevik") for a different time and place. Kotkin's classic study of Stalinism shows that mastering the ideological language of the state was empowering for Soviet subjects, and performing those categories—"speaking Bolshevik"—was constitutive of Soviet power. Kotkin, *Magnetic Mountain*, chap. 5. There was no totalitarian state coercing the Persian cosmopolis into existence, and invoking a model in many ways specific to mass politics and the modern state may seem provocative. At a minimum, the analogy reminds us of the political stakes of composing a poetic verse or producing a legal opinion.

99. Most people did just that most of the time, given that around 90 percent of the population during the preindustrial period was agrarian. Crone, *Pre-Industrial Societies*, 15.

Just as important as refining these models is distancing ourselves from those that may seem more familiar, unlearning what we think we know. The Persianate does not signal an ethnicity, or even a single language. It was not the cultural residue of a bygone Iranian empire, nor did it constitute an imagined community. Islam was not reducible to scripture, nor were Turkic or Persian texts any less Islamic than Arabic ones. Instead, the chapters that follow offer a picture that needs to be appreciated on its own terms—terms set by the centuries of likeminded predecessors to the Islamic scholars of Bukhara.

Chapter 2

Centering Bukhara

The Reconstruction and Mythologization of an Abode of Knowledge

In March 1912, the inaugural issue of *Bukhara the Noble*, Central Asia's first Persian-language newspaper, asserted an immutable Islamic pedigree for the eponymous city: "Bukhara the Noble is of the bosom of Islam and the noblest of Islamic homelands; it was and has always been a source of ulama and fount of learned men."[1] Writing in the 1870s, the Russian traveler N. A. Maev had been similarly impressed: "We entered through crowded, narrow streets . . . past mosques, madrasas, and pillar-like minarets. And then there she was, this center of Islam, Bukhara the Noble."[2] By the second half of the nineteenth century, Bukhara's status as a timeless beacon of Islam was well-established. This claim to timeless fame is generally taken for granted in the secondary literature—which takes at face value the Russian sources which, in turn, uncritically accepted assertions of the ulama.[3] To quote the city's most popular pilgrimage

1. *Bukhārā-yi sharīf*, no. 1 (March 11, 1912), f. 1. The official Ashgabat newspaper *Zakaspiiskoe obozrenie* included a Persian supplement as early as 1903, and a Hebrew-script Persian newspaper appeared in the Farghana Valley in 1910. For comparison, the first fully Persian-language newspaper anywhere was in Calcutta in 1822; the first Iranian newspaper appeared in 1837. In Central Asia, Persian periodicals trailed Turkic ones by several decades.

2. Maev characterized Bukhara as "noble," using the Russian word *blagorodnaia* translated directly from the Arabic *sharīf*. Maev, *Ocherki Bukharskago khanstva*, 63.

3. Russian observers arrived at the peak of the mythologization project, asserting that "Bukhara has long been considered the center of Muslim learning." Khanykov, "Opisanie Bukharskogo

guide: "In every century since antiquity Bukhara has been the gathering place for the ulama of the age."[4]

Bukhara was indeed an important city from the first centuries of Islam, and the same processes that elevated it in the ninth century continued—and even accelerated—in the nineteenth. Elite throughout the Islamic world endeavored to write even the most modest of hometowns into the grand narratives of sacred history, and Bukhara was hardly unique in this regard. Yet Bukhara stands as a particularly striking example of this phenomenon because the city's champions had an especially rich body of material at their disposal and because that rhetoric was matched with physical infrastructure.[5] Intellectuals drew on traditions shared as far away as Morocco, as well as cultural material specific to the Persian cosmopolis, without drawing any clear lines between the two. This mythologization project manifested both in writing and in the physical world, which together constituted a process devoted to asserting the city's eternal centrality.

Yet Bukhara's historical trajectory as a center of Islamic learning was far more uneven than the city's advocates allowed, and the illusion of timelessness was something scholars had to actively maintain. Most of the city's iconic architectural monuments are no older than the sixteenth century, and even the epithet that most vividly conjured Bukhara scholarly allure—"Abode of Knowledge" (*Dar al-Ilm*)—appears to date to the long nineteenth century.[6] Bukhara the city was an ancient urban center of considerable importance, but Bukhara the idea was the outcome of a project that reached new heights during the period covered in this book.

This chapter historicizes the ascent of Bukhara by focusing both on investments in physical religious infrastructure and on textual mythologization,

---

khanstva," 206. Claims by the ulama about Bukhara's eternal sanctity are repeated in Crews, *For Prophet and Tsar*, 252; Khalid, *Islam after Communism*, 31. Interestingly, both Khalid and the Bukharan scholars creating Bukhara's sacred history (e.g., Muʿīn al-Fuqarāʾ) quoted Juwaynī's Mongol history *Tārīkh-i jahān gushāyī* on this point (though Khalid does not imply that Bukhara's status remained unchanged in the centuries following Juwaynī). Muʿīn al-Fuqarāʾ, *Risāla-i Mullā-zāda*, f. 2b. Although I generally cite the manuscript version, there is also an edited version of the text: Muʿīn al-Fuqarā, *Tārīkh-i Mullā-zāda; dar żikr-i mazārāt-i Bukhārā*.

4. *Risāla-i Mullā-zāda*, f. 2b.

5. On the coconstitutive relationship between paper and space, see Green, *Making Space*.

6. The moniker *Dār al-ʿIlm* may not have entered into circulation until the nineteenth century, and is especially common in poetical anthologies composed in Bukhara around the turn of the century such as those of Muḥtaram and Pīrmastī. In tenth-century Baghdad the same term referred to an institution that housed more than 10,000 books. Sourdel, "Dār al-ʿIlm." "Bukhara the Noble" (*Bukhārā-yi Sharīf*), an even more widespread epithet attached to Bukhara, appears to have entered into usage earlier than *Dār al-ʿIlm*, but was likely also a post-Timurid phenomenon. Subtelny, "The Making of Bukhārā-yi Sharīf," n. 2. Russian travelers explicitly, and erroneously, dated *sharīf* to the fourteenth century, attributing it to Ibn Baṭṭūṭa. Olsuf'ev and Panaev, *Po Zakaspiiskoi voennoi zheleznoi doroge*, 220.

whereby Bukhara was discursively centered within the larger Perso-Islamic cosmopolis. These mutually reinforcing efforts had roots in the deep past, reemerged in the sixteenth century, and reached a crescendo in the nineteenth century.[7] The early modern chapter of this story, particularly urban construction of religious infrastructure under the Shibanid and Ashtarkhanid dynasties, has received scholarly attention. The nineteenth century, however, is better known for colonial defeat and stagnation. This chapter argues that the Manghit era marked the city's cultural apex, inheriting all of the prestige and infrastructure from previous eras, and building on them substantially.

Centering Bukhara within the Perso-Islamic tradition conjures an apparent contradiction: enacting cosmopolitan high culture definitionally entails embracing the distant and unfamiliar rather than the customary and parochial.[8] Yet the premise of this chapter suggests that the ulama of Bukhara were doing the opposite: valorizing the local rather than the cosmopolitan. How can we resolve this paradox? And how could the likes of Bukhara ever compete with Mecca or Isfahan?

Bukhara's efforts in the cultural arena were all the more critical because of the city-state-cum-protectorate's political weakness. All Muslim rulers invested in religious infrastructure to varying degrees. But the fact that Central Asia's age of sprawling steppe empires had ended made soft power disproportionately important and explains the fevered pitch of madrasa construction and mythologization. A boom in madrasa construction beginning in the sixteenth century produced larger cadres of Islamic scholars and grounded their social networks. These scholars penned manuscripts asserting Bukhara's central role in sacred Islamic history and Persianate epics.[9] This was not an early instance of proto-nationalism, or even an imagined Bukharan community, but rather the localization of a transregional cosmopolis.[10] By tying the universal and abstract to the immediate and concrete,

---

7. This trajectory stands in some tension to that proposed by V. V. Barthold, who argued that by the nineteenth century Khiva and Khoqand had surpassed Bukhara in terms of cultural output. Barthold, *Four Studies on the History of Central Asia*, 67. However, the argument here is supported by Ivanov, "Kul'turnaia zhizn' narodov Srednei Azii v XVIII–pervoi polovine XIX v.," 217.

8. In using the concept of "centering," I follow Mimi Hanaoka in conceptualizing the centripetal force binding the universal to the local: "Perspectives from the Peripheries"; *Authority and Identity in Medieval Islamic Historiography*. Hanaoka's approach differs in her understanding of "centering" as a process of identity formation, whereas I situate it within the cosmopolis paradigm.

9. Catharine Edwards and Greg Woolf demonstrate the interplay between architecture and imagination in "Cosmopolis: Rome as World City."

10. This is not necessarily to assert that such thing as a Bukharan community or identity did not exist. Instead, it is to clarify that the phenomenon of "centering the cosmopolis" explored in this chapter should not be confused with such a claim. This approach differs somewhat from Rian

Bukhara's mythologization project exemplifies an understudied process with parallels throughout the preindustrial world.

Bringing Mythic History Down to Earth

The antiquity of Bukhara's splendor continues to be taken for granted to the present day. Yet Bukhara's claim to splendor was not always so iron-clad.[11] The city's regional centrality ebbed and flowed from ancient times to the early modern period. For much of its precolonial history, Bukhara was hardly a backwater, nor was it yet the cosmological pole that it was later imagined to be.

Bukhara's rise as a dominant, fortified economic center can be traced to the fifth century CE, just barely predating the emergence of Islam.[12] From this point through the Islamic conquests (late seventh–eighth centuries), Bukhara was an important regional city-state, albeit one overshadowed by neighbors such as Balkh and Samarqand. Even within the Bukharan oasis, the city seems to have been second in importance to Paykand, and possibly ranking after Ramitan as well.[13] Unlike Samarqand and Balkh (as well as Merv and Khujand), though, Bukhara is absent from the corpus of Pahlavi (Middle Persian) writing, including the sole surviving geographical work.[14] The seventh-century Chinese Buddhist pilgrim Xuanzang mentioned Bukhara only in passing, lavishing far greater detail on Samarqand and Kesh

---

Thum's monograph, which convincingly argues for "an imagined community before the arrival of nationalist worldviews." *The Sacred Routes of Uyghur History*, iv.

11. On Bukhara's fluctuating importance, see also Liechti, "Books, Book Endowments, and Communities of Knowledge in the Bukharan Khanate," 27.

12. Bukhara was one of several important Sogdian cities, and one that emerged relatively late. de la Vaissière, *Sogdian Traders: A History*, 5, 105. Bukhara is not mentioned in any chronicles of Alexander the Great's conquests, though archeologists have dated pottery fragments to the centuries immediately thereafter. Gangler, Gaube, and Petruccioli, *Bukhara, the Eastern Dome of Islam*, 19. The name Nawak-mēthan ("New Residence"), referring to a capital of the Bukharan oasis, appears in Chinese sources and proto-Sogdian fragments from Kultobe dating well before the fifth century. However, it is unclear if Nawak-mēthan occupied the same site as the later city of Bukhara, and in any case Nawak-mēthan appears in the fragments to take fourth-place importance after Samarqand, Kesh (later Shahrisabz) and Nakhshab (later Qarshi). Sims-Williams and Grenet, "The Sogdian Inscriptions of Kultobe," 98, 101, 107. The earliest textual reference to the name Bukhara in an Iranian language seems to be a demonym from a Bactrian document from 698 AD (references on coins appear earlier). Sims-Williams, *Bactrian Documents from Northern Afghanistan*, 1:96–97.

13. Muzio, "An Archaeological Outline of the Bukhara Oasis," 49–50. Paykand was referred to as "the original, ancient Bukhara" (*Bukhārā-yi aṣlī-yi qadīmī ān ast*). Gulshanī, *Tārīkh-i humāyūn*, f. 5b. By the late Sogdian period, the Bukharan oasis "no longer seems to have been organized around a central town." de la Vaissière, "Sogdiana iii. History and Archeology."

14. Daryaee, *Šahrestānīhā ī Ērānšahr*, 18. Samarqand, Balkh, and Khorezm (along with Khujand) are mentioned in this work and in the *Bundahišn* ("First Creation," a Zoroastrian cosmological work,

(Shahrisabz).[15] Even rare surviving Sogdian documents refer to Samarqand rather than Bukhara.[16]

During the Islamic conquests in the seventh and eighth centuries, Bukhara was a city of regional importance, as well as a fount of incessant resistance against Arab occupying forces. Early Islamic rule mostly consisted of seasonal raids from the garrison town of Merv, which targeted neighboring city-states of equal or even greater standing.[17] Arab armies annihilated Paykand in reprisal for a rebellion, which created space for Bukhara to emerge as the central hub of the oasis.[18] Much like the emergence of New Persian language and literature, the rise of Bukhara was tied to the rise of Islam.

Even so, Bukhara was not yet the peerless center of learning in Central Asia that it would later become. Bukhara's star glittered during the time it served as the capital of the Samanid dynasty (900–999), but even geographical works that flourished during that same period often place other cities on a higher footing.[19] Bukhara was the subject of a significant local history—Narshakhi's *Tarikh-i Bukhara* ("History of Bukhara")—but so too were other cities in the neighborhood (e.g., Balkh and Samarqand).[20]

Along with its champions, Bukhara had its detractors. Yaqut al-Hamawi wrote in his thirteenth-century geographical treatise that Bukhara was "among the grandest cities of Central Asia."[21] But then Yaqut continued:

---

which additionally mentions Merv, Herat, and what is probably Kabul), whereas Bukhara is absent from both.

15. Xuanzang makes Samarqand's political centrality during this period explicit. Xuanzang and Bianji, *The Great Tang Dynasty Record of the Western Regions*.

16. Livshits, *Sogdiiskie dokumenty s gory Mug*, 2:105. Vaissière also argues for the centrality of Samarqand during the pre-Islamic period. *Sogdian Traders: A History*, 17. "Bukhara" (*pwx'r*) does not occur in Sogdian documents as a proper toponym, though it does appear as a demonym and coinage type. Lur'e [Lurje], "Istoriko-lingvisticheskii analiz sogdiiskoi toponimii," n. 65.

17. Gibb, *The Arab Conquests in Central Asia*, 18.

18. By the time of the composition of the tenth-century *Ḥudūd al-ʿalam*, Paykand was described as a minor city (*shahrak*) of 1,000 homesteads (*ribāṭ*). *Ḥudūd al-ʿalam*, 394.

19. C. E. Bosworth writes that the Samanids favored Bukhara over Samarqand because "Bukhara had ancient traditions as a capital." *The Ghazvanids*, 30. Until the Samanids, Bukhara had not been the capital of anything but the oasis of Bukhara (and even then often as a tributary of Samarqand). Bukhara is given pride of place as the Samanid capital in *Ḥudūd al-ʿālam* and praised accordingly, but the description of Samarqand is similar. *Ḥudūd al-ʿālam*, 393–94. Muḥammad Bakrān mentions Bukhara, but not on his list of cities known for their excellence (*khūshī*). Bakrān, *Jahān-nāma*, 70. Both works have been translated: *Hudud al-Alam. The Regions of the World: A Persian Geography*; *Dzhakhan-name (Kniga o mire)*.

20. Narshakhī's history is available in translation: Narshakhī, *The History of Bukhara*. See also Azad, *Sacred Landscape in Medieval Afghanistan* (on the thirteenth-century *Fażāʾil-i Balkh*), as well as Paul, "The Histories of Samarqand." There were important differences between these different locally focused texts, but all provided justification for the specialness of the city in question and its inhabitants.

21. Yāqūt, *Muʿjam al-buldān*, 353. Zakarīyāʾ al-Qazwīnī, a geographer also writing in the thirteenth century, concurred, describing Bukhara as an "assembly of jurists, repository of wise ones, and source of rational sciences (*ʿulūm al-naẓar*)." *Aṡār al-bilād wa-akhbār al-ʿibād*, 510.

"Despite what we have described about the virtue of the city, poets have criticized it for its filth and the prevalence of uncleanliness in its streets, since there are no toilets."[22] He substantiated this assertion by directly quoting verses by poets who held Bukhara in somewhat less esteem than most of the ulama discussed in this book. Just like later Bukharan scholars, the poet Muhammad ibn Dawud had a theory about the etymology of the word Bukhara, albeit a less flattering one:

> Lo, a town made wholly of shit; and its denizens worms within!
>
> That would be Bukhara, meaning "fecal steam"; So thick not even aloeswood incense can cut it.[23]

"Fecal steam" was a combination of *bukhar* ("steam") and *khara* ("defecating"), which together approximated the name "Bukhara."[24] In other words, for many, medieval Bukhara was a great city of Central Asia, but for others it was quite literally a shithole.[25]

Whiff of excrement notwithstanding, these were the centuries that produced much of the raw material nineteenth-century scholars would later build on. Bukhara was one of several incubators for the rise of New Persian literature, and a succession of scholarly dynasties produced many of the legal works that became indispensable to Hanafi Muslims everywhere, not just in Bukhara.[26] The memory of these developments would become central to the mythologization project that lasted from the sixteenth century to the early twentieth.

Yet whatever strides the city had made under the Samanids and their successors, the Mongol conquest in the thirteenth century profoundly diminished its status. Although the Mongols did not destroy every city they conquered, they devastated Bukhara not once but thrice.[27] During Ibn Battuta's extensive travels in the Islamic world in the fourteenth century, the explorer elected to travel directly from Khorezm to Samarqand, lingering in Bukhara

---

22. Yāqūt, *Muʿjam al-buldān*, 354.

23. Yāqūt al-Ḥamawī, *Muʿjam al-buldān*, 354.

24. The Persian *bū* ("smell") combined with the Arabic *kharāʾ* ("excrement") is another effective pun, as noted by Hanaoka, *Authority and Identity in Medieval Islamic Historiography*, 211.

25. For discussion of a similar etymology of Bukhara provided by another medieval Arab geographer—Muḥammad al-Muqaddasī—as well as an overview of other, more serious etymologies of the word "Bukhārā," see Hanaoka, 211–12.

26. McChesney, "Central Asia's Place in the Middle East: Some Historical Considerations," 44–48; Subtelny, "The Making of Bukhārā-yi Sharīf," 80.

27. The Mongols sacked Bukhara in 1220, 1273, and 1276, and the city reportedly remained uninhabited for seven years after the third disaster. Yuri Bregel, "Bukhara iii. After the Mongol Invasion."

only briefly at a shrine complex outside of the city proper.[28] He justified this decision on the grounds that Bukhara had been laid to waste by the Mongols and had become a den of sectarian fanaticism.[29] Powerful new scholarly dynasties replaced the ones wiped out by the Mongol conquest, but in the period that immediately followed the political patronage shifted in focus. Under Timurid rule Bukhara played second fiddle to the capital of Samarqand and even third and fourth fiddle to other regional cities such as Balkh and Herat.[30]

Bukhara again grew in importance as the seat of power of the Shibanids (1500–1599), and the city remained the capital of the Ashtarkhanid dynasty (1599–1747).[31] Although historians note that the quality of construction was somewhat inferior to that of the Timurid period, the Shibanid and Ashtarkhanid dynasties of the early modern period nevertheless began concentrating material investment on construction in Bukhara rather than Samarqand.[32] This process continued under the Manghits and reached its zenith.[33]

Bricks, Mortar, and Bukhara's Architectural Landscape

The Manghit dynasty (1747–1920) that ruled Bukhara for the entirety of the long nineteenth century is generally regarded as decadent and weak, an impression reinforced by its crushing defeat by Russia in 1868. Yet it was on its watch that a significant portion of Bukhara's ostensibly ancient religious infrastructure reached skyward. The madrasas constructed during Manghit rule were individually lesser in scale than some of the most famous landmarks of their

28. This was the Bākharzī shrine complex, which stands to the present day, the custodians of which impressed Ibn Baṭṭūṭa with their erudition.

29. This "fanaticism" was characterized as *taʿaṣub*, or unifying belief that binds factions together. Ibn Baṭṭūṭa, *Riḥla*, 237. Florian Schwarz has astutely pointed out inconsistencies in Ibn Baṭṭūṭa's account and challenges the degree of the Mongol devastation. "Politische Krise und kulturelle Transformation im mongolenzeitlichen Iran," 2. Even by Schwarz's reckoning, the city had suffered a relative loss of political prestige vis-à-vis other urban centers.

30. Gangler, Gaube, and Petruccioli, *Bukhara, the Eastern Dome of Islam*, 28. In the tumult following the Mongol conquest, the powerful Burhānī family was displaced by their Maḥbūbī rivals, the latter of whom managed to hold on to power in Bukhara into the fourteenth century. McChesney, "Central Asia's Place in the Middle East: Some Historical Considerations," 46. See also Schwarz, "Politische Krise und kulturelle Transformation im mongolenzeitlichen Iran."

31. McChesney, "Economic and Social Aspects of the Public Architecture of Bukhara in the 1560's and 1570's."

32. Asanova and Dow, "The Ṣarrāfān Baths in Bukhara," 191. Before ʿAbdallāh retook Samarqand, his rivals there had been invoking the city's Timurid heritage; investment in Bukhara's infrastructure served as a counterbalance. Welsford, *Four Types of Loyalty in Early Modern Central Asia*, 235.

33. Much of the secondary literature views the Manghit period as marking deterioration. For instance, Gangler, Gaube, and Petruccioli, *Bukhara, the Eastern Dome of Islam*, 29.

predecessors, such as the massive Mir-i Arab, but they were far greater in number and supported a vast religious establishment (see figure 3). Moreover, this construction was not inhibited by the Russian conquest of Central Asia, and even picked up steam in the decades leading up to the Bolshevik Revolution.[34]

The scale of Bukhara's madrasa establishment was staggering. By the early twentieth century, Bukhara boasted over 200 separate madrasas—most supported by associated endowments and containing living quarters (*hujra* or cell).[35] Russian observers in 1910 put the number of madrasa students at 4,000, which seems to be a conservative estimate when compared with the total capacity provided by madrasa cells as reported in local writing (around 7,000).[36] Writing less than a year later, Muhammad "Gulshani" estimated the number of students in Bukhara at 50,000—an incredible figure, given that he reckoned a total population of 180,000.[37]

Even assuming that Gulshani's is an exaggerated number, it is meaningful that he imagined Bukhara to be a city of students. Muslims studied in sufi lodges, mosques (of which there were upward of 360 in the city), and private study circles.[38] After all, Gulshani was counting *talib-i ilm*, which is usually translated as "student," but literally means "one who is seeking knowledge."[39] Whatever the statistical reckoning, "Abode of Knowledge" seems a well-deserved title for this Central Asian college town.

---

34. The indirect effect of Russian expansion on madrasa construction is a conclusion supported by Paolo Sartori's work on the Khivan case: "On Madrasas, Legitimation, and Islamic Revival in 19th-Century Khorezm," 107, 119.

35. Russian and Bukharan estimates are remarkably similar. Gulshanī put the total number of madrasas at 199 (*Tārīikh-i humāyūn*, f. 3a), while Żiyā'—writing about a decade later—put it at 204 (*Ẕikr-i asāmī-yi madāris-i dākhila-i Bukhārā-i sharīf*). Russian captain Fenin reported in 1910 that there could be up to 220 separate institutions. RGVIA F 400 O 1 D 3914, f. 35a. This is double the number (103) posited in Khanykov's well-known account. Gangler, Gaube, and Petruccioli, *Bukhara, the Eastern Dome of Islam*, 61. It is even possible that Żiyā''s estimate was a conservative one, as a study has recently cataloged 300 separate institutions: Jumanazar, *Buxoro ta'lim tizimi tarikhi*.

36. Report by Captain Fenin, a Russian military intelligence agent (*razvedchik*) studying Uzbek and Persian in Bukhara in 1910: RGVIA F 400 O 1 D 3914, f. 35a. According to Żiyā', there were 3,863 cells (*ḥujra*); given that cells usually accommodated two (and rarely went empty), the actual number may have been close to double Fenin's estimate. Also worth considering is the fact that Allen Frank puts the number of Tatar students studying in Bukhara alone at 3,000; it seems doubtful that Bukhara's student body was three-quarters Tatar, which is a point in favor of Gulshanī's estimates. Frank, *Bukhara and the Muslims of Russia*, 7.

37. Or rather "one *lak* eighty thousand souls within the city's confines." Unusually, Gulshanī uses the Indian unit *lak* (Hindustani: *lākh*) for his figures, which is equivalent to 100,000. Gulshanī, *Tārīkh-i humāyūn*, f. 3a; see also RGVIA D 483 O 1 D 132, f. 72b. Gulshanī's estimate of Bukhara's population is close to that of British Indian agent Mohan Lal, who put the population at 170,000 in the 1840s. Lal, *Travels in the Panjab, Afghanistan, & Turkistan, to Balk, Bokhara, and Herat*, 129.

38. Meiendorf, *Journey of the Russian Mission from Orenbourg to Bokhara*, 37.

39. By contrast, Fenin was counting *mullā-bacha* (lit. "children of the mullas"). RGVIA F 400 O 1 D 3914, f. 35a. Probably they had broadly the same collection of individuals in mind.

The sheer scale of Bukhara's educational establishment is all the more remarkable when considered in a comparative perspective. O. Kerenskii, for instance, was impressed by the number of well-funded madrasas in Khoqand, which amounted to thirty-four separate institutions in 1892—roughly equivalent to the number of madrasas constructed under the last two Manghit rulers alone (see figures 3 and 4).[40] Although paling next to Bukhara, the scale of the madrasa establishment in Samarqand was almost twice that of Khoqand, at fifty-eight by the end of the nineteenth century, of which over half had been founded in the nineteenth century (and ten since the Russian conquest).[41] Khiva, which engaged in a similar project of state-building and madrasa construction (before and during Russian protection), boasted sixty-two by the early twentieth century.[42] Bukhara's religious infrastructure was at least on par with that of the capital of the most powerful empire in the Islamic world and seat of the caliphate, and perhaps even slightly grander in scale: Ottoman Istanbul was home in the nineteenth century to somewhere between 150 and 200 madrasas, which is marginally fewer than the number found in Bukhara.[43]

How was it, then, that a diminutive amirate-cum-protectorate came to rival the Ottoman capital in terms of religious infrastructure? Bukhara was imagined during this period to be an ancient locus of Islamic sanctity and education. Yet most of the astonishing capacity described by Gulshani was the culmination of only several centuries of sustained investment, with the Manghits continuing and by some measures even accelerating a project initiated by their predecessors. Shah-Murad (r. 1785–1800) oversaw a campaign to systematically rewrite and update endowments (*waqfs*) for the city's madrasas and other religious establishments, thus clarifying their administration and restoring confidence in their continued funding.[44] This attention to religious infrastructure continued throughout the nineteenth century and up to the Bolshevik Revolution, with hundreds of endowments dedicated to

40. Kerenskii, "Nashi uchebnyia zavedeniia: Medrese Turkestanskago kraia," 3/20.

41. Khalid, *The Politics of Muslim Cultural Reform*, 85.

42. Baltaev, *Khiva esdaliklari*, f. 7a; Sartori, "On Madrasas, Legitimation, and Islamic Revival in 19th-Century Khorezm," 106.

43. Cahid Baltacı lists over 115 madrasas in Istanbul already by the end of the sixteenth century. *XV–XVI. Asırlarda Osmanlı medreseleri*. By the eighteenth century, that number had grown to 200. Zilfi, *The Politics of Piety*, 44. However, in 1869 only 166 remained, the others having been removed for competing infrastructure projects or lost to natural disasters (though the same author counts up to 500 madrasas constructed at various points in the preceding centuries). Akgündüz, *Osmanlı medreseleri XIX*, 23.

44. McChesney, "Waqf, Central Asia," 92–94. See also Reichmuth, "Semantic Modeling of Islamic Legal Documents," 14.

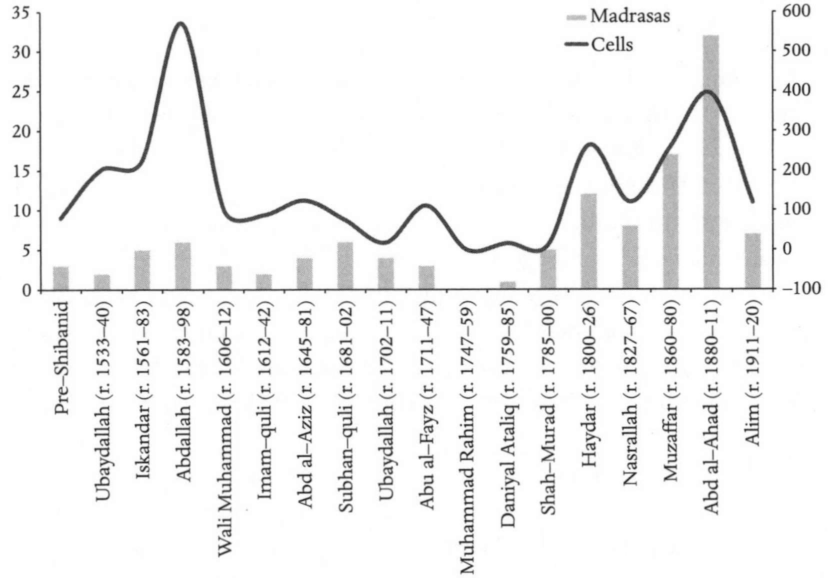

FIGURE 3. Madrasa construction over time, calculated in terms of the number of structures and student capacity.

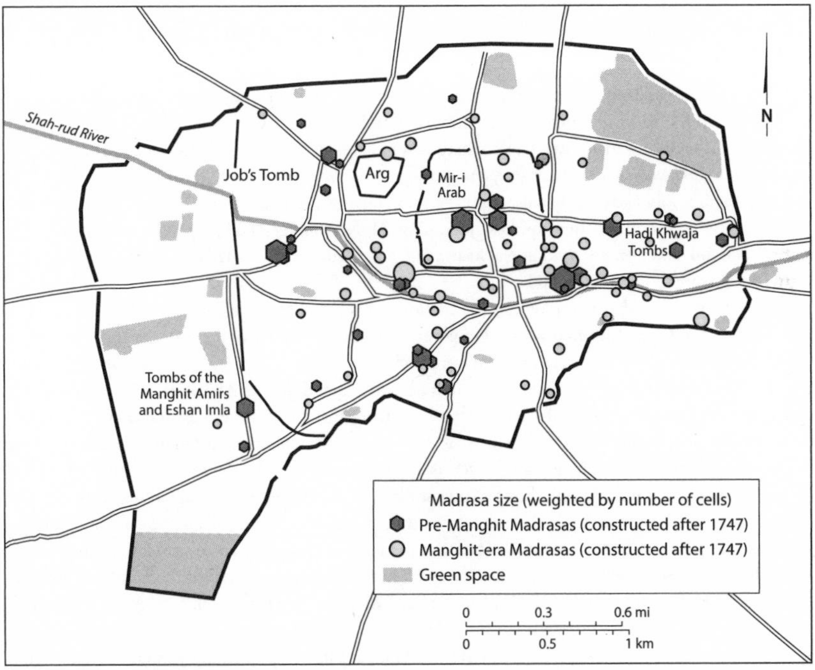

FIGURE 4. Map of city of Bukhara with madrasas sized by student capacity. Coordinates for still-standing sites were taken either from Google or personally with a handheld GPS device. Coordinates for sites that no longer exist were georeferenced from colonial-era maps, and deduced from Bregel, *An Historical Atlas of Central Asia*, 80–81; Sukhareva, *Kvartalnaia obshchina pozdnefeodal'nogo goroda Bukhary*; Gangler, Gaube, and Petruccioli, *Bukhara, the Eastern Dome of Islam*.

establishing new madrasas (as well as sufi lodges and mosques, which were often also institutions of higher learning) and augmenting existing ones.[45]

Considering the chronology of Bukharan madrasa construction in aggregate is useful for appreciating the scope of Bukhara's transformation over the long nineteenth century.[46] Even by the most conservative interpretations of available sources, Bukhara's capacity for accommodating students increased by 30 percent during the Manghit dynasty through the establishment of at least eighty new madrasas.[47] Though not as sizable as some of the madrasas built during the sixteenth century, such as the famous Kokaltash (147 cells) or Mir-i Arab (111 cells), these madrasas could nevertheless accommodate well over 2,000 additional students.[48]

These figures indicate that decline in one domain (military) could be accompanied by prosperity in another (education and culture).[49] Not only did the Russian subjugation of Bukhara in 1868 fail to put a halt to the city-state's investment in educational infrastructure, it also freed Bukharan rulers to devote even more attention to it. Under Nasrallah (r. 1827–60), who led the most sustained period of military expansion during the precolonial period of the Manghit dynasty's rule, only 0.2 madrasas were constructed per year,

---

45. Gulshanī counted seventeen sufi lodges (*khānaqāh*), 391 mosques within the walled portion of the city (or 657 mosques including the suburbs), and 195 primary schools (*maktab*). Although this section focuses on the madrasas, students studied in *maktabs* beforehand and often continued their education in a *khānaqāh* afterward (see chapter 4).

46. Żīyā''s *Ẕikr-i asāmī-yi madāris* serves as a starting point for these figures, which are also informed by numerous other sources, including Abdukholiqov et al., *Architectural Epigraphy of Uzbekistan: Bukhara—Part 1*; Sukhareva, *Kvartal'naia obshchina pozdnefeodal'nogo goroda Bukhary*; Zhumanazar, *Buxoro ta'lim tizimi tarikhi*.

47. It is possible that some of the foundation dates listed by Żiyā' were renovations of older structures—a not-uncommon practice. However, this would not change the broader story, as renovation constitutes an investment in new infrastructure.

48. The average number of cells per madrasa constructed under ʿAbdallāh was ninety-five versus fourteen under the Manghits and forty-one during the Shibanid and Ashtarkhanid dynasties. It is possible that smaller madrasas constructed during prior epochs had fallen into disrepair and were not accounted for in the sources. Allen Frank writes that, unlike the rest of Turkestan, cells in Bukharan madrasas usually only housed one student at a time because "Bukharans were quick to assume that when two students sharing a *ḥujra* they were likely homosexuals." Frank, *Bukhara and the Muslims of Russia*, 102. Kerenskii wrote that madrasa cells usually accommodated three to four individuals. "Nashi uchebnye zavedeniia," 1/18. Sadriddin Ayni certainly described multiple students being packed into a single cell, as did Hāmid ibn Baqā Khwāja: *Tanzīl al-amṡāl*, f. 2a; Ayni, *Yāddāsht-hā*, 100–101.

49. In Ottoman and Mughal studies the "decline paradigm" has generally been shifted to questions such as the decline *of what* and *for whom* and *for how long*? Studies that highlight the flourishing culture and commerce during eras of supposed decline are Doumani, *Rediscovering Palestine*; Hasan, *From Pluralism to Separatism: Qasbas in Colonial Awadh*. For discussions of the decline paradigm in Central Asia, see Sela, *The Legendary Biographies of Tamerlane*, chap. 6; Levi, "The Ferghana Valley at the Crossroads of World History."

while under his successor Muzaffar (r. 1860–85), whose rule spanned the pre-colonial and colonial periods, the rate was 0.85. The high point in madrasa construction was the reign of Abd al-Ahad (r. 1885–1911), under whose reign almost every year saw the construction of one or more new madrasas on average (1.03). The rate of construction over the Manghit period as a whole was 0.47 madrasas per year, versus under 0.15 during the Shibanid and Ashtarkhanid dynasties (considered together).

The Russian conquest meant that Bukharan rulers no longer had to worry about asserting sovereignty over outlying city-states; it was guaranteed by their imperial "benefactors." Although Muzaffar lost the important city of Samarqand, he leveraged both active Russian support and the threat of imperial force to secure control over Shahrisabz, Hisar, and mountainous provinces (e.g., Badakhshan, Darwaz, Khatlan: the Kuhistan), which Bukhara had only rarely and partially controlled in ages past. This allowed for a steadier flow of revenues, which in turn led to patronage, which in turn led to endowments.[50] Meanwhile, a new crop of merchants enriched themselves from trade with Russia, which facilitated *waqfs* from another direction.[51] These factors led to a growth in madrasa construction across the region, but the sheer scale of expansion set Bukhara apart.[52]

Unfortunately, chronological data is unavailable for over half of Bukhara's madrasas. If we assume that if nineteenth- and early twentieth-century authors were less likely to be aware of the foundation date of older madrasas and less likely to allocate the unaccounted madrasas to the previous two dynasties, the rate of investment in infrastructure from 1500 to 1747 appears on par with the Manghit period. Even that scenario would support the argument that the long nineteenth century witnessed a continuation of a mythologization project dating to the sixteenth century, and with roots stretching even further back. However, this assumption is dubious given that many of the madrasas lacking firm construction dates likely predate the Shibanid dynasty, and others were probably built during the nineteenth century. With those qualifications in mind, it is certain that the late nineteenth century was a period of major infrastructural expansion, at least matching the early modern period, and likely surpassing it by a significant margin.

---

50. The structural impact of semicolonial status on Bukhara's internal politics has yet to be the subject of rigorous inquiry, but on how the Russian presence strengthened the hand of the amirs, see Khalid, "Society and Politics in Bukhara, 1868–1920."

51. Mirbabaev, *Istoriia madrasa Tadzhikistana*, 31 passim.

52. Increased profits from merchant activity and cotton cultivation led to a boom in madrasa construction within Russian Turkestan as well. Khalid, *The Politics of Muslim Cultural Reform*, 84–85.

This chapter focuses on the effect of the dramatic increase in madrasa capacity. Motivations are difficult to assess, particularly when the historical actors in question did not leave memoirs detailing their thought processes. Some scholars have argued that the Manghits, unlike their predecessors, could not boast direct descent from Genghis Khan, and that a turn toward Islamic forms of legitimacy played a role in the physical manifestation of piety.[53] Others point out that madrasas had an overtly practical function as well: to produce the government administrators necessary for running a state.[54] But the phenomenon also likely owes something to opportunity, rather than just intention: as the Manghits expanded and consolidated power, they endowed madrasas as new resources became available. This is perhaps why we see so few madrasas constructed over Amir Haydar's long but fraught reign, and so many under Abd al-Ahad, the first ruler whose entire rule was guaranteed by the Russian Empire. Finally, the ambition to center Bukhara within the Persian cosmopolis stands as another factor in the madrasa construction boom—perhaps not a cause of the expansion of educational infrastructure, at least not consciously, but as its consequence.

Sacred Geography, Sacred History

Investment in infrastructure was central to Bukhara's success in edging out competitor city-states, but the city's scholars and rulers were building a narrative that rested on more than bricks and mortar. Their ambition was to mythologize Bukhara's status as a peerless center of religion and learning not only for their time, but for all time.[55] By blending Persian high culture with Islamic sacred history they localized the universal, thereby centering the cosmopolis. Bukhara's mythologization project was not unique to the long nineteenth century: just as madrasas built on top of older monuments and funded with new endowments, nineteenth-century writers built on what had gone before.[56] The process of compilation and amalgamation was inherently creative, despite the illusion of timelessness.

---

53. Von Kügelgen, *Legitimatsiia sredneaziatskoi dinastii Mangitov*, 84 passim. Other scholars have criticized the legitimacy paradigm generally, and with regard to madrasa construction in particular. Welsford, *Four Types of Loyalty in Early Modern Central Asia*, 15–16; Sartori, "On Madrasas, Legitimation, and Islamic Revival in 19th-Century Khorezm," 100–104.

54. Sartori, "On Madrasas, Legitimation, and Islamic Revival in 19th-Century Khorezm," 108–9.

55. "Myth" and "mythologization" in this usage are not dismissive. Islamic scholars were concerned with sources and historicity, and the resultant legendary history of the city was entirely plausible in its cultural context. The terms certainly are not intended to play into the "myth of [post-Enlightenment] mythlessness." Coupe, *Myth*, 5–6.

56. In a sense, this process can be viewed as parallel to Shāh-Murād's campaign to copy, amalgamate, and update *waqf* deeds for madrasas and other religious institutions in the city of Bukhara. See also Antrim, *Routes and Realms*, chap. 2.

The phenomenon of centering a particular place within a much larger cosmopolis has deep roots in the Islamic world and is evident from the earliest centuries of the religion's existence.[57] The process has received the most attention as an instrument for nativizing Islam, tying religious symbols and sacred history to local figures and sites.[58] Despite these origins, the same dynamic was still present in early modern Bukhara, long after the majority of the population had become Muslim. I first focus on the ways Bukhara was centered within the Islamic world writ large; and then consider how the city was centered within the concentric Persianate sphere more specifically. It is critical to emphasize that these were part of the same process: the Persianate was inherently Islamic.

Bukhara's religious infrastructure rested on top of centuries of accumulated lore, which was attested in textual productions across multiple genres. Many of these works explicitly referenced and built on one another, particularly pilgrimage guides and city histories. The earliest such work was Narshakhi's tenth-century *Tarikh-i Bukhara*, which continued to be consulted through the twentieth century.[59] Its popularity was dwarfed by Mu'in al-Fuqara's fifteenth-century *Risala-i Mulla-zada*, which was reproduced with abandon through the long nineteenth century.[60] Core traditions captured in these texts were repeated in new synthetic works composed in the long nineteenth century, for both distant and local audiences, including one notable pilgrimage guide written by a prince of the ruling Manghit dynasty.[61]

57. Savant, *The New Muslims of Post-Conquest Iran*.

58. DeWeese, "Sacred History for a Central Asian Town"; Antrim, *Routes and Realms*, chap. 2; Hanaoka, *Authority and Identity in Medieval Islamic Historiography*, chap. 7.

59. For instance, Narshakhī's work appears on the list of ʿAbdallāh Balkhī's personal book collection. *Jung-i ʿAbdallāh Balkhī Kātib*, f. 701a. ʿAbdallāh Balkhī is further discussed in chapter 7. For a discussion of the problem of authorship, and how pilgrimage guides and sacred histories tended to build upon one another, see Paul, "The Histories of Samarqand," 76–77.

60. Most extant copies of this work date to the long nineteenth century. The al-Biruni Institute of Oriental Studies, for instance, holds copies from 1804, 1815, 1819, 1828, two from 1830, 1835, two undated copies from the mid-nineteenth century, 1860, 1877, 1879, 1895, 1897, an undated copy from the late nineteenth century, and 1900. The Institute of Oriental Studies in Dushanbe has a few earlier copies (from 1649, 1662, and an undated copy from the seventeenth century), but there too the majority are from the nineteenth century: 1830, two from 1835, 1841, 1847, 1867, 1873, 1888, and 1896. So frequently was this work copied that it shows up under different titles. The most frequent variation are *Tārīkh-i Mullā-zāda* and *Kitāb-i Mullā-zāda*. Occasionally it is even misidentified: the *Taẕkira-i shuyūkh-i Bukhārā* (copied in 1844) in the Oriental section of St. Petersburg National University Library (Biblioteka Vostochnogo Fakul'teta, Sankt-Peterburgskii Gosudarstvennyi Universitet no. 593). The work was eventually lithographed in Kagan (New Bukhara) in 1904, with Narshakhī's *Tārīkh-i Bukhārā* included in the same volume. See also Storey, *Persidskaia literatura*, 2:1115. It is also present as an untitled manuscript in the library of the University of Mecca.

61. Descriptions of Bukhara's sacred geography appear in collections in the Volga-Urals region of Russia, such as a *Ziyārāt-i Bukhārā*, which is a near-copy of *Tārīkh-i Mullā-zāda*, as well as a Turkic-medium guide lithograph (*Tārīkh-i Bukhārā wa tarjumat al-ʿulamā*ʾ). Muḥammad Nāṣir al-Bukhārī (Manghit),

Descriptions of sacred sites and legendary events appear across other genres as well, such as Gulshani's geographical-historical work *Tarikh-i humayun* (1911), and Sadr-i Ziya's *Zikr-i awa'il-i Bukhara* (the late 1920s).[62] These works, written in different time periods, enjoyed varied readership and exemplified diverse writing styles, which makes their common sensibilities and apparent aims all the more striking.[63]

If an animating motivation for these authors was to impress readers with Bukhara's Islamic sanctity, there was no more effective means of doing so than connecting the city directly to the Prophet Muhammad and his Companions. The Arabs did not conquer Central Asia during the Prophet Muhammad's lifetime (or that of any of the Rightly Guided Caliphs, r. 632–661), but numerous strategies for overcoming inconvenient details such as this had been in place for centuries (both in Bukhara and elsewhere). Hadiths asserting a transcendent connection between the Prophet and Bukhara were circulated already in Narshakhi's tenth-century history.[64] These tropes continued to circulate in early modern and even colonial-era texts, conveying to new generations of readers that Bukhara's title "Fakhira" ("distinguished, superior") had been revealed to the Prophet directly by the angel Gabriel, and glossing over the fact that the hadith had since been classified as "unsound."[65]

Similarly, Ziya included hadiths about Bukhara attributed to Narshakhi's history that do not appear in surviving versions of the work:[66]

Tuḥfat al-zā'irīn. This is likely a version of *Hādī al-zā'irīn* by the same author, included in a volume compiled by none other than Żiyā'. See also Paul, "The Histories of Samarqand," 80–81.

62. Żiyā', *Ẕikr-i awā'il-i Bukhārā*.

63. Assessing the audience of manuscripts inevitably involves a great deal of guesswork, particularly because the contents could be memorized and recited orally. *Risāla-i Mullā-zāda* was written earlier and copied multiple times, while I am only aware of one copy of the other two, so it seems fair to conclude that the former enjoyed the widest audience, though it is impossible to know for sure.

64. For instance, some hadiths circulated through these texts wherein the Prophet foresaw the incorporation into Islam of a holy city revealed to him by God, but which he never saw with his own eyes. Hanaoka, *Authority and Identity in Medieval Islamic Historiography*, 212–14, 92–98.

65. *Risāla-i Mullā-zāda*, f. 2b. On the *Fākhira* traditions as recounted by Narshakhī, see Hanaoka, 212–13. In the long nineteenth century, this epithet shared space with the more popular *Sharīf* and *Dār al-'Ilm*, but in the early modern period *Fākhira* was used more exclusively; for instance, Muṭribī Samarqandī, *Taẕkirat al-shu'arā'*, 150, 167, 191 passim. This particular tradition (whose transmitter was identified as Salmān al- Fārisī by Narshakhī, but unspecified by Mu'īn al-Fuqarā') appears in a work by al-Zamakhsharī, who was a collector of rare hadiths. Zamakhsharī, *Rabī' al-'Abrār*, 272. See also the editor's footnote (no. 15) in Narshakhī, *Tārīkh-i Bukhārā*, 201–2.

66. The tradition may have been in Żiyā's version of Narshakhī's text. We know from a list of his personal book collections that he had a volume containing both Narshakhī's history and *Risāla-i Mullā-zāda*. Vohidov and Erkinov, "Le fihrist (catalogue) de la bibliothèque de Ṣadr-i Żiyâ." The tradition also appears in Yāqūt al-Ḥamawī's *Mu'jam al-buldān* and Abū Yaḥyā Zakarīyā' al-Qazwīnī's *Aṯār al-bilād*, so Żiyā may also have followed the precedent of other such amalgamative texts and added a new touch.

"There lies a city in Khurasan from beyond the Oxus river, which is named Bukhara. It is a land enveloped by sanctity and surrounded by triumphant angels. Its denizens [even while] sleeping in their beds are vigilant on the path of God."[67] Interestingly, Ziya stopped short of relaying the full hadith, in which the Prophet continued that beyond Bukhara lay a city known as Samarqand, a city blessed by a sacred stream flowing straight from heaven and the grave of one of the prophets; and beyond that would be conquered the land of Qatawan, where 70,000 martyrs and their ancestors would be granted intercession by the house of the Prophet on the Day of Judgment.[68] Not only did Ziya elide the equally sacred status of the other cities referenced in the hadith, he also appropriated those motifs—that is, prophet tombs and special intervention for a city's inhabitants—for Bukhara. Thus traditions that enjoyed a genuinely antique pedigree advanced a narrative particular to the early modern period: one could imagine the same hadith being used during the Timurid era to instead exalt Samarqand.

Beyond divine inspiration, relics were an important way to tie Bukhara's geography to Islam's most sacred figures—and like hadiths, these traditions continued to evolve into the nineteenth century.[69] Unlike Narshakhi's tenth-century history, Mu'in al-Fuqara's fifteenth-century text was organized entirely around burial sites.[70] Although tombs were immobile, relics could be divided into smaller pieces and moved.[71] According to Mu'in al-Fuqara, strands of the Prophet's hair were buried in the graves of various holy scholars, such as the tomb complexes of Imam Sha'bi and Qazi Abu Zayd Dabusi (d. eleventh century).[72] These traditions were kept alive in works produced in the nineteenth century, which continued to coach pilgrims in the proper etiquette when visiting a relic-bearing site.[73] According to one early

67. Żiyā', *Ẕikr-i awā'il-i Bukhārā*, f. 235a.

68. Qaṭawān was a village located not far from Samarqand. Yāqūt al-ḥamawī, *Mu'jam al-buldān*, 4:375.

69. For a discussion of relics and sacred geography in Islam more generally, see Wheeler, *Mecca and Eden*.

70. On the meaning attached to saintly topography, see Amster, *Medicine and the Saints*, 22. Relics played an important role in other local histories written in the same time period. Hanaoka, *Authority and Identity in Medieval Islamic Historiography*, 198–201.

71. This is excluding Timur's legendary transfer of the Prophet Daniel's tomb from the Iranian city of Susa to Samarqand. Both modern cities now boast tombs of Daniel, as does the Iraqi city of Kirkuk.

72. *Risāla-i Mullā-zāda*, f. 7a. The text also relayed special instructions for the proper veneration of hairs from the Prophet. *Risāla-i Mullā-zāda*, ff. 7b–8a.

73. For instance, Muḥammad Nāṣir al-Bukhārī reproduced this tradition from the *Risāla-i Mullā-zāda* in *Tuḥfat al-zā'irīn*, 18.

twentieth-century source, a cloak worn by the Prophet could attract more than 100,000 pilgrims in a season.[74]

Relics and tombs were critical for illustrating the continuity of Bukhara's glory. In modern Uzbekistan, the antiquity of Bukhara's architectural splendor takes center stage, a sensibility inherited from the Soviet period. Historical sites have been sanitized, objectified, and selectively presented to emphasize the difference between a past way of life and the present. For this reason, it is generally the older tombs and madrasas that the Soviets preserved for posterity, whereas many of the Manghit-era constructions depicted in figure 4 have been demolished or repurposed.[75] In stark contrast, during the early modern period Bukhara's connections to sacred history were used to demonstrate that the city remained part of a living tradition, that the ulama of the current age were the peers of their predecessors, and that Bukhara's sacred past flourished in the present.

For instance, Mu'in al-Fuqara's pilgrimage guide described the tombs of the Mahbubi family dynasty of scholars prominent in Bukhara immediately following the Mongol conquest.[76] He also wove the acolytes of Yusuf Hamadani (d. 1141) into that same tapestry, noting that several of them were buried near Imam Bakr Hamid, which also happened to be the resting place of one of the hairs of the Prophet Muhammad.[77] The Manghit prince Muhammad Nasir's early twentieth-century pilgrimage guide carried that torch, establishing scholars of his age as essential parts of Bukhara's sacred landscape. He remarked that Damulla Inayatallah Khwaja's (d. 1856/57) shrine was situated just to the southeast, thus putting a scholar from living memory in the same company as some of the most famous Hanafi legal scholars in history

---

74. One l<u>akh</u> of pilgrims, using the Indian measure. Gulshanī, *Tārīkh-i humāyūn*, f. 81b. The shrine in question was located in Langar Ata. Situated in the mountains south of Shahrisabz, Langar Ata is more firmly in Samarqand's hinterland than Bukhara's, yet rhetorically appropriated for Bukhara's glory in this text. For references on the shrine's history, see Welsford, *Four Types of Loyalty in Early Modern Central Asia*, n. 137.

75. On changes to Bukhara's architectural landscape during the Soviet period, see Gangler, Gaube, and Petruccioli, *Bukhara, the Eastern Dome of Islam*, chap. 12.

76. Muʿīn al-Fuqarā, *Tārīkh-i Mullā-zāda; dar ẕikr-i mazārāt-i Bukhārā*, 23–25. The graves of both ʿUbaydallāh Ṣadr al-Sharīʿa and Maḥmūd Tāj al-Sharīʿa were included in the description, both of whom wrote numerous works that remained part of the legal curriculum in Bukhara and beyond into the twentieth century, and their names would have been familiar to visitors (see chapter 4 on madrasa curriculums).

77. Muʿīn al-Fuqarā, *Tārīkh-i Mullā-zāda; dar ẕikr-i mazārāt-i Bukhārā*, 67–68. Imām Bakr Ḥāmid was one of the "four Bakrs" of the Chahār Bakr shrine complex just outside of Bukhara. Muʿīn al-Fuqarā and Muḥammad Nāṣir were both careful to point out that Hamadānī's tomb was in Merv, and therefore focus on his followers' tombs in Bukhara, but that did not stop Bukharan residents of the Kār-khāna / Nūr-ābād neighborhood from frequenting a shrine dedicated to him. Sukhareva, *Kvartal'naia obshchina pozdnefeodal'nogo goroda Bukhary*, 244.

(the Mahbubis), one of the most famous sufi shaykhs (Hamadani), and even the Prophet himself via sacred relic.[78]

The Abrahamic Prophet Job (Ayyub) similarly illustrates the power of the distant past in elevating Bukhara during the long nineteenth century. Narshakhi's tenth-century text made no mention of Job, and the tradition connecting the prophet with Bukhara probably emerged in the medieval period.[79] However, Mu'in al-Fuqara's fifteenth-century text invoked Narshakhi to link Job to Bukhara, even while acknowledging that the historicity of the tradition was questionable at best.[80] This qualification did not prevent the author from describing other legends about Job's tomb in Bukhara, such as a tree that remained green even during winter and under which lay a spring that flowed forth from heaven.[81] For the average pilgrim, it was the miraculous tales rather than the historicist qualifications that rose to the surface: an account asserting Bukhara as Job's final resting place and recounting the story of the heavenly spring was carved into a wooden plaque above the burial chamber.[82]

Once again, the same pattern emerges: antique origins, early modern expansion, nineteenth-century embellishment. Just as with stories about the Prophet Muhammad, traditions associated with Job remained vibrant and were even expanded on. Sayyid Muhammad Nasir al-Bukhari followed Mu'in al-Fuqara's lead in questioning the veracity of Job's resting place, but added to it that the prophet's actual tomb was in the land of the Houris (heavenly nymphs attested in the Qur'an), seeming to endow the spring at Job's tomb with role of a conduit.[83] Ziya recounted the legend as fact, relaying the same

---

78. Muḥammad Nāṣir, *Tuḥfat al-zā'irīn*, 98. This is the same ʿInāyatallāh nicknamed "Qāżī-yi Kalān Taḥt-i Minārī."

79. The "discovery" of ancient tombs in ahistorical locales was not unique to Bukhara; Ali's shrine in Balkh and Daniel's in Samarqand appeared in roughly the same period. Paul, "The Histories of Samarqand," 80. For a discussion of this and other legendary resting places of Job, see Wheeler, *Mecca and Eden*, 102.

80. Muʿīn al-Fuqarā' quoted Ḥasan al-Baṣrī (d. 728, credited as an early figure in many sufi lineages) from Narshakhi's *Tarikh-i Bukhara*, stating that Job visited Bukhara and was treated well by its inhabitants, prompting him to say a prayer blessing the city. *Risāla-i Mullā-zāda*, f. 3a. He also noted that Job was in fact buried in a village near Damascus. *Risāla-i Mullā-zāda*, f. 3b.

81. On this point Muʿīn al-Fuqarā' quoted Muḥammad ibn Aḥmad Ghunjār and Asbāṭ ibn Ilyasaʿ al-Bukhārī. The former wrote a history of Bukhara that is now lost. Muʿīn al-Fuqarā' did not specify whether he had access to a copy, but may well have been quoting the plaque physically located on the doorway to the burial chamber, which explicitly quoted Ghunjār. Abdukholiqov et al., *Architectural Epigraphy of Uzbekistan*, 395. On Ghunjār, see Samʿānī, *al-'Ansāb*, 78–79, as well as Narshakhī, *Tarikh-i Bukhara / Istoriia Bukhary*, 102; Narshakhī, *The History of Bukhara*, 103.

82. Abdukholiqov et al., *Architectural Epigraphy of Uzbekistan*, 395. The wooden plaque is still on display.

83. The author attributes this tradition to Muḥyī al-Dīn al-Nūrī. Muḥammad Nāṣir al-Bukhārī, *Tuḥfat al-zā'irīn*, 8. The author cites the *Risāla-i Mullā-zāda* as one of his sources. Muḥammad Nāṣir

tradition from the same source, but without any of Mu'in al-Fuqara's incredulity.[84] Moreover, Ziya claimed that the original source had been quoting none other than Muhammad ibn al-Hasan al-Shaybani, whose scholarship forms the basis of the Hanafi school of Islamic law.[85] Many of these shrine guides married a sense of genuine historicity (citing sources and assessing reliability) with a flair for the dramatic, directing pilgrims even to tombs of questionable provenance.[86] For instance, Muhammad Nasir's pilgrimage guide mentioned that Bukharan residents frequented a tomb erroneously believed to be the final resting place of al-Ghazali (d. 1111), a scholar famous for reconciling sufism and Islamic law, but nevertheless advised potential visitors as to the shrine's location.[87]

In Ziya's writing, Job's association with Bukhara takes on a decidedly presentist bent. Ziya expanded on a long-attested account of the hospitality Job found in Bukhara when he first arrived in the city by following the prophet from Bukhara to Tashkent (then Chach), where denizens of Tashkent stole the prophet's donkey. Just as Job blessed Bukhara for their hospitality, he damned Tashkent for its treachery.[88] By way of conclusion to his story, Ziya advised the reader that thievery remains the motto of the people of Tashkent.[89] It does not seem a coincidence that Tashkent had by the time of his writing overshadowed Bukhara as a regional center in the financial sphere, which made the city's spiritual claims all the more important.

Just as Ziya spun stories about the Abrahamic prophet for contemporary relevance, the graves of more recent figures mushroomed up around Job's tomb; for instance, the Mahbubi family of scholars was buried nearby.[90] During the Soviet period, the tombs connecting Bukhara's ancient past to figures

---

was the son of the Bukharan amir ʿAbd al-Aḥad; only the lithograph version of the work survives. *Sokrovishcha vostochnykh rukopisei*, 10.

84. Żiyāʾ attributed the information to Muḥammad ibn Aḥmad Ghunjār's now lost *Tārīkh-i Bukhārā*. Ghunjār's work is not listed as part of Żiya's library, but two copies of *Risāla-i Mullā-zāda* are. Vohidov and Erkinov, "Le fihrist (catalogue) de la bibliothèque de Ṣadr-i Żiyâ,'" secs. 243–44.

85. Żiyāʾ, *Ẕikr-i awāʾil-i Bukhārā*, f. 235a. The "original source" refers to Ghunjār's lost *Tārīkh-i Bukhārā*.

86. Muʿīn al-Fuqarāʾ cautioned that even though the graves of Companions of the Prophet were famous among the people of Bukhara and popularly visited, reliable historical sources demonstrate that their respective resting places lie elsewhere. He also endorsed their continued veneration and association with Bukhara, arguing that if the belief of the pilgrim were sincere, he or she would still receive full blessing for the pilgrimage. *Risāla-i Mullā-zāda*, f. 10a.

87. Muḥammad Nāṣir, *Tuḥfat al-zāʾirīn*, 98.

88. *Dar Ḥaqq-i Ēshān bad kard.*

89. Żiyāʾ, *Ẕikr-i awāʾil-i Bukhārā*, f. 235a.

90. Of the pre-Islamic prophets the figure of Job looms largest, but other Abrahamic holy men are also referenced in these texts, even if somewhat more vaguely. ʿAbd al-Raḥmān "Tamkīn" attributed Bukhara's very foundation to the Qur'anic prophet Idris. Wennberg, *On the Edge*, 88. One notes that the

FIGURE 5. Job's Tomb in 1927, with surrounding tombs still intact. Photograph (no. 3-1350) courtesy of the Central State Archive of Film and Photo Documents of Uzbekistan.

of the intervening centuries were cleared away, and today a well-manicured park stands in its place (see contrast between figure 5 and figure 6). But Job's grave was previously the centerpiece of a single pilgrimage site integrating a millennium of sacred history, with the long nineteenth century merely the latest chapter.

Bukhara's mythologization project married textual production with physical infrastructure, and Job's tomb was no exception. From 1770 through 1917 at least forty-five *waqfs* were endowed toward the maintenance of the Job (Hazrat-i Ayyub) mosque, which had been founded by Timur in 1383/84.[91] In the marginalia of one of these endowments is a note specifying that the lands associated with the *waqf* had been enveloped by sand until 1914/15 when the Manghit amir intervened and restored the lands to their original state.[92] Thus the renovation project provided a concrete artifact substantiating written production.

prophet Idris is often credited with the development of writing in Islamic sources (fitting with the d-r-s root in his name, the same as "madrasa"), making his association with Bukhara all the more appropriate.

91. TsGARUz F i-323 O 1 D 396/1–2, 404–31. The tomb section of the complex was founded by Timur, at least according to epigraphy on the tomb. Abdukholiqov et al., *Architectural Epigraphy of Uzbekistan 1*, 391.

92. TsGARUz F i-323 O 1 D 396/1.

FIGURE 6. Job's Tomb in 2014. Photograph by author.

For all of the textual embellishments composed by Ziya and his predecessors, and despite a rich courtly chronicle tradition, no one ever produced a universal narrative situating the Manghit dynasty in the long run of Islamic history.[93] Yet these texts mythologizing Bukhara as a place served some of the same functions, explaining the place of the city and its rulers in relation to the earliest caliphates and Arab conquests. For instance, Mu'in al-Fuqara emphasized the fact that the Arab general Qutayba erected the congregational mosque of Bukhara in 712, the same decade as the Umayyad Mosque's construction in Damascus, thus linking Bukhara to a sacred monument over 2,000 miles distant.[94] Gulshani similarly focused attention on Qutayba's congregational mosque (as well as six others constructed in Bukhara by the

93. The universal history was a common genre in the Islamic world, which generally begins with pre-Islamic Abrahamic history (sometimes including an account of the Sasanians), then moves to Prophetic history, then the early caliphates, and culminates with the ruling dynasty in question.

94. *Risāla-i Mullā-zāda*, f. 2a. Qutayba's mosque had long since collapsed and had been renovated and rebuilt numerous times in previous centuries. The current structure dates to the Timurid-Shibanid transition in the early sixteenth century (with construction having begun earlier), although apparently the minaret dates to 1127. Gangler, Gaube, and Petruccioli, *Bukhara, the Eastern Dome of Islam*, 48, 90.

famous general), but rather than connecting it to the Umayyad Mosque, he linked it to the mythological prophet Khizr, who miraculously instructed Qutayba how to build the Qibla such that it correctly faced Mecca.[95] Elsewhere Gulshani asserted that the Arab inhabitants of Waghanza district were the direct descendants of Qutayba's troops, having remained behind as wardens of the eastern domains.[96] The common thread connecting these different testaments was Bukhara's place in the grand narrative of Islamic history.[97]

Muhammad Nasir took the additional step of adding the Manghit dynasts into the pilgrimage circuit.[98] Thus figures like Shah-Murad and Amir Haydar were inserted into the same landscape as famous medieval monarchs such as Isma'il Samani (r. 892–907) and his heirs. Muhammad Nasir explicitly compared Shah-Murad to the Caliph Umar (r. 634–644), remarking that they were both the second of their line, and that only their rulership was steeped in the radiance of the Prophet's good character.[99]

Just like Job's shrine, or Isma'il Samani's mausoleum, the Manghit tombs were surrounded by the resting places of famous Islamic scholars. Many of these adjacent graves, however, dated only to the last couple centuries. The past Manghit rulers were located closest to Habiballah, one of the first sufis to bring the Mujaddidi branch of the Naqshbandiyya to Central Asia, and Eshan Imla, another famous scholar of the eighteenth century.[100] Imla

---

95. Gulshanī, *Tārīkh-i humāyūn*, f. 2b. Gulshanī also clarified that the congregational mosque built by Qutayba was by his day known as the Masjid-i Kalān. Khiżr (or sometimes al-Khażir), the "Green Man," is a revered figure in Islam possessed of great wisdom sometimes considered to be a prophet; he also figures prominently in Persian Alexander romances. Wensinck, "al-Khaḍir." Both Amir Timur (r. 1370–1405) and the first Manghit dynast Muḥammad Raḥīm Khan (r. 1747–70) claimed descent from this figure. Von Kügelgen, *Legitimatsiia sredneaziatskoi dinastii Mangitov*, 429–30.

96. Gulshanī, *Tārīkh-i humāyūn*, f. 13a.

97. For numerous traditions connecting Bukhara to the Rightly Guided Caliphs, see Żiyā', *Ẕikr-i awā'il-i Bukhārā*, f. 235a. Similarly, Gulshanī wrote that the caliph Uthman's son Sayyid Aḥmad's tomb was a popular pilgrimage site in the adjacent district of Khutfar (*Tārīkh-i humāyūn*, f. 25b), just as Mu'īn al-Fuqarā' had previously placed one of Uthman's other sons in Bukhara proper.

98. The water cistern (*sardāba*) near the Manghit mausoleum was haunted, according to local tradition. Sukhareva, *Kvartal'naia obshchina pozdnefeodal'nogo goroda Bukhary*, 161.

99. *Ḥażrat-i Amīr al-Mu'minīn Shāh-Murād Ma'ṣūm Ghāzī, kih s̱ānī-yi khulafā'-i rāshidīn wa 'Umar 'Abd al-'Azīz būda, kih bi-juz-i ēn ḥażarāt-i khamsa hīch yak az salāṭīn-i mutaqaddimīn ū muta'akhirīn bi-sīrat-i ḥażrat-i Rasūl-i Allāh salṭanat bi-tāb na-rafta* . . . Muḥammad Nāṣir, *Tuḥfat al-zā'irīn*, 94. Since there were two Manghit rulers before Shāh-Murād, but only one Rightly Guided Caliph before 'Umar, logically this would seem to compare the first Manghit ruler, Raḥīm Khan, to the Prophet, though the author does not mention a grave site for the founding Manghit dynast.

100. Muḥammad Nāṣir, *Tuḥfat al-zā'irīn*, 90–93, 95; ḥabībāllāh's controversial revivalist ideas were not well received: he was killed by an angry mob, even though his ideas ultimately triumphed. DeWeese, "'Dis-Ordering' Sufism in Early Modern Central Asia," 263–64.

mentored the children of Hadi Khwaja, whose family shrine complex formed another major pilgrimage destination elsewhere in the city, and whose legacy is a major focus of chapter 7.[101]

Madrasas and minarets were critical to Bukhara's stature as an Islamic center. Texts discussed here provided a story to go with the physical infrastructure, one that rooted shared Islamic tradition in that sacred landscape. In this manner, scripture broke its textual fetters, made manifest all around for anyone to see and touch. In this respect, it shared much with a Persianate literary complex inseparable from Islam.

Imagining Bukhara's Epic Past

Nothing in the discussion thus far significantly differentiates the mythologization of Bukhara from other mythologization projects elsewhere. Relics were carried all over the Islamic world and beyond, and by the middle ages there was hardly a village that could not boast at least a minor shrine or pilgrimage site. What made Bukhara's cultural landscape specifically Persianate? What did the city share with Lahore, for instance, but not Timbuktu?

Scholars have emphasized the importance of processes similar to those discussed above for conversion to Islam, when local sacred sites helped new Muslims endow traditions that had originated very far away with indigenous significance. Indeed, the very formation of the Persian cosmopolis was wound up in such a process. However, by the early modern period the "band wagon" period of conversion had long since passed, and for the majority of the population Islam had long since become a native religion.[102] Yet traditions connecting the Prophet to Bukhara remained important for establishing the city's centrality within a broader cultural tradition. Even children studying in a *maktab* (primary school) would have had a reference point for understanding the power of such an assertion. And those same schoolchildren were simultaneously immersed in a world of Persianate culture layered on top of, and integrated with, the Islamic tradition, memorizing Persian verses of Hafez and Suras of the Qur'an.

This point is clarified with even a cursory reading of many texts glorifying Bukhara. Nasafi's ode to the city glorified shrines and monuments throughout Bukhara with scriptural allusions.[103] Within the same verses, Nasafi also

---

101. Muḥammad Nāṣir, *Tuḥfat al-zā'irīn*, 97.

102. Bulliet, *Islam*, 38.

103. For instance, Nasafī compared Bukhara's mosques to the celestial "frequented house" of the angels (*bayt al-ma'mūr*). Paul Losensky describes his collection poem as a "walking tour" of the city. Losensky, "Sāqi-Nāma (Book of the Cupbearer)."

likened the Great Minaret's penetrating gaze to the snakes growing out of Zahhak's shoulders, referring to a dragon creature from the *Shah-nama* with deep roots in pre-Islamic Persian culture.[104]

This is not to say that all Persian-medium works were equally referent to the cultural traditions with pre-Islamic roots. Both Mu'in al-Fuqara and Muhammad Nasir's respective pilgrimage guides are relatively light on allusions to the Persian literary canon. Yet even Mu'in al-Fuqara relayed a tradition attributing etymology of the name Bukhara to the Zoroastrians' (*Mughan*) phrase for "congregation of knowledge" (*majma'-i ilm*), noting that term was also close to that of the Uyghur Buddhists word for "temple" (*vihara*).[105] Mu'in al-Fuqara and Muhammad Nasir Manghit both repeated a well-known tradition that the Samanid dynasty (the tombs of which were adjacent to Job's shrine complex) was descended from Bahram Chubin, a Persian noble who briefly usurped the Sasanian throne in the sixth century.[106]

Ziya's writing went even further in drawing explicit ties between Bukhara and Persian epic literature. In particular, he strove to connect Bukhara's landscape to events depicted in Ferdowsi's *Shah-nama*, perhaps the single most famous work of Persian literature.[107] Just like the pilgrimage guides, Ziya's work elaborated on ideas that had already been in circulation for the better part of a millennium. Narshakhi's tenth-century history provided the initial scaffolding for Ziya's synthesis. In mythic antiquity, according to Narshakhi's account, Bukhara (then known as Abgir) had been misruled by Abrawi, the shah of Paykand, and the region's denizens petitioned the king of Turkestan to intervene. The king complied, sending in his stead his son Sherkishwar, who then proceeded to liberate the province, kill the evil shah Abrawi, and lay the foundations of the city of Bukhara.[108]

---

104. "If a frightened thief falls into his grasp; [The Mināra-i Kalān, the sole surviving pre-Mongol minaret of Bukhara] will eat his brain, just like one of the snakes [growing] from Żahhāk's [head]." Nasafī, *Kulliyāt-i as̱ār*, 29.

105. Mu'īn al-Fuqarā, *Tārīkh-i Mullā-zāda; dar z̤ikr-i mazārāt-i Bukhārā*, 3–4. Richard Frye considers this etymology (i.e., *vihāra*, the same etymology as the modern Indian state of Bihar) less likely than a Sogdian or Turkic origin. "Bukhara i. In Pre-Islamic Times," *Encyclopædia Iranica* vol. 4.

106. Mu'īn al-Fuqarā, 25. The Jūybārī shaykhs, custodians of the Chahār Bakr shrine complex, claimed descent from a Samanid princess, and were therefore implicitly also tied to Chūbīn: Schwarz, "From Scholars to Saints: The Bukharan Shaykhs of Ǧūybār and the Ziyārats to the Four Bakr," 42.

107. Did Żiyā' envision his "vintage" interpretation of Bukharan history as a rebuttal to emergent "Chaghatayism," which claimed Tamerlane and Turkic vernacular writing as the patrimony of the Uzbek nation? Khalid, *Making Uzbekistan*, 16 passim. It is possible since żiyā''s writing overlapped chronologically with the modernist ideas of the Jadids.

108. Żiyā', *Z̤ikr-i awā'il-i Bukhārā*, f. 225a. Żiyā' was summarizing from an introductory section of Narshakhī's *Tārīkh-i Bukhārā* added centuries later. Narshakhī, *Tārīkh-i Bukhārā*, 7–10.

So far, Ziya's text merely summarized Narshakhi's much more venerable account of Bukhara's foundation. However, following Sherkishwar's defeat of Paykand, Ziya seamlessly continued the story into the narrative of the *Shah-nama*. Though Sherkishwar may have laid the initial foundations of the city, it was Siyawush, son of Kaykawus, who founded the famous *arg* (fortress) of Bukhara. Siyawush was also mentioned as the *arg*'s founder in Narshakhi's work, but without the reference to the stories about him that would become popularized in the centuries following the writing of Ferdowsi's eleventh-century rendition of the epic.[109] The *Shah-nama* hero Rustam was not mentioned anywhere in Narshakhi's *Tarikh-i Bukhara*, but Ziya reminded readers in his version that it was Rustam who trained Siyawush in his earlier years. Ziya also recounted the story of Siyawush and Sudaba, in which the Iranian prince Siyawush was forced to flee Iran to avoid the advances of the queen Sudaba and the shame to his family such an affair would bring. Like Rustam, Sudaba is absent from Narshakhi's account, but figured prominently in Ziya's. Siyawush temporarily found refuge in Turan and married into the family of Afrasiyab, another famous character from the *Shah-nama*, who gave him land in Bukhara to build the *arg*.[110]

Some discrepancies exist between Ziya's account and the *Shah-nama*, which mentions Khotan rather than Bukhara as the province out of which Siyawush carved his domain, and indeed a Khotanese shrine exists to the present day challenging Bukhara's claim as Siyawush's final resting place.[111] The connection between Siyawush and Central Asia runs deep, with pre-Islamic Buddhist texts connecting the hero to Khotan and Pahlavi (Middle Persian) ones positing Samarqand as his birthplace.[112] Siyawush's

109. Narshakhī, 32–33.

110. Żiyā', *Ẕikr-i awā'il-i Bukhārā*, ff. 225a–225b. The *Shāh-nāma* does not specify that it was in Bukhara that Afrāsīyāb granted Siyāwush land. The epic does go into some detail about the fortress Siyāwush built in Turkestan (*kang-diz*), which Żiyā' identified with the *arg*. Yarshater, *The Shahnameh*, Siyāwush line 1601. Afrāsīyāb's incorporation as a Turkic hero has deep roots in Central Asia: Payne, "The Making of Turan," 30.

111. Yarshater, *The Shahnameh*, Siyāwush line 1568. However, Żiyā''s account is not truly irreconcilable with the *Shāh-nāma*, since the city of Khotan itself is associated with Siyāwush's father-in-law, Pīrān, and the epic does not specify just how far away Siyāwush built his city—which was known as Sīyāwakhshgard (rather than either Khotan or Bukhara). Yarshater, *The Shahnameh*, Siyāwush line 1687. Ferdowsi seems to have had a location more in the direction of western China in mind, since a versified description of Siyāwush's fortress (*kang-diz*) appearing in one *Shāh-nāma* manuscript describes the fortress city as one month travel from an unnamed river of China. Yarshater, *The Shahnameh* 2:308–9 ("Ṣifat-i Kang-diz-i Siyāwush ba Turkistān" section). Rian Thum describes a process of localization and rearticulation in the case of Khotan remarkably similar to that of Bukhara. *The Sacred Routes of Uyghur History*, 12–27. Towns in western China were sometimes known as "little Bukharas." Fletcher, "V.A. Aleksandrov on Russo-Ch'ing Relations in the Seventeenth Century," 165.

112. Siyāwush appears in Buddhist text as Kunāla, son of the Indian monarch Ashoka, with China filling in as the enemy of Khotan in place of the Iran-Turan rivalry found in the *Xwadāy-*

association with Bukhara enjoys comparable pedigree, however. Narshakhi wrote that denizens of Bukhara continued to sing odes mourning Siyawush's tragic death even centuries after the Islamic conquests.[113] In all cases the pre-Islamic Siyawush narrative local to Central Asia was reintegrated with the Perso-Islamic version reinvigorated by Ferdowsi and once again localized to regional centers.

This process places in stark relief not only the centering of the cosmopolis—that is, centering Bukhara within the Persianate tradition—but also the subordination of the local to the universal. Traditions that seem to have begun their lives locally in Bukhara, such as the founding of the *arg*, were sanitized and blended with stories that circulated much more broadly. There was a creative energy inherent in this project, but that energy was also destructive. Our view of local culture in the past is almost always refracted through a cosmopolitan lens, and Bukhara's mythic history was no exception.

Ultimately, both Narshakhi's and Ziya's respective histories were based on the original Arsacid/Sasanian historical epic (*Xwaday-namag*) tradition.[114] Ferdowsi's *Shah-nama* was one of many works produced in the centuries following the Islamic conquests based on these now lost Sasanian histories.[115] The original Arabic version of Narshakhi's *Tarikh-i Bukhara* was written in the mid-tenth century—earlier than Ferdowsi's *Shah-nama* and hence before that particular rendition of the *Xwaday-namag* stories had become the single most popular work of Persian literature in history and mandatory reading for nobles and scholars alike throughout the Persianate world.[116] The "Turan" remembered by the *Shah-nama* was a mythical other to juxtapose against Iran with only a vague geographical connection to Central Asia and

---

nāmag tradition. Apparently, the origins of this conflation can be traced to the Kushan dynasty (50 BC–225 AD), which ruled from Balkh but maintained connections in western China. Skjærvø, "Eastern Iranian Epic Traditions I: Siyāvaš and Kunāla." The hero also appears in the brief Pahlavi work *Shahrestānīhā ī Ērān-shahr*, though in this text he is invoked as the founder of Samarqand, not Bukhara. According to this work, Kay-Khusraw, son of Siyāwush, was also born in Samarqand. Daryaee, *Šahrestānīhā ī Ērānšahr*, 18. Of course, the Pahlavi version is not fully compatible with the *Shāh-nāma*, since Samarqand is referenced as an extant city when Siyāwush travels to Turkestan (e.g., Ferdowsi, *The Shahnameh*, Siyāwush line 877).

113. The minstrels performing these odes were known as *kēn-i Siyāwush*. Narshakhī, *Tārīkh-i Bukhārā*, 24.

114. Narshakhī's work sometimes refers to these sources broadly as *kutub-i pārsīyān.*, 23.

115. On the *Xwadāy-nāmag* and the use of Ferdowsi's *Shāh-nāma* as a historical source, see Pourshariati, *Decline and Fall of the Sasanian Empire*, 10–18.

116. The Arabic version of Narshakhī's history is now lost; only Abū Naṣr Aḥmad al-Qubāwī's translation into Persian remains. Maria Subtelny described the *Shāh-nāma* as "required reading" in the Shibanid court—a prerequisite that did not distinguish that particular dynasty in the least. "Art and Politics in Early 16th Century Central Asia," 145.

none of the ethnic connotations of Turkestan.[117] In a sense, Ziya brought the project Narshakhi had begun full circle by reconnecting heroes from the *Xwaday-namag* tradition to tangible Bukharan geography while simultaneously updating them with the most popular tales in the *Shah-nama*.

Similarly, Gulshani's geography connected Bukhara's geography not only with Islamic scriptural history, but the Persian literary tradition as well. Once again, local color from Bukhara's environs is repainted with a cosmopolitan brush. For instance, Gulshani wrote that the district of Ramitan was named after Afrasiyab's daughter and was home to an ancient ruin associated with her. According to local legend, the daughter traveled throughout the provinces of Bukhara looking for a cure, only to become well upon her arrival in Ramitan.[118] Gulshani associated many of the pre-Islamic ruins with Afrasiyab, mentioning another ancient fortress attributed to the legendary king in the province of Karmina.[119] Alexander the Great and his associated legendary exploits were part and parcel of this tradition as well, popularized not only through Ferdowsi's *Shah-nama*, but also Nizami's version.[120] Though references to Alexander are absent from Narshakhi's history, Gulshani wrote of a ruined fortress in Nur-Ata believed to have been built by the great conqueror, as well as a nearby shrine containing his footprint that served as a popular pilgrimage destination.[121]

Though the ultimate origins of the Arabic "shadow cosmopolis" and the Persian cosmopolis were distinct, already by the eleventh century they had been synthesized into a cohesive Persianate tradition legible throughout vast swaths of Eurasia. Protectorate-era authors such as Ziya and Gulshani were not innovating in this respect; the amalgamation of Islam and Persian high

---

117. In fact, Ferdowsi imposed the ethnic designations (such as "Turk") from his own time (tenth and eleventh centuries) onto the mythical history of the *Xwadāy-nāmag* tradition. Kowalski, "The Turks in the Shāh-Nāma," 126.

118. Gulshanī explained the etymology of Ramitan as "tranquil body" (*ārām-tan*), referring to the princess's regained health. He did not specify whether this was the same princess (i.e., Farangēs) who married Siyāwush in the *Shāh-nāma*. Gulshanī, *Tārīkh-i humāyūn*, ff. 10a-10b. Interestingly, Narshakhī relayed a different tradition involving Ramitan and a princess. Narshakhī, *Tārīkh-i Bukhārā*, 10.

119. Gulshanī, *Tārīkh-i humāyūn*, f. 15a.

120. For an overview of the Persianate Alexander romance tradition (Iskandarʾnāma), see Hanaway, "Eskandar Nāma"; Cornwall, "Alexander and the Persian Cosmopolis, 1000–1500."

121. Gulshanī, *Tārīkh-i humāyūn*, f. 24b. Alexander legends seemed to have been quite common in Central Asia and not limited to Bukhara, necessarily. The population of Darwāz in Bukhara's mountainous hinterland believed itself to be descended from Alexander and tied local landmarks to him. "The Amir's proceedings in Wakhan and Shighnan," f. 3. Alexander also appears in connection with Central Asia in Pahlavi texts, though in an entirely negative light, fitting with his maligned legacy in Sasanian Iran. Alexander was alleged to have burned sacred Zoroastrian texts kept in a fire temple in Samarqand and then cast them into a sea (though there are no seas very close to Samarqand). Daryaee, *Šahrestānīhā ī Ērānšahr*, 18.

culture began with the inception of New Persian literature. Following the example of their forebears (such as Narshakhi), Ziya reminded the reader that Afrasiyab was a descendant of the prophet Noah and that Kaykawus (father of Siyawush) was the same individual as Nimrod, thus marrying the Abrahamic and Persian traditions in the course of narrating Bukhara's ancient history.[122] He noted that Siyawush was buried in the *arg's* east gate, adding later that a descendant of Abu Hanifa was buried under a nearby cupola.[123] Mu'in al-Fuqara's *Risala-i Mulla-zada* generally focuses more in integrating Bukhara into specifically Islamic sacred history, but even he remarked that one of the aforementioned hairs of the Prophet was buried in the tomb of a Sogdian noble, thus similarly connecting Bukhara's Persian and Islamic traditions.[124] In this manner, the Central Asian ulama wove Bukhara right into the center of a larger Perso-Islamic historical tapestry.[125]

In centering the Perso-Islamic cosmopolis, Bukhara was in good company.[126] For instance, Mahmud ibn Wali's sixteenth-century history illustrates a very similar process of tying the neighboring city of Balkh both to Islamic history and the more specifically Persianate tradition.[127] The difference is that by the long nineteenth century, Bukhara's mythologization project continued, whereas that of Balkh lay dormant. But Samarqand produced a major pilgrimage guide in the late nineteenth century, which reflected continue engagement with the cosmopolis even under Russian rule. Just as in the case of Balkh, the text attributed Samarqand's founding to legendary figures from the *Shah-nama* throughout the same pages in which it connected the city to early figures in Islamic history.[128]

---

122. Żiyā', *Ẕikr-i awā'il-i Bukhārā*, ff. 225a–225b.

123. Żiyā', *Ẕikr-i awā'il-i Bukhārā*, ff. 225b, 246b.

124. *Risāla-i Mullā-zāda*, f. 7a. See also Subtelny, "The Making of Bukhārā-yi Sharīf," 86–87.

125. The memory of figures such as Afrāsīyāb was later incorporated into Soviet nationalisms, which could serve as a source of both tension and common ground with other Persianate societies. See, for instance, Pickett, "Soviet Civilization through a Persian Lens," 815.

126. Chitralekha Zutshi's work on the "centering" (not a term she uses) of Kashmir has many parallels with the Bukharan case. *Kashmir's Contested Pasts*.

127. To anticipate some of the arguments to come in relation to Bukhara, Maḥmūd ibn Walī wrote that Balkh was the capital of Luhrāsp, a legendary Iranian king of the *Shāh-nāma* tradition. This discussion of legendary Persian history was woven into descriptions of the city's sacred Islamic geography, including religious infrastructure and saintly tombs. Maḥmūd ibn Walī, *Tārīkh baḥr al-asrār fī manāqib al-akhyār*, 384. Even Turkic-medium mythologization efforts revealed their Persianate roots: for instance, the Turkic sacred histories of Sayrām describe figures from Persianate epics, such as Jamshid and Nurshirvan, in addition to more universally Islamic tropes and more narrowly Turkic ones. DeWeese, "Sacred History for a Central Asian Town," 254, 262–64.

128. Abū Ṭāhir Khwāja (whose family dynasty is discussed in chapter 7) wrote that Samarqand's earliest foundations can be traced to Kaykāwus, who—incidentally—was Siyāwush's father. Another heroic figure from Persian mythology, the dragon-slaying Garshāsp, later discovered buried treasure in the vicinity, and used it to erect a fortress and walls. Abū Ṭāhir ibn Abī Sa'id, *Samariyya*, 5. Another tradition attributes the founding of Samarqand to Afrāsiyāb, a figure also connected to Bukhara, and

Thus Bukhara's mythologization project was not uncontested, and certainly not unprecedented, even though it was unusually well developed.

Centering the Cosmopolis

The poet Sayyidayi Nasafi's (d. ca. 1707) ode to Bukhara opens with the following lines:

> O' the beauty of the city of steam [*bukhar*], and its pure earth;
> From the soil of which flows powdered musk.[129]

Nasafi's predecessor, Muhammad ibn Dawud, also focused on the "steam" (*bukhar*) in the city's name to make a much less flattering comparison. Yet by the early modern period, it was Nasafi's vision that predominated, and dreams of flowery musk became all the more fragrant as the long nineteenth century wore on.

Bukhara's mythologization project was not unique in kind. What set it apart was the scale on which the city combined a textual mythologization project with an unparalleled boom in the construction of tangible architecture. Partisans of humbler towns carried out many of the same rhetorical moves as those of Bukhara. But they could not match the rhetoric with infrastructure, at least not anywhere near on the same scale as the Abode of Knowledge. Bukhara's institutions produced the very intellectual cadre who inscribed the city into sacred history: madrasas and texts were two sides of the same coin.

The universality of Perso-Islamic high culture was what lent it such power, offering mobility to those who mastered it, and providing a common discourse throughout the Persianate space. This power was enhanced by anchoring the universal to the local, since it asserted a constitutive role for Bukhara in shaping the contours of the cosmopolis—both in the present and in a mythic past. Explaining Bukhara's place in the cosmopolis, and demonstrating that connection through the physical landscape, justified the ability of Islamic scholars to wield its power.

Even with the emphasis on Bukhara's particular place in cosmopolitan high culture, this was not an exclusivist project. Rather than an early instance of an "imagined community," the mythologization of Bukhara was instead one of the last instances of a cosmopolitan style of valorizing

---

whose name now serves as the eponym of the Sogdian archaeological site outside of Samarqand. Abū Ṭāhir ibn Abī Saʿid, 6.

129. Nasafī, *Kulliyāt-i aṣār*, 28.

the local in universalist terms. Nationalists such as the Jadids (who were contemporaries of early twentieth-century figures in this study) emphasized what was unique and special about the Muslims of Turkestan as a community, whereas the scholarly elite of this study asserted Bukhara's centrality in, and connectedness to, a broader cultural tradition.[130] It was not necessary, or even desirable, for the ulama of Bukhara to claim the Persian cosmopolis as something uniquely Bukharan; its status as a pivot of a much larger phenomenon was the basis of the city's allure. Confusingly, those same nationalists seized on many individual features of Persianate culture, such as the *Shah-nama* (the Persian epic of kings), but they did so by connecting it to the national heritage of a particular people and using novel categories.[131]

Bukhara's efflorescence was not the first time the premodern cosmopolis was centered on the local, but it was one of the last such examples.[132] The modern era and the -isms brought with it marked the end of elite, cosmopolitan forms of cultural production, and the mythologization project that centered Bukhara in the Persian cosmopolis was not an example of proto-nationalism. The fact that Bukhara's mythologization project coexisted with Islamic modernist movements elsewhere (and, by the twentieth century, in Bukhara itself) that were imagining new forms of collective identity has led historians to misunderstand the late cultural history of Bukhara by prioritizing modern categories not prominent in the sources themselves. In this narrow sense, the Jadids represented exactly the sort of radical break with the past they imagined themselves to be.

The Jadids took Bukhara's timelessness for granted, but they also conflated the premodern cultural complex on which that timelessness rested with stagnation—a view echoed in Soviet writing, and eventually Western scholarship as well.[133] This chapter argues that something else entirely

---

130. Khalid, *The Politics of Muslim Cultural Reform*. Insofar as the architects of Bukhara's mythologization had a community in mind, it was the community of Muslims as a whole (*umma*)—though even that border was porous (see example of the Persianate-Jewish poet Ẓabīḥā in the introduction, or voluminous recent scholarship on Hindu actors in Persianate India).

131. The "invention of tradition" was "so unprecedented that even historic continuity had to be invented." Hobsbawm and Ranger, *The Invention of Tradition*, 7. This observation aptly applies to the Jadids. On the processes by which modernists appropriated the Persianate for national aims, see Kia, "Indian Friends, Iranian Selves, Persianate Modern"; Pickett, "Soviet Civilization through a Persian Lens."

132. Mid-nineteenth-century Arcot stands as another example of relatively late patronage of Persianate high culture. Schwartz, "The Curious Case of Carnatic."

133. For instance, "This was a difficult period in the history of Bukhārā-yi Sharīf. At a time when other centers of Islamic learning in the east, such as Kazan and Baku, were undergoing a cultural revival in the new climate of Islamic educational reform, Bukhara had become a closed city." Subtelny, "The Making of Bukhārā-yi Sharīf," 109.

was going on. Though perhaps not a "Bukharan Enlightenment," as some revisionist scholarship would have it, there was indeed a flowering in the cultural-religious sphere during the long nineteenth century. Just as with Mughal expansion into Kashmir, or even Arab expansion into Central Asia a millennium prior, upheaval and subsequent political consolidation opened space for an explosion of cultural activity.[134] The Manghit dynasty had achieved a degree of stability and state-building leading up to the Russian conquest of 1868, but their control of their hinterland was tenuous at best. Nevertheless, as first among equals in an arena of competing and aspiring states, they invested heavily in religious infrastructure. Counterintuitively, capacity for investment increased under Russian protection, as merchants leveraged new resources, and the borders of the amirate were guaranteed by colonial troops. The refurbished and expanded physical landscape fueled the imagination of scholars wishing to project Bukhara's stature across space and time. The broader Perso-Islamic cultural world was critical to the first part of that equation—that is, weaving Bukhara into the longue durée of the cosmopolis. The next chapter turns toward the spatial: just how far did this vision of Bukhara center reverberate, and for whom?

---

134. Żiyā, *The Personal History of a Bukharan Intellectual*, 18 passim; Shukurov, *Khurāsān ast īn jā*, 114–15, 121–22; Zutshi, *Kashmir's Contested Pasts*.

CHAPTER 3

Bukhara Center

Islamic Scholars as a Network of Human Exchange

Bukhara was imagined as a pivot of Persianate high culture, an Abode of Knowledge within a much larger cosmopolis. Bukhara did not enjoy the timeless patrimony that its denizens imagined. Instead, it was the product of a deeply rooted mythologization project that accelerated in Central Asia's long nineteenth century. This chapter shifts the focus from cultural discourse to social history to assess the human impact of Bukhara's efflorescence. To what extent did Bukhara's cosmological centrality manifest in actual networks of human exchange? How far did Bukhara's allure extend, and from what points of origin were people willing to travel there for education in its colossal madrasa establishment?

The cosmopolis has most frequently been conceptualized as a literary phenomenon.[1] We know that educated people in Delhi were reading many of the same texts as their contemporaries in Istanbul, Isfahan, and Kazan. And we know that a handful of individuals physically traversed that space (though we also know that many more stayed much closer to home). Yet the question remains: is the concept applicable outside of literature? Is a framework arising from *intellectual* and *cultural* history resonant for *social* history?[2]

1. See chapter 1.
2. Green, *Terrains of Exchange*, 3.

One strategy for applying the Persianate concept to social history is to consider the cosmopolis as a shorthand for describing the variegated forms of knowledge an individual could leverage to advance his (or, in rare cases, her) standing in society. Even though the *Shah-nama* (the Persian "Book of Kings") as a text circulated throughout the entire Persianate space, this chapter argues that most Bukharan scholars traveled through more circumscribed regional networks. The ulama were faced with the challenge of reconciling their lived experience in the city-states of Central Asia with the far vaster Perso-Islamic cosmopolis that shaped the cultural ecology of their world. As illustrated in the preceding chapter, the ulama discursively "centered" Bukhara within the cosmopolis. This chapter argues that the mythologization process produced "little Persianate spheres" of actual human exchange, overlapping networks of scholarly activity within which the forms of knowledge that intersected in Bukhara were especially potent.

At its core, the logic underpinning these networks is straightforward. Even though the circulation of the *Shah-nama* sometimes serves as a synecdoche for the Persian cosmopolis writ large, literature was but one component of a much larger curriculum.[3] This canon seamlessly integrated not only Persian literary texts, but also Arabic-medium Hanafi legal manuals, Turkic chancery practices, and more. Residents of Isfahan shared a literary culture with natives of Bukhara, but not religious sect (with Iranians predominantly Shi'i, and Central Asians overwhelmingly Sunni-Hanafi). Bukharan and Ottoman subjects alike were versed in the poetry of Hafez but were separated by vernacular literature in Ottoman Turkish.[4] This chapter posits that the more these skills and knowledge forms overlapped regionally, the more an individual scholar was able to channel his training into social currency—which in turn facilitated more frequent human movement across distance.[5] These locally circumscribed exchange networks are conceptualized as little Persianate spheres—with dynamics shaped by the larger cosmopolis of high culture, but not reducible to it.

The story of centering the cosmopolis for a regional constituency and of deploying the corresponding social currency within that context is one that could equally be told about any number of other Persianate nodes: Lahore,

3. On the madrasa curriculum, see the next chapter.

4. Like Central Asian Turkī (aka Chaghatay), Ottoman was a Turkic vernacular of Persian; but it was a parallel, separate vernacular. Only a few Ottoman texts circulated in Central Asia (although Ottoman versions of Chaghatay works were not uncommon).

5. It is important to note that these different disciplines were mastered by a single social milieu; that is, "jurists" and "poets" were not separate social groups, but rather separate social roles simultaneously mastered by Islamic scholars.

Isfahan, Istanbul, and beyond. Bukhara was not unique in this regard. However, this pivot between cosmopolitan high culture and social power dynamics at the subregional level remains terra incognita. Texts were resonant across vast swathes of territory, but the mechanics of the world undergirding them are left to the imagination in much of the extant scholarship. Yet these ideas were not merely floating in the ether, and the paths taken by the ulama of Bukhara can perhaps shed light on the social world producing, and produced by, cosmopolitan transculturation. Ultimately, the chapter traces the geographical trajectories of the Islamic scholars at the heart of this study, revealing a regional cultural-religious network that revolved around Bukhara the Noble, the Abode of Knowledge.

Bukhara as the Pole of a Nonstate Transregional Network

By the end of the nineteenth century, Bukhara had achieved renown as a major educational hub, a city blessed personally by the Prophet Muhammad, the ancient seat of Afrasiyab's Turanian empire, and final resting place of Children of Israel, Companions of the Prophet, and sufi saints alike. Yet the notion that Bukhara was second in sanctity only to Mecca would have been news to Muslims living in Jerusalem, for instance, or Istanbul, where Bukhara was distant and its claims unknown. So just how far did Bukhara's allure extend?

By the second half of the nineteenth century, Bukhara was firmly established as the center of a little Persianate sphere of human exchange that included Balkh, Badakhshan, and the Farghana Valley as its inner ring, as well as Khorezm, western China (Xinjiang), Siberia, and the Muslim territories of Russia as an outer ring. In exceedingly broad terms, scholars originating from the inner ring were well represented in the upper ranks of the ulama.[6] Scholars originating from the outer ring traveled to Bukhara in large numbers but were less likely to "make it" and remain in Bukhara for the long term, and more frequently returned home after finishing their educa-

6. This chapter and chapter 5 draw conclusions in part from prosopography, or "collective biography," a methodology designed to avoid "generalizing from a handful of eloquent examples" in the face of scarce information. Verboven, Carlier, and Dumolyn, "A Short Manual to the Art of Prosopography," 36. In this book, the aggregate figures are drawn from biographical dictionaries (mostly of poets, and one devoted to calligraphers) by Wāżiḥ (late 1860s), Żiyā᾽ (early 1900s), Muḥtaram (1908), Pīrmastī, ʿAbdī (1904), and Sharʿī. The figures are out of a total of 200, excluding those for whom no biographical data was provided. These numbers illustrate some trends in broad strokes, but they are not significant in any statistical sense. For comparison, biographical dictionaries produced in the earliest centuries of Islam are vast, sometimes including thousands of scholars: Ahmed, *The Religious Elite of the Early Islamic Ḥijāz*.

tion.[7] Still less integrated—particularly in terms of ulama migration—were Iran, southern Afghanistan, and northern India, despite sharing many common features of Persianate high culture. Students from those territories still turned up in Bukhara, but more often gravitated toward the epicenters of little Persianate spheres closer to home, imagined to be every bit as central as Bukhara.

Any attempt to delineate a nonstate network of exchange must be made in terms of gradients and patterns, not borders or ironclad rules.[8] After all, this was a time period in which the vast majority of the sedentary population stayed put. Nevertheless, certain regional origins cropped up in Bukharan biographical dictionaries more than others, and my focus here is on those villages, provinces, and cities that sent their best and brightest to Bukhara instead of competing Perso-Islamic scholarly centers such as Qom, Basra, Lahore, or Delhi.

As common sense dictates, the most common origin of Bukharan scholars was the immediate environs of Bukhara, with just under 40 percent from the oasis, and just over 25 percent originating from the city.[9] Also exceedingly well-represented were Samarqand and adjacent provinces such as Shahrisabz and Urgut, together accounting for 17 percent of the total.[10] It is not surprising then that these core territories of what is conventionally understood as "Central Asia" are well represented, but the figures nevertheless serve as a benchmark for comparing territories further afield.

By the second half of the nineteenth century, eastern Khurasan (including areas such as Balkh, Maymana, and Kunduz) had become northern

7. This second generalization is more impressionistic than that related to the "inner ring." Scholars from the outer ring of Bukhara's little Persianate sphere are all but absent from the Bukharan *tażkiras*. However, in biographical dictionaries produced about those regions (when available), Bukhara appears prominently as a prestige destination for scholars who returned home after "graduation."

8. To be clear, states of various stripes will constantly make appearances in the pages to come. By "nonstate," I am emphasizing that these networks were not reducible to any single state. A state-rich environment, with a plentitude of competing city-states, protectorates, and empires, meant that there were many potential patrons and employers on offer.

9. That is, including immediate suburbs, such as Ghijduwan and Wabkand.

10. One notes that many of the poetical anthologies of the seventeenth century were written in Samarqand, and scholars originating from Samarqand are correspondingly better represented (e.g., in Muṭribī's *tażkira* they make up around 20 percent of the sample, exactly on par with Bukhara). Muṭribī Samarqandī, *Tażkirat al-shuʿarā*; Malīḥā Samarqandī, *Tażkira-i mużākir al-aṣḥāb (yā tażkira al-shuʿarā-yi Malīḥā-yi Samarqandī)*. This shift supports the chronology advanced in the previous chapter on the mythologization of Bukhara, even though similar efforts continued in Samarqand well into the twentieth century.

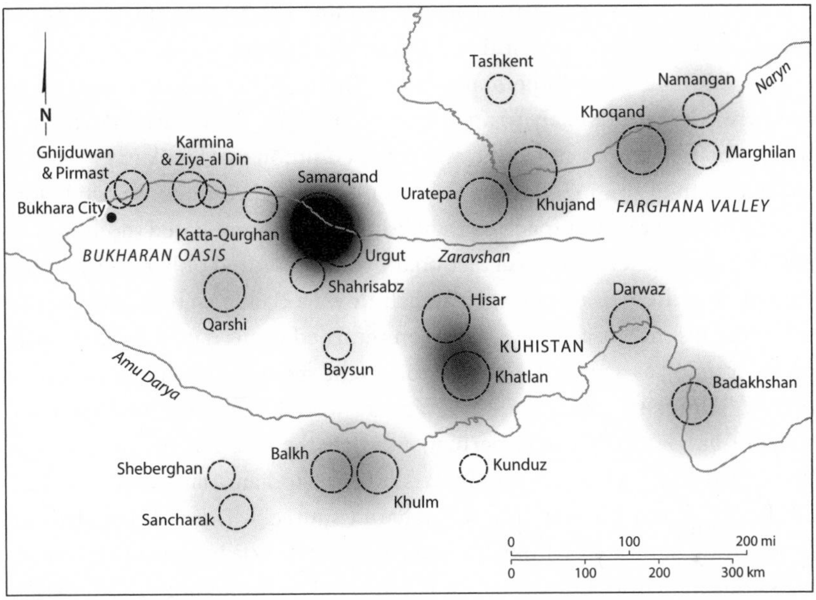

FIGURE 7. Heat map of scholarly migration in Central Asia, with circles proportionate to the number of scholars originating from that location (excluding the city of Bukhara itself). Map designed by author.

Afghanistan.[11] The political integration of these territories into the emergent Afghan state did not, however, preclude their social integration with Bukhara.[12] Khurasan was only slightly less represented than the Samarqand region, accounting for nearly 10 percent of the origins of elite Bukharan scholars. For instance, two such scholars, Jamal al-Din and his brother Qawwam al-Din, were born in the sometimes-autonomous city-state of Khulm (a.k.a. Tashqurghan) but traveled to Bukhara for madrasa education. Jamal al-Din, and possibly his brother, found patronage as court poets under Amir Muzaffar (r. 1860–85) and later the governor of the quasi-independent province of Hisar, only to meet a violent end during the Russian conquest.[13] It is worth noting that Khulm lies almost 200 miles closer to Kabul than Bukhara,

11. Even though historically Khurasan encompassed a much broader region than just the eastern reaches, for the sake of brevity I refer to it as "Khurasan." As understood here, eastern Khurasan is roughly coterminous with the Chahār Wilāyat (i.e., Maymana, Andkhoy, Sar-i Pul, and Sheberghan).

12. See also the discussion of ʿAbd al-Wāḥid Ṣarīr Balkhī's patronage network of immigrants from Khurasan in chapter 6.

13. Sources differ as to whether they were killed in Jizakh in 1865 or several years later in Ḥisār. Wāżiḥ, *Tuḥfat al-aḥbāb*, ff. 61–63, 162–63. Żiyāʾ, *Tażkār-i ashʿār*, 290.

albeit connected by more treacherous terrain, a fact that underscores the social integration over political and geographic factors.

Scholars like the brothers al-Din of Khulm, who chose to remain in Bukhara, were more likely to appear in biographical dictionaries devoted to the luminaries of that city. But it was more common for the ulama to return to their point of origin following the completion of their madrasa education. After all, Bukhara's vast madrasa establishment accommodated thousands of students, but the biographical dictionary genre captured only hundreds: the elite of the elite. For instance, Izzatallah Khwaja Balkhi went to Bukhara to complete his madrasa studies, but then returned to his native Balkh to pass on his training as a *mudarris* (instructor) in the madrasa adjoining the shrine of Ali.[14] Ordinarily, Bukharan biographers would likely not have included a figure like Izzatallah who permanently left the city, but because he was descended from a famous family of shrine custodians (*mutawalli*), Izzatallah Balkhi found his way into a Bukharan source.[15] The political division between the amirate of Bukhara and Afghanistan was irrelevant to Izzatallah's education: the skill set demanded of scholars throughout this territory was near-identical and he sought the most prestigious education he could conceive.

Other types of sources offer further support for Khurasan's firm and continued integration into Bukhara's orbit well after its political separation. One legal opinion clarified the definition of "travel" (*safar*) from the perspective of Hanafi law specifically for locales in Central Asia and Khurasan.[16] Muslims considered to be traveling are subject to different prayer requirements than Muslims in residence, but Bukhara, Balkh, and Qarakol were sufficiently close and frequently traversed that it was not obvious when moving between them constituted formal travel. The ruling specified that even if the intention (*niyyat*) of travelers of Balkh origin was to reside in Bukhara, not Qarakol, the full prayer regimen was still incumbent upon them if they settled there.[17]

Even more indicative of the region's scholarly integration is an endowment (*waqf*) from 1867. In October–November of that year one Mizrab Biy ibn Rahim Biy endowed his candle shop to finance the students studying in Bukhara but originating from his native Andkhoy, a town now lying in the

14. On the famous tomb of ʿAlī in Mazār-i Sharīf, see McChesney, *Waqf in Central Asia*.

15. Wāżiḥ, *Tuḥfat al-aḥbāb*, ff. 140–43.

16. This particular fatwa was copied into a *jung* collection. On the nature of *jung* as the textual category, see the introduction.

17. Ḥusaynī, *Jung-i majmūʿa-i riwāyāt*, ff. 87b–88a.

northern Afghanistan province of Faryab.[18] In exchange for the scholarship, those students were to gather every Friday and Monday evening to recite the Qur'anic Surah Hazrat al-Mulk to the credit (*sawab*) of the Prophet Muhammad as well as Mizrab Biy.[19]

These two documents demonstrate that the scholarly exchange network between Bukhara and Khurasan extended beyond the elite scholars captured in the biographical dictionaries.[20] Students of more modest means from Khurasan gravitated to Bukhara for their education, which they transformed into gainful employment both north of the Amu River, where they received their training, and south of it, where they were born. Yet for those students and scholars originating from Khurasan, Bukhara was hardly foreign: the skills they picked up in Bukhara were equally useful in both locales, and much further afield as well.

It is important to disaggregate Khurasan from the rest of Afghanistan also because of the picture that emerges from Afghan sources. When the focus is shifted south of Khurasan to emergent urban centers such as Kabul, it is remarkable how few ulama originated from the Bukharan oasis and its neighboring territories. For instance, in an anthology of poets prominent in the court of Timur-Shah Durrani (r. 1722–93), not a single individual hailed from a territory north of the Amu River, or even immediately south of it.[21] Instead, of the twenty-six individuals listed, the vast majority was attracted to Kabul from educational complexes in India (19 percent), Herat (19 percent), and Qandahar (11 percent).[22] In other words, the Durrani Empire seemed to split the difference between little Persianate spheres rooted in the respective Safavid and Mughal Empires from which Afghanistan was carved.[23] This

18. More specifically, Miżrāb Biy stipulated that a tenth of the shop proceeds would go to the *mutawallī*—who was to be recruited from his own kin—and that the remainder would be distributed evenly among the students from Andkhoy.

19. TsGARUz F i-323 O 1 D 127. Sūrat al-Mulk (67) is one of the "one of the best-known and most frequently recited *sūrahs* of the Quran," and often recited to avert trials and hardship—which seems appropriate in this case. Nasr et al., *The Study Quran*.

20. Russian sources also attest to the extensive presence of Afghans studying in Bukhara, often complaining of the rowdy behavior. RGVIA F 400 O 1 D 3914, f. 44b, 50b.

21. One of these scholars, Abū Saʿīd Khwāja, studied sufism and other Islamic sciences in Kabul's Masjid-i Ūzbakān ("Mosque of the Uzbeks"). He may have originated from Central Asia, but the text does not specify his birthplace. Fūfalzāʾī, *Taymūr Shāh Durrānī*, 487.

22. Fūfalzāʾī, 462–91. Nor does this picture change much if one consults the same author's list of famous calligraphers (*khaṭṭāṭān*), doctors (*ṭabībān*), or the demonyms on a simple list (absent biographical information) of the notable men of the realm. Fūfalzāʾī, 413–25, 490–97. One exception is the doctor and historian Muḥammad Nāṣir Badakhshī, who originated from a region well represented in Bukhara (i.e., the Kuhistan). Fūfalzāʾī, 495.

23. Herat, in particular, was described as an important educational center for scholars that ended up in Kabul. Fūfalzāʾī, *Taymūr Shāh Durrānī*, 471. Texts such as Aṣīl al-Dīn al- Ḥusaynī's guide to

changed in the latter half of the nineteenth century, when Kabul established firmer control over Khurasan, and some evidence shows that even at the turn of the nineteenth century educational connections were being established through scholarships to study in Bukhara offered under Shah Zaman Durrani (r. 1793–1801).[24] Thus Bukhara's reputation carried currency in Kabul, and Bukhara-trained ulama were present in Kabul—just not in the numbers one finds Khurasanis in the upper Bukharan elite.

A region integrated into the Bukharan orbit to a slightly greater extent than Khurasan, on a scale comparable to Samarqand, was the Farghana Valley, which accounted for approximately 17 percent of elite Bukharan scholars described in biographical dictionaries. Many of these individuals settled and became some of the most powerful scholars in Bukhara.[25] In one sense, this finding is not surprising. Both Khoqand (the amirate that controlled the Farghana Valley) and Bukhara were "Uzbek" khanates absorbed by the Russian and Soviet empires, and eventually fell into the "Central Asia" category. Yet this reasoning is retrospective and teleological. Most locales in Khurasan and the Farghana Valley were roughly the same distance from Bukhara, around 600 miles away. The Farghana Valley and eastern Khurasan were both subject to varying degrees of control by the Bukhara-based Ashtarkhanid dynasty (1599–1747) before that empire fractured into city-states.[26] Like Bukhara, Khoqand was ruled by a Turkic dynasty before being directly annexed by the Russian Empire, but then so were many of the city-states of Khurasan before being conquered by an ethnically dissimilar dynasty. In other words, there was nothing natural or inevitable about the strong representation of Farghani migrants in Bukhara, whose numbers were not much greater than those from Khurasan (i.e., what became northern Afghanistan).

---

the city's shrines was quite similar to that of Mullā-zāda for Bukhara (as discussed in the previous chapter), serving to elevate Herat as the center of its own little Persianate sphere. In a few instances, the text even provides evidence of cross-pollination between the two centers, such as Ākhund Mullā ʿAbdallāh Fāżil Bukhārāʾī, who apparently came to Herat sometime in the nineteenth century for sufi training, and ended up teaching at the Madrasa-i ʿĀliyya. Ḥusaynī, *Risāla-i mazārāt-i Harāt: Maqṣad al-Iqbāl al-Sulṭāniyya*, 187–88.

24. Fūfalzāʾī, *Durrat al-Zamān: Tārīkh-i Shāh Zamān*, 402–4; Ziad, "Traversing the Indus and the Oxus," 557.

25. For instance, the Tatar scholar Shihāb al-Dīn Marjānī characterized the Khoqandi transplant ʿAbd al-ʿĪsā al-Khūqandī (d. 1823–24) as "the most famous Bukharan scholar of his time." Marjānī, *Wafiyyat al-aslāf*, f. 157b.

26. The shared Ashtarkhanid legacy of many of the most closely integrated territories outside of Bukhara's *political* control in the long nineteenth century is suggestive, and likely played an indirect role in shaping many of the other factors this chapter considers formative to Bukhara's little Persianate sphere.

Nor is the integration of Farghana into Bukhara's orbit easily attributed to colonial-era imperial networks. A Russian officer sent to Bukhara in 1910 for Uzbek and Persian language training noted in a report that Muslim students were flocking to Bukhara from Russian Turkestan despite colonial efforts to regulate that traffic (or at least monitor it). The officer reported that efforts by the Turkestan governor-general to require formal requests from Russian Muslim subjects had been entirely futile because such regulations required the cooperation of the Bukharan madrasa instructors, who ignored these imperial demands without consequence. The officer explained Bukhara's allure in terms of Bukhara's mythologized sanctity, rather than the imperial grid: "One must not forget that Bukhara, or 'Bukhara the Noble,' is considered a center of Muslim learning in Turkestan to the present day, and students (*Mullo-bachi*) who received their education there enjoy a special respect, as illuminated with the sanctity of Bukhara."[27]

The city of Khoqand boasted thirty-six madrasas and continued to attract students from the Farghana region, but Abd al-Ahad (r. 1885–1911) alone had constructed nearly two-thirds that amount in Bukhara (at least twenty-four). Thus the era during which the two city-states had vied for regional supremacy was long gone by the end of the nineteenth century.[28] Students of means flocked to Bukhara for their education, just as their colleagues from Khurasan did. Jami Qazi-Khwaja, for instance, traveled to Bukhara from the Farghana city of Margilan to immerse himself in Perso-Islamic forms of knowledge, skills that were perfectly transferable back to his home city. Upon his return to Margilan, he acquired the prestigious position of *qazi* (judge), likely under Russian rule or the years leading up to it.[29]

The third spoke of this little Persianate sphere was formed by the Kuhistan, Bukhara's mountainous hinterland to the east, which included Badakhshan, and which would eventually become Soviet Tajikistan.[30] In stark contrast to Khurasan and the Farghana Valley, which were increasingly politically distant from Bukhara during the nineteenth century, the Bukharan

27. RGVIA F 400 O 1 D 3914, f. 35a.

28. Ostroumov, "Narodnoe obrazovanie," 165. Ostroumov also counted the number of students studying in Khoqand to be 2,262—as against the 50,000 students studying in Bukhara estimated by Muḥammad Ṣādiq Gulshanī. There is some evidence that increased student stipends (indirectly consequent of improved irrigation methods in the Farghana Valley) may have lured students back to Khoqand madrasas around the turn of the century. Nalivkin, *Tuzemtsy, ran'she i teper'*, 97–98.

29. Muḥtaram, *Tażkirat al-shuʿarā*, ff. 108b–109a. Dāmullā Ḥasan Zāyir had a similar trajectory vis-à-vis Khujand. Muḥtaram, *Tażkirat al-shuʿarā*, f. 112a.

30. What I am calling "the Kūhistān" was administratively referred to as "east Bukhara" in colonial sources during the protectorate period. In these figures, it consists of Badakhshan, Khatlan, Qarategin, and Darwaz.

amirate gained control of the Kuhistan in the 1870s under Russian backing.[31] In a poetical *tazkira* (biographical dictionary) written before Bukhara's military advance into these mountainous territories, only 7 percent of the scholars included were specified as of that origin, whereas the aggregated figures (with all other sources written after Bukhara's incorporation of the Kuhistan) amounting to 14 percent.[32] If one includes Hisar in that mix, a province of lower elevation that was more firmly within Bukhara's political reach in the preceding decades, the percentages jump to nearly 19 percent.[33] Looking from the other direction, over a fourth of the scholars featured in a 1930s anthology of Badakhshani poets studied in Bukhara.[34] In other words, Bukhara's military conquest of the Kuhistan certainly advanced the region's social integration with Bukhara, but only to a level still roughly on par with the Farghana Valley and Samarqand.[35]

The Outer Ring of Bukhara's Little Persianate Sphere

One might reasonably expect Khorezm, the region northwest of Bukhara across the Qizilqum desert and directly south of the Aral Sea, to be firmly intertwined with this little Persianate sphere.[36] After all, Khiva (the city-state controlling this territory and sometimes used interchangeably with the term Khorezm) was—alongside Bukhara and Khoqand—one of the "three khanates" of Central Asia. Yet the volume and regularity of scholarly traffic between Bukhara and Khorezm appear to have been a full gradation below that of Khurasan, Farghana, and the Kuhistan—thus confining Khorezm to the outer ring of Bukhara's little Persianate sphere. In the late nineteenth century Bukharan biographical dictionaries, the representation of Khorezmians is virtually nil.[37]

---

31. Khalfin, *Rossiia i Bukharskii emirat na zapadnom Pamire.*

32. Wāżiḥ, *Tuḥfat al-aḥbāb.* Moreover, representation from the Kuhistan is less pronounced in poetical anthologies from the seventeenth century (when the region was outside of Bukhara's control); for example, under 4 percent, including Hisar, in Muṭribī's collection: Muṭribī Samarqandī, *Tażkirat al-shuʿarāʾ.*

33. Hisar (and nearby Dushanbe, which would become the capital of the Tajik SSR) was considered part of "east Bukhara" during the protectorate period.

34. Yumgī, *Armaghān-i Badakhshān.* Of those, a disproportionate number hailed from Darwaz, which was located slightly closer to Bukhara; and many Badakhshani scholars studied in India as well.

35. See also Dudoignon, "Faction Struggles among the Bukharan Ulama."

36. On the relationship between Khorezm and Bukhara, see Pickett, "Enemies beyond the Red Sands."

37. One exception was a poet and *mudarris* identified only by his pen name "Nūr," who traveled to Bukhara from his native Urgench to study, where he apparently remained. ʿAbdī, *Tażkirat al-shuʿarā,* f. 170a. There are also a small number of scholars identified in *tażkiras* as Turkmen, who very likely

Conceptualizing Khorezm as part of the outer ring of this little Persianate sphere did not mean that Khorezmian students were absent from Bukharan madrasas, just that they rarely rose to the top of the Bukharan scholarly elite. Many of them did quite well for themselves upon returning home. For instance, in a mid-eighteenth-century biographical account of the Naqshbandi sufis, Muhammad Tahir wrote that his great grandfather, Mawlana Hazrat-i Dawlatshah had studied in Bukhara during the reign of Abdallah Khan (r. 1583–98), a tradition carried on by both Hazrat-i Dawlatshah's son Mawlana Baqi and then Muhammad Tahir himself in the eighteenth century (apparently skipping a generation).[38] Sa'dallah, one of Muhammad Tahir's sons, also studied in Bukhara, while another trained in Khiva and remained there as a *mudarris* (college instructor).[39] Similarly, one of Muhammad Tahir's sufi masters, Mawlana Aman Tirmizi, was also by origin from Khorezm, but studied in Bukhara and pursued various scholarly pursuits in Balkh and Termez as well.[40] Families of scholars split between the two domains moved back and forth with some frequency, and Muhammad Tahir noted numerous Khorezmian colleagues who traversed between Bukhara and Khiva.

Other sources from the later period indicate significant movement between these regions. For instance, a fatwa assisted a Khorezmian who ventured to Bukhara in the hopes of reclaiming his runaway wife.[41] And Bukharan government correspondence with the Russian political agent from the early twentieth century addressed some of the legal ramifications of Khorezmian students traveling to Bukhara for madrasa study.[42] The majority of students originating from the inner ring (Samarqand, Khurasan, the Kuhistan, and the Farghana Valley) mostly returned home after completing madrasa study as well; the difference is that some of those students also remained in Bukhara and prospered, whereas far fewer Khorezmians appear to have done so.

Khorezm's separateness from Bukhara's educational network (relative to the inner ring, that is) is likely the result of several related factors. Khorezm was much more firmly anchored within an emergent Turkic vernacular cultural milieu than Bukhara. Unlike Bukhara, Khiva's administration was primarily

---

had roots in Khorezm. For instance, Yaḥyā Khwāja was identified as the Turkmen descendant of the famous sufi saint Sayyid Ata, and also studied under a famous calligrapher (Chappa-Nawīs). Żīyā', *Taẕkirat al-khaṭṭāṭīn*, f. 191b. Yaḥyā Khwāja's prestige must have been considerable, since he was sent as an ambassador to Russia following Bukhara's defeat in 1868. RGADA F 1385 O 1 D 652, f. 1a.

38. Muḥammad Ṭāhir Khwārazmī, *Taẕkira-i Ṭāhir Ēshān*, ff. 351a–352a.

39. Muḥammad Ṭāhir Khwārazmī, *Taẕkira-i Ṭāhir Ēshān*, ff. 353a–353b.

40. Muḥammad Ṭāhir Khwārazmī, *Taẕkira-i Ṭāhir Ēshān*, ff. 346b—49b. Amān Tirmiẕī also studied in Damascus while on the Hajj.

41. *Jung-i riwāyāt i maḥżarā*, f. 288a.

42. Pickett, "Enemies beyond the Red Sands," 174–78.

conducted in Turkic, its chronicles were written in Turkic, and the nineteenth century witnessed the coordinated translation of a wide variety of Persian and Arabic texts into Turkic.[43] Many Bukharan scholars knew Turkic as well, and many composed poetry in that language.[44] Moreover, the vernacular Turkic textual culture assumed and built upon the Perso-Islamic one. Nevertheless, the jump from a cosmopolitan milieu to an equally sophisticated vernacular one was nontrivial and may have played a role in dissuading Khorezmian students from making a permanent career in Bukhara. Even more important is the fact that—unlike Khoqand or Shahrisabz—Khiva survived the Russian conquests as a protectorate, which allowed it to continue to invest in a madrasa establishment anchoring a little Persianate sphere of its own, one not referent to Bukhara.[45]

The Volga-Urals, Siberia, and the Kazakh steppe belt can perhaps be considered to part of the outer ring, similar to Khorezm; these areas were very much integrated into Bukhara's orbit, but less so than Farghana, Khurasan, and the Kuhistan. Muslims living in the Volga-Ural region of the Russian Empire increasingly oriented themselves toward Bukhara during the eighteenth century, and a Siberian biographical dictionary reveals Bukhara's importance as an educational center for the steppe region as well.[46] According to Allen Frank, the number of Tatars studying in Bukhara by the early nineteenth century numbered as many as 3,000.[47]

Yet, much like Khorezm, Russian Muslims are absent from the biographical dictionaries devoted to Bukharan luminaries produced in the late nineteenth and early twentieth centuries, despite the opposite trend in sources produced in the Volga-Urals.[48] This suggests that the relationship was weighted in one

43. Sartori, "On Madrasas, Legitimation, and Islamic Revival in 19th-Century Khorezm," 113; Erkinov, "Persian-Chaghatay Bilingualism."

44. Moreover, communication between Russian Turkestan and adjoining Bukharan provinces was often conducted in Turkic, apparently without issue (see, for instance, TsGARUz F i126 O 2 D 163); however, the Russian Political Agent communicated with the Bukharan government in Persian.

45. As discussed in chapter 1, Turkic can be considered a "vernacular" of Persian in that it borrowed extensively from Persian terminology, symbolism, and literature. Paolo Sartori argues that Khiva's own madrasa program was related to the influx of migrants from the Russian Empire. "On Madrasas, Legitimation, and Islamic Revival in 19th-Century Khorezm," 107, 119. Sartori even suggests that Khiva suffered from an "inferiority complex" vis-à-vis Bukhara as an Islamic center. Sartori, "On Madrasas, Legitimation, and Islamic Revival," 102.

46. Frank, *Bukhara and the Muslims of Russia*; Khālidī, *An Islamic Biographical Dictionary of the Eastern Kazakh Steppe 1770–1912*.

47. Frank, *Bukhara and the Muslims of Russia*, 7.

48. At least 5 percent of the entries in volume 6 of Marjanī's *Wafiyyat al-aslāf*, which covers not only Tatar ulama, but scholars from the entire world, hail from Bukhara and its environs.

direction and that Russian Muslims had greater difficulty integrating themselves into Bukharan society than their peers originating from Farghana, the Kuhistan, and Khurasan. As is evident from Tatar-produced biographical dictionaries, Russian Muslim students usually returned home, where they were able to leverage Bukhara's prestige to great effect. Those who remained were apparently isolated from the ranks of elite intellectuals composing Bukharan biographical dictionaries.

This greater social distance was likely a consequence of the sheer physical expanse between the Volga-Urals and Bukhara, as well as cultural differences. Tatar and Khorezmian literary and chancery culture was much more thoroughly Turkic than Bukhara's.[49] To be clear, the Volga-Urals and Khorezm were both home to sizable collections of Persian manuscripts and scholars capable of reading them, but Tatars generally wrote in either Turkic (just as in Khiva) or Arabic.[50] These differences posed a problem for some students visiting Bukhara for educational purposes. For instance, Hamid Muhammad al-Qazani was born on the outskirts of the Volga-Ural city of Kazan (annexed by Russia in 1552) but elected to remain in Bukhara until his death.[51] Hamid Muhammad was very successful in integrating himself into Bukharan life. He was a master at *tajwid* (Qur'anic recitation), which allowed him to preach at many mosques in Bukhara and teach in various madrasas. Hamid Muhammad had one problem: his spoken Persian was lousy, which made it difficult for him to attract students.[52] His plight was not unique, and likely shared by students from other parts of the outer ring and partly explains why so many others also found that their acquired social currency went further back home than it did in Bukhara.

References to scholars from elsewhere in the Russian Empire are even fewer. Evidence of migrants from the Caucasus in Bukhara's madrasa system is almost nonexistent. However, unlike the Volga-Urals, this lack of connectivity runs in both directions. In a biographical dictionary of ulama

49. Under Russian rule, official documentation in the Muslim parts of the empire was predominantly in Russian. However, the chancery language of the Golden Horde had been Turkic, and Turkic (especially Tatar) continued to be the primary indigenous language of publication.

50. In contrast with Central Asia, Tatars continued to publish original works in Arabic into the late nineteenth century, such as Marjānī's biographical dictionary (*Wafiyyat al-aslāf*).

51. Ḥamīd Muḥammad went back and forth between these cities at least twice before settling. Marjānī, *Wafiyyat al-aslāf*, f. 179b.

52. "He was weak in speaking Persian, and for that reason very few students wished to study under him." Marjānī, *Wafiyyat al-aslāf*, f. 198a. On language challenges faced by Russian Muslim students, see also Frank, *Bukhara and the Muslims of Russia*, 142–43. Ḥamīd Muḥammad's personality flaws did not help either: Marjānī wrote that he was quick to anger and resort to curses (*'ājil bi'l-shatm*). *Wafiyyat al-aslāf*, f. 197b.

from Dagestan, no references to Bukhara exist, though there are one or two references to Samarqand.[53] Abdallah al-Daghestani al-Shirwani (d. 1842/43) stands as an exception that proves the rule. Following his exile from the Caucasus—presumably for activities deemed subversive by Russian authorities, given that the Caucasus campaigns were raging at the time—Shirwani took up residence in Kazan. Only *after* integrating into the Tatar educational network did he migrate to Bukhara for his education.[54]

Altishahr (situated in the southern half of the Chinese province of Xinjiang, and sometimes referred to as eastern Turkestan) also fits into the outer ring of the little Persianate sphere shared by Khorezm and the Volga-Urals. Like those regions, its geographic and cultural distance from Bukhara limited its social integration relative to the likes of Farghana, Khurasan, and the Kuhistan.[55] Moreover, Altishahr enjoyed an internal coherence separate from Bukhara, tightly integrated through pilgrimage networks between the settlements dotting the rim of the Tarim Basin.[56] East Turkestan had a modest madrasa establishment of its own (eighteen in Kashgar, between thirty and fifty in Yarkand by the end of the nineteenth century), supporting an internal educational network nested within Bukhara's outer orbit.[57] For these reasons, few of Bukhara's elite bore demonyms like "al-Kashgari" or "al-Yarkandi," marking them or their ancestors as residents of one of the "six cities" (the literal meaning of Altishahr).[58]

By contrast, Bukharan-trained teachers were common in Altishahri madrasas, which meant that even students from that region who did not make it to Bukhara were nonetheless indirectly integrated into the city's educational network.[59] When a scholar from one of the towns rimming the Tarim Basin yearned for training beyond that which Kashgar's madrasas

---

53. Durkilī al-Tūnī, *Die Islamgelehrten Daghestans und ihre arabischen Werke*; Durgeli, *Uslada umov v biografiiakh dagestanskikh uchenykh*. As in the case of Iran, this likely has to do with the inapplicability of the Hanafi school of jurisprudence emphasized in Central Asian madrasas, which would have had little currency in the predominantly Shafiʾi Caucasus.

54. Marjānī, *Wafiyyat al-aslāf*, f. 196a.

55. Despite Altishahr being more thoroughly Turkic in terms of vernacular textual production, east Turkestani scholars who returned from Bukhara to more prestigious positions back home were not infrequently singled out for their mastery of Persian literature. Muḥammad Qāsim Amīn Turkistānī, *al-I ʿlām li-ba ʿż rijālāt Turkistān*.

56. Thum, *The Sacred Routes of Uyghur History*, 12–14 passim.

57. Ildikó Bellér-Hann quotes these rough figures from various European travelers, especially Martin Hartmann: *Community Matters in Xinjiang 1880–1949*, 329, 331. These figures notwithstanding, anecdotally (e.g., in Muḥammad Qāsim, *al-I ʿlām li-ba ʿż rijālāt Turkistān*), Kashgar seems to have been more of a hub than Yarkand.

58. The identity and number of those cities were variable. Thum, *The Sacred Routes of Uyghur History*, 6.

59. Bellér-Hann, *Community Matters in Xinjiang 1880–1949*, 329–32.

could offer, Bukhara was often the destination. Muhammad Ibrahim of Khotan dreamed of studying under the famous Indian scholar of Farangi Mahall, Abd al-Hayy Laknawi, but scholars in Khotan convinced him to instead travel to Bukhara—advice he took, setting out in 1911 at the age of seventeen.[60] Similar trajectories—traveling from one of the towns of the Tarim Basin to Kashgar for the initial study, and then continuing on to Bukhara—are common among biographies of east Turkestanis.[61] For instance, Shaykh Abd al-Qadir (l. 1799/1800–1880/81), a chief judge (*qazi-yi kalan*) of Kashgar, boasted a Bukharan madrasa pedigree.[62]

The handful of references in other genres of sources to Altishahri ulama active in Bukhara are generally at lower rungs of the social ladder. For instance, sometime in the late nineteenth century Qazi Abd al-Wahid Sadr informed the Bukharan government that one Hajji Abdallah Khotani had abandoned his post as an imam of a village mosque outside of Ghijduwan, several kilometers from Bukhara.[63] The reason given was that Hajji Abdallah had returned to "his own province," presumably referring to the city of Khotan in Chinese Turkestan.[64] Perhaps he realized that his advancement would be more assured on home turf, where a Bukharan education was more unusual and impressive.

Altishahr was oriented toward Bukhara as an educational and spiritual pole, and if a stalwart soul was to travel beyond the Tarim Basin for an education, the Abode of Knowledge was a likely destination. Altishahri students in Bukhara were less common than their colleagues from Farghana but hardly unknown.[65] Muhyi al-Din ibn Sabir al-Kashgari was born in Kashgar

60. Fażlī, *Tarjimat wālidī*, 12. Assuming this is indeed the ʿAbd al-Ḥayy of Lucknow who Ibrāhīm had in mind, he would have been disappointed had he not taken the advice of his elders, since that scholar passed away in 1886 (at the age of thirty-nine, so it would not have been an unreasonable assumption that the shaykh was still among the living).

61. For instance, in a sizable modern compendium of east Turkestani ulama biographies, scholars such as Shams al-Dīn Dāmullām (d. 1938), Shaykh ʿAbdallāh Dāmullām (d. 1962/63), or Shaykh ʿUs̱mān Aʿlam Akhund (d. 1883/84), all of whom returned home after completing their study: Muḥammad Qāsim, *al-Iʿlām li-baʿż rijālāt Turkistān*, 382, 432; 512. Although I have not analyzed this collection quantitatively, anecdotally it is the more celebrated scholars (judging by honorifics, length of entry, etc.) who made the trip to Bukhara (or India). Many more east Turkestani scholars studied in their hometown madrasa or traveled just to Kashgar and then returned.

62. ʿAbd al-Qādir initially trained in Kashgar, then spent around four years in Bukhara, and returned to Kashgar knowledgeable in Hadith, Qur'anic exegesis (*tafsīr*), and inheritance law, as well as Persian literature (on those subjects in relation to madrasa instruction, see next chapter). Muḥammad Qāsim Amīn Turkistānī, *al-Iʿlām li-baʿż rijālāt Turkistān*, 512.

63. This is almost certainly the same Qāżī ʿAbd al-Wāḥid Ṣadr Ṣarīr Balkhī (d. 1885/86), whose family dynasty is discussed in chapter 6.

64. TsGARUz F i-126 O 1 D 1953, f. 5a.

65. The Turkic Muslims of western China are now known as Uyghurs, but that term was not yet used in the nineteenth century. On how this population became Uyghurs, see Brophy, *Uyghur Nation*.

and received his initial training there, but traveled to Bukhara in 1910/11 to complete his education, after which point he continued on to Mecca on the Hajj.[66] The fact that Bukhara had been subjugated by Russia did not diminish its appeal, nor did the Chinese and Russian borders he had to pass through in 1910 prove a decisive hindrance.[67]

The Russian imperial apparatus even assisted eastern Turkestan's Bukharan connection in some cases.[68] Correspondence between the Russian Resident in Bukhara and the Qushbegi's office show that Russian officers reached out to their colleagues in the Kashgar consulate to solve inheritance disputes when Bukharans died in Xinjiang. In May 1917, the Russian consul in Kashgar wrote to the Russian resident that a merchant named Sayyid Khwaja Ruzybaev had passed away and left property behind and inquired as to whether he had any living relatives in Bukhara to collect it. The resident forwarded the request to the Qushbegi (a position sometimes translated as prime minister), whose office investigated the matter—ultimately without uncovering a widow or heir.[69] Though Sayyid Khwaja was referenced in the correspondence as a merchant, his name suggests the possibility of religious authority as well, and the incident illustrates patterns of mobility between the regions more generally.

Little Persianate Spheres beyond Bukhara's Orbit

What of the Ottoman, Qajar, and Mughal/British Indian realms, which constituted the most powerful Eurasian political entities of the day? These regions were effectively beyond even the outer ring of Bukhara's little Persianate sphere. Some of the reasons for this varied between each case, but all three boasted little Persianate spheres of their own, separate from, and on equal footing with, Bukhara.

As caliphs and guardians of Mecca and Medina, the Ottoman sultans enjoyed conceptual prestige in the minds of Central Asian scholars, but movement between those realms was decidedly limited until the late nine-

---

66. Muʿallimī, *Aʿlām al-Makayyain*, 786.

67. The Bolshevik Revolution was a different story; a scholar from Turfan aiming to study in Bukhara was forced to turn back in Khoqand in 1917. Muḥammad Qāsim, *al-Iʿlām li-baʿż rijālāt Turkistān*, 436.

68. For a broader discussion of some of the specific ways the advancing Russian and Chinese empires affected the nature of migration, see Pickett, "The Darker Side of Mobility."

69. TsGARUz F i-126 O 2 D 6100, f. 3a-4b. In a similar inquiry a year earlier—which also came up empty—it was the *qāżī-yi kalān*'s office, which investigated the matter in Bukhara. TsGARUz F i-126 O 2 D 6172.

teenth century.[70] After Russia connected Bukhara to the Volga-Ural region with railroads, that avenue became the most popular means of going on the Hajj.[71] By the early twentieth century, the Jadids had become fascinated by the Ottoman Empire as a model of reform, and many of them spent time in Istanbul.[72] Before that, however, the eastern pilgrimage route through India was likely more common than the one through Ottoman lands and references to Anatolia are infrequent in the sources, aside from occasional diplomatic contact. Muhammad Parsa Khwaja-i Salam (d. 1853/54), for instance, served as an ambassador to the Ottoman Empire, where he may have lived out his days.[73]

Isolated examples such as Muhammad Parsa notwithstanding, for the purposes of the little Persianate sphere centered on Bukhara, the Ottoman Empire was a realm firmly apart: although Central Asian Muslims traveled to Ottoman lands in significant numbers, not a single Ottoman-trained scholar appears among the ranks of elite Bukharan ulama in any of the sources considered in this study.[74] Ottoman scholars had their own "abodes of knowledge" toward which to orient themselves, and the Ottoman religious establishment (*ilmiye*) was systematically integrated into the state in a manner that had no real parallel elsewhere, least of all Central Asia.[75] Both areas were Persianate in the domain of high culture, but the skill sets cultivated in Ottoman and Central Asian madrasas were not fully interchangeable. Ottoman Turkish can be considered a vernacular of Persian in the same way that eastern Turki/Chaghatay was, but one that constituted a much larger linguistic jump for Central Asians: texts written Ottoman Turkic did not circulate in Central Asia.[76] Thus, before the Jadids, Ottoman centers of learning held no particular allure for the Central Asian ulama, nor did Bukharan madrasas attract Anatolian students.

Though geographically adjacent, and despite the fact that Iran is now the unit most readily associated with "Persianate" as a concept, Qajar Iran

70. Burton, "Relations Between the Khanate of Bukhara and Ottoman Turkey, 1558–1702."

71. Brower, "Russian Roads to Mecca," 579; Kane, *Russian Hajj*; Can, *Spiritual Subjects*.

72. Khalid, "Central Asia between the Ottoman and the Soviet Worlds."

73. Wāżiḥ, *Tuḥfat al-aḥbāb*, ff. 45–46. The sources disagree about whether Muḥammad Pārsā died in Istanbul or Bombay. Żiyā', *Nawādir żiyā'īya*, f. 48b

74. For instance, a Russian diplomat in Cairo reported in 1896 that around 200 Central Asian families were living in Egypt at the time. RGVIA 400-1-1936, f. 4b; see also Can, *Spiritual Subjects*. In the seventeenth century, Central Asian acolytes of the Naqshbandiyya-Mujaddidiyya established prominent communities in Ottoman territories as part of the same movement from India that spread the branch to Central Asia itself. Weismann, *The Naqshbandiyya*, 73–76.

75. Zilfi, *The Politics of Piety*.

76. However, certain Arabic legal texts composed by Ottoman scholars were part of the madrasa curriculum in Bukhara.

was just as removed from the Bukharan orbit as the Ottoman Empire. Since the sixteenth century, Iran's population was predominantly Shi'i, which limited its potential for social integration with Central Asia. This wall was by no means impermeable, and Robert McChesney has debunked the "barrier of heterodoxy" paradigm that once framed much of the literature.[77] Bukhara itself was even home to a sizable Shi'i community, which had been forcibly relocated there by Shah-Murad (r. 1785–1800) following his conquest of Merv.[78] During an 1860 Qajar campaign in Merv against Turkmen slavers, Mirza Muhammad Tihrani "Taqi Haft Qalam" was taken prisoner following the Qajar army's catastrophic defeat and was eventually sold as a slave in Bukhara.[79] As a *sayyid* (descendant of the Prophet), trained calligrapher, and poet, Muhammad Taqi found employment (albeit in bondage) in the service of the Bukharan Qushbegi, which he pursued until he became ill and was freed to return to his homeland.[80]

Muhammad Taqi's story was not unique, and other educated Iranians found that many of their skills were fully transferrable to administrative positions, particularly in direct service to the Turkic military elite.[81] By the mid-nineteenth century, former Iranian captives were disproportionately represented in newly established Bukharan artillery and infantry units.[82] Moreover, Iranian poets were frequently integrated into Bukharan poetical anthologies, even those who never left their homeland—something that cannot be said of Indian poets, despite a rich tradition of Persian poetry, and despite the wild popularity of poets such as Bedil.[83]

Nevertheless, the Shi'a-Sunni split between Central Asia and Iran meant that many of the functions that made up the occupational mainstay of the Bukharan ulama were closed to non-Sunnis.[84] Judicial appointments

---

77. McChesney, "'Barrier of Heterodoxy'?" Sectarian boundaries were hardening during the long nineteenth century, for reasons articulated in Pickett, "Nadir Shah's Peculiar Central Asian Legacy." See also discussion of the discourse of blasphemy in chapter 6.

78. Kimura, "Sunni-Shi'i Relations in the Russian Protectorate of Bukhara."

79. On the slave trade in Central Asia, a significant portion of which was the sale of Iranian slaves, see Eden, *Slavery and Empire in Central Asia*.

80. Wāżiḥ, *Tuḥfat al-aḥbāb*, ff. 50–51.

81. As time went on, the Manghit dynasty of Bukhara became increasingly reliant on Iranians (as well as Russian slaves and British deserters) to run its military. Holzwarth, "The Uzbek State as Reflected in Eighteenth Century Bukharan Sources," 100. To the present day, some communities in Bukhara identify as "Iranian."

82. Holzwarth, "Bukharan Armies and Uzbek Military Power, 1670–1870," 323–25.

83. For instance, Wāżiḥ, *Tuḥfat al-aḥbāb*, and Muḥtaram, *Tazkirat al-shuʿarā*. By contrast, the author of a well-known poetical *tazkira* from the early modern period, Muḥammad Muṭribī Samarqandī, traveled to India and updated his anthology to include Indian poets.

84. For an interesting partial exception to this rule, see the case of Jahāngīr Majnūn in the next chapter. Despite his Iranian Shi'i origins, Jahāngīr Majnūn competed for religious authority as

depended on a mastery of Sunni Hanafi law, which was not practiced in Shi'i Iran. The sufi communities of Central Asia had an overwhelmingly Sunni orientation, whereas institutionalized sufism been mostly eliminated from Iran during the sixteenth century.[85] These hurdles meant that Iran was a step removed from other areas more firmly integrated into Bukhara's scholarly network, despite sharing a common literary culture.[86] Needless to say, with Persianate centers of learning in Isfahan, Shiraz, and Qom, the Qajar realm did just fine without Bukhara.[87]

India's relationship with Bukhara is perhaps the most nuanced of the Persianate spaces that I argue to have been essentially outside of Bukhara's scholarly orbit, containing numerous little Persianate spheres in its own right. Delhi was not as geographically distant from Bukhara as Istanbul, nor was it isolated by sect like Iran, and the two regions enjoyed a legacy of sizable population transfers.[88] Moreover, Central Asia was intimately connected with India by merchants, some of whom were also Islamic scholars (though many were Hindu) and used their travel as an opportunity to study in Bukharan madrasas.[89] For instance, one Muhammad Amin Hakim's father was born in India and came to Bukhara as a merchant in the late nineteenth century; he spent the proceeds of this activity giving his son the best education money could buy, which Muhammad Amin deployed to earn his place among Bukhara's scholars rather than its merchants.[90]

There is likewise evidence of Bukharans traveling to India and back. A sealed letter dated June–July 1855 from the Nizam of Hyderabad guaranteeing safe (and duty-free) passage for a Bukharan residing in the Indian

---

a *maddāḥ*, something like a minstrel or folk preacher. Jahāngīr's biography (written by an Islamic scholar) contains profuse criticisms of his lack of formal madrasa training.

85. Because the Safavid dynasty was itself the continuation of a sufi community, rival sufi groups were suppressed early in Safavid history, as core tenets of sufism (such as veneration of the house of the Prophet) were absorbed into mainstream Shi'ism. Arjomand, *The Shadow of God and the Hidden Imam*, 109–19. See also Anzali, *Mysticism in Iran*.

86. Abdul-Karim Rafeq demonstrates that *maẕhab* affiliation shaped educational networks even within Sunni domains. Syrian Hanafi ulama gravitated toward Istanbul for education, whereas their Shafi'i counterparts went to Cairo in greater numbers. "Relations between the Syrian 'Ulamā' and the Ottoman State in the Eighteenth Century," 76–78.

87. One also notes that Iranian poets show up much more prominently in early modern anthologies written before the sectarian divide hardened. For instance, over 12 percent of the poets included in Muṭribī's seventeenth-century *taẕkira* originated from Iran, which was more even than those from the Farghana Valley. Muṭribī Samarqandī, *Taẕkirat al-shu'arā'*.

88. See Kumar, *The Emergence of the Delhi Sultanate*.

89. Levi, *The Indian Diaspora in Central Asia and Its Trade, 1550–1900*.

90. Muḥammad Amīn Ḥakīm is also discussed in chapter 5 in terms of his expertise in medicine and geomancy (an occult science); for a broader discussion of the tendency of merchant families to buy their way into the learned elite, see the next chapter.

princely state found its way to the chancellery of the Bukharan amirate. While the letter does not state whether one Mawlawi Ala al-Din Bukhari was residing in Hyderabad in a scholarly capacity, it does specify that he was transporting fifteen books on a bullock cart back to his homeland.[91] This stands as evidence of the constant movement of texts from India to Central Asia, which is also demonstrated by the numerous lithographs published in locales such as Lucknow and Lahore now residing in Central Asian collections. This new technology was often used to dramatically increase the availability of classical texts in the early nineteenth century, long before lithography was introduced in Central Asia.[92] This does not, however, stand as proof of India's integration into Bukhara's educational orbit (or little Persianate sphere), even if they shared a common thought world (or cosmopolis).

Certain legal documents reinforce the evidence for the conceptual proximity between India and Bukhara. One fatwa copied into a *jung* (notebook of miscellany) offered an opinion related to the death of a Bukharan residing in India. Funeral rites (*janaza*) had been carried out in India by the permission of the Mughal emperor, but without the presence of a representative from the deceased's family, without the permission of a *qazi*, and despite the fact that the body had not putrefied by the time it arrived in Bukhara.[93] This legal opinion highlights not only the physical movement of people, but also the legal interlegibility of the two similarly Hanafi spaces. India was not imagined by the author of this opinion to be so far removed that it was either irrelevant or outside the bounds of his legal judgment.

Where does this leave integrated scholarly movement between India and Central Asia? Sufi networks—especially that of the Naqshbandiyya-Mujaddidiyya and particularly in the latter half of the eighteenth century—stand next to merchants as another major qualification to this study's conceptualization of India as standing essentially outside of Bukhara's little Persianate sphere. But even this exception is only partial. India's Naqshbandi-Mujaddidi revivalist networks were not sending students to Bukhara to train in its madrasa establishments in large numbers. Rather, this movement was a consequence of Naqshbandi-Mujaddidi efforts to induct Central Asian Muslims into the order and thereby instruct them in the teaching of

91. TsGARUz F i-126 O 1 D 1293. The document does not specify whether ʿAlāʾ al-Dīn's books were manuscripts or lithographs. The cart is referred to by the Hindustani term *manzil-bandī*.

92. ʿAbd al-ʿĪsā al-Khūqandī (d. 1823–24) was especially well known for his early adoption of Indian-produced books, probably in the 1810s. Marjānī, *Wafiyyat al-aslāf*, f. 157b.

93. The fatwa ruled that it was lawful for the deceased's family to perform funeral rites again once the body arrived in Bukhara. Ḥusaynī, *Jung-i majmūʿah-i riwāyāt*, f. 110a. The Mughal emperor is referred to as *pādishāh-i waqt, imām-i zamān-i Hind*.

Ahmad Sirhindi, the seventeenth-century founder of this offshoot of the Naqshbandiyya—efforts that were overwhelmingly successful.[94] In terms of physical movement, these migrations (both of Central Asians traveling to India for training, and Indian sufis moving to Central Asia to establish offshoots) were limited both chronologically and in quantity of individuals.[95] After an initial period of outreach, the Naqshbandiyya-Mujaddidiyya quickly became indigenized to Central Asia, such that sufi knowledge was passed from generation to generation without necessarily involving travel to the parent nodes of the order in India.[96] After the initial missionaries from India founded a node in the sufi network, or after a Central Asian scholar traveled to India for training, subsequent initiates could receive instruction closer to home.

By the end of the eighteenth century, most of the established ulama in the city of Bukhara had embraced the Naqshbandi-Mujaddidi revivalist teachings, and even rulers of Bukhara (Shah-Murad and Amir Haydar) had become part of the network.[97] As a result, most of the Naqshbandi-Mujaddidi ulama were Bukharan Naqshbandi-Mujaddidis. The Indian branches of the Naqshbandi-Mujaddidi community continued its tradition of dispatching missionaries northward to establish circles of their own into the nineteenth century, including in the hinterlands of Central Asia, where Bukhara's direct influence was less pronounced.[98] For instance, sometime in the mid-nineteenth century, a scholar named Shah Abd al-Wahid Tashqurgani left his native Khulm not to study in Bukhara, but to seek Naqshbandi-Mujaddidi training in Delhi, after which he returned to his native Khulm to pass on what he had learned.[99] Mulla Nur Muhammad Kulabi's trajectory was nearly identical, except that he passed the knowledge he acquired in Delhi on to disciples in the Kuhistan rather than Khulm, as did Mulla Muhammad Mir Qaratigini.[100] These accounts stand as evidence for India's centrality for Bukhara, rather than vice versa.

---

94. A major new study of this phenomenon is Ziad, "Traversing the Indus and the Oxus."

95. Jo-Ann Gross shows that migration of the non-Mujaddidi Naqshbandiyya had petered out by the late eighteenth century. "The Naqshbandīya Connection," 240.

96. See Babadzhanov, "On the History of the Naqshbandiya Mujaddidiya in Central Mawara'nnahr in the Late 18th and Early 19th Centuries"; von Kügelgen, "Rastsvet Nakshbandiia-Mudzhaddidiia v Srednei Transoksanii s XVIII–do nachala XIX vv.: Opyt detektivnogo rassledovaniia"; Ziad, "Traversing the Indus and the Oxus," 518.

97. This transition played out over the course of the eighteenth century, and the Naqshbandī-Mujaddidī takeover was met with stiff resistance early on. DeWeese, "'Dis-Ordering' Sufism in Early Modern Central Asia," 264–65; Ziad, "Traversing the Indus and the Oxus," 526.

98. These findings are corroborated in Ziad, "Traversing the Indus and the Oxus," 681–82.

99. Tash-Qurghan is another name for Khulm. Mujaddidī, *Manāqib al-ahmadiyya*, ff. 217b–218a.

100. Muḥammad Maẓhar Mujaddidī, *Manāqib al-ahmadiyya*, ff. 221a–221b; 222b–223a.

Another Naqshbandi-Mujaddidi text similarly illustrates the brotherhood's aggressive expansion into areas at the fringes of Bukhara's orbit—and outside of the Sunni Hanafi fold. Timur Khan Bajuri (d. 1810/11) was inducted into the order in northern India by Shams al-Din Habiballah Janan-i Janan, who traced his intellectual lineage directly to Ahmad Sirhindi.[101] After twenty-two years of training, Timur Khan returned to his native Bajur (located between Kabul and Peshawar), where he began training disciples of his own—so many that he needed to slaughter twenty to thirty sheep every evening to feed them. Timur Khan used Bajur as a base of operations to launch missionary expeditions northward into Central Asia—which included jihad against infidels in the mountainous areas of Badakhshan.[102] The text makes a special point of emphasizing that Timur Khan gained fame among the Muslims of Central Asia, and that when the ulama of that region made the mistake of engaging him in the debate about points of religion, he emerged victorious. Nevertheless, one notes that his activities (as well as those of his son and successor, Muhammad Ma'sum) primarily focused on the edges of Bukhara's influence.[103]

Rare missionaries attempting to found new study circles after much of the Bukharan ulama had already indigenized the Naqshbandiyya-Mujaddidiya were frequently unsuccessful.[104] Raz Muhammad Qandahari traveled far and wide throughout India seeking knowledge, before eventually traveling north to Balkh, Bukhara, and then Samarqand.[105] Learning of this new arrival, the amir of Bukhara secretly sent an agent to test Raz Muhammad's piety, and—after the test was passed successfully—invited him to a royal audience,

---

101. Incidentally, Shams al-Dīn himself had roots in Central Asia; his father had immigrated to India from Qarshi (Nasaf) and served in the Mughal military. *Biografiia sheikhov Naqshbandiia i Mudzhadddidiia*, f. 59b. Shams al-Dīn was eventually martyred in 1785/86 for defying the Mughal Emperor over a point of Islamic doctrine. *Biografiia sheikhov Naqshbandiia i Mudzhadddidiia*, f. 60b.

102. The text refers somewhat vaguely to the "dark-skinned infidels who resided in the mountains around Kabul, Badakhshan, and Bajur": *kuffār-i siyah* [*sic*] *pūst kih dar jibāl-i Kābul ū Badakhshān ū aṭrāf-i Bājūr sākin and*. *Biografiia sheikhov Naqshbandiia i Mudzhadddidiia*, f. 61b. Probably some of these "infidels" were Isma'ilis, against whom the Naqshbandiyya-Mujaddidiyya had been making inroads since the eighteenth century. Beben, "The Legendary Biographies of Nāṣir-i Khusraw," 230–31. Others may have been non-Muslims of Nuristan, or Hazaras. In other instances, members of the Naqshbandiyya-Mujaddidiyya preached tolerance for Shi'as: Ziad, "Traversing the Indus and the Oxus," 542.

103. *Biografiia sheikhov Naqshbandiia i Mudzhadddidiia*, f. 61b and ff. 61b–62a. On Naqshbandī-Mujaddidī expansion under the Afghan Durrani dynasty, see Ziad, "From Yarkand to Sindh via Kabul."

104. Similarly, see Waleed Ziad's case study of Fażl Aḥmad Ma'ṣūmī, whose forced departure from Bukhara was rhetorically tied to his mastery of Bedil's poetry. Ziad, "Traversing the Indus and the Oxus," 686–87.

105. The text notes only that Rāz Muḥammad did not "find solace" in Balkh or Bukhara (*taskīn na-yāfta*). Muḥammad Maẓhar Mujaddidī, *Manāqib al-Ahmadiyya*, ff. 237b.

which the sufi refused. Soon thereafter Raz Muhammad returned to his shaykh in India, intending to eventually return to Samarqand, but dying on the way near Ghazni.[106]

If anything, Naqshbandi-Mujaddidi missionary activity provides evidence of Bukhara's integration into an India-centered little Persianate sphere.[107] Central Asians traveled to India for training and then returned home, or Indian-trained sufis migrated to Central Asia and remained. With some exceptions, there is scant evidence that Indian Muslims moved to Bukhara for the express purpose of receiving Islamic training in any significant numbers. Nashbandi-Mujaddidi migrants integrated into the more locally circumscribed Bukharan madrasa network within a generation or two.

Indian Muslims situated themselves in relation to their own "abodes of knowledge" and anchored their own "little Persianate spheres" in places such as Delhi, Lucknow, and Lahore. Occasionally, this point is spelled out explicitly. A 2002 Urdu publication about the history of Rampur's Madrasa-i Aliya states that the institution was conceived of as "the Bukhara of India," but after local scholars had established themselves in the eighteenth and nineteenth centuries it became instead "the envy of Bukhara."[108] Rampur was not so distant from Central Asia that it was unmoved by Bukhara's bid for Islamic prestige, but was sufficiently established in its own right to compete rather than defer. In other words, India was more thoroughly integrated with Central Asia than the Qajar or Ottoman realms, but nevertheless more aptly conceptualized as the home to numerous "little Persianate spheres" of its own rather than a node in Bukhara's wide-reaching scholarly network.

Weaving the Social Back into the Cosmopolis

Bukhara's scholarly elite replenished their numbers predominantly from an inner ring consisting of the Farghana Valley, the Kuhistan (mountainous territories to the east), and eastern Khurasan (now northern Afghanistan). Most students from the inner and outer rings alike could never hope to make it into a biographical dictionary of the greatest scholars of the age, but they could still find success back home, or in more modest positions within Bukhara. Islamic scholars who returned home to become a village imam in Tatarstan,

106. The source does not explicitly attribute causality between Rāz Muḥammad's departure from Samarqand and refusing the amir's request; nor does it offer an alternative explanation. Muḥammad Maẓhar Mujaddidī, *Manāqib al-Ahmadiyya*, ff. 237a–237b.

107. For an in-depth illustration of this point, see Ziad, "Traversing the Indus and the Oxus," chap. 12.

108. Khan, *Madrasa-i ʿālīya-i Rāmpūr*, 9.

for instance, or a provincial judge Xinjiang, primarily relied on their knowledge of the Islamic scriptures and Hanafi law, core facets of the Bukharan madrasa curriculum that were fully transferable. Training in these skills was also on offer locally, but there was an implicit hierarchy of educational centers. Scholars originating from Bukhara rarely traveled to Khiva, Kazan, or Kashgar for education, whereas the reverse was quite common. Cities such as these served as mid-level educational hubs within Bukhara's broad orbit, servicing the majority of regional ulama, with Bukhara serving as a prestige educational destination for families of greater means and ambition.

Where the overlap of disciplines cultivated in Bukhara was even less pronounced, such as in the Ottoman or Qajar realms, students had no reason to venture to Central Asia. As I argue in the following chapters, it was the intersection of multiple forms of knowledge that paved the path to scholarly influence in the sophisticated urban environment of Bukhara. Where consensus over what constituted the Perso-Islamic canon began to unravel (such as the Ottoman Empire and Qajar Iran, along different vectors), or where peer competitors claimed equal centrality in the Persian cosmopolis (such as India, as well as the Ottoman and Qajar territories), sustained educational migration was far more limited. Whether the ulama of Bukhara liked it or not, there were limits and gradations to the city's centrality.

An implication of this fact is that Bukhara's centrality was not always so ironclad, and serious competitors had previously vied successfully for similar status. In the rubble of Nadir Shah's empire after 1747, a panoply of city-states emerged throughout Central Asia that might each have emerged as the paramount regional center instead of Bukhara, and many of them competed with Bukhara for a time to attract Islamic scholars. The most serious such challenger was Khoqand, a Farghana city not founded until 1740, but which became a city-state in its own right and received substantial investment from the late eighteenth through mid-nineteenth centuries.[109] In many instances, the sources reveal direct efforts by Bukharan rulers to siphon off the intellectual talent from other city-states, especially Khoqand and Shahrisabz.[110]

109. ʿUmar Khan's efforts could not be ignored even by partisan Bukharan authors writing much later, including those used for many of the aggregate figures in this chapter: "It is befitting that the shah of Bukhara should be submissive to you [i.e., ʿUmar]; for ʿUmar is worthier of the throne of justice (*takht-i ʿadālat*) than Haydar [i.e., the Bukharan monarch r. 1800–1826]." Indeed, ʿUmar Khan himself was a celebrated poet and was included in Wāżiḥ's collection under the heading of his apt penname "Amir." Wāżiḥ, *Tuḥfat al-aḥbāb*, f. 145 and ff. 29–30.

110. ʿUmar Khan went to elaborate lengths to attract Sulṭān Khwāja Aḥrārī "Adā" (d. 1834) away from Bukhara, even offering him the title "king of poets." But in 1829 Amir Naṣrallāh Manghit (r. 1827–60) enticed him into the Bukharan fold, appointing him *shaykh al-Islām* after several rebuffed

By the late nineteenth century Bukhara was the Abode of Knowledge its partisans claimed it to be—from the perspective of those living within the orbit traced in this chapter. The city's religious infrastructure dwarfed that of other Central Asian cities, and in terms of educational capacity it competed with any other city in the Islamic world. These networks of human, intellectual, and cultural exchange integrated this little Persianate sphere in a manner not reducible to the numerous and overlapping political boundaries of Central Asia, which fluctuated throughout this time period. As the examples in this chapter make evident, those political boundaries and institutions were far from irrelevant, but the cosmopolis too played a formative role, anchoring the universal to the local and shaping educational exchange patterns.

---

overtures. Wāżiḥ, *Tuḥfat al-aḥbāb*, f. 13; Muḥammad ḥakīm Khān, *Muntakhab al-tawārīkh*, vol. 1, 429; Sayyid Mīr ṣadīq Tūra Ḥashmat, *Taẕkirat al-shu ʿarā ʾ*, 12b marginalia. On efforts by the Keneges rulers of Shahrisabz to compete with Bukhara for Islamic scholars, see Pickett, "Written into Submission," 837–39.

CHAPTER 4

Patricians of Bukhara

Turkic Nobility, Persianate Pedagogy, and Islamic Society

Who created, recreated, and maintained the Persian cosmopolis? Who were the agents behind this domain of writing, learning, and exchange? Despite the carefully constructed illusion of timelessness, cultural centers do not just appear out of thin air: they are built and enacted by people.

Islamic scholars are the focus of this book, but they were not the only patricians of Bukhara, and they cannot be understood outside of the larger ecosystem.[1] They shared their elite status with merchants, competed for spiritual and cultural leadership with street preachers, and were reliant on a Turkic military elite for their wellbeing. No formal barriers existed between these categories, and nonscholarly patricians frequently invested their resources to educate themselves and become ulama. Even though there were many ways to wield influence in Bukhara (as in all societies), only the scholarly elite and the Turkic nobility were explicitly valorized as such, albeit by fundamentally distinct justifications. Merchants and preachers might also be considered patricians, but they lacked a formal place in the cosmopolis and

1. I occasionally use the terms "patriciate" and "patrician" to refer to the elite strata as a whole (i.e., inclusive of and extending beyond the ulama) as a homage to Richard Bulliet's pioneering study *The Patricians of Nishapur*.

were rhetorically subordinated to the twin pillars of the patriciate: Turkic nobility and the ulama.

Received understandings of the ulama as an ethnically Iranian, urban stratum to be contrasted with Uzbek nomad-warriors, or as austere preacher-jurists standing disapprovingly aloof, ultimately miss the mark. Indeed, there were only two paths to the patriciate in Central Asia during its long nineteenth century: by the pen or by the sword.[2] Neither path was a birthright or governed by ethnicity, and the way of the pen was an inclusive one, encompassing jurists, government officials, occultists, calligraphers, doctors, and more.

Patricians Outside the Scholarly Fold

Before examining the many social roles embodied by the ulama, it is important to first emphasize that there were other paths to elite status separate from the Islamic discursive tradition governed by entirely separate logics of power.[3] Especially in Eurasia, but in the Islamic world more broadly as well, there existed a centuries-old social division between the military estate—dominated by Turkic clans stratified by kinship loyalties—and civil administration and education, which was permeated by Perso-Islamic cultural forms.[4] The ulama can be understood only in relation to their counterparts: the Turkic nobility.[5] The career of one member of this class serves as an instructive counterpoint to the scholarly path.

Turkic nobles did not, for the most part, write about themselves and rarely appeared in biographical dictionaries unless their social function overlapped with that of the ulama. In the late nineteenth century, the Russian orientalist Alexander Kuhn (1840–88) convinced Abdallah Beg Udaychi to narrate his

2. Naṣīr al-Dīn Ṭūsī deployed this formulation in his famous eleventh-century work on ethics: *The Nasirean Ethics*, 230.

3. The phrase "logic of power" is used to differentiate the two dominant forms of power in the time and place covered in this book, in the sense suggested by Moshe Halbertal: "While members of the community may disagree about specific beliefs and practices, they do agree about what is the proper way of justifying them." *People of the Book*, 8.

4. Bregel, "The Role of Central Asia in the History of the Muslim East," 5. Although I embrace this basic structural bifurcation, the ethnic dimension of the generalization is much more accurate in one direction; that is, sedentary communities (sometimes referred to as "Tajiks" or "Sarts") did not usually participate in the clan military system, though they were recruited as soldiers in ʿAlim Khan of Khoqand's "ghalcha" army. Levi, "The Ferghana Valley at the Crossroads of World History," 228.

5. Beside *ʾumarāʾ*, an emic term more specifically approximating the idea of "nobility," is the idea of "white boned" (*aq söyek*), which generally refers more specifically to descendants of Genghis Khan—and therefore exclusive of virtually all of Bukhara's nobles, including the ruling Manghit dynasty. Bregel, "Uzbeks, Qazaqs and Turkmens," 231.

career to Mirza Abd al-Rahman, Kuhn's hired scribe.[6] This account offers a glimpse into the professional trajectory of an individual's advancement separate from that of the ulama.[7]

Abdallah Beg came from a line of governors of various provinces, but especially Panjikent, a town located sixty-five kilometers up the Zarafshan Valley from Samarqand (in what is now Tajikistan). His mother was from a Samarqandi Tajik family, and it was in Samarqand that Abdallah Beg spent the first twenty years of his life. On his father's side, Abdallah Beg's family was from the Yuz tribe and distinguished itself with the hereditary title *dad-khwah*, a Persian conjunction used by the Turkic nobility meaning "petitioner for justice."[8]

By the nineteenth century, the upper rungs of the Turkic aristocracy no longer derived their authority exclusively from military skills cultivated on the steppe, and it seems that shared Turkic ethnicity, culture, or identity were not critical factors either, given that Abdallah Beg was raised in an urban Persianate environment.[9] Abdallah Beg made no mention of attending madrasa or any other formal schooling, although other nobles were known to initially attend madrasa before training in the martial arts.[10] Instead, the pivotal factor that determined his elite status was a bloodline tied to "the collective memory of the Mongol conquests of the early thirteenth century and the roles played by the amirs' ancestors during that time"—in other words, noble

6. AV IVR RAN F 33 O 1 D 149.

7. The source is unusual in that it fits neatly neither into the category of colonial knowledge, given that it was recorded in Persian by a *mīrzā* (scribe) directly from ʿAbdallāh Beg's own words, nor into any indigenous genre of writing. Though uncommon in the Central Asian context, it resembles the "newswriting" (*wāqʿia-nawīsī*) phenomenon in India as appropriated by the British. See Bayly, *Empire and Information*.

8. The Yuz tribe was prominent in Uratepa, a city (and sometimes city-state) located further up the Zarafshan valley (now called Istaravshan). "Zhizneopisanie Abdully-beka," f. 1b.

9. However, the performative dimension of military prowess retained importance. Allsen, *The Royal Hunt in Eurasian History*, 124 passim. Moreover, rank-and-file Turkic horsemen were feared well into the nineteenth century: "an Oozbek is part of his Horse, and he takes an Afghan out of the saddle with his spear, as you would take up meat with a spoon." "Narrative of a journey through Toorkistan made by Futteh Muhummid." By the eighteenth century, "the critical social distinction in the Bukharan state was evidently not conceptualised between 'nomad' and 'sedentary' but between 'warrior'/'Uzbek' and 'subject.'" Holzwarth, "The Uzbek State as Reflected in Eighteenth Century Bukharan Sources," 97.

10. For instance, ʿAbd al-Muʾmin, grandson of Amir Muẓaffar, attended "elementary madrasa" (*al-madrasa al-ibtidāʾiyya*) in Guzar, and then trained in firearms and horsemanship. ʿAbd al-Muʾmin, *Ażwāʾ ʿalā tārīkh Tūrān*, 159. According to McChesney, biographical references to amirs receiving literary education are almost nonexistent, despite the important role of the Turkic elite in patronizing the arts. "The Amirs of Muslim Central Asia in the XVIIth Century," 46, 49. Private tutoring in the Mughal case seems to have been more extensive. Faruqui, *Princes of the Mughal Empire, 1504–1719*, 78–81.

lineage.[11] "Turkic" as employed here does not refer to ethnicity, but rather the moral-political traditions governing the world of the warrior elite. Noble lineage was a necessary condition for acquiring positions of influence within the Turkic fold, but not by itself sufficient.

Rather than immersion in the arcane proficiencies of the ulama, the Turkic path to prominence revolved around proximity to the person of the amir. Abdallah Beg did not offer great detail about the career of his father, Yamaq Dad-khwah, but proudly emphasized that Yamaq was personally given a golden staff by the amir of Bukhara. Yamaq Dad-khwah died when Abdallah Beg was twenty years old, and the young noble was immediately summoned to Bukhara and assigned to Amir Nasrallah's (r. 1827–60) royal entourage, where he served for eight years and received considerable favor.[12] Having gained the personal trust of the amir, Abdallah Beg was appointed *yasawul-i mahram* (personal assistant to the amir) for six years and then for six months as *shighawul* (in charge of tax collection) until Amir Muzaffar (r. 1860–85) was elevated to the throne. Soon after Muzaffar came to power, Abdallah Beg was appointed *udaychi*, a position involved with organizing audiences with the amir and overseeing his travel.[13]

Just as Abdallah Beg's advancement depended on the favor of the amir alone, the monarch's displeasure posed the corresponding potential for danger. The rest of Abdallah Beg's autobiography is peppered with references to instances of unemployment as Abdallah Beg fell foul of princely ire and rivals. In one instance he earned disfavor through a faux pas at another noble's wedding, and in another situation for failing to manage the appropriate ceremonial distance at which petitioners were supposed to sit or stand from the amir—one of the principal duties of the *udaychi*.[14]

---

11. McChesney, "The Chinggisid Restoration in Central Asia: 1500–1785," 286.

12. What I am translating as "royal entourage" is from an irregular form of *maḥram*, which refers to the ruler's private household, where only the most trusted servants were allowed: *qaṭār-i maḥramiyya*.

13. In this position ʿAbdallāh Beg supervised the collection of annual taxes from the provinces, supervising ten individuals engaged in inspecting the quantities of grain and other taxes sent to Bukhara. AV IVR RAN F 33 O 1 D 149, marginalia—f. 1b. In the sixteenth century, the *shīghāwul* was essentially a chamberlain. McChesney, "The Chinggisid Restoration in Central Asia: 1500–1785," 286. In the margins of the text ʿAbdallāh Beg's interviewer describes the responsibilities of the *yasāwul-i maḥram* as those of a chief of staff; that is, the individual controlling personal access to the amir and delegating orders of the amir to others within the court. AV IVR RAN F 33 O 1 D 149, marginalia—f. 1b. On the power wielded by these court appointees, see Sartori, "The Evolution of Third-Party Mediation in Sharīʿa Courts in 19th- and Early 20th-Century Central Asia." Timur Beisembaev suggests that the term *ūdaychī* may have originated from the Arabic plural for "gifts" (*hadāyā*) as the individual tasked with presenting a tribute to the khan. "Farhang-i wāzhigān wa iṣṭilāḥāt-i dīwānī." On the etiquette of proximity to the khan, see McChesney, "The Amirs of Muslim Central Asia in the XVIIth Century," 49.

14. AV IVR RAN F 33 O 1 D 149, ff. 1b–2a.

Ultimately, Abdallah Beg's loose tongue got him exiled from Bukhara entirely. Shortly after the Russian conquest of Tashkent in 1865, Abdallah Beg complained to a friend: "I have served as *udaychi* twice now but have enjoyed nothing but hardship. Now everything is being conquered by the Russians anyway—what prestige does the position of *udaychi* carry?" His friend turned out to be close to the amir, and Abdallah Beg's grumbling resulted in an exile of sorts in the form of tax inspection duties in Nur-Ata province.[15] Despite his dim view of Russian expansion, in the end Abdallah Beg took advantage of the new borders as a way to escape the reach of the amir by returning to the home of his mother's family in Samarqand after it was conquered by Russia in 1868. There he remained until the scribe in Kuhn's employ interviewed him.[16]

Abdallah Beg inhabited the same world as that of the ulama, serving as a *yasawul-i mahram*, but never a *mufti* (writer of legal opinions). He spent time in the amir's retinue, but not the madrasa. Had his career risen further, he might have become a regional governor, but never a *qazi-yi kalan* (chief judge).[17] It is no accident that the names of the positions open to Abdallah Beg are nearly all etymologically Turkic or Mongolian, and those of the ulama are near-exclusively Arabic in origin, but this was a consequence of the power models underpinning their advancement, the respective "scripts" the two social strata were playing from—not ethnicity or even way of life. Abdallah Beg was no roving pastoralist; he spent his formative years in an urban environment and came from a mixed ethnic background, just like most people in the region. His success hinged on the memory of the military exploits of his ancestors combined with personal proximity to the royal court.

The majority of this book focuses on the ulama, which makes it all the more important to always keep in view the alternate path to the patriciate. State-organized coercive force is not the only kind of power, but it was the kind over which nobles such as Abdallah Beg enjoyed a monopoly. It is a kind of power sometimes invisible in accounts written by the ulama, but it was ever-present—indispensable, but inaccessible.

---

15. AV IVR RAN F 33 O 1 D 149, f. 2a.

16. ʿAbdallāh Beg probably went into early retirement in Samarqand. As Alexander Morrison has shown, unlike the British in India, the Russian Empire did not rely on a local, landholding elite as intermediaries, so the steppe tradition making ʿAbdallāh Beg a patrician in the Bukharan context was inoperative in Russian Turkestan. Morrison, *Russian Rule in Samarkand, 1868–1910*, chap. 3.

17. A short biographical notice in the Bukharan chancellery archive on one Mahdī Khwāja Biy paints a similar picture, charting his career jumping between numerous government posts before being rotated between various governorships in the protectorate in two-year intervals. TsGARUz D i-126 O 1 D 1160.

However, the reverse was not the case: Turkic nobility could educate their way into the ranks of the ulama, as the next section will demonstrate, but no amount of madrasa-schooling could unlock Abdallah Beg's career path for an aspiring scholar.

Noble Scholars and Scholarly Nobles

The Turkic nobility–Islamic scholar dichotomy is a crucial heuristic for understanding the Central Asian patriciate. But like all heuristics, it disguises a more complicated reality. The bifurcated model of the Central Asian elite rests on rubrics of power, one of them based exclusively on lineage and proximity to more powerful Turkic nobility (especially the amir himself) and the other on learning. The latter stratum was dramatically more permeable than the former. Turkic elite such as Abdallah Beg could potentially educate themselves into the ranks of the ulama, should the vicissitudes of the day call for such a move—and the latter half of the nineteenth century was a particularly turbulent period for the Turkic nobility.

Turkic lineage had the potential to indirectly advance the career of aspiring scholars. Even though the two paths to the patriciate rested on fundamentally distinct logics of power, the intersection between them could lead to transformative outcomes. Turkic nobles who found themselves disqualified from advancement into a career track similar to that of Abdallah Beg often had material resources at their disposal to secure an education. As the fourth son of Amir Muzaffar, Sayyid Mir Siddiq Tore "Hishmat" is a particularly famous example of this trajectory. During his father's rule, Mir Siddiq was pursuing a typical career path for a Turkic noble, serving as governor of the province of Charjuy. Perhaps realizing his dubious future as a noble given the still-active tradition of tanistry, Mir Siddiq honed his scholarly talents while still serving as governor by personally scribing a lavish Qur'an.[18] After taking the throne, his brother, Amir Abd al-Ahad (r. 1885–1911), placed Mir Siddiq under a house arrest that lasted thirty-two years, ending only when he fled to Afghanistan, along with the rest of the royal court, after the Bolshevik conquest in 1920.[19]

---

18. Mīr Ṣiddīq "Ḥishmat" 's brother, Sayyid Akrām Khan Töra, managed to stay in favor even after the succession; but one wonders if he was hedging his bets by ensuring that his son, ʿAbd al-Muʾmin, received a madrasa education. ʿAbd al-Muʾmin, *Ażwāʾ ʿalā tārīkh Tūrān*, 159. Peter Golden describes tanistry as "a system in which the ablest member of the charismatic clan seized power, killing those relatives who challenged or threatened to challenge him." *Nomads and Sedentary Societies in Medieval Eurasia*, 13.

19. Żiyāʾ, *Tażkār-i ashʿār*, 291–92.

Mir Siddiq did not sit idle while captive in his dwelling near Lab-i Hawz (the central water cistern) in Bukhara. Instead, he reinvented himself as an Islamic scholar, burnishing his credentials by amassing one of the most impressive libraries in Bukhara and personally authoring a poetic anthology.[20] Despite Mir Siddiq's obvious prestige and material advantages derived from his royal lineage, biographical anthologies legitimate his stature referencing only his scholarly achievement; references to lineage or military exploits were out of place (and potentially even a liability) in the scholarly world, even though they were potent for other constituencies. Just like so many of his peers, he was praised for his mastery of a vast array of Islamic sciences, particularly astrology and calligraphy, but also Islamic law, etiquette, and the occult.[21] In his "unique" erudition and eclecticism Mir Siddiq had much in common with other ulama, but the instrumental source of his prestige—that is Turkic lineage—set him apart. Interestingly, one of his biographers explicitly mentioned his lack of formal training in a madrasa, suggesting that his acquisition of the scholarly skill set through "sheer dedication" made his achievements all the more impressive.[22] In short, Mir Siddiq effectively translated his royal lineage into an asset within the context of a distinctly Perso-Islamic logic of authority.

In addition to princes from the ruling dynasty, Turkic nobility from rival tribes also ameliorated their inherent political liability by refashioning themselves as ulama.[23] Eighteenth- and nineteenth-century Central Asia was a constantly shifting mosaic of city-states, semi-vassals, and loose confederations, and the periodic elimination of some such polities led to a steady flow of politically suspect members of the Turkic aristocracy into Bukhara as prisoners or refugees. For instance, after Bukhara extended its reach over the Shahrisabz region in 1870, Mir Siddiq offered his tutelage and patronage to help the recently captured noble Abdallah Beg Yakkabaghi become of Bukhara's all-time greatest calligraphers.[24]

Other examples similarly illustrate the potential for refugee nobles to become scholars. Shah-Murad (r. 1785–1800) devoted an enormous amount of energy to subjugating Merv, which was then ruled by the Iranian-appointed governor Bayram Ali Khan.[25] In a battle on the city's outskirts in 1786/87

20. Mīr Ṣiddīq Ḥishmat, *Taẕkirat al-shuʿarā*ʾ, 61. Mīr Ṣiddīq's *taẕkirat* for the most part replicates information found in Wāżiḥ's *Tuḥfat al-aḥbāb*.

21. Muḥtaram, *Taẕkirat al-shuʿarā*, ff. 102a–102b; Żiyāʾ, *Taẕkār-i ashʿār*, 291.

22. *Saʿy wa taraddud* ("sheer dedication"). Żiyāʾ, *Taẕkār-i ashʿār*, 291.

23. Mīr Ṣiddīq's brother, Nūr al-Dīn "Hayāʾ" similarly refashioned himself into a poet of some stature. Muḥtaram, *Taẕkirat al-shuʿarā*, f. 102b.

24. On Abdallāh Beg Yakkabāghī's trajectory, see Pickett, "The Darker Side of Mobility."

25. Ḥakīm Khan, *Muntakhab al-tawārīkh*, 1:364.

Shah-Murad scored a decisive victory, killing Bayram Ali Khan and bringing back his head to display in Bukhara. Though the city of Merv itself managed to hold out for another year, Shah-Murad cut off their food and water supply, eventually forcing Hajji Muhammad Husayn Khan, the city's leader and Bayram Ali Khan's son, to surrender. Hajji Khan (as he is referred to in the sources), along with the majority of Merv's population, was forced to permanently relocate to Bukhara and embrace Sunnism.[26]

Hajji Khan was treated with considerably more respect than his father, and as Shah-Murad's honored guest he trained under the esteemed scholar Damla Mirak A'lam.[27] This training was enough to earn him remembrance as a great Bukharan scholar and poet, but the hospitality was not enough to convince him that he would not eventually share Bayram Ali's fate. Hajji Khan fled first to Shahrisabz, then Khoqand—competitor city-states actively seeking to attract ulama. In the case of the former, when Shah-Murad demanded that his political prisoner be returned, and offered a sizable ransom, Niyaz Ali Diwan-begi, the ruler of Shahrisabz, thumbed his nose at his rival by asserting that "even if you offered me seven years' income, I would never turn over an honored guest. After all, we are Uzbeks."[28] Eventually, Hajji Khan managed to escape Central Asia and lived out his days in the holy Iraqi city of Najaf. For his scholarly peers, however, Hajji Khan's branding as an enemy of the state was irrelevant next to his poetical acumen, and his biographer eschewed any reference to the political controversy, mentioning only cryptically that he left Bukhara "for a certain reason."[29]

Turkic nobles who were deposed from their city-states sometimes fled to Bukhara as refugees to avoid Hajji Khan's fate. The ancestors of Hamid Beg Eshik Aqabashi ibn Amjad Qilich Ali Biy (d. 1910/11) ruled the province or sometimes quasi-independent state of Jowzjan, located near Maymana, and Sar-i Pol in Khurasan (what is now northern Afghanistan).[30] When Amir Abd al-Rahman (r. 1880–1901) of Kabul conquered the province, Hamid Beg fled to Bukhara, where he served in the Bukharan military. Perhaps finding himself out of place in the configuration of Turkic tribal loyalties specific

26. *Hama musalmān shudand*. Muḥammad Yaʿqūb Bukhārī, *Risāla*, f. 6b. These refugees (or at least some of them) retain their Shiʿism even to the present day, forming a distinct community in Bukhara. Kimura, "Sunni-Shi'i Relations in the Russian Protectorate of Bukhara."

27. Wāżiḥ, *Tuḥfat al-aḥbāb*, f. 68.

28. Ḥakīm Khan, *Muntakhab al-tawārīkh*, 1:365. In this quote, the Keneges and Manghits were both "Uzbeks" in that they were sub-branches of the same Uzbek super-tribe, not necessarily in the modern ethnic sense.

29. Wāżiḥ, *Tuḥfat al-aḥbāb*, f. 68.

30. *Eshik āqā-bashi* is itself a Turkic title, translating to "head of the threshold." Like so many of the positions held by ʿAbdallāh Beg Ūdaychī, it denotes personal proximity to the ruler.

to Bukhara, Hamid Beg threw himself into his studies, also earning himself a reputation as a cunning chess player. He eventually became sufficiently skilled in the Islamic sciences that he debated in scholarly discussion circles (*majlis*), though some of his detractors slandered him for being uncultured.[31] Some lingering resentment of his metamorphosis on the part of the other ulama notwithstanding, like the other Turkic elite considered here, Hamid Beg mastered Islamic forms of knowledge to claim a different form of elite status than that afforded by his Turkic lineage.

The figures in these anecdotes have much in common: noble bloodlines that might otherwise have elevated them instead became a liability, which drove them to pursue separate avenues to the patriciate. Many of them commanded financial resources and family connections that were helpful for making the transition into the learned class. But once they did so, their claim to high status was articulated almost entirely through the prism of intellectual accomplishments, drawing from the same script as their new scholarly colleagues. In exploiting material resources to become scholars, these Turkic nobles had much in common with another influential social group: the merchants.

The "Sometimes Ulama"

Even if dividing the elite into either Turkic nobility or ulama constitutes a useful heuristic, it is a messy one, and the military elite were not the only social group that bled into the ulama in practice: merchants too stood as an influential elite social group that could refashion themselves into ulama. Even so, the model of the patriciate used here remains a bipartite one rather than tripartite. This is because—unlike belonging to a Turkic tribal group—financial resources did not stand as an independent, self-justifying source of influence. No matter how influential, merchants did not commission texts glorifying "the great traders of the realm"—in contrast especially with the ulama, but also in some cases with the Turkic nobility. Rather, merchants and tradesmen tended to use their largesse to become ulama. Much like the Turkic nobility, merchants and tradesmen often faded into the background of sources written by the ulama (which is to say, most sources). Merchants were influential, but that did not mean that either Turkic nobles or ulama were rushing to style themselves merchants on attaining influence.

Merchants were adept at using their resources to become scholars. Nine percent of the scholars in Muhtaram's *tazkira* (biographical dictionary) came

31. *ʿAdam-i salīqa*: "uncultured." Muḥtaram, *Tazkirat al-shuʿarā*, ff. 100a–100b.

from a merchant background. Unlike jurisprudence, sufism, or the other vocations discussed in the next chapter, merchantry was not intrinsically associated with the ulama, though it does not seem to have been considered a dishonorable pursuit.[32] In Central Asia, many merchants were non-Muslim, with a sizable migrant population of Indian merchants, both Hindu and Muslim.[33] In other words, while many scholars were also merchants, most merchants would not have been considered part of the ulama.[34]

Merchantry did not mesh equally well with all the other scholarly functions. In particular, merchants rarely held concurrent positions as public functionaries. None of the seventeen merchants in Wazih's or Muhtaram's respective biographical dictionaries were also judges (*qazis*), public morality enforcers (*muhtasibs*), or *muftis*, and only one was a *mudarris* (madrasa instructor). These positions were connected to a reliable stream of revenue, which may have reduced the need to make a living in the bazaar.[35]

Though merchants were uncommon in the courtrooms and madrasas, compensating scholarly activities earned some of their members places in biographical dictionaries. Many merchants were also *mirzas* (scribes; 18 percent of the merchants), which is understandable given that their profession's emphasis on record keeping and arithmetic dovetailed with that of the *mirza*.[36] They also embodied the myriad other social roles of the ulama, serving as poets, calligraphers, astrologers, sufis, and physicians.

Certain aspects of the merchant profession were particularly synergetic with scholarly activities. For instance, Fazl Diwana-i Katib-i Shikast-nawis traveled to Bukhara from India during the reign of Amir Haydar (r. 1800–1826) laden with manuscripts, including an exhaustive collection of exquisitely penned works of Bedil, whose enigmatic mystical poetry caught

32. Merchants and trade in Central Asia are a relatively well-studied topic. Burton, *The Bukharans*; Warikoo, "Central Asia and Kashmir:"; Dale, *Indian Merchants and Eurasian Trade, 1600–1750*; Levi, *India and Central Asia*; Khazeni, "The City of Balkh and the Central Eurasian Caravan Trade in the Early Nineteenth Century."

33. Hindu merchants even enjoyed the advantage of being able to lend money at interest, though Scott Levi points out that prohibitions against usury did not necessarily prevent Muslim merchants from doing the same in practice. Levi, *The Indian Diaspora in Central Asia and Its Trade, 1550–1900*, 185–87.

34. On the relationship between sufi networks and long-distance trade, see Sultonova, "Trade Relations between Bukhara and Yarkend Khanates in the 16–Earlier 17 Centuries"; Lydon, *On Trans-Saharan Trails*.

35. This also explains why the ratio of merchants in the Żīyā'ʾs biographical dictionary of calligraphers (*Tażkirat al-khaṭṭāṭīn*) is far lower (2 individuals out of 108), as scribing constituted a concrete service with a somewhat predictable source of income.

36. This was particularly true in the colonial period, when Russian officials pressured often-reluctant Bukharan merchants to document financial transactions in writing: AVPRI F 147 O 486 D 49, ff. 3a–4b.

fire during the late eighteenth and nineteenth centuries in Central Asia.[37] When the amir learned of Fazl Diwana's magnificent collection, he honored him with a royal visit and offered to purchase the books at an exorbitant fee. To the astonishment of all, Fazl Diwana refused to sell, prompting Haydar to issue a proclamation far and wide of a handsome reward for anyone who could produce copies of the poetic volumes within forty days.[38] Fortunately for Fazl Diwana, he was also a skilled calligrapher, and the merchant-cum-scholar sequestered himself for the specified duration, and on the morning of the fortieth day he rode to the royal palace with not one but two copies of each of Bedil's works. He used the generous proceeds from his scholarly feat to further another of his pursuits—*qalandarism* (mendicant sufism)—building a mosque across from a *qalandar* lodge and donating the remainder to the ascetics.[39]

Moving forward in time to the late nineteenth century, Abd al-Rasul "Tajir" (d. 1914/15) was a rare exception to the trend of merchants generally not holding salaried posts.[40] Abd al-Rasul abjured the trading occupation of his forebears and spent his family's substantial merchant capital on learning, securing himself a spot studying under Abd al-Shakur (d. 1888/89), an influential scholar who served for a time as *qazi-yi kalan*.[41] His financial resources and scholarly devotion eventually paid off when Abd al-Rasul was appointed *mudarris* of the mid-sized Muhammad Nazar Parwanachi madrasa.[42] Thus the resources afforded by Abd al-Rasul's background were instrumental in his scholarly career, but in pursuing the new path he left his previous vocation behind him.

Similarly, the changing pen names of one Mirza Shah illustrate the desirability of transitioning from the financial world to the scholarly one. Mirza Shah came from a family of moneylenders, and so when he first began composing poetry he used the alias of "Sarraf" (lit. "money changer"). Upon attaining the status of a scholar, Mirza Shah exclaimed: "Praise be to God

37. On Bedil's reception elsewhere in the Persianate world, as well as his Soviet legacy, see Schwartz, "The Local Lives of a Transregional Poet."

38. The duration of forty days—whether in the retelling or actual proclamation—bears religious significance, particularly in sufism. Pious individuals would often seclude themselves in prayer for forty days (called a "chilla") and special houses were endowed for the practice (*chihil-khāna*).

39. Żiyā', *Tazkirat al-khaṭṭāṭīn*, ff. 92b–93a.

40. ʿAbd al-Rasūl's poetic pen name (*takhalluṣ*) literally means "trader, merchant," hinting that there was something unusual about a merchant being included in the biographical dictionary and suggesting that the merchants and ulama were distinct communities, albeit with significant overlap.

41. Muḥtaram, *Tazkirat al-shuʿarā*, f. 95a.

42. Pīrmastī, *Afżāl al-tazkār*, f. 53a–53b. This madrasa was destroyed during the early Soviet period. Żiyā', *Zikr-i asāmī-yi madāris*.

that I have cleansed myself of the profession of tradesman and entered the ranks of the learned."[43] To mark this elevation in status, Mirza Shah was bestowed with a new pen name: Fa'iz (lit. "victorious").[44]

Merchants were not the only group that frequented the bazaar—though they were the ones with the most ties to ulama. A few craftsmen also made it into the biographical dictionaries. One poet was noted to be an excellent watchmaker and tailor, and another took up his father's career in the Russian textile industry (*urus-bafi*) after finishing his madrasa studies.[45] By and large, however, craftsmen, unlike merchants, lacked the means to attain the necessary education to elevate themselves into the ranks of exemplary scholars.[46]

Curriculums, Perso-Islamic Learning, and Social Mobility

As already stated, both Turkic nobles and merchants could become Islamic scholars and did so in significant numbers. This was possible because the second pillar of the patriciate was based on knowledge, and—in theory—open to anyone. But just what did embarking on this scholarly path entail? Which disciplines constituted the madrasa knowledge system? This section traces the path by which an intellectual wayfarer might become one of "those who are knowledgeable," the literal translation of "ulama." It addresses curriculum questions; the broader world of pedagogy and learning beyond the "formal" madrasa study circle; and social mobility. Specifically, it considers the following puzzle: how was it that students transformed themselves into polymaths of Islam, masters of a dizzying array of disciplines ranging far beyond most reading lists that have come down to us?

No state dictated a set of textbooks for madrasas in Bukhara, nor anywhere else in Central Asia.[47] Nevertheless, with caution and a few important

43. Żīyā', *Taẕkār-i ash'ār*, 320.

44. It was the poet Muḥtaram who bestowed the new nickname upon Mīrzā Shāh, with whom he was romantically involved (on the figure of the Beloved, see chapter 6). Mīrzā Shāh met his end in the aftermath of the Bolshevik Revolution. Żīyā', *Taẕkār-i ash'ār*, 320; Muḥtaram, *Taẕkirat al-shu'arā*, ff. 144b–145b.

45. Pīrmastī, *Afżāl al-taẕkār*, ff. 66b–67a. Judging by his name, this individual, ḥājjī Sayyid Aḥmad Khwāja Samarqandī "'Ajzī," was possibly a descendant of the Prophet (*sayyid*) and had also completed the Hajj; both distinctions would have elevated his religious esteem in the eyes of the ulama. Muḥtaram, *Taẕkirat al-shu'arā*, f. 137a.

46. Even so, tradesmen did cultivate their own literary sphere, written in more colloquial Persian and Turkic. Dağyeli, *Gott liebt das Handwerk*.

47. Bukharan rulers did, however, specify reading lists in *waqfs*, which they endowed in their capacity as individuals. Liechti, "Books, Book Endowments, and Communities of Knowledge in the Bukharan Khanate," 304–405.

caveats, one can speak of a loosely standardized madrasa curriculum in Bukhara.[48] Surviving lists of texts taught in the madrasas overlap a great deal and are consistent in excluding certain forms of knowledge from the "formal" madrasa curriculum, thereby approximating an internal understanding of curricular versus elective/postgraduate learning.[49]

The core madrasa curriculum taught students how to teach themselves and how to continue their intellectual journey under new mentors in other disciplines.[50] It inculcated the fundamental skills necessary for mastering a much larger array of interrelated fields after "graduation," or at least after meaningful progress in the core sequence. Before beginning madrasa study, students achieved basic literacy through Qur'anic recitation in primary school (*dabiristan* or *maktab*). Then, at the initial stage of madrasa training, students were introduced to basic Arabic grammar and syntax through Persian-medium primers.[51] As emphasized in chapter 1, Arabic was

48. Even in the far more systematized Ottoman case historians have been reluctant to fully embrace the term "curriculum" along with its modern connotations of standardization and systemization. Nevertheless, as a heuristic (and because of the close parallels with European scholasticism), I use analogical terms such as "curriculum," "diploma," "graduation," and "extracurricular."

49. Over 60 percent of the twenty titles listed in a 1909 Russian report on madrasas in Samarqand overlapped with those listed in Sadriddin Ayni's autobiography. RGIA F 1396 O 1 D 342, ff. 138–51; Ayni, *Yāddāsht-hā*, 135. Looked at in another way, every one of the titles on Ayni's much shorter list of fourteen texts is also accounted for in the 1909 Samarqand report and in Alexander Kuhn's commissioned list. Kuhn, OR RNB F 940, no. 144. Moreover, some sources mention a "Bukharan curriculum"; for instance, one student was described as studying in the city of Guzar, but according to the "Bukharan method" (*manhaj al-ta'līm fī Bukhārā*). 'Abd al-Mu'min, *Ażwā' 'alā tārīkh Tūrān*, 159. The usual madrasa sequence with specific titles has been detailed elsewhere, and will not be recapitulated here. See, for instance, Khan, *Muslim Reformist Political Thought*, chap. 1. As far as the day-to-day texture of madrasa life in Bukhara, see Frank, *Bukhara and the Muslims of Russia*, chaps. 4–5.

50. Much of what Anthony Grafton and Lisa Jardine argue about the displacement of European scholasticism in favor of humanism might equally be asserted about the madrasa system vis-à-vis the new method schooling of the Islamic modernists (the Jadids): "the triumph of humanist [or Jadidi] education cannot simply be explained by reference to its intrinsic worth or practical utility. On the contrary, the literary education of the humanists [or Jadids] displaced a system far better adapted to many of the traditional intellectual and practical needs of European [or pre-Soviet Central Asian] society." *From Humanism to the Humanities*, xii. To continue the interpolation: "At the level of the school [*maktab*], it offered literacy in Latin [Arabic and Persian] of a sort to thousands of boys. At the higher level of the university arts course [madrasa], it [scholasticism] provided a lively and rigorous training in logic and semantics. At the higher level still of the professional faculties of law, medicine and theology [mostly pursued in post-graduate study after making significant progress in the core madrasa curriculum], it trained men for employment in powerful and lucrative occupations." Grafton and Jardine, *From Humanism to the Humanities*, xii–xiii. For a discussion of parallels, and possible interactions, between European scholasticism and the classical madrasa system, see Makdisi, *The Rise of the Colleges: Institutions of Learning in Islam and the West*, chap. 4.

51. This meant that some students (such as Muḥammad Ḥiṣārī) required tutoring in written Persian before beginning madrasa study, presumably in order to access the Persian-medium primers on Arabic (titled *Bi-dān* and *Awwal-i 'ilm*). According to Ayni, an informal tutor was called a *dāmullā-yi kunjakī*. Ayni, *Yāddāsht-hā*, 135.

effectively a "shadow" cosmopolis to the Persian one, meaning that Persian literature took for granted the vast Arabic corpus layered on top of it. Thus, the first step in becoming a Persianate intellectual was years devoted to Arabic grammar and syntax, which accounted for around 30 percent of the curriculum.[52] Next came logic (*mantiq*; studied for at least five years, and similarly making up around 30 percent of the listed texts) and rhetoric (*balaghat*; accounting for approximately 7 percent of the texts).[53] Philosophy (*hikmat*; around 7 percent of the texts) and theology (*kalam*; close to 20 percent of the texts) were covered in the final six years of study.[54] This core sequence of texts usually took around a decade to complete, though especially esteemed scholars sometimes boasted of having finished it in six years.[55]

The madrasas of Central Asia were hardly "*qazi* mills," churning out a class of lawyers. The curriculum was aimed at cultivating intellectuals who were capable of grasping the underlying principles of their subject matter.[56] When students studied law, the emphasis was initially on jurisprudence, the science of deriving substantive law (*usul al-fiqh*), rather than memorizing content.[57] Despite this theoretical training, independent reasoning for the purpose of deriving law (*ijtihad*) was not something that many scholars of

52. This figure is out of thirty-one texts listed in Kuhn, OR RNB F 940, no. 144. Of course, not all texts were studied for the same amount of time. However, in a reading list that stipulates months and years devoted to each text, students studied grammar (*naḥw*) and syntax (*ṣarf*) for around 30 percent of the total time they were in the madrasa as well. RGIA F 1396 O 1 D 342, ff. 138–51.

53. Again, the percentage of texts comes from Kuhn, OR RNB F 940, no. 144, and the duration comes from RGIA F 1396 O 1 D 342, ff. 138–51. The 1909 Samarqand report does not include rhetoric at all. However, there is ample evidence that Taftāzānī's work on rhetoric, *al-Muṭawwal*, was generally a core part of the Bukharan curriculum, given that it is well accounted for on Bukharan book endowment lists; the work also appears in Safavid, Ottoman, and Indian curriculums. Liechti, "Books, Book Endowments, and Communities of Knowledge in the Bukharan Khanate," 403; Robinson, *The 'Ulama of Farangi Mahall and Islamic Culture in South Asia*, 48–52, 240–51. For a lively description of the back-and-forth between teacher and student while studying logic in modern Iran, discussing one of the very same texts taught in Bukhara, see Mottahedeh, *The Mantle of the Prophet*, 71–75.

54. Kuhn, OR RNB F 940, no. 144.

55. Musayyab Bukhārī, *Kitāb-i maqāmāt-i mashā'ikh*, f. 678a. Another scholar was lauded for having completed his training by the age of twenty. Fawzīya Turkistānī, *al-Qurrā' fī Turkistān*, 8. Raḥmatāllah ibn 'Atā'allāh Khwāja spent twelve years completing the "core texts" (*jam'-i kutūb-i mutadāwila*). Musayyab Bukhārī, *Kitāb-i maqāmāt-i mashā'ikh*, f. 729a. From the very genesis of the madrasa system, there was no set duration, with different students spending different amounts of time mastering the texts. Makdisi, *The Rise of the Colleges: Institutions of Learning in Islam and the West*, 96. According to Allen Frank, five to six years was a typical length of study in a village madrasa of the Volga-Urals. *Muslim Religious Institutions in Imperial Russia*, 223.

56. For a defense of the term "intellectual" in relation to Islamic scholars, see Binbaş, *Intellectual Networks in Timurid Iran*, 2.

57. This is not so different from American law schools, in which students spend their formal education studying jurisprudence (*usūl al-fiqh*), leaving the task of memorizing substantive law (*furū' al-fiqh*)—that is, the Bar—for after graduation. Although many graduates went on to become local mosque imams, it is difficult to see how logic or *usūl al-fiqh* would be crucial for that task. By contrast,

the long nineteenth century would claim to do, the canonical Hanafi interpretations having been consolidated many centuries prior.[58] Thus students who received a diploma (*ijaza*) for completing this course of study were not qualified to perform any of the most prestigious social roles of the ulama, not even that of the jurist.[59] Rather, the diploma marked them as worthy of continuing their pursuit of knowledge across diverse disciplines, either through self-study or in apprenticeship to new mentors.

This common core of grammar, syntax, logic, theology, as well as rhetoric and principles of jurisprudence is well substantiated in surviving reading lists, and was common throughout much of the Islamic world. Over 40 percent of the titles on a 1909 Samarqand reading list can be found in the "Dars-i Nizami" curriculum of the late Mughal Empire.[60] Overlap with the Ottoman curriculum was about the same, and even the Safavid curriculum overlapped with that of Bukhara by at least 30 percent.[61] A core layer of grammar, syntax, logic, and rhetoric was quite similar throughout the Islamic world, whereas sectarian differences manifested most acutely in exegetical, theological, and legal texts, which accounts for the lower percentage of common texts in the Safavid sequence.[62]

---

training in rhetoric was very useful for an imam, especially when delivering the *khuṭba*. Jones, *The Power of Oratory in the Medieval Muslim World*, chap. 3.

58. This statement is not meant to rekindle the "closing of the gates of *ijtihād*" debate; there were some scholars who claimed to be *mujtahids*, such as Hādī Khwāja. Siddīq, *Zhizneopisanie bukharskogo uchennogo sheikha*, f. 151b. Rather, it is to emphasize that for most scholars of the long nineteenth century, such a claim would amount to the height of arrogance, seemingly placing the scholar on equal footing with the classical scholars who first formulated the Sharia. See also Sartori, *Visions of Justice*, 262–63.

59. I have not seen many physical *ijāzas* in Central Asian collections. However, published exemplars emphasize the transmission of knowledge, attesting from whom the student's teacher learned the discipline in question, and from whom that teacher learned the discipline, as far back as possible. For instance, an *ijāza* procured by a scholar from Khotan in the Hijaz, after finishing a Bukharan education: *Ijāzat al-Imām Muḥammad Zāhid*. On the legitimate transmission of textual knowledge, see Messick, *The Calligraphic State*, 89.

60. The Dars-i Niẓāmī list is considerably longer (around forty separate works are listed) than most of the Central Asian lists (from twenty to just over thirty works are listed). Nevertheless, nearly 20 percent of the Dars-i Niẓāmī titles can be found in the Central Asian exemplars (i.e., Kuhn, Ayni, and the 1909 Russian report). If one (a) includes works known to have been read in Bukharan madrasas based on endowment deeds, and (b) counts commentaries of works on Central Asian lists in addition to the original works as overlap, then nearly 50 percent of the Dars-i Niẓāmī curriculum coincided with that of Central Asia. A major source of discrepancy is the fact that the Indian system included mathematics, a subject absent from the Central Asia "core" (and which does not appear in the supplementary book lists reported by Kuhn, although mathematical texts certainly circulated in Bukhara).

61. Ahmed and Filipovic, "The Sultan's Syllabus"; Robinson, *The 'Ulama of Farangi Mahall and Islamic Culture in South Asia*, 244–48.

62. This foundation was common as far away as West Africa. Hall and Stewart, "The Historic 'Core Curriculum' and the Book Market in Islamic West Africa," 118–28.

The curriculum was remarkably stable over time.[63] The average date of writing of works appearing on madrasa reading lists was sometime in the fifteenth century.[64] Yet this stability did not mean that the curriculum was static, even though it was certainly conservative. For instance, Muhammad al-Mubarak Lahuri's commentary on Muhibballah Bihari's (d. 1707) *Sullam al-ulum* was listed as one of the core texts on logic, likely illustrating the direct influence of the Indian Dars-i Nizami curriculum (of which Bihari's work was a constituent element) on Central Asia.[65] Bukharan scholars likewise continued to write updated commentaries of older works: Ata'allah Khwaja wrote a commentary on Mulla Yusuf al-Qarabaghi's theological work, which appears as a core madrasa text in its original form.[66] Similarly, Sayyid Alim Khwaja "Hatif" (d. 1852–53) wrote a commentary on the *Tafsir-i bayzawi*, which was frequently studied in madrasas (appearing in Ottoman and Indian curriculums as well).[67] Muhammad Sharif ibn Ata'allah would scribe hadiths into the margins of philosophy texts, relating them to the principle at hand.[68] Even if these newer texts were not adopted into the core curriculum, they were undoubtedly important resources for students and point to continued intellectual engagement with an enduring canon.[69]

But what is to be made of the conspicuous absences? If not in the madrasa, where did scholars learn to quote hadiths from memory, compose Persian

63. For instance, nearly all of the texts (over 70 percent) found in nineteenth-century curricula are also found in book endowments from the sixteenth century. Lists of titles in sixteenth-century book endowments are provided in Liechti, "Books, Book Endowments, and Communities of Knowledge in the Bukharan Khanate."

64. This chronological trend coincides with findings in a statistical survey of the West African curriculum, for which texts produced in these centuries formed the foundation. Hall and Stewart, "The Historic 'Core Curriculum' and the Book Market in Islamic West Africa," 144. The Jadids were vociferous critics of the "medieval" madrasa curriculum. Ayni was not entirely off base when he remarked that the madrasa curriculum had not changed since the fifteenth century. Ayni, *Yāddāsht-hā*, 136. But, from the perspective of the ulama, that was a feature, not a bug: the system endured because it worked.

65. Kuhn, OR RNB F 940, no. 144. It is perhaps not a coincidence that the development of the Dars-i Niẓāmī (eighteenth century) coincided with the influx of Naqshbandī-Mujaddidī scholars into Central Asia.

66. Muʿaẕi, *Tārīkh-i Bukhārā wa tarjumat al-ʿulamāʾ*, 17; Żīyāʾ, *Nawādir-i żiyāʾīya*, f. 43a. Kuhn, OR RNB F 940, no. 144. This would make ʿAtāʾallāh's work a commentary on a commentary on a commentary, since al-Qarabāghī's work is itself a commentary on al-Dawwānī's *Kitāb-i Mullā Jalāl* (ubiquitous on Central Asian reading lists), which is a commentary on Ażud al-Dīn al-Ījī's *al-ʿAqāʾid*.

67. Wāżiḥ, *Tuḥfat al-aḥbāb*, ff. 241–42.

68. *Dar ḥawāshī-yi* Ḥikmat al-ʿayn *baʿżī-yi aḥādīṡ-i nabawī rā (ṣallā Allāh ʿalāyhi wa sallam) bi-qawāʿid-i falsafa taṭbīq namūda-and*. Musayyab Bukhārī, *Kitāb-i maqāmāt-i mashāʾikh*, f. 811a.

69. As Wael Hallaq points out, the fact that one work is a "commentary" on another work tells us much about how the author understood canonical authority, but little about whether or not the ostensible commentary was "innovative" or "dynamic." Commentaries may appear at first glance to merely explain an older, more authoritative work, but depart radically by implication. Hallaq, "Takhrij and the Construction of Juristic Authority," 321 passim.

couplets on the fly, debate sufi metaphysics, and adjudicate law? These subjects were studied simultaneously with the madrasa curriculum (and often physically within the walls of the madrasa as electives of sorts) and mastered afterward. Where differences exist between the attested lists of Central Asian madrasa texts, it is often in these areas—particularly Hadith, Qur'anic exegesis, and legal topics. That such electives were absent from most lists of core texts is not indicative of their unimportance, nor does it suggest that they were rarely studied. Rather, their absence from most core sequences of texts is due to the fact that the core was necessary to access the electives in the first place.

Substantive law (*furu al-fiqh*, lit. "branches of law) is, in some ways, the trickiest subject to pin down in relation to the standard madrasa curriculum. Substantive legal texts do appear as part of the "core" on some reading lists, but the genre is conspicuously absent on others.[70] In Alexander Kuhn's commissioned list of madrasa texts, *furu al-fiqh* texts are included, but separately from the main sequence.[71] It seems that in Central Asia substantive law was often considered separate from the core but because so many career paths revolved around it, a large proportion of students studied it both simultaneously with the core curriculum and after graduation.[72]

What is indisputable is that even students destined for modest imamships studied some amount of substantive law, either on the side or integrated into the curriculum. For instance, when a local *qazi* was faced with the minor administrative hiccup of the mosque's imam having abruptly left town, his replacement was required to read eleven lines from a section of the *Hidaya* (the paramount Hanafi legal manual throughout Eurasia which, according to one list, was studied for five years in the madrasa) on prayers according to

70. According to the 1909 Russian Samarqand madrasa report, students spent four years studying the *Mukhtaṣar al-wiqāya* already in the first level. RGVIA F 1396 O 1 D 342, f. 139a. However, Ayni claimed that students in Bukhara received their diplomas without ever touching such texts. Although Ayni was particularly indignant at the lack of *tafsīr* (Qur'anic exegesis) in the core curriculum, his list of texts also lacks any references to *furū' al-fiqh*. Ayni, *Yāddāsht-hā*, 135–36.

71. Above the list of *furū' al-fiqh* texts is written "studying [legal] issues is in the following manner" (*taḥṣīl-i mas'ala bar ēn rawīsh* [*sic*]). Kuhn, OR RNB F 940, no. 144.

72. This understanding helps reconcile a debate in the literature over whether or not *furū' al-fiqh* was taught in Central Asian madrasas. It was taught physically inside of the madrasas (along with a number of other subjects outside the core curriculum), but outside of some (though perhaps not all) incarnations of the standard reading list. On the debate, see Frank, *Bukhara and the Muslims of Russia*, 120–21; Khalid, *The Politics of Muslim Cultural Reform*, 33. This division seems active in a different form in the Ottoman realm as well, where madrasas were organized hierarchically into beginning and advanced institutions. A curriculum of one of the advanced institutions focuses nearly exclusively on subjects I have characterized as "extracurricular" / "postgraduate" in the Central Asian case, such as substantive law, Hadith, and *tafsīr*. Ahmed and Filipovic, "The Sultan's Syllabus," 207.

the rules of Arabic grammar, translate the meaning, and correctly expound on the issues contained therein.[73] Another account depicts a candidate for local imamship botching his explanation of the Hajj section of the *Hidaya* and losing favor on those grounds.[74] Thus the core madrasa curriculum provided students with the requisite tools for pursuing more specialized fields, such as *furu al-fiqh*, which were essential for even a relatively modest position such as that of imam.

Considering substantive law as an elective, layered on top of a core of grammar, syntax, logic, rhetoric, and theology, provides a model for understanding other forms of knowledge. Much like *furu al-fiqh*, Hadith and *tafsir* (Qur'anic exegesis) appear on reading lists elsewhere in the Islamic world, but inconsistently in Central Asian curricula.[75] Yet Ata'allah Khwaja received separate diplomas for mastering Hadith and *tafsir* as part of his madrasa study.[76] Ata'allah's son, Rahmatallah, taught a famous thirteenth-century *tafsir* by Nasir al-Din Bayzawi to students studying in the Muhammad Sharif madrasa. This was the same text included on Ottoman and Mughal reading lists.[77] Rahmatallah's brother was known to recite from memory pages of *tafsir* at a time during madrasa lessons, both from Bayzawi and lesser-known commentators.[78]

That the author felt the need to draw special attention to Rahmatallah's instruction of *tafsir* might point to its quasi-extracurricular status (i.e., not part of the "core," but nevertheless widely studied).[79] Similarly, Muhammad Ibrahim, an east Turkestani student from Khotan (a city in what is now western China), began madrasa study in Kashgar and then received diplomas from

---

73. RGIA F 1396 O 1 D 342, ff. 138–51.

74. *Tetrad' s razlichnymi zapisiami*, f. 26b and f. 27b.

75. The fourteenth-century Hadith collection *Mishkāt al-maṣābīḥ* appears as the capstone of the reading list commissioned by Kuhn, on madrasa endowment lists (along with associated commentaries), and on Indian and Ottoman lists as well. This is apparently quite different from the curriculum of the first madrasas from the eleventh century, which started with the scriptures. Makdisi, *The Rise of the Colleges Institutions of Learning in Islam and the West*, 80.

76. Musayyab Bukhārī, *Kitāb-i Maqāmāt-i Mashāyikh*, f. 678a.

77. Riżawī, *Manāqib wa maqāmāt-i ʿAṭāʾallah*, f. 64b. Nāṣir al-Dīn al-Bayżawī's Qur'anic *tafsīr* also appears extensively in Bukharan madrasa book endowment lists, and Żīyāʾ's personal library contained two copies. Liechti, "Books, Book Endowments, and Communities of Knowledge in the Bukharan Khanate," 404; Vohidov and Erkinov, "Le fihrist (catalogue) de la bibliothèque de Ṣadr-i Żiyâ.'"

78. Musayyab Bukhārī, *Kitāb-i maqāmāt-i mashāyikh*, f. 815a.

79. This further account seems to suggest something slightly out of the ordinary in the family's emphasis on scripture from the very earliest stages of madrasa study: "[ʿAtāʾallāh's] mastery of *tafsīr* and Hadith was unmatched. From the very beginning of his study, his father [Hādī Khwāja] instructed him to memorize three hadiths daily along with the associated transmitters." Riżawī, *Manāqib wa maqāmāt-i ʿAṭāʾallah*, f. 72b.

numerous instructors in Bukhara.[80] After Bukhara, Muhammad Ibrahim traveled to Tashkent, where he received separate diplomas for Hadith and *tafsir*, and to Andijan, where he received yet another diploma for Qur'anic recitation.[81] Again, the core subjects were bundled together in a diploma (*ijaza*) separate from the elective and postgraduate disciplines (*tafsir*).

So far, we have considered only Arabic disciplines. But the categories, technical terms, and symbols permeating those disciplines also infused Persian writing (and, by extension, Turkic as well). If there is some ambiguity as to whether substantive law was part of the core curriculum, it is eminently clear that Persian literature (e.g., poetry, sufi treatises) generally was not.[82] Yet training in Persian literature may be less categorically distinct from substantive law than initially meets the eye. Kuhn's commissioned list of madrasa texts also included the most important works of Persian literature, such as the *Shah-nama* and the poetry of Hafez.[83] Like *furu al-fiqh*, literature appears alongside the core madrasa texts as the common domain of madrasa students, even if studied outside of formal study circles.[84]

Muhammad Karim al-Bulghari's trilingual Arabic-Persian-Turkic dictionary provides a striking illustration of the integration of core and extracurricular curricula. Al-Bulghari's dictionary was expressly aimed at conveying wisdom necessary to Tatars hoping to study in Bukhara, where they would be required to know not only Arabic and Persian, but also the dialectical idiosyncrasies of Central Asian colloquial Turkic; after all, core texts were in Arabic, and supplementary lessons were in Persian, but many Bukharans spoke

---

80. Muḥammad Ibrāhīm's son and biographer states that he received *ijāzas* in Bukhara for "completing his study," a statement that supports the notion of a more or less standard "core." Moreover, the texts he mentions having started studying in Kashgar (and presumably finishing in Bukhara) are well represented on Central Asian curriculum lists, such as Taftāzānī's commentary on Nasafī's *ʿAqāʾid* (theology), and Taftāzānī's commentary on Qazwīnī's *Talkhīṣ al-miftāḥ* (rhetoric). Fażlī, *Tarjimat wālidī*, 12–14.

81. Fażlī, *Tarjimat wālidī*, 15.

82. Even this rule is not ironclad. Rumi's *Masnawī* was apparently taught in some Ottoman madrasas in the nineteenth century. Akgündüz, *Osmanlı medreseleri XIX*, 156.

83. Kuhn, OR RNB F 940, no. 144, f. 3a. Moreover, literary works such as the *Dīwān* of Hafez and Attar's *Conference of the Birds* appear on Bukharan madrasa book endowment lists. Liechti, "Books, Book Endowments, and Communities of Knowledge in the Bukharan Khanate," 404. More recent works of poetry, such as the eighteenth-century poets Bedil and Mashrab, were also included, as were the Turkic works of Alisher Navoi—even though these "literary" materials were sometimes collectively glossed as *Fārsī*.

84. Which texts were "literary" (a category with no direct emic equivalent) is far from straightforward (for more on this, see chapter 6). On another list (also commissioned by Kuhn), Persian poetry, *tafsīr*, and substantive law texts are all thrown together into a common list of "texts we study." Kuhn, OR RNB F 940, no. 150.

Turkic.[85] The introduction to al-Bulghari's lexicon explains the importance of the Persian language in terms of the fusion of Islamic and Persian history (discussed in chapter 2) in relation to Bukhara as a city. First, al-Bukhari proffers an unsound hadith to the effect that "the language of heaven is Arabic and Persian."[86] Then—in mixed Turkic and Arabic—the author attributes to the Persian language a divine (*ilahi*) provenance as the language spoken by sons of Noah and the legendary kings of Iran alike.[87]

The integration of Persian into the madrasa environment is similarly illustrated by other texts. Abd al-Wahid Sadr Sarir Balkhi (d. 1885/86) had little to say in his personal notebook (*jung*) about his formal schooling but waxed nostalgic about his schooldays in Bukhara's Tursunjan madrasa.[88] He portrayed the informal nocturnal gatherings convened by the students as a magical time, especially one particular night in 1838–39 when he discovered the famous Indo-Persian poet Abd al-Qadir "Bedil."[89] After studying Bedil's poetry, Abd al-Wahid and his friends composed their own verses in the style of the great poet and took turns reciting them in the madrasa after hours by candlelight. The core courses by day were a necessity, but poetry was a pursuit of passion.[90]

Sufism has been aptly described as "the postgraduate creed of Islam"; in other words, a body of knowledge and practices pursued in addition to the madrasa curriculum.[91] After receiving a madrasa diploma, and not infrequently additional diplomas for collateral subjects, students continued

85. Bulghārī, *Sabab-i taqwiyat*, f. 1b. Al-Bulghārī distinguishes between Central Asian and Tatar Turkic dialects with the following phrasing: *al-lughāt al-Turkīya al-ghayr al-Bulghārī*. The text is predominantly Tatar-inflected Turkic, but the author shifts in and out of Arabic, as in this phrase.

86. More specifically, the text specifies *al-Fārsī al-Darī*, but referring to the late antique language, not the modern language of Afghanistan, as the text clarifies elsewhere. Muḥammad Karīm al-Bulghārī, *Sabab-i taqwiyat*, f. 3a. Elsewhere, al-Bulghārī provides a remarkably detailed typology of Persian dialects, delineating seven different types of Persian, including four "archaic"/"abandoned" (*mahjūr*) ones (which are also the only western Iranian languages in the group)—Harawī, Shikrī (perhaps Sagzi), Zāwulī (Zabuli), Sogdian—as well as three still in use (*musta ʿmal wa mashhūr*)—Pahlavi (likely here referring to Parthian), Dari, and Farsi. Al-Bulghārī seems to be building on models from classical Arabic literature (e.g., Ibn Muqaffaʿ), though the origin of this particular seven-partite sequence is unclear. Bulghārī, *Sabab-i taqwiyat*, f. 4a.

87. Al-Bulghārī builds on the work of early Arabic-medium historians to connect the Persian language to a grandson of the prophet Noah, and to the legendary Kayanian kings of Iran, as well as to Jamshid. Bulghārī, *Sabab-i taqwiyat*, ff. 3a–3b.

88. Tursūnjān was a relatively new madrasa at the time, constructed in 1805/6. Żiyāʾ, *Ẕikr-i asāmī-yi madāris*.

89. Bedil is included on Kuhn's reading list. OR RNB F 940 (Kun), no. 144, f. 3a.

90. *Jung-i ʿAbd al-Wāḥid Ṣadr Ṣarīr Balkhī*, f. 102a.

91. Jafri, "Madrasa and Khānaqāh, or Madrasa in Khānaqāh? Education and Sufi Establishments in Northern India," 74. See also Eickelman, "The Art of Memory: Islamic Education and Its Social Reproduction."

their study under the tutelage of a shaykh in a sufi lodge (*khanaqah*), which was often part of the same complex as the madrasa.[92] However, tutelage in sufism did not necessarily begin after graduation. There is some evidence that sufi forms of knowledge were taught at the madrasa stage, albeit separately from the formal lessons. For instance, a short biography of the Dahbidi shaykh Tash Muhammad (d. 1815/16) states: "The habit of the *akhund* [i.e., Tash Muhammad] was to have his students spend four days out of the week studying the traditional Islamic sciences (*ilm-i qal*) [likely referring to the core madrasa curriculum] and during the three days off engage in mystical exercises (*ilm-i hal*)."[93] Similarly, Qari Mir Muhsin's biographer wrote that as a young boy he came to Bukhara and completed the madrasa curriculum (*ilm-i qal*) and also studied *ilm-i hal* under sufi teachers until he became a sufi deputy (*khalifa*).[94]

Khuday-berdi began studying under sufi shaykhs at several shrines in Bukhara even before he was old enough to begin formal madrasa study; at these shrines he would study both silent and vocal *zikr* (trance-inducing ritual chanting) and engage in fasting.[95] After beginning his madrasa study, Khuday-berdi would often spend all night studying his madrasa texts at shrines situated beyond the city limits, making it back to the madrasa at daybreak just before class. The hagiography's author seems to imply that the otherworldly presence of Amir Kulal, a famous sufi shaykh, aided Khuday-berdi in his study: "Beneath the standard of Amir Kulal I practiced my lessons, weeping."[96] At these sufi shrines the madrasa core blended into mystical practices as Khuday-berdi engaged in discussions (*munazara*) with custodians of the holy sites.[97]

---

92. The term *ijāza* (translated as "diploma") is also used to indicate completion of sufi training and license to train others.

93. Musayyab Bukhārī, *Kitāb-i maqāmāt-i mashāyikh*, f. 659a. Contrasting the traditional Islamic sciences with sufi forms of knowledge (i.e., *ʿilm-i ḥāl* vs. *ʿilm-i qāl*) is a standard formulation in hagiographical sources, and one that parallels the identification of all learned individuals (e.g., *ʿulamāʾ ū fużalā*ʾ). Direct equation between *ʿilm-i qāl* and the madrasa curriculum was made by Ḥiṣārī, who wrote that he spent ten years pursuing *ʿilm-i qāl* after procuring a cell at the ʿAbdallāh Khān madrasa: *Wa muddat-i dah sāl mustaqīm būda bi-ḥuṣūl-i ʿilm-i qāl saʿī-yi mawfūr bi-ẓuhūr āwarda*. Ḥiṣārī, *Yāddāsht-hā*, ff. 13a–13b.

94. Muḥtaram, *Tazkirat al-shuʿarā*, f. 148a.

95. Since *zikr* can induce an ecstatic "state" (a literal translation of *ḥāl*) of proximity to God, it may be that this is exactly what other authors had in mind by *ʿilm-i ḥāl*. Moreover, the term *taṣawwuf* was not synonymous with *ʿilm-i ḥāl*, and tended to be associated with more senior scholars—perhaps more of a postgraduate field of study.

96. Saʿādatallāh, *Luṭf-i buzūrg*, f. 25 a and ff. 25a–25b.

97. Saʿādatallāh, *Luṭf-i buzūrg*, f. 26a. Khudāy-berdi's biographer wrote that he was often only one step ahead of the night watchman (*mīrshab*) during his nocturnal traipsing, and that his classmates tried to scare him by telling him stories of ferocious dogs roaming the streets. Ibid.

Conceptualizing the madrasa experience in terms of core curriculum versus elective and postgraduate study can only take us so far. As we have seen, students pursued fields of study far beyond the scope of the putative core curriculum. Different madrasa instructors integrated different extracurricular disciplines into the core: some drilled Hadith study from an early age, and others emphasized substantive law. Students did not necessarily regard any of those subjects as more authentically part of a standard curriculum than others, even if there are observable patterns in terms of which disciplines were most consistently included and expected to be mastered in advance of others.

It is also the case that the core fields that show up on nearly every reading list—grammar, syntax, logic, rhetoric—are also the ones with the most consistent overlap throughout the Islamic world. But that common core was only the beginning. The fact that the concept of "ulama" remained a flexible category—one without a specific legal or theological definition—did not stop a Central Asian scholar from writing the following: "By the Sharia, a scholar (*alim*, sg. of ulama) is one who is characterized by the quality of [knowing] the religious sciences, [including] jurisprudence, *tafsir*, Hadith, and the fundamentals of the law (*usul al-fiqh*)."[98] Notably, the fact that this minimum resume of a bona fide scholar mostly lists fields beyond those emphasized in madrasa curriculums suggests that the examples recounted above constituted the norm rather than the exception.

Although discrepancies existed between broadly overlapping curriculum lists, those disparities were not a product of institutional differences between madrasas. Madrasas did not have rigid corporate identities, and in that sense "college" is slightly misleading as a translation. Students were not limited to attending lessons at the same madrasa as their *hujra* (lit. " 'cell," effectively a dorm room funded by a modest stipend), but rather mixed and matched study circles throughout the city.[99] For example, Khuday-berdi shared a room at the celebrated Diwan-begi madrasa, where he would spend several days at a time studying, before rotating to lessons at the Qushbegi and Kokaltash madrasas for several days of the week.[100] Certainly, some madrasas were more prestigious than others (especially Mir-i Arab and Kokaltash), but when it came to discriminating between study circles, the emphasis was

98. *Bi-sharīʿat ʿālim kas-ē bāshad kih mutaṣaf bi-ṣifat-i ʿulūm-i dīnī . . . wa ʿilm-i fiqh ū tafsīr ū ḥadīs̱ ū uṣūl-i fiqh bāshad*. Even though this opinion is written in a *jung* notebook, it is accompanied by three seals of endorsement (uncommon for *jung*). The full opinion is about the permissibility of switching teachers without authorization, which is frowned upon; defining what it means to be "learned" (*ʿālim*) is merely the setup for the main point. Ḥusaynī, *Jung-i majmūʿah-i riwāyāt*, f. 225a.

99. These findings are corroborated by Frank, *Bukhara and the Muslims of Russia*, 100.

100. Saʿādatallāh, *Luṭf-i buzūrg*, ff. 36b–37a.

on the individual teacher rather than the institution.[101] A scholar named Damulla Hasan Akhund even turned his own home into a madrasa, dividing and expanding a portion of it to house students.[102] Thus the nature of the madrasa is best conveyed by the literal definition of the Arabic term: a "place of learning," any place in which a student could find a *mudarris*.

In theory, if a willing teacher could be found and an endowed cell with a stipend could be secured, anyone could become a scholar, regardless of economic background. Of course, reputation and resources helped, and some families managed to ensure access to the best training for their children for generations. But the system was relatively open to students who came from modest backgrounds. Sources do not allow easy assessment of social mobility in any systematic fashion, but rags-to-riches stories are quite common in biographies of prominent scholars.

Khuday-berdi's family history stands as a fairly explicit example of the capacity of education to fundamentally change one's social status.[103] His ancestors had migrated from the environs of Bukhara to Maymana, a province in eastern Khurasan, at the behest of the Shibanid ruler Abdallah Khan (r. 1583–98), but the encroachment of Afghan troops in the mid-eighteenth century sent the clan (along with Khuday-berdi's father) fleeing back to Bukhara.[104] Uprooted from the family's holdings, the young Khuday-berdi apprenticed himself to the village tailor (*muza-duz*) to make ends meet. In his free time, the boy would frequent mosques and shrines in the environs of his village. One day, someone remarked to Khuday-berdi: "What reason do you have to run to and fro between these shrines? If your goal is God's approval, then you will not gain it without knowledge. Only after you acquire knowledge should you put good deeds into action."[105] Heeding the

101. For instance, these madrasas provided larger instructor salaries and student stipends. Jumanazar, *Buxoro ta'lim tizimi tarikhi*, 94–104. The diplomas (*ijāza*) listed an entire chain of teachers by name, sometimes stretching back hundreds of years, but were often silent on the venue of study. The concept of *khiẕmat* ("service") is frequently used to describe the relationship between teacher and student, suggesting the centrality of the individual relationship over the institution.

102. "Soobshchenie o prepodavateliakh bukharskikh medrese v epokhu pravleniia emirov Muzaffara i Abdulakhada," f. 10b. The biography goes on to describe how Dāmulla Ḥasan used the proceeds from a loan collected from another scholar to further embellish the madrasa section of his home.

103. Jumʿa-Qulī "Khumūlī," whose rural background is discussed in the introduction, is another such example.

104. Saʿādatallāh, *Lutf-i buzūrg*, f. 19a, 21b. By way of explanation, the author merely states that the Afghans "committed great injustice." I am not certain what specific Afghan encroachment the text is referring to, but it may have had something to do with Nadir Shah's conquests.

105. *Luṭf-i buzūrg*, 24a. The author is alluding to the sufi maxim that action (ʿ*amal*) and knowledge (ʿ*ilm*) must go together.

advice, Khuday-berdi sought out an elementary *maktab* teacher and began attending his school.

Khuday-berdi's *maktab* teacher was simultaneously the village imam; shadowing the imam "day and night" in all his activities was part of the boy's education.[106] This service was partly vocational training, but also compensation for the imam's services as a teacher. For instance, Khuday-berdi would help the imam by fetching water and collecting straw for fuel when it was cold.[107] Conversely, his better-off peers were able to compensate the *maktab* teacher with their family's wealth—a fine cloak, sweets, and even a stipend in some cases.[108] Students from elite families also benefited from almost invariably receiving early instruction from their relatives, concurrent with or even preceding the *maktab*. Nevertheless, even privileged students attended the same *maktabs* and the same madrasas as students of humbler backgrounds, such as Khuday-berdi.

Co-ed Primary Schooling in a Bastion of Patriarchy?

The account of Mawlawi Muhammad Sharif ibn Ata'allah Khwaja's primary schooling opens with a curious setup: "The esteemed Mawlawi had two primary school instructors, one male, and one female."[109]

Initially, Muhammad Sharif studied in a boy's *maktab*.[110] When his father died suddenly in 1795/96, Muhammad Sharif showed no inclination to mix with others and sequestered himself for two full years in mourning.[111] Once he was ready to socialize, his mother considered sending him back to the boy's school, but decided against it because of their idle talk and obnoxious behavior.[112] Instead, his mother decided to send Muhammad Sharif to a girl's primary school under a Bibi Khalifa.[113]

106. Saʿādatallāh, *Luṭf-i buzūrg*, f. 24a. This was characterized as "service" (*khiẕmat*) from the student to the teacher, in exchange for "benefit" (*ifāda*). These core concepts have deep roots in relation to Islamic learning. Chamberlain, *Knowledge and Social Practice in Medieval Damascus, 1190–1350*, 111–13, 128.

107. Saʿādatallāh, *Luṭf-i buzūrg*, f. 25a–25b.

108. Musayyab Bukhārī, *Kitāb-i maqāmāt-i mashāʾikh*, f. 791b.

109. Musayyab Bukhārī, *Kitāb-i maqāmāt-i mashāʾikh*, f. 791a.

110. As a general rule, boys and girls were taught separately. Whereas boys could go on to study at madrasa, for most girls the *maktab* was the end of the road. Frank, *Muslim Religious Institutions in Imperial Russia*, 225.

111. Musayyab Bukhārī, *Kitāb-i maqāmāt-i mashāʾikh*, f. 792a.

112. *Wālida-i mājida-i Ēshān khwāsta kih Ēshān-rā bi-dabīristān sipārand, laykin az harza-gūyī ū parīshān-aḥwālī-yi kūdakān-i maktab-i rijāl andīsha namūda.*

113. These figures, also known by the Turkic term *otin*, are more visible in colonial / Soviet sources, and later anthropological research. Fathi, "Otines."

The *maktab* could therefore be a place of mixing not only between classes but also genders. The learned elite were overwhelmingly men—and in Central Asia perhaps even more uniformly so than other parts of the Islamic world.[114] Or, at least, the scholars visible in sources (written by men) are overwhelmingly men.

It is interesting that the Bibi Khalifa, who instructed Muhammad Sharif during his formative years is extolled using similar language as that used for her male counterpart (albeit with greater emphasis on her exemplary chastity), seeming to put her on equal or near-equal footing. She received the same remuneration (an honorary cloak and tray full of sweets), was credited with similarly heroic feats of piety (e.g., praying for days on end without rest), and was praised for reading out loud books on ritual piety to other adult women.[115] The Bibi Khalifa also penned magical scrolls capable of curing illness.[116]

One wonders what a biographical dictionary of the great Bibi Khalifas of Bukhara might have looked like, had one ever been penned.[117] This account of a Bibi Khalifa's intellectual activities is unusual, but that does not mean that such figures were rare. Much like the *maddahs* (a panegyrist and narrator of the lives of deceased holy men), they did not easily fit into the "script" from which most ulama were writing. However, just because they lacked the resources to speak for themselves (a forte of their male counterparts) does not make their presence any less real.

Looking beyond the standard madrasa curriculum, and emphasizing the remarkable breadth of study both in and outside the institutional boundaries of the madrasa, lays the groundwork for a core argument in the chapters to come: namely, the unity of the ulama as a social group, mastering myriad forms of knowledge at the same time and performing social roles associated with those disciplines as shifting circumstances dictated. Their eclecticism was grounded in Bukhara's vast educational establishment.

114. For an example of a particularly accomplished such scholar in late fifteenth- and early sixteenth-century Damascus, see al-Baʿuniyyah, *The Principles of Sufism*.

115. Musayyab Bukhārī, *Kitāb-i maqāmāt-i mashāʾikh*, f. 792b.

116. Far from "folk magic," cleanly separable from the madrasa education, this social function was one she shared with the male ulama as well (see next chapter).

117. More sources detailing the lives of female ulama seem to have survived in the case of the Farghana Valley. Kılıç-Schubel, "Writing Women." See also Shanazarova, "A Female Saint in Muslim Polemics."

Religious Authority without a Madrasa Education

The madrasa system was the only form of formal education on offer in Central Asia before the twentieth century. Even Turkic nobles who received education through private tutoring were still madrasa-adjacent, since their tutors were often madrasa instructors. This madrasa training outside of the madrasa allowed them to more easily fashion themselves as ulama should circumstances necessitate such a transition.[118] Yet the lack of alternative formal educational venues does not mean that the ulama were without competitors. Although often diminished in written sources, Central Asia was home to a kaleidoscope of figures with a different kind of training, whose expertise intersected with that of the ulama, and who competed for religious authority.

One such profession was that of the *maddah*. Described in other contexts as "professional story-tellers of the urban milieu" and "begging singers of the streets," these figures' relationship with the scholarly class was sometimes strained because of their lack of formal education.[119] So strained, in fact, that despite occupying a space devoted to inculcating religion among the masses (along with entertainment), *maddahs* are rarely mentioned in the *tazkiras*.[120] From the perspective of the madrasa-trained elite, then, the *maddah* was an entertainer, not one of their own.

A partial exception to this general rule offering a rare insight into this group is the figure of Mirza Jahangir Majnun Irani.[121] Despite his lack of madrasa training, Jahangir Majnun was included in a *tazkira* alongside some of the most illustrious ulama of the realm—with profuse qualifications but included nonetheless. Before immigrating to Bukhara, Jahangir Majnun served in the courts of various Iranian noblemen, scribing and reciting poetry. Jahangir's biographer afforded him a certain amount of respect for his skill in writing poetry in the style of Rumi's *Masnawi* and because he

118. Central Asian sources are generally light on details on what exactly princely tutoring entailed, other than the fact that it could be a source of patronage and prestige for the ulama. For example, Wāżiḥ, *Tuḥfat al-aḥbāb*, f. 49. However, many of the disciplines emphasized in the education of Mughal princes mirror those of the madrasa, with the addition of subjects such as military tactics. Faruqui, *Princes of the Mughal Empire, 1504–1719*, 78–81.

119. Quoted from Boratav, "Maddāḥ."

120. In directly ruled Turkestan, the Russian colonial authorities sought to take advantage of this perceived schism and use the *maddāḥs* against the ulama. Erkinov, "Islamskii institut maddakhov—propovednikov v Turkestanskom krae." See also Alexandre Papas, *Thus Spake the Dervish*, 183–87.

121. Jahāngīr Majnūn is also discussed in the next chapter in the context of his similarly problematic guise of apothecary (*'attār*), a profession that competed with the formally trained physicians (*ṭabīb*) in the same way that *maddāhs* competed with formerly trained poets.

performed the Hajj and was trained by scholars in Mecca and Medina to properly recite the virtues of the saints (*manqabat-khwani*).[122]

Even so, Jahangir's biographer viewed his fame among the ulama as essentially illegitimate because he had not received a proper madrasa education. A laundry list of Jahangir's disciplinary deficiencies underscores the range of training a scholar was expected to receive: "Nevertheless, [Jahangir Majnun] had never studied even a bare minimum of the rational or transmitted sciences, or the fundamental or applied Sharia; and he was utterly unacquainted with (Arabic) grammar or syntax, logic, rhetoric, philosophy (*hikmat*), theology (*kalam*), law, the rules of inheritance, Qur'anic exegesis, Hadith, language, and philosophical mysticism (*tasawwuf*)—[of all of these disciplines he was ignorant] except the poetry of the great Persian poets, history, the Prophet's biography, and the virtues of the saints."[123] The implication was that it was highly unusual, bordering on scandalous, for a Persian poet to lack training in the standard array of Arabic madrasa disciplines.

To echo the argument advanced in chapter 3, one notes that as an Iranian, Jahangir's training in Persian poetry made him a partial fit for the intersectional skill set that characterized the ulama of Bukhara, but the narrower knowledgebase of the *maddah* overlapped more comfortably with his literary background. Even so, by most standards Jahangir was already a polymath of considerable breadth—just not relative to his madrasa-trained competitors. Jahangir was included in the *tazkira* in part to set him apart from other *maddahs*, as the best of a bad lot. But even his less respectable peers sang the poetry of Sa'di, Hafez, and Alisher Navoi.[124] Jahangir's case demonstrates that the overlap between the respective domains of scholars and folk performers could occasionally earn some *maddahs* a place in the ranks of the ulama.

That acceptance was partial, qualified, and grudging. In one sense, the *maddahs* were a conduit between the ulama and the masses. They frequented tea houses and barbershops, came out of the woodwork during festivals such as the Persian New Year (Nawroz), and gravitated toward bazaars frequented by peasants coming into the countryside.[125] For this audience, they synthesized elements of the Perso-Islamic knowledge base for a popular audience.

122. Shar'ī, *Tazkirat al-shu'arā*, ff. 75b–76a.

123. Shar'ī, *Tazkirat al-shu'arā*, f. 76a.

124. Rempel', *Dalekoe i blizkoe*, 66.

125. Rempel', *Dalekoe i blizkoe*, 66. In an autobiography of sorts, 'Abd al-Ghafūr Turkistānī wrote that on a certain day when "10,000" people thronged to a sufi shrine in Ramitan, a village outside of Bukhara, numerous *maddāḥs* congregated as well. The author was a teenager when he wrote this

However, the ulama did not see the need for intermediaries, and often rejected the vocation of the *maddah* as one of superstitious nonsense. Like the ulama, *maddahs* claimed authority in passing on Islamic knowledge, but unlike the ulama the *maddahs* did not subscribe to a canon of knowledge similar to that embodied in the madrasa education and accompanying extracurricular pursuits. That made them competitors, not partners. In a biographical entry ostensibly in praise of Jahangir, considerable space was devoted to criticizing by name Jahangir's fellow *maddahs* as charlatans who took advantage of the naivete of the common people for personal monetary profit.[126] Nor was Jahangir spared from such criticism, suffering the allegation that his *masnawi* mishandled intertextual scriptural references, and that his poems did not actually make much sense.[127] The nonsensical nature of his poetry was what earned him the poetic alias Majnun (meaning "crazy").[128]

Jahangir Majnun seems to have been aware of these criticisms about the gaps in his resume, and—to justify his status as a legitimate scholar—his admirers spread stories testifying to his brilliance as a legal mind. Jahangir encouraged the circulation of an anecdote in which he was able to solve a religious question that stumped even the most erudite of ulama, earning him the gratitude of Bukhara's *qazi-yi kalan*. His biographer dismissed the tale as rubbish.[129] But even so, these criticisms were a consequence of the fact that Jahangir was pushing the boundaries of what qualified one as a legitimate scholar, and in a manner convincing to many. Jahangir's activity as a *maddah* was subversive in the same way as his apothecary trade. Ultimately, Jahangir

---

account and was taking his *maktab* classmates to visit the shrine and listen to the storytellers. ʿAbd al-Ghafūr-i Turkistānī, *Bayān-i dāstān*, f. 78b.

126. Sharʿī does not pull his punches: "Those stories that [the *maddāḥs*] recite in public haven't even the faintest trace of wisdom or learning among rational, eloquent, and wise people—they are only liked by the ignorant and stupid (*juhalā ū sufahā*)." Sharʿī, *Tażkirat al-shuʿarā*, f. 76b.

127. "Although [Majnun] inserted a great quantity of Qur'anic Suras, passages from the Hadith, and yearnings for mystical philosophy (*māyil-i taṣawwuf*) into his [*maṡnawī*], they were not informed by any degree of exegesis or proper explanation (*tafsīr ū sharḥ*)." Sharʿī, *Tażkirat al-shuʿarā*, ff. 75b–76a.

128. "Some simpletons (*sāda-dilān*) incapable of discerning beautiful poetry or speech imagine [Jahāngīr] to be a master poet entirely without evaluating [the quality of his words]. His poetry is great in number and widespread, but very few of them are above criticism (*naqd ū taṣḥīḥ*). Many of them are unsalvageable unless unrelated meanings are applied to the poetry on [Jahāngīr's] behalf—which is how he was given the alias Majnūn." Sharʿī, *Tażkirat al-shuʿarā*, f. 76b.

129. To illustrate his disdain for the tale, Sharʿī began his rendition of it under the header *min al-ḥikāyāt al-każbiyya*: "from the false tales." It is possible that Sharʿī's allegations were spurious and motivated by personal rivalry, but the point here is what those allegations tell us about the social environment. Sharʿī, *Tażkirat al-shuʿarā*, ff. 77a–77b.

could not be ignored because he had pulled off the rare feat of breaking into the scholarly milieu, but without the same pedigree.

Pillars of the Patriciate

This chapter has taken a panoramic view of the patricians of Bukhara, and how they achieved their patrician status. The ulama were an important pillar of the patriciate, but the scholarly milieu cannot be understood in isolation from the larger ecosystem within which they operated. The Turkic nobility inhabited a different array of social roles, based on a fundamentally distinct logic of power, even though they frequently traversed the gap and became scholars themselves. Merchants stood as another influential group, but—unlike scholars and Turkic nobles—one whose authority was achieved instrumentally. When merchants achieve mention as personages of importance, it is often because they were able to claim mastery of Islamic training, rather than because wealth was deemed worthy of emulation. Meanwhile, street preachers and storytellers such as the *maddahs* stood apart from the patriciate in that they lacked any kind of institutionalized authority, but competed with the ulama for popular religious influence.

Thus the ulama were far more than monkish university professors. The core madrasa curriculum provided them the necessary background to pursue a wide spectrum of disciplines both in tandem with madrasa study and afterward. Law (the field most conventionally associated with the ulama) was only the tip of the iceberg, and not necessarily even studied as part of the core curriculum. Rather, law was one of many fields in which the ulama would continue their intellectual journey after completing the madrasa sequence. The remaining chapters of this book narrow in focus to a single pillar of the patriciate—the ulama—and expand our understanding of the constitution of that social group. The madrasa was a stepping-stone into the world of the high Persianate intellectual.

Chapter 5

High Persianate Intellectuals

The Many, Many Guises of the Ulama

Abd al-Qadir's biographer wrote: "In the view of his peers and superiors he achieved great mastery in languages, history, biography, epistolography, prose, poetry, medicine, astrology, astronomy, trigonometry, jurisprudence, theology, ethics, sufism, art, music, and calligraphy."[1] This cornucopia of competencies is breathtaking—and yet, Abd al-Qadir's eclecticism was far from extraordinary among the ulama. Abd al-Qadir was not a representative of a narrow professional cadre of jurists, the vocation that has often characterized the ulama. Rather, he was a high Persianate intellectual.

The ulama were not the only patricians of Bukhara, but they were the only elite cadre whose claim to authority rested on the mastery of Perso-Islamic knowledge. Scholars such as Abd al-Qadir were not merely sufis, jurists, poets, or musicians, confined to a particular trade or social identity. Instead, they were a cohesive milieu of multitalented polymaths who invoked jurisprudence, or performed the role of wandering ascetic, as the social context dictated.

The scholars introduced in this book stood at the apex of a historical synthesis integrating a wide range of Perso-Islamic knowledge forms into a

1. Sharʿī, *Tazkirat al-shuʿarā*, ff. 66b–67a.

single whole. Just as Islamic and pre-Islamic Persian forms were inexorably intertwined in the city's mythologization, so too were the disciplines and social roles of the ulama. By the nineteenth century tens of thousands of graduates were emerging from Bukhara's madrasas and it was not enough to simply have mastered Arabic grammar and theology: scholars distinguished themselves through their "extracurricular" and "postgraduate" scholastic pursuits. Never before had scholars had so much in common across such an eclectic range of competencies, nor would they again, following the rise of reformist Islam and the Soviet transformation.

The High Persianate Intellectual in Islamic History

Just how novel was the "high Persianate intellectual"? And how does this figure factor into the longue durée of Islamic history? Classical scholars such as al-Farabi (d. c. 950) or al-Biruni (d. 1048) were also polymaths, boasting mastery of an impressive array of disciplines. Certainly, ulama of Bukhara were not the first polymaths of Islam. But they were more uniformly eclectic than ever before.

Much of the fabric of Islamic culture was tangible centuries before the period addressed in this book, and the ulama were shaped by patterns reaching back to the seventh century. Despite the lack of any hegemonic religious institution comparable to the Catholic Church, broad consensuses repeatedly emerged, allowing the absorption of new cultural-religious elements into Islam. This sedimentary process of canon formation began with the compilation of the Qur'an at the inception of Islam, continued in the first few centuries of its existence with the consolidation of theology and discrete schools of law, and still later added a layer of sufism.[2] After a formative period in which it competed with Arabic, Persian literature settled into a canon of its own, inextricably embedded on the theological, legal, and exegetical canons that came before.[3]

This picture that emerges is one of centuries of innovation, amalgamation, and reconciliation between forms of knowledge that had indeed once been embodied by discrete social groups. In early centuries of Islamic history,

2. Richard Bulliet has dubbed this pattern the "big bang, big crunch" meta-theory of Islamic history, arguing that the religion was characterized by periods of remarkable heterogeneity, followed by forceful moments of contraction whereby scholars canonized and embraced discreet elements of the faith while simultaneously rejecting the fringe. Bulliet, "Islamic Reformation or 'Big Crunch'? A Review Essay," 12.

3. Losensky, *Welcoming Fighānī*, 2 passim; Keshavmurthy, *Persian Authorship and Canonicity in Late Mughal Delhi*, 2, 103.

the collective term *alim* (the Arabic singular of the plural ulama, "one who knows") is rarely encountered in the sources because on an individual basis, a more specific term would be more appropriate, such as jurist (*faqih*) or Qur'an reciter (*qari*).[4] As the centuries ticked on, fields that were once the contentious projects of a discreet group were accepted into the canon and became the knowledge base expected of all learned people.

For all these twists and turns throughout Islamic history, the term "ulama" ties the scholar of this study to those of medieval Damascus, for instance, or early modern Bijapur. The agents discussed in this book actively advanced exactly such a narrative that might tempt us to overstate how much in common the ulama of those periods would have had with the high Persianate intellectuals of Bukhara. For instance, the Tatar historian Shihab al-Din Marjani's six-volume biographical dictionary of the ulama begins with scholars living in the time of the Prophet and continues through 1889, placing Tatar and Bukharan scholars next to their colleagues from India to North Africa.[5] This is despite the fact that the ulama did not represent a hereditary caste or socio-economic group, nor was their membership defined in Islamic law, despite frequently being invoked as a conceptual category in jurisprudence and the Hadith.[6] Marjani followed precedent in imposing an imagined continuity and uniformity that did not fully exist.

The enduring category of "ulama," identifiable in Islamic texts across a thousand years and many languages, has led to numerous superb studies (though none to date about Central Asia).[7] "Ulamologies" constitute some of the best entries into Islamic social history, particularly in the premodern period.[8] These pioneering studies have informed this one in important ways. Ira Lapidus conceptualizes ulama as an expansive category encapsulating multiple professions—not just jurists, but also sufis, scribes, and bureaucrats.[9]

4. Bulliet, *Islam*, 105.

5. Shihāb al-Dīn Marjānī, *Wafiyyat al-aslāf.*

6. Humphreys, *Islamic History*, 187. The term ulama appears in the Qur'an (26:197, 35:28), though never to refer to a social class of scholars as such. Already in the Hadith, the word seems to have been attached to a social collective of some kind. For instance, a famous hadith states that the ulama are the "heirs of the prophets": *al-ʿulamāʾ warathat al-anbīyāʾ* (Sunan Abī Dāwud, 3:317).

7. For instance, Ahmed, *The Religious Elite of the Early Islamic Ḥijāz*; Brockopp, *Muhammad's Heirs*; Bulliet, *The Patricians of Nishapur*; Chamberlain, *Knowledge and Social Practice in Medieval Damascus, 1190–1350*; Petry, *The Civilian Elite of Cairo in the Later Middle Ages*; Zaman, *Religion and Politics under the Early ʿAbbāsids*.

8. "Ulamalogy is a noble science—at least we have to think so, because it is almost all the Islamic social history we will ever have for this period [i.e., the Middle Ages]; but we need not take the *ulama* at their own high estimate." Mottahedeh, "Review of The Patricians of Nishapur: A Study in Medieval Islamic Social History by R.W. Bulliet," 495.

9. Lapidus, *Muslim Cities in the Later Middle Ages*, 107–9.

Richard Eaton takes this logic a step further, describing religious elite in terms of social role or function rather than any kind of corporate identity.[10]

This chapter builds on those approaches and pushes them a step further. The aforementioned studies make it clear that even in the medieval period, the ulama were a colorful cadre of polymaths.[11] Yet in the centuries separating those studies from this one, many of the activities and knowledge forms that had once been the purview of contained social groups had been integrated into the mainstream Perso-Islamic canon.

Sufism as a Spectrum of Activities

The history of Islam in Central Asia can appear all but synonymous with the history of sufism. Surveys of the region's history do not fail to emphasize its importance as the home and final resting place of Baha al-Din Naqshband, and scholarship even on the post-Soviet period is resolute in its focus on sufism.[12] This section focuses on the figure of the sufi as the first persona—or rather, personas—of the ulama.

Even formulating "ulama" as a category inclusive of sufi practices of various stripes is at odds with much of the extant literature. Scholarship on Central Asia frequently posits a distinction between sufis and ulama as separate social groups, factions, or practitioners of distinct religious practices.[13] One facet of sufism, *tasawwuf* (sometimes translated simply as "sufism," but here designated as "mystical philosophy" to allow "sufism" a more capacious connotation), appeared in the tenth century, and sufis were often separate from, and even in competition with, the ulama.[14] By the twelfth century, sufi groups were beginning to organize along various patterns, until many communities began congealing around an institutionalized "order" or "brotherhood" (*tariqa*), characterized by master-disciple transmission of knowledge and authority along with detailed guidelines for spiritual wayfaring (*suluk*).[15] During

10. Eaton, *Sufis of Bijapur, 1300–1700*, xxxii passim.

11. R. Stephen Humphreys observed that when defining the ulama "it is easier to say what they are not." *Islamic History*, 187.

12. For a comprehensive historiographical review, see DeWeese, "Re-Envisioning the History of Sufi Communities in Central Asia."

13. See, for instance, Babadzhanov, "On the History of the Naqshbandiya Mujaddidiya in Central Mawara'nnahr in the Late 18th and Early 19th Centuries," 392.

14. Chamberlain, *Knowledge and Social Practice in Medieval Damascus, 1190–1350*, 108–28; Bulliet, *The Patricians of Nishapur*, 43. In Mamluk Egypt, sufis were opponents of the ulama and often lacked a formal education. Knysh, *Islamic Mysticism*, 173. A more rigorous definition of *taṣawwuf* might be an "internal Islamic discursive domain concerned with right belief and practice." Bashir, *Sufi Bodies*, 10.

15. DeWeese, "Re-Envisioning the History of Sufi Communities in Central Asia," 37–38.

these early centuries of organized sufism, the ulama might be considered those learned individuals who lacked such membership, and lines quickly began to blur.[16] Nevertheless, in many contexts, the "sufis" and "ulama" appear to have been meaningfully distinct social groups into at least the early modern period.[17]

This conceptual binary is not merely an artifice of the secondary literature: a sufi-ulama dichotomy is routinely invoked in Central Asian primary sources of the nineteenth century. For instance, before beginning his memoir, Muhammad Hisari included separate odes in praise of the sufis and ulama.[18] Similarly, the renowned intellectual Sadr-i Ziya described the reign of Amir Haydar (r. 1800–1826) as characterized by madrasas stuffed with learned men and the sufi lodges full of masters (*murshidan u mashayikh*).[19] Such proclamations, which seem to refer to separate groups of people, are likely drawing on stock formulas from earlier centuries when such a bifurcation had a firmer basis in social reality. By the long nineteenth century, the operative distinction was the social context: in the example above, the distinct activities of the madrasa and the sufi lodge were carried out by a single group of people, as will be shown.

It is difficult to find an individual scholar of this period who was not engaging in "sufi" practice of some form or another. Moreover, sufi communities had long since ceased functioning as discrete, exclusive entities. Single individuals routinely traced spiritual lineage (*silsila*) through multiple lines at once, and religious disputes about a ritual practice that had once played out between *tariqas* instead took place within those communities.[20] It is suggestive that when Sadr-i Ziya imagined Amir Haydar's reign as a golden age for both the ulama and sufis in the quote above, he made no mention of specific sufi orders who packed into the lodges, but did emphasize that both vocal and silent recitations (*zikr*) were practiced.[21] Only several centuries earlier, separate sufi brotherhoods competed aggressively with one another for

---

16. Ernst and Lawrence, "What Is a Sufi Order?," 239.

17. This fits the picture offered in Eaton's study of the sufis of Bijapur, in which he considers sufis as an identifiable group separate from the ulama, but which overlapped with the ulama and served many of the same social functions in practice. *Sufis of Bijapur, 1300–1700*, 129–31. Devin DeWeese places the fusion of sufis and ulama around the sixteenth or seventeenth century. "Re-Envisioning the History of Sufi Communities in Central Asia," 52.

18. Ḥiṣārī, *Yāddāsht-hā*, ff. 8a–8b.

19. Żiyāʾ, *Nawādir-i żiyāʾīya*, ff. 42b–43a.

20. DeWeese, "'Dis-Ordering' Sufism in Early Modern Central Asia."

21. Żiyāʾ, *Nawādir-i żiyāʾīya*, ff. 42b–43a. Sufis in nineteenth-century Central Asia were particularly invested in a debate about whether to ritually invoke the name of Allah (i.e., *z̤ikr*) silently or vocally. See DeWeese, "Foreword."

dominance, but by the long nineteenth century another moment of consolidation stripped them of their divisiveness.[22] Doctrinal disputes remained but debates, corporate identities, and even textual production were not organized along the lines of *tariqas* as they had been previously.

In reassessing the relationship between sufis and the ulama, it is not sufficient to merely observe that the two terms no longer referred to separate social groups. Even if sufism is conceived in terms of practice rather than group identity, the problem remains that sufism as a term aggregates various practices and knowledge forms. It is an etic category, imposed from the outside, not one with a single analog in the sources (not even *tasawwuf*).[23] Practices that have traditionally been considered sufi appear in the *tazkira* (biographical dictionary) genre under a number of guises: as forms of knowledge, as ascetic practice, as recitation of litanies, as ecstatic performance, as sacred descent, and as social organizations.

Hardly the purview of a separate social group, sufism—under various headings—was a major intellectual pursuit of the ulama. As discussed in the previous chapter, the sufi lodge was in some respects a postgraduate educational institution for the ulama, where they continued to study metaphysics and advanced spiritual doctrine. Scholars lauded in the biographical dictionaries for their mastery of mystical philosophy (*tasawwuf*), or spiritual wayfaring (*suluk*), were not necessarily the same individuals as those identified with a leadership role within the organizational structure of a sufi community (e.g., a shaykh or *murshid*). For instance, Abd al-Alim al-Qazani (d. 1817/18) traveled from the Volga-Urals to Bukhara for madrasa study, just like thousands of his peers. Just as he "took" (*akhaza*) knowledge from the great ulama of Bukhara, he "took" knowledge of *tasawwuf* from a shaykh in Kabul for his "postgraduate" education. Upon returning to his homeland, Abd al-Alim taught in a madrasa, served as an imam, and passed on his knowledge of *tasawwuf* to disciples (*murids*).[24] Many other ulama were casually attributed mastery without any reference to disciples or other organizational features of sufism associated with the knowledge form. *Tasawwuf* as a body of

---

22. For instance, on the bitter struggle between the Naqshbandiyya and Yasawiyya in Central Asia, see DeWeese, "The Masha'ikh-i Turk and the Khojagan."

23. Shahzad Bashir is worth quoting at length in this regard: "It is notable that while Muslims started using the adjective *Sufi* to describe certain types of religious attitudes quite early in Islamic history, *Sufism* is not, in its origins, an internal term but a descriptor employed by Western observers to refer to a diverse array of intellectual and social phenomena relating to those who have called themselves Sufis. This is to say that the presumption that all things described as being Sufi cohere into a system—becoming an *ism*—is a modern terminological invention." Bashir, *Sufi Bodies*, 19.

24. Marjānī, *Wafiyyat al-aslāf*, ff. 152a–53b.

knowledge was separable from the *tariqa* as an institution and expected of any esteemed Islamic scholar.[25]

This is not to say that no connection existed between sufism as a body of knowledge and sufism as an organization. Many Islamic scholars performed specific social roles and held positions associated with teaching sufi disciplines: *murshid*, *pir*, and shaykh, all of which refer to a mentor passing on sufi knowledge to a group of students, usually in a sufi lodge (*khanaqa, zawiyya*) or shrine (*mazar*).[26] These terms referred to a vocation and activity, which could be temporary or long term, and encompassed only a subset of those who necessarily claimed mastery of *tasawwuf*.

For instance, Hajji Ni'matallah "Muhtaram," author of a *tazkira*, wrote that after going on the Hajj he returned to Bukhara and crawled into a secluded corner in a sufi lodge to bask in the tutelage of Hazrat Eshan Kuti Wali-khan Urguti, who was "shorn of worldly attire" and approaching the "rank of the divine" (*rutbat-i jabaruti*)."[27] The language here is unmistakable: Muhtaram was following the sufi path in a classic master-disciple relationship, recognizable since at least the twelfth century.[28] However, the important point is that sequestering himself in the sufi lodge was a temporary activity for Muhtaram, not a career or dominant identity. Before studying under the sufi shaykh, Muhtaram had finished the madrasa curriculum in Bukhara and then spent seventeen months on pilgrimage to Mecca and Medina, where he continued his education under masters of Hadith, Qur'anic exegesis (*tafsir*), and other Islamic sciences.[29] After completing an unspecified amount of time in Kuti Wali-khan Urguti's tutelage, Muhtaram went into the service of Abd al-Ahad's (r. 1885–1910) court, where he was ordered to write an anthology of poets, before eventually meeting his demise during the chaos of the Russian civil war.[30]

25. *Taṣawwuf* and (more commonly) *sulūk* were not the only terms used to refer to sufi forms of knowledge. *Ma'rifa* was sometimes contrasted with *'ilm* (both meaning "knowledge") as the more mystical of the two, just as *'ilm-i ḥāl* was contrasted with *'ilm-i qāl* to make the same distinction.

26. The forms of knowledge associated with the *khānaqāh* were generally associated with one type of "knowledge" (*ma'rifa*), whereas the spectrum of activities linked to the madrasa were understood as another sort of "knowledge" (*'ilm*). McChesney, "Earning a Living," 96.

27. Muḥtaram, *Tażkirat al-shu'arā*, ff. 157b–158a. In typical sufi cosmologies, *nāsūt* and *jabarūt inter alia* represent different realms of being, the former the realm of mortals and the latter a higher realm of power. For a discussion of poetical *tażkiras* as a genre, see Losensky, *Welcoming Fighānī*, chap. 1. "Ḥażrat" was an honorific used when identifying any venerable scholar or authority figure in Central Asia; "Ēshān" referred to his status as a sufi mentor; the *nisbat* "Ūrgūtī" refers to Kūtī Walī-Khān's origin in the town of Ūrgūt, a town not far from Samarqand.

28. DeWeese, "Organizational Patterns and Developments within Sufi Communities," 330.

29. Muḥtaram, *Tażkirat al-shu'arā*, f. 157b.

30. Żiyā', *Tarjuma-i aḥwāl-i 'Abd al-Shakūr*, f. 125b; Żiyā', *Tażkār-i ash'ār*, 342–43.

Hence Muhtaram possessed the necessary pedigree to be considered a sufi if one bears in mind that such a designation did not imply a permanent career path or dominant corporate identity. Rather, it was a specific activity he engaged in, a limited phase in his broader Islamic education—and not a defining one at that, for he was most famous as a court poet in the eyes of his contemporaries.[31] By contrast, his mentor Kuti Wali-khan Urguti was apparently the fulltime master of a Bukharan *khanaqah* (sufi lodge), which would have been funded by a *waqf* endowment. Even in Kuti Wali-khan's case, however—and in the case of many of his contemporaries holding similar positions—no specific sufi brotherhood is mentioned.[32] His status as a sufi shaykh should be considered as a vocation and activity, and one he may have left in favor of other pursuits or held simultaneously with other careers. Every Islamic scholar was a "sufi" in some sense, given the enormous scope the term has come to encompass, but what that entailed varied a great deal.[33]

Of the 192 scholars described by Muhtaram, thirteen (7 percent) were characterized as performing the professional functions of a shaykh; of the shaykhs, only six appear to have performed that function exclusively. Khalifa Husayn, for instance, served as the master of a madrasa and *khanaqah* simultaneously and was eventually appointed by Amir Muzaffar (r. 1860–85) to give the Friday sermon (*khutba*) at the Masjid-i Kalan—positions commonly associated in the secondary literature with the ulama.

The logic implicit in the above figures is made explicit in the short biography of Muhammad Sharif:[34] "Through his status as a *khwaja* and son of a *mawlawi*, [Muhammad Sharif] became a *mufti* [legal opinion writer] and *mudarris* [teacher] within the [city] of Bukhara. His shaykh-liness was of a greater degree than his scholarly knowledge (*ilm*), but despite that, he was appointed *qazi-yi kalan* (chief judge)."[35] Even as the passage preserves the

31. Żiyā', *Tażkār-i ash'ār*, 342–43. All of the ulama included in this collection were poets, but Muḥtaram was unusual in that he received direct patronage from the amir for his production. Muḥtaram, *Tażkirat al-shu'arā*, f.179b.

32. This was likely in part because the Naqshbandiyya-Mujaddidiyya had subsumed and incorporated other sufi communities that had formerly represented viable alternatives.

33. Not only is the term "sufi" an etic term in emic disguise (it is rarely used in the sources to refer to the same figures glossed in English as "sufi"), when it *is* used in the Bukharan context it often refers to a *mu'azzin* (the reciter of the call to prayer).

34. I believe this is Muḥammad Sharīf ibn Atā'allāh, whose family dynasty is discussed in chapter 7.

35. TsGARUz R-2678, f. 8a. The meaning of *khwāja* varied by time and place: in earlier centuries in Central Asia it could refer to a descendant of the Prophet or the early Arab settler community, or in the plural (*khwājagān*) to a sufi community preceding the Naqshbandiyya, but by the nineteenth century it had become a common title for sufis in Central Asia. Etymologically related to the word

distinction between sufi and legal knowledge forms, the two are mutually reinforcing, and Muhammad Sharif moves between these social roles fluidly.[36]

Even in centuries prior it was not unheard of for Muslims to be members of multiple spiritual lineages simultaneously, but by the eighteenth and nineteenth centuries the very relevance of the *tariqas* as embodying distinct *silsilas* seems to have diminished.[37] In terms of organized sufi *tariqas*, the Naqshbandiyya-Mujaddidiyya was the only game in town, which meant that even scholars identified with one or another forms of sufism were often distinguished by other activities. For instance, the sufi credentials of Asrar Khwaja Urguti "Muftaqir," Kuti Wali-khan's brother and close friend of Muhtaram, were also emphasized by his biographers, but like his brother Asrar Khwaja was not placed under the aegis of any specific spiritual lineage, and like Khalifa Husayn his professions consisted of teaching, writing fatwas, and preaching.[38] Most ulama claimed spiritual lineages, but not all performed the function of a shaykh.

Spiritual lineages persisted not only as bundled *silsilas*, but also as blood lineages.[39] Indeed, sacred lineage manifests as yet another distinct meaning attached to the umbrella term "sufi." While active, exclusive membership in a sufi order was rarely specified for an individual scholar in the *tazkiras*, the names of venerable brotherhoods often appear in association with a specific ancestor, who lived in a time when those terms *did* connote more rigid boundaries and inter-*tariqa* competition. One of the most frequently claimed sacred lineages was to Sayyid Ata, whose associated sufi order, the Yasawiyya, had been all but subsumed by the Naqshbandiyya.[40] Muhammad

---

for "lord" (*khudā*), *khwāja* was comparable in connotation to *mawlawī*, a sufi title with a similar meaning ("master").

36. This source was composed in 1940, written in Persian by a Bukharan, but commissioned by a Soviet orientalist, which may have reinforced the conceptual distinction (even if still overlapping) between "sufi" and "scholar."

37. Multiple *silsila* affiliations are evident since at least the sixteenth century. This phenomenon was not specific to Central Asia; it was evident in India as well. Hermansen and Lawrence, "Indo-Persian Tazkiras as Memorative Communications," 160. See also DeWeese, "'Dis-Ordering' Sufism in Early Modern Central Asia." Sufi doctrinal manuals frequently provided instructions for multiple *silsilas* within the same volume; e.g., Walī-allāh, *al-Qawl al-jamīl fī bayān sawā ʾ al-sabīl*.

38. Hence Asrār Khwājah was most certainly a sufi in some sense, but he was also a *muftī*, imam, *mudarris*, and poet. Muḥtaram, *Taẕkirat al-shuʿarā*, ff. 162a–162b; ʿAbdī, *Taẕkirat al-shuʿarā*, no. 64, f. 159b.

39. The persistence of distinct sufi orders in the popular imagination explains why Russian statisticians were able to neatly separate surveyed shaykhs by *silsila*. For instance, in 1900 a Russian census reported seventy Naqshbandī shaykhs, forty-four Qādirī shaykhs, and one ʿIshqī shaykh in the Samarqand oblast. RGIA F 821 O 6 D 612, p. 160.

40. Sayyid Atā lived in the fourteenth century, with two intermediaries between him and Aḥmad Yasawī in terms of spiritual succession from the community's founder. DeWeese, "Atāʾīya Order."

Tahir Khwarazmi, the author of a mid-eighteenth-century sufi *tazkira*, made a strong point of claiming descent from Sayyid Ata through his mother's side, despite being firmly situated in the Naqshbandi order.[41]

A century later, Muhammad Parsa Khwaja-i Salam (d. 1853/52) likewise placed great import on his status as a descendant of Sayyid Ata, even going so far as to explicitly recall that this sacred lineage ensured his ancestors the privilege of being appointed to the ranks of Naqib and Sadr.[42] Like his ancestors, Muhammad Parsa enjoyed the patronage of the amirs, but unlike them he was not a Naqib (though he was granted the rank of Sadr) and did not appear to be filling any social functions that can reasonably be characterized as sufi (e.g., shaykh or *khalifa*).[43] Instead, his primary employment was that of an *elchi* (ambassador) under Amir Nasrallah (r. 1827–60).[44]

Other sufi holy figures are also routinely invoked in *tazkira*, such as Baha al-Din Naqshband, Khwaja Ubaydallah Ahrar, Mawlana Kasani (all foundational figures of the Naqshbandiyya). However, this did not necessarily entail any kind of active, *khanaqah*-based activities. Individuals enjoying such bloodlines were seen to be sufi in that they enjoyed the blessing (*barakat*) associated with the holy person. They leveraged that social capital to pursue a myriad of activities in professions, sometimes including the administration of a sufi lodge and training of disciples, but just as often to pursue other career paths without any particular connection to sufism by any definition (such as *qazi*).

As discussed in chapter 3, the Naqshbandiyya-Mujaddiyya seems to retain some semblance of the *tariqa*-as-order model, exhibiting coherence as a distinct transregional institution into the nineteenth century, by which time it

---

According to legend, Sayyid Atā converted Özbek Khan of the Golden Horde to Islam and, as a result, his descendants were exclusively awarded the rank and position of *naqīb* under the Ashtarkhanid dynasty, though by the seventeenth century Naqshbandi sufis had begun to wrest this privilege from the Yasawiyya. DeWeese, "The Descendants of Sayyid Ata and the Rank of Naqīb in Central Asia." By the Manghit period, the Naqshbandiyya had absorbed the Yasawiyya from the inside out. DeWeese, "The Mashaʾikh-i Turk and the Khojagan."

41. Muḥammad Ṭāhir's goal in connecting himself to Sayyid Atā was to establish his pedigree as a *sayyid* (descendant of the Prophet), which he could also do directly through ʿAlī on his father's side. Muḥammad Ṭāhir, *Tazkira-i Ṭāhir Ēshān*, f. 352b.

42. This is not the same individual as Muḥammad Pārsā Khwāja ibn ʿInāyatallāh Khwāja, who had the same pen name of "Pārsā" and also served as an *elchi*, albeit a decade or so later.

43. Wāżiḥ, *Tuḥfat al-aḥbāb*, ff. 45b–46a.

44. "Ambassadorship" is a loose translation of the Turkic concept of *elchi-gī* as *elchis* appeared to have performed an internal function as well in Central Asia. For instance, Mīrzā Bābā Ḥisarī reported registering in the *elchi-khāna* (embassy) in the Bukharan province of Khuzār after emigrating from the capital. Ḥiṣārī, *Yāddāsht-hā*, f. 16b. This was true in Khorezm as well. Bayānī, *Shajara-i Khwārazmshāhī*, fol. 369b.

had been domesticated in Central Asia.[45] Indian shaykhs continued to send acolytes to proselytize the order through the colonial period, and the Mujaddidiyya continued to serve as a corporate organizing framework to some degree even after the other orders had been "dis-ordered."[46] For instance, Mulla Nur Muhammad Kulabi traveled to India in the mid-nineteenth century to study under the famous shaykh Shah Ahmad Sa'id Faruqi (d. 1860/61), received his license (*ijazat*) to take on his own disciples as Shah Ahmad's deputy (*khalifa*), and then returned to his native Kulab in Bukhara's mountainous, contested hinterland.[47] Nur Muhammad quickly gained renown to the extent that he began attracting the students of a rival Qadiri shaykh. According to his fellow Mujaddidi biographer, at least, the rival shaykh recognized that Nur Muhammad's rank was upon the heavenly throne (*arsh*), while the Qadiri shaykh's remained on the ground, which caused his students to flock to Nur Muhammad.[48]

This does not prove that the students viewed the choice between the two shaykhs as a zero-sum choice between the Qadiriyya and the Naqshbandiyya-Mujaddidiyya. Other sources illustrate that bundling *silsilas* was increasingly common during this period, especially for the Mujaddidis (following the example of Mujaddidi founder Ahmad Sirhindi). For instance, the Indian Mujaddidi scholar Ghulam Ali Shah (better known as Abdallah al-Dihlawi) was noted for his simultaneous belonging to the very *silsila* with which his colleague Nur Muhammad was competing—the Qadiriyya.[49] Thus the Naqshbandiyya-Mujaddidiyya seems to represent an in-between case, one where inter-*tariqa* rivalry was still evident, but also one where those distinctions were beginning to dissipate as *tariqa* memberships were bundled together, and the Mujaddidis absorbed their rivals.

The landscape of sufism had evolved dramatically since the Middle Ages. For many, such as Hajji Ni'matallah Muhtaram, sufism was a temporary activity, a form of postmadrasa education and spiritual contemplation. For others, like his mentor Kuti Wali-khan or Naqshbandiyya-Mujaddidiyya missionaries, it was a vocation—though not necessarily an exclusive one. Still

45. The Naqshbandiyya order was native to Central Asia, but from the end of the seventeenth century missionaries from a branch of the order "renewed" by Shaykh Aḥmad Sirhindī (d. 1624) began arriving in Central Asia from India preaching against innovation (*bid'a*) in Islam and promoting silent *ẕikr*; ties were maintained between the non-Mujaddidī Naqshbandiyya branches in Central Asia and India, albeit less successfully. Gross, "The Naqshbandīya Connection," 240.

46. DeWeese, "'Dis-Ordering' Sufism in Early Modern Central Asia."

47. Muḥammad Maẓhar Mujaddidī, *Manāqib al-Aḥmadiyya*, ff. 221a–221b.

48. Muḥammad Maẓhar Mujaddidī, *Manāqib al-Aḥmadiyya*, f. 221b.

49. *Az nisbatayn-i sharīfatayn-i Qādiriyya ū Naqshbandiyya bar dāshtand wa az rūḥāniyyat-i mashāyikh bashārat-hā yāftand. Biografiia sheikhov Naqshbandiia i Mudzhadddidiia*, f. 60b.

for others it amounted to a blood or spiritual ancestry. Yet even these faces of sufism do not fully capture the range of possibilities. Another archetype appearing in the sources is that of the wandering holy fool, often referred to by terms such as *qalandar*, *faqir*, and *darwish*. This figure was often associated with pious madness and ecstatic behavior.[50] Although this activity emerged gradually between the thirteenth and fifteenth centuries as a reaction against the formal sufi orders, by the nineteenth century the *qalandar* had been domesticated into an expected feature of Islamic society, even while retaining his ascetic and antisocial character.[51]

Russian statisticians conceived of a clear distinction between *qalandars* and sufi shaykhs (sometimes also differentiating between *eshan* and *pir* in the latter case) and placed them in separate census categories.[52] However, I am using the abstract term "archetype" intentionally, as the *qalandar* was as much a collection of tendencies and personality types as an activity, and some scholars were more ecstatic than others.[53] When the term *qalandar* appears in *tazkiras* it is typically accompanied by descriptors or substitutes such as *mashrab* (intoxicated, ecstatic), *la-ubali* (uninhibited), and *majzub* (renouncing worldly concerns). Secondary literature tends to pose *qalandarism* "as a reaction against the institutionalized, rigorously legalistic framework of established religion, as an inherent threat to the rationality of the *mulla* and the *qazi*, and the purism and puritanism of Islamists."[54] However, in the long nineteenth century, *qalandarism* constituted another potential virtuous role and activity for the ulama.[55]

A mid-nineteenth century scholar by the name of "Arsi" was popular among the Turkic nobility for playing the fool in court and daring to tell brazen jokes, a role fitting with his "*qalandar* nature."[56] He did not adopt

---

50. This figure was someone "who has withdrawn from the world and who wanders about like a vagabond; a man who has renounced all worldly things and who has seen the truth, a philosopher." Yazıcı, "Qalandar."

51. According to Ahmet Karamustafa, in the late medieval Ottoman Empire, "the antinomian rejection of society represented by deviant dervish groups developed concomitantly with, and primarily in reaction to, the organized Sufism of the socially respectable *ṭarīqas*." *God's Unruly Friends*, 86. Robert McChesney hints that this domestication of *qalandarism* was already underway by the seventeenth century. "Earning a Living," 95.

52. RGIA F 821 O 6 D 612, p. 164b.

53. Literature on sufism often posits two poles in tension with one another: "sober" mysticism, and "ecstatic" mysticism. Needless to say, *qalandars* fell on the ecstatic extreme.

54. Frembgen, "Divine Madness and Cultural Otherness," 248.

55. Even in South Asia, religious terrain generally considered to be more hospitable to "holy fools," wandering *darwīshes* came under harsh criticism from the scripturalist Islamic modernists, not to mention the colonial authorities. Green, "Transgressions of a Holy Fool."

56. Unusually, this individual was identified only by his *takhalluṣ* (pen name), which comes from the Arabic *arṣ*, meaning "igniting, stirring up, exciting." Most Persianate poets wrote under a pen

the role of a court buffoon for lack of other prospects but rather opted into the occupation after completing his studies at a madrasa, having migrated from Hisar to Bukhara for that express purpose.[57] Nor were *qalandars* limited to such activities. Arsi penned poetic verses as well; Usman Beg Katib (d. 1900/1901) did not let his ecstatic nature get in the way of becoming one of the finest Qur'anic scribes of the age; nor did it hinder Muhammad Burhan "Qani" from teaching Islamic sciences in a madrasa, or Wafa Khwaja "Wahshi" (d. 1914/15) from doing the same (at the side of the *qazi-yi kalan* no less) and then rising to the position of provincial judge.[58] Qasim Zhinda Makhdum, a sufi poet from Maymana in eastern Khurasan, was described by his biographer as sometimes donning the tattered garb of the *qalandar* when fraternizing with fellow ecstatic types, implying that he set the robes aside when engaging in other pursuits.[59] Mulla Ahmad Makhdum leveraged his renown as a *qalandar-mashrab* to climb to the rank of the amir's personal *mufti*—a sober, legal position that seemingly could not be further removed from *qalandarism*.[60]

It is important to again emphasize that there was a spectrum of *qalandar* activity. Although specifics are sparse in the sources, it is unlikely that individuals such as Wahshi and Arsi were living in caves and begging on the street, like *qalandars* on the more extreme end of the spectrum. Nevertheless, their antisocial behavior served the same function as it did for the more ecstatic *darwishes*, allowing them to get away with actions and expressions unimaginable under normal circumstances. For instance, Wahshi (whose pen name, not coincidentally, means "wild," "untamed") was known for writing caustically slanderous poetry (*hajw*) about his colleagues.[61]

Ecstatic, ascetic *darwishes* more strictly embodying the *qalandar* ideal appear in biographical dictionaries (particularly sufi ones). Mulla Haybat Akhundzada entered the tutelage of a Naqshbandi-Mujaddidi shaykh in India, but shortly after his initiation he abruptly fled into the countryside

name, often self-selected, and generally worked the term (usually referring to a quality for which they were known) into the final line of a poem.

57. Wāżiḥ, *Tuḥfat al-aḥbāb*, f. 20a.

58. Żiyā', *Taẕkirat al-khaṭṭāṭīn*, f. 72a; Muḥtaram, *Taẕkirat al-shu'arā*, f. 149a; Pīrmastī, *Afżāl al-taẕkār*, f. 160b; 'Abdī, *Taẕkirat al-shu'arā*, ff. 183a–183b.

59. "Sometimes he [Qāsim Zhinda] donned the tattered (*zhinda*) clothing of the *qalandars* and would sit with them on their bench (*maṣṭaba*)." Wāżiḥ, *Tuḥfat al-aḥbāb*, f. 168a.

60. The position of *muftī-yi jalaw* (lit. "*mufti* of the reigns") was associated with the amir's personal retinue, though it is a position I have only seen referenced in this particular source. TsGARUz R-2678, f. 8a.

61. "Few people escaped the fetters of his calumnious prose (*hajw*) or leapt from the trap of his caustic writing (*tasṭīr-i ẕamm*)." Meanwhile, Waḥshī was also famed for his mastery of philosophy. Muḥtaram, *Taẕkirat al-shu'arā*, f. 174a.

to seclude himself in asceticism. He was next encountered in Khurasan by another of the shaykh's disciples, Mulla Mir Malik, who was ultimately successful in bringing Haybat Akhundzada back into the Naqshbandi-Mujaddidi fold. Mir Malik's problem was not Haybat Akhundzada's ecstatic behavior per se, but the fact that it prevented him from performing the five daily ritual prayers. "You are a learned person (*alim*)," remonstrated Mir Malik, "Perform the prayers with calm and repose." Ultimately cured, Haybat Akhundzada went on to train "thousands" of sufi adepts himself.[62] In this example, Haybat moved from one social role to another, both of which are conventionally categorized under the common rubric of "sufi." Others seemed to seamlessly embody the role of shaykh and holy fool at the same time.[63]

The *darwish*-figure as an uneducated mendicant, separate from the ulama, is a trope particularly pervasive in colonial writing. Yet evidence for the overlap of these groups seeps into even Russian sources. A Russian intelligence report from 1914 expressed concern about a holy fool (*dewana*) from Yarkand who had crossed into east Bukhara from Afghanistan after completing the Hajj. The author of the report expressed surprise that this unnamed figure was in fact extremely educated, and spent most of his time teaching students about the life of the Prophet.[64]

Far from being seen as the antithesis of the sober ulama, therefore, by the nineteenth century *qalandarism* too had been assimilated into the broad array of virtuous social roles and activities pursued by individual scholars. There may have been unschooled *qalandars* as well, but the individuals appearing in the sources considered in this study are near-uniformly madrasa-products. Describing an esteemed colleague as having a *qalandar*'s nature was usually a compliment and performing the role of "holy fool" was an acceptable—even valorized—pursuit. Engaging in *qalandar* activities was often a temporary occupation and did not preclude other simultaneous activities. Though *darwishes* and *qalandars* are generally considered sufis in secondary literature, they were rarely designated as part of any particular order in the sources, and their activities do not necessarily have any direct relationship to the other forms of sufism considered here, such as lineage, serving as a shaykh or administering a *khanaqah*.

In other words, there is nothing inherently logical about even grouping these categories and social functions together into a sufi*sm*, suggesting a

62. Mujaddidī, *Manāqib al-Aḥmadiyya*, f. 241a and ff. 240b–241a.

63. Muḥtaram, *Tazkirat al-shu ʿarā*, f. 168.

64. The reason Russian officials took an interest in the Yarkandi *dēwāna* was that he was allegedly inciting the local populace of Qurghan-Tepa against the empire. RGVIA F 1396 O 2 D 2088, f. 13b.

coherent system—especially given that sufi concepts had come to permeate most genres and facets of Islam. These sufi roles were but a few of the many hats worn by the ulama.

Public Faces of the Ulama

The notion that virtually *all* Islamic scholars dabbled in sufi activities of various stripes is quite different from the dominant portrayal in secondary literature of two separate, sometimes mutually antagonistic constituencies. More familiar are the public faces of the ulama: clerk (*mirza*), public morality enforcer (*muhtasib*), *mudarris*, *mufti*, and *qazi*. When the term "ulama" is deployed in modern studies, it is these figures that the author generally has foremost in mind. Alongside the more esoteric social roles, these ones were indeed a mainstay of the ulama.

Just how widespread were these different positions among the ulama? Was there a typical career trajectory? Unlike the various sufi roles and forms of knowledge discussed in the previous section, it is more straightforward to assess the public faces of the ulama prosopographically: as an ostensibly appointed position, either an individual scholar served as a *qazi*, or he did not.[65] These figures are illustrative but by themselves do not provide a full picture: most of these *tazkira* purport to detail poets (and calligraphers in one case). To my knowledge no biographical dictionary specifically of the ulama was produced in Bukhara during this period, even though *tazkiras* branded that way were written elsewhere (the Volga Urals and India, for instance). This is less of a limitation than it may seem because while not all scholars were necessarily poets, nearly all poets were scholars. Abdi made this point explicit when he noted that his work was concerned with "the characteristics and poetry of the perfectly virtuous poets, by which I mean the *qazis*, *muhtasibs*, *muftis*, *mudarrises*, and learned scholars."[66] In combination with other kinds of evidence, these rough proportions offer a sense of the occupations a typical high Persianate intellectual pursued.

Of the 133 poets described by Wazih, forty-four (31 percent) performed at least one of the four roles described by Abdi as characterizing the most learned of scholars: *qazi*, *muhtasib*, *mufti*, or *mudarris*.[67] Muhtaram's biographical dictionary, also concerned exclusively with poets but written four decades later in

65. On prosopography ("collective biography") and the sources behind this dataset, see chapter 3.

66. ʿAbdī, *Tazkirat al-shuʿarā*, 10.

67. Wāżiḥ included in his collection a handful of Iranian poets from the Qajar court, as well as a slightly larger sampling of Khoqandi poets from the reign of Muḥammad ʿUmar Khan (r. 1810–22).

1908, offers a similar picture at 34 percent. Forty-five percent of the scholars in a *tazkira* targeted specifically at calligraphers (with a sample size of 107) served one of these four roles at some point in their careers. In all three sources, *qazis* and *mudarrises* are the most numerous, hovering at around 18 percent of the respective samples. *Muftis* and *muhtasibs* came in second at 7 to 10 percent, though Wazih reported fewer *muftis* than the others (3 percent). For comparison, recall from the previous section that the number of individuals specifically described as fulfilling the role of sufi shaykh was around 7 percent.[68]

This data does not demonstrate that a plurality of the ulama as a whole during this period were *qazis*, one of the most prestigious positions attainable for a scholar: these biographical dictionaries cataloged the elite of the elite. The more commonplace roles associated with Muslim congregational life, such as the imam or muezzin (prayer caller), are less visible in these texts but were much more prominent in the social landscape. In the early twentieth century, the city of Bukhara alone had well over 350 mosques, each of which would have had an imam.[69] Yet this profession is mentioned in association with scholars included in *tazkiras* only occasionally: 5 percent in all three *tazkira* considered in the aggregate. Even this figure is somewhat misleading since those rare individuals specified as imams gave sermons at mosques of special prestige. Abd al-Rahim Tarabi "Yari" (d. 1904/5), for instance, preached to Amir Muzaffar himself at the mosque in the Arg fortress of Bukhara. Moreover, Yari was also a *mudarris* and sufi shaykh, not to mention calligrapher and personal tutor of Muzaffar's children, so he hardly exemplified the garden-variety imam.[70] Other more common professions, such as the muezzin, occur only once in two of the collections but not in the third (i.e., that of Wazih).

The cadre of scholars detailed in these *tazkiras* (particularly those written at the turn of the nineteenth century) overlap to such an extent in part because the upper crust of Bukharan society was a relatively small cadre of individuals. These biographical anthologies were unified in their aspiration to document the lives of the best of the best, and the most esteemed and influential scholars tended to be *mudarrises* and *qazis*, often simultaneously.[71]

I omitted these individuals from the dataset since the author appeared to know them only from collections of their poetry, lacking any concrete biographical information. Wāżiḥ, *Tuḥfat al-aḥbāb*.

68. According to Ulfat Abdurasulov, in nineteenth-century Khorezm these "public faces" of the ulama had so thoroughly coalesced with their sufi guises that they appear as conjunctions. For example, *qāżī-ēshān*, *mudarris-ēshān*, and it was just as often that an *ēshān* would found a madrasa as a *khānaqāh*. Abdurasulov, "And the Išān's Consciousness Flew Out of His Head."

69. Gulshanī, *Tārīkh-i humāyūn*, f. 3a. Maev, *Ocherki Bukharskago khanstva*, 70–71.

70. Muḥtaram, *Taẕkirat al-shu'arā*, f. 178b;

71. It is often difficult to tell from the sources when positions were held concurrently and when they were held consecutively, and the figures here do not distinguish between those possibilities.

Of the twenty-four *qazis* mentioned by Muhtaram, for instance, seven also taught in the madrasa. In Wazih's collection, the overlap is even higher, with nine individuals serving both functions despite a smaller sample size. Although the occupation of *mufti* appears slightly less often than that of *mudarrise* and *qazi*, this is likely because—excluding state positions such as the military *mufti* (*mufti-yi askari*)—the *mufti*'s position was often less formalized than the former two.[72] Of the eighteen *muftis* included in Muhtaram's *tazkira*, all but five also performed the functions of a *mudarris* or *qazi*.

What to make of the small, but significant, cadre of morality police (*muhtasibs*, in the Central Asian context synonymous with the office of *ra'is*) among the ranks of poets and calligraphers?[73] In classical Persian poetry the figure of the *muhtasib* often appears as the buzz-killing nemesis of the poet, stepping in to shut down the fun when a party got out of hand. In the Islamic tradition, *hisba* refers to the public servant "forbidding wrong" on behalf of the state.[74] Didactic manuals produced in early modern Central Asia, such as the *Majma al-arqam*, stuck to the classical formulation, defining the position as "[supervising] the people's observance of the Sharia."[75] Unlike *qazi* and *mufti*, this position was abolished in Russian Turkestan.[76]

Certain *muhtasib* positions were powerful, particularly the city *muhtasib* of Bukhara.[77] Both Abd al-Shakur "Ayyat" and his rival Badr al-Din "Raja"

There are specific examples of scholars teaching and serving as a *qāżī* at the same time, such as Abū'l-Fażl Balkhī "Sayrat," who was described as remaining dedicated to his students even while *qāżī* of Shahrisabz. Sharʿī, *Tażkirat al-shuʿarā*, f. 56a.

72. In theory, any Muslim of sufficient erudition (vaguely conceived) could submit a fatwa to the *qāżī* presiding over a particular case, which accounts for the overlap between these legal functions in the prosopographical figures. Isogai, "Seven Fatwa Documents from Early 20th Century Samarqand." Beyond fatwa writing, muftis wrote protocols of the claim (*maḥżarāt*) necessary to initiate legal proceedings. Sartori, "The Evolution of Third-Party Mediation in Sharīʿa Courts in 19th- and Early 20th-Century Central Asia," 318.

73. The deduction that *muḥtasib* and *raʾīs* were synonymous was made prosopographically (e.g., in Muhtaram's *tażkira*, all of the *muḥtasibs* are also *raʾīses*) and based on direct equation in some sources (e.g., *bi-riʾāsat-i dār al-iḥtisāb*: Pīrmastī, *Afżāl al-tażkār*, f. 160b). See also Petrov, "Bukharskii mukhtasib v nachale XX veka." In medieval Khurasan, the *raʾīs* had been a separate position with responsibilities akin to a town mayor. Bosworth, "Raʾīs," 403. In classical Islamicate societies, the *muḥtasib* was "the person who is effectively entrusted in a town with the application of this rule [i.e., commanding right and forbidding wrong] in the supervision of moral behaviour and more particularly of the markets." Cahen et al., "Ḥisba," 485. For a monograph-length treatment of the *muḥtasib* in the context of Mamluk Egypt, see Stilt, *Islamic Law in Action*.

74. Cook, *Commanding Right and Forbidding Wrong in Islamic Thought*, 447–48.

75. Levi and Sela, *Islamic Central Asia*, 271.

76. Morrison, *Russian Rule in Samarkand, 1868–1910*, 252.

77. In Franz Wennberg's estimation, the *raʾīs* (*muḥtasib*) "was the second rank after the chief judge, *qāżī-yi kalān*, who was responsible for all higher appointments in the judicial administrations." *An Inquiry into Bukharan Qadimism*, 11–12.

used the position as a stepping-stone to the *qazi-yi kalan* of Bukhara. Outside the capital, however, the position is mentioned infrequently (6 percent of Muhtaram's sample, 8 percent of Wazih's and Ziya's, respectively), and is often associated with younger scholars. Nazrallah ibn Mulla Mahmud (who actually went by the pen name "Muhtasib" in his poetry) died young in 1890/91, having immediately gone on from the madrasa to serve as *muhtasib* in numerous provinces, including the mid-sized province of Qarakol.[78] The *muhtasib/ra'is* was a mid-level position enforcing Islamic law at the provincial and even village level.[79] Outside of Bukhara it was attainable immediately after graduating from a madrasa, but for most senior scholars captured in *tazkiras*, their days serving the function of *muhtasib* had already been forgotten, perhaps, or were deemed unworthy of mention.

The most frequent entry-level position was that of the *mirza*. The term *mirza* originally meant "prince" *(amir-zada)*, but by the nineteenth century in Central Asia it was used interchangeably with *munshi*, meaning "clerk" or "scribe."[80] *Mirzas* accounted for 9 percent of Muhtaram's and Wazih's poets, respectively, and 14 percent of Ziya's calligraphers. (It comes as no surprise that the figure is higher for a biographical dictionary commemorating calligraphers, given the overlapping skill sets.) One needed relatively little schooling to become a *mirza* once basic penmanship and literacy had been acquired. The Russian orientalist A. L. Kuhn wrote that the scribe he hired to record notes for an expedition to lake Iskanderkul spent only two years in a Samarqand madrasa following his primary education in a *maktab* before working for Kuhn.[81]

Scribal services were required not only for government business, but also for Bukhara's merchant activity, and one bazaar *mirza*—Qari Azim Bukhari "Amlah" (d. 1894/95)—even managed to gain notoriety as a poet.[82] Unlike Amlah, most of the *mirzas* making up the 9 percent were young rising stars in the various royal courts.[83] For the scribes that appear in the *tazkira* genre,

78. Muḥtaram, *Taẕkirat al-shu'arā*, f. 155a.

79. The *Majma' al-arqām* suggests that the *fayżī* and *mīr-i asad* served the function of *muḥtasib* outside of Bukhara proper. Levi and Sela, *Islamic Central Asia*, 271. This distinction does not seem to be borne out, however, in either *taẕkiras*, fatwa collections, or Russian colonial sources. See also the description in Vambery, *Travels in Central Asia*, 222–23.

80. Żiyā' even goes so far as to claim that the conflation of these meanings originated with the famous Timurid ruler Ulugh Beg, whose calligraphy was so exquisite that the term came to be associated with writing. Żiyā', *Tarjuma-i aḥwāl-i Abd al-Shakūr*, f. 117a.

81. SPIVAV, F33 O1 D218, f. 4ba.

82. Pīrmastī, *Afżāl al-taẕkār*, f. 34b.

83. In his biographical account of the Manghit dynasty, Żiyā' tends to equate the scribes (*munshīyān*) with the courtesans and secretaries (*nadīmān wa dabīrān*). Żiyā', *Nawādir-i żiyā'īya*, f. 49b.

serving as *mirza* was merely a first step before moving on to more influential positions.

Thus, the typical career progression of a polymath of Islam begins to take shape. A recent madrasa graduate might immediately work as a *mirza*, imam, or perhaps a *muhtasib*—quite likely while continuing to advance in "postgraduate" forms of knowledge at a *khanaqah*. Those who distinguished themselves might move on to be appointed as madrasa instructors, *qazis*, or *muftis*. And at the very top, singular positions such as *qazi-yi kalan*, *shaykh al-Islam*, or *muhtasib* of the city of Bukhara awaited.

This array of social roles crystalized much earlier in Islamic history than those associated with sufism.[84] Most of them depended on mastery of substantive Islamic law, which in turn depended on a canonical set of scriptural sources. During the first three centuries of Islam, hadith collectors and legal theorists were not necessarily the same individuals. By the eleventh and twelfth centuries, however, one canonization had integrated the regionalized hadith traditions, a second had consolidated theology into a specific set of Ash'ari-Maturidi doctrines, and a third moment of canon formation had whittled the proliferation of legal schools into the four major Sunni *mazhabs* that dominate to the present day. Moreover, in the case of Central Asia, Turkic dynasties actively favored the Hanafi legal school, and in the two centuries leading into the Mongol period, a picture of legal pluralism gave way to a Hanafi consensus.[85]

Already by the twelfth century, all of the social roles discussed in this section were recognizable in some form in Central Asia. *Muhtasibs*, *qazis*, and *muftis* enforced the legal-theological Maturidi-Hanafi consensus; that consensus was strengthened and reproduced by the instruction of *mudarrises*. Many scholars moved between these functions with great frequency or held them simultaneously. Yet there were more canonization processes to come, integrating new forms of knowledge and social roles into the expected repertoire of the ulama. Even pushing past the sufi-ulama dichotomy does not capture the full range of options open to the ulama of Bukhara.

The Arts and Beyond

Sufism was one "postgraduate creed of Islam"—that is, a body of knowledge and associated occupations pursued in addition to the hard Islamic sciences of the madrasa. Other postgraduate career paths were poetry and calligraphy.

84. Brockopp, *Muhammad's Heirs*, 21.

85. Madelung, "The Spread of Maturidism and the Turks."

There seems little need to defend the critical role of Persian literature in defining a common high culture stretching from Ottoman lands to India and Western China. Poetry was so prevalent that it was taken for granted as an expected pursuit of the ulama.

Poetry was much more than a hobby, however pleasurable. Mirza Baba ibn Damulla Safar Muhammad Hisari (d. ca. 1878) was not mentioned in the biographical dictionaries concerned with Bukhara's most prominent scholars. He was neither a *qazi* nor a *mudarris* but enjoyed modest success as a bureaucrat in provinces such as Khuzar, Jizzakh, and Ziya al-Din. While he enjoyed the off-and-on patronage of local governors, work was inconsistent and at times he compared his penury to that of a "shepherd's dog."[86] Despite his middling status as a *mirza*, Hisari interspersed his memoir with poetic verse, including praises to reigning Amir Nasrallah—nothing out of the ordinary within the scholarly milieu.

More interestingly, Hisari described how his poetic acumen allowed him to obtain work utterly unrelated to that particular skill. When Hisari moved to the province of Jizzakh—located not far from Tashkent and for the most part controlled by Bukhara before the Russian conquest—he was without friends, patrons, or work. Learning that the governor frequented a particular mosque located near the town fortress, Hisari made sure to be there, carefully scribing spiritual poetry during the governor's favored time for prayer.[87] The governor took notice, studied Hisari's prose intently for a few moments, and then offered him a job.[88] The position had little to do with Hisari's extracurricular poetic talent but rather consisted of tax-related accounting.[89]

This is a revealing example of the larger argument at hand. The governor was not looking for a court poet or calligrapher. Yet because the many social roles were so thoroughly integrated, Hisari was advertising his quality as a high Persianate intellectual. By illustrating his talent in penmanship and prose, Hisari signaled that his skills and refinement went beyond the core curriculum of the madrasa, despite the fact that those skills (particularly literacy, logic, and rhetoric) were precisely the ones that he would use the most as a bureaucrat.[90]

---

86. Ḥiṣārī, *Yāddāsht-hā*, f. 23b.

87. "In innovative fashion I penned poetical excerpts (*qiṭʿa*) . . . and with a steel pen I accommodated the Divine Word in poetic form." *Bi-ṣanāʾiʿ-i jadīda qiṭʿāt-i jallī mē-nawishtam . . . wa bi-khāma-i fūlādīn chandī az suwar-hā-yi kallām-i rabbānī-rā bi-miṣrāʿ-i jallī gunjāyish mē-dādam*. Ḥiṣārī, *Yāddāsht-hā*, ff. 27b–27a.

88. Ḥiṣārī, *Yāddāsht-hā*, f. 27a.

89. The term used to refer to these activities, *sar-rishta-i istīfāʾ*, was common across Persianate societies. Ḥiṣārī, *Yāddāsht-hā*, f. 28a.

90. The economic concept of "signaling" is helpful for understanding this dynamic: a firm (in this case the governor) is unable to directly observe the quality of a potential employee, which leads

Just as every scholar was a sufi in some sense of the word, every scholar seemed to be a poet of some caliber. Admittedly, the fact that the majority of Bukharan *tazkiras* were specifically conceived as poetic anthologies constitutes a serious sampling bias: definitionally, all the ulama captured in those sources were poets. These sources reveal that all poets were also ulama but tell us little about the proportion of ulama who were poets. Still, the fact that most of the surviving *tazkiras* were defined as biographical dictionaries of the poets, and not the ulama, is indicative of the popularity of literature as a discipline.

Other sources not specifically geared toward poetry also reveal its widespread mastery by the ulama. For instance, Abu al-Nizam Rahmatallah (d. 1846/47) was a Bukharan scholar described in an Arabic-medium, Tatar-authored biographical dictionary dedicated broadly to the ulama as a group, yet his poetry is listed alongside his judgeship as one of the meritorious achievements of his life.[91] As with Hisari, poetry did not necessarily factor into Abu al-Nizam's day job, but his literary talents nevertheless served to justify his inclusion among the ranks of great Islamic scholars.

For a handful of individuals poetry amounted to a full-time profession, but these were rare—even in the poetical anthologies. The *mirzas* that formed a ruler's retinue of courtiers, such as Hisari, were expected to compose verses and recite the verses of others, but they also fulfilled other practical functions, including scribing. As a young man Hajji Ni'matallah Muhtaram was hired by Abd al-Ahad (r. 1885–1910) to compose a poetical anthology, but even this constituted a discrete assignment rather than a career path.[92]

The poet Muhammad Rajab Hisari "Pari" is an exception that proves this broader trend.[93] Pari was described as illiterate and uneducated, presumably lacking a madrasa education, but so delightful were the verses that sprung from his lips that he captivated the high functionaries of Hisar.[94] No mention was made of any concurrent or subsequent positions held by

to an asymmetry of information. The firm focuses on a different trait (in this case poetry) that tends to be correlated with the desired qualification.

91. Marjānī, *Wafiyyat al-aslāf*, f. 204a. Incidentally, Abū al-Niẓām's biographer, Shihāb al-Dīn Marjānī, was invested in elevating his stature partly to defend the controversial figure Naṣr al-Dīn al-Qūrṣāwī (Kursavi) (d. 1813), whose reformist teachings they both followed. Qūrṣāwī lived much of his life in Bukhara until the ulama drove him out for advocating active interpretation (*ijtihād*) of the core Islamic scriptures. Keller, *To Moscow, Not Mecca*, 12.

92. Żiyā', *Tarjuma-i aḥwāl-i Qāżī ʿAbd al-Shakūr*, f. 125b.

93. Muḥammad Rajab's pen name (*takhalluṣ*) refers to magical denizens of another world synonymous with *jinn* (genies).

94. *Bā wujūd-i ʿāmī būdan, dar naẓm-i aṣnāf-i shiʿr qudrat-i tamām dāshta.* Wāżiḥ, *Tuḥfat al-Aḥbāb*, ff. 44–45.

Pari, which would almost certainly have been closed to him, given his lack of formal schooling. Pari's success in rising to the stature of a court poet stands as an anomaly in the sources, and the fact that the author made a point of emphasizing it is indicative of just how unusual his career trajectory was. Poetry was a knowledge form mastered by the ulama, not a separate profession.

Poetry and calligraphy were integral to the repertoire of a well-rounded scholar not just because of the doors these skills opened up, but also because of the opportunity for innovation and creativity. It is an interesting coincidence that in neighboring Persianate societies—Tatarstan and India, for instance—the resurgence in production of biographical dictionaries specifically detailing the ulama as a collective was contemporaneous with Muslim reform movements seeking to reengage the Islamic tradition, often with an emphasis on "returning" to the core texts (i.e., the Qur'an and Hadith) in order to meet the challenges of colonialism and modernity.[95] Although there was no shortage of innovative engagement with the Islamic sciences in Central Asia before this (especially in the commentary tradition), the prominence of poetry as the dominant rubric for biographical dictionaries is nonetheless striking.

The creative energy surrounding the calligrapher's vocation is particularly palpable in Sadr-i Ziya's *Tazkirat al-khattatin*, a biographical dictionary of calligraphers. Ziya treated the scribal trade similarly to sufi *tariqas*, tracing the flow of knowledge from master to disciple through the generations. Distinct calligraphic styles were treated as separate *silsilas* (artisanal lineages), usually originating only a handful of generations prior. Mawlawi Saqi Muhammad Balkhi Sanchariki (d. early eighteenth century) developed a variant of *nastaliq* script so unique that it was referred to as "Saqi-gi," and enticed many students to follow in his footsteps.[96]

In marked contrast to language used in relation to the Islamic sciences—and even poetry to a lesser extent, for which imitation (*taqlid*) of earlier scholars was viewed as meritorious—in the domain of calligraphy, Ziya was keen to emphasize the invention (*ikhtira*) of a new technique. In contrast with

95. In India, for instance, all but one specimen of the biographical dictionary genre were dedicated to sufis rather than the ulama prior to the close of the eighteenth century. Metcalf, *Islamic Revival in British India*, 44. In Central Asia, by contrast, the biographical dictionaries concerned with the ulama as a social group that were reproduced during the early modern period were generally reproductions of classical works in Arabic about medieval scholars.

96. Żiyā', *Tazkirat al-khaṭṭāṭīn*, f. 82a. Żiyā' possessed eight different manuscripts scribed by *Sāqī* in his personal library: Vohidov and Erkinov, "Le fihrist (catalogue) de la bibliothèque de Ṣadr-i Żiyâ.'"

sufism, in which the founding figures were almost invariably considered superior to their successors, in the domain of calligraphy students routinely surpassed their forebears. For instance, Sadiq-jan "Kufri" "Kuydarakhti," who lived during the reign of Amir Haydar (r. 1800–1826), initially imitated (*taqlid karda*) Saqi's style of calligraphy, but as his fame grew he invented his own exquisite style, "the likes of which had never been seen before."[97] Later on, in the middle of the century, Inayatallah Khwaja "Qazi-yi Qalan Taht-i Minari" similarly innovated a style equal to that of Saqi Balkhi.[98]

Like poetry, calligraphy was rarely the sole occupation of an individual scholar. Calligraphers were also poets (9 percent), imams (5 percent), *mirzas* (14 percent), *mudarrises* (19 percent), and public legal functionaries (i.e., *muhtasib*, *mufti*, and *qazi*; 36 percent). Of the 102 individuals covered in *Tazkirat al-khattatin*, two were described as *qalandars* and four as performing the functions of a sufi shaykh. Around one-third of the calligraphers were not identified with any other profession, but these entries tend to be the tersest, so it is likely that even they were not full-time calligraphers.

Masters of Medicine

Medicine is a narrowly professionalized vocation today, but it too was one of the many hats worn by the polymaths of Islam. It was not near-universally pursued, like sufism or poetry, nor was it a mandatory component of the madrasa curriculum. Because no separate medical institution existed, all physicians (*tabib*) were also madrasa-trained ulama. Much like poetry and sufism, medicine stands as one of the paths scholars pursued to elevate their standing.

Physicians appear among the ranks of ulama infrequently, constituting 4 out of Muhtaram's 192-person sample and 7 out of Wazih's 133 poets (around 2 to 5 percent between them).[99] Abd al-Qadir "Sawda be Pul" "Pishak-baz" (d. 1873/74) mastered the standard Islamic sciences (*ulum-i mutadawila*) until he became captivated not only by medicine (*tibb*) but also by music (*musiqi*) and the occult sciences (*ulum-i ghariba*), including astronomy/astrology (*nuzum wa hay'a*).[100] Abd al-Qadir's variegated interests earned him a spot in Amir Muzaf-

97. Żiyā', *Tazkirat al-khaṭṭāṭīn*, ff. 85a–85b.

98. Żiyā', *Tazkirat al-khaṭṭāṭīn*, f. 88b. This figure and his intellectual lineage are discussed further in chapter 7.

99. When the Indian traveler Ḥāfiẓ Muḥammad Fāżil Khan visited Bukhara in 1812, he was generally impressed with the Bukharan amirate, with the notable exception that he found the quality and quantity of physicians and hospitals deplorable. Fazil Khan, *The Uzbek Emirates of Bukhara & Khulum*, 38.

100. Shar'ī, *Tazkirat al-shu'arā*, ff. 66b–67a. "Pishak" (sometimes "pushak") is a uniquely Central Asian word for "cat"; 'Abd al-Qādir's second nickname means "one who plays with cats" or "cat-

far's retinue and the honorary rank of *uraq*.[101] Although no mention is made of him making use of his medical skills, Muzaffar commissioned Abd al-Qadir's to draw on his expertise in trigonometry (*handasa*) to make a map of the Bukharan Emirate.[102] Like so many of his peers, Abd al-Qadir was capable of performing a wide range of social roles, and even the knowledge forms he was not actively using served to bolster his overall status as a high Persianate intellectual.

Other physicians seemed to be more focused on the practice of medicine. Abd al-Zahir Makhdum Bukhari (d. early twentieth century), for instance, specialized in curing *khanazir*, a kind of goiter or glandular swelling in the neck.[103] The disease seems to have been quite common, afflicting several of his colleagues and killing at least one.[104] Even a specialist like Abd al-Zahir was noted for his mastery of poetry and the principles of language as much as for his medical capabilities.[105]

The classical Greco-Islamic medical sciences had deep roots in Central Asia, originating from a synthesis produced by the translation movement of the ninth century.[106] By the early nineteenth century, indigenous medicine was facing competition in new techniques from Europe, which were built on a common foundation of received Greco-Islamic medicine.[107] When then-prince Nasrallah learned of Amir Haydar's death in 1826, he rushed from his governorship in Qarshi toward Bukhara to claim the throne before falling severely ill. Rather than consulting a *tabib* like Abd al-Qadir or Abd al-Zahir, he went to Christian doctors (*atba-i masiha*), though even they proved ineffectual.[108] By the nineteenth century, the indigenous Nestorian

---

lover" and was given to him because of the animal's omnipresence in his household, perhaps invoking the image of the famous companion of the Prophet Muḥammad, Abū Hurayra, who was also named for his affinity for felines. Żiyā', *Tażkār-i ash'ār*, 379.

101. When the *Majma' al-arqām* was written in 1798, *uraq* referred to a *muḥtasib* specifically for the military. Levi and Sela, *Islamic Central Asia*, 271. By the late nineteenth century, it had apparently transitioned into an honorary scholarly rank third in importance after *ṣadr* and *ṣudūr*. Żiyā, *The Personal History of a Bukharan Intellectual*, 1.

102. Żiyā', *Tażkār-i ash'ār*, 308–9.

103. 'Abdī, *Tażkirat al-shu'arā*, f. 116a.

104. A scholar named Mullā Shahāb al-Dīn "Afsar" perished from the affliction in 1895/96. Muḥtaram, *Tażkirat al-shu'arā*, f. 89a.

105. 'Abdī, *Tażkirat al-shu'arā*, f. 116a.

106. In Arabic the word *ṭabīb* simply means "doctor," but the presence of Western medical science led to a bifurcation between the *ṭabīb*, which came to refer to a traditionally trained physician or even folk healer, and doctors trained in foreign techniques who were generally referred to by imported words such as "doctor" or the Russian *vrach*. In India, the term "Yunani" came to refer to Greco-Islamic medicine (*ṭibb*) in the modern period.

107. As is well known, a Latin translation of Ibn Sina's (Avicenna) Canon of Medicine (or *Qānūn*) served as a medical textbook in Europe through the eighteenth century.

108. Ḥakīm Khan, *Muntakhab al-tawārīkh*, 417. The association between Christians and medicine can be traced even into the Sasanian period, and Abbasid monarchs relied on them as well.

Christian communities of the Silk Road era were long gone, and the text does not clarify the identity of these mysterious Christian doctors. They may have been Armenian or Russian.

By the second half of the nineteenth century, some of the ulama interested in medicine had taken it upon themselves to embrace European medical techniques after completing their madrasa studies. Muhammad Amin Hakim (d. early twentieth century) translated Russian and European (*farangi*) medical manuals into Persian. Interestingly, he also translated Islamic medical treatises into Russian and other unspecified European languages, suggesting that he viewed the new methods as complementing, rather than displacing, the traditional ones.[109] His contemporary, Habiballah "Zuhuri," studied first in Bukhara but then went on to work in a Russian hospital in Samarqand (*tababat-khana*)—which did not prevent him from gaining renown as an expert in the poetry of Hafez.[110] It seems that at the end of the nineteenth-century European medicine was in the process of being adopted as yet another social role of the ulama to complement rather than displace *tibb*.

The apparent unpopularity of medicine as a profession among the ulama is partly explained by a competitor profession, the perfumer (*attar*), who also served as an apothecary. Because perfumery did not require a madrasa education and was considered to be a less prestigious profession than that of the *tabib*, the term is encountered only infrequently in biographical dictionaries.[111] In this sense, *attar* was a figure somewhat analogous to that of the *maddah* (minstrel), more of a competitor to the ulama than one of their guises.

For instance, Abd al-Azim Shar'i included Mirza Jahangir Majnun Irani in his biographical compilation not to praise him but to question his learning and place among the ulama. Among his charges was that though Mirza Jahangir was a competent perfumer, that expertise did not translate into any real knowledge of treating illnesses. Shar'i noted that both useful and harmful information was included in the practical books of remedies ubiquitous in the bazaars and used by everyone. Yet knowledge of those practices was

109. Muḥtaram, *Taẕkirat al-shuʿarā*, f. 92a. As Devin DeWeese has pointed out, simple dichotomies between "Western" and "Islamic" medicine are of limited use in appreciating how Central Asian medicine was practiced and conceptualized. "Muslim Medical Culture in Modern Central Asia," 3–4.

110. ʿAbdī, *Taẕkirat al-shuʿarā*, f. 108a—marginalia.

111. Examining biographical dictionaries from the medieval period, Doris Behrens-Abouseif demonstrates that medical practice gradually split into medical theory, which was still popular among the ulama, and medical practice, which became associated with craftsmen of lower status (perhaps analogous to the ʿaṭṭār in this case). "The Image of the Physician in Arab Biographies of the Post-Classical Age." According to Lapidus, however, apothecaries and other craftsmen were also included in medieval biographical dictionaries. *Muslim Cities in the Later Middle Ages*, 109.

not the same as real medical knowledge; hence, Mirza Jahangir should not be considered a true *tabib*.[112] Mirza Jahangir's inclusion in Shar'i's collection—to refute his status as a scholar rather than endorse it—is fortuitous in that it reveals a dichotomy between a medical practices embraced by the ulama as distinct from a popular practice considered beneath it.[113]

N. S. Lykoshin, a Russian administrator and orientalist, personally encountered in Chimkent what he characterized as a folk healer (*znakhar'*)—at first glance a figure not unlike the *attar*. Lykoshin was suffering from an eye ailment and agreed to have it treated by a local healer named Rahmatallah. First, the Russian official paid the healer to purchase a sheep, slaughter it, and distribute the meat to the needy so that they might pray on behalf of Lykoshin. Then the healer asked for Lykoshin's name, wrote it down on a piece of paper, and proceeded to analyze the letters of his name to see his fortune and discern a cure for the ailment. Next, to Lykoshin's confusion, the Rahmatallah drew a series of dots in horizontal rows on a separate piece of paper, which he then connected with lines of varying lengths. Then the two sat facing each other, knee-to-knee, and Rahmatallah read verses from the Qur'an, occasionally pausing to blow into Lykoshin's afflicted eyes.[114]

Lykoshin did not emerge from the experience a happy customer, having dismissed the healer's craft as "folk superstition" (*tuzemnoe sueverie*) from the start. The orientalist may have been correct that Rahmatallah had not mastered the science of *tibb*. However, that did not mean that Rahmatallah was an *attar*, and Lykoshin was incorrect to dismiss him as "uneducated."[115] Rather, like many of his colleagues, Rahmatallah was a practitioner of a sophisticated array of occult sciences—as evidenced by the details and technical terms Lykoshin himself recorded.[116] Rahmatallah scrutinized the letters

112. Sharʿī, *Tazkirat al-shuʿarā*, f. 77b.

113. Similarly, Ṣāliḥ ibn Muḥammad Qandahārī Qāʾinī, author of a notable nineteenth-century medical treatise, cautioned that "physicians should themselves study medicines rather than leaving their preparation to sellers of drugs and perfumes (that is, to ʿaṭṭārs)." DeWeese, "Muslim Medical Culture in Modern Central Asia," 9.

114. Lykoshin, *Pol zhizni v Turkestane*, 260–66. The healing power of breath distinguishes this as prophetic medicine (*al-ṭibb al-nabawī*), as distinct from Greco-Islamic medicine (although the ulama performed both). Lykoshin connected this to the sufi practice of *tawajjuh* (a kind of spiritual focus and transmission)—and he may well have been correct, which stands as further evidence for the broader argument in this chapter for polymathy. Lykoshin, *Pol zhizni v Turkestane*, 262–63. Moreover, occultism had been intellectually integrated with sufism for centuries: Melvin-Koushki, "Astrology, Lettrism, Geomancy," 143 passim.

115. Lykoshin, *Pol zhizni v Turkestane*, 256, 262.

116. Even while dismissing the healer's craft as "folk practice" and "superstition," Lykoshin's own evidence points to the opposite conclusion. Trying to make sense of what he was witnessing, Lykoshin kept hearing references to a nineteenth-century encyclopedic work with sections detailing *jafr* and *raml*, Ḥakīm Wājid ʿAlī-Khān's *Maṭlaʿ al-funūn*, and proceeded to discuss the work's content.

in Lykoshin's name because he was a master of *jafr* (lettrism). Rahmatallah was connecting the dots, so to speak, because he was also a practitioner of *raml* (geomancy). Lykoshin lampooned Rahmatallah's explanation of his craft as related to the "science of the astrolabe," but both *jafr* and *raml* had been integrated into the science of astrology since the at least the fourteenth century.[117] Rahmatallah was indeed a healer, but less folksy than Lykoshin assumed. Instead, Rahmatallah was embodying another social role of the ulama: the occultist.

Masters of the Unseen

Just like sufi practices of various stripes, poetry, and calligraphy, the occult sciences (*ulum-i ghariba*) were yet another domain mastered by high Persianate intellectuals.[118] Like medicine, occultism was an elite practice—not mastered by everyone, and certainly far less prevalent than poetry, law, or sufism. Yet Rahmatallah was far from alone: somewhere between 2 and 5 percent of his colleagues were fellow occultists, a figure roughly on par with *tibb*.

Sihr (magic) is theoretically forbidden in Islam because it is associated with deception and falsehood. This principle was not absolute, and there was no phenomenon of witch hunts on any scale comparable to Christendom.[119] However, "occultism" was not understood as *sihr*, a term that does not appear in the *tazkiras*. Over the course of centuries, it came to be understood as *Islamic* science—an unproblematic, respectable skill set for the ulama.[120] This was made possible by an epistemology shared across the gamut of Islamic intellectual thought, rooted in Neopythagorean panpsychism along with its associated idea of a chain of being and ultimate oneness of existence.

Scholars were frequently described as experts in astronomy (*ilm-i nujum*), including practical astrological applications, such as deducing the influence of the stars on human destinies. Also popular was geomancy (*ilm-i raml*, lit.

Lykoshin, *Pol zhizni v Turkestane*, 266. To pose the same question as Johannes Fabian in a different historical context: Was Lykoshin "out of his mind"? Fabian, *Out of Our Minds*.

117. Melvin-Koushki, "Persianate Geomancy from ṭūsī to the Millennium"; Melvin-Koushki, "Astrology, Lettrism, Geomancy," 143–44.

118. See also Melvin-Koushki and Pickett, "Mobilizing Magic."

119. Melvin-Koushki, "How to Rule the World," 142. Some Arabic literature differentiates between good and bad *siḥr*, with the former generally performed by higher beings such as angels. Ohtsuka, "Magic," 502.

120. Lettrism, for instance, "by the early fifteenth century, was widely considered to be not only the most Islamic of all the occult sciences, but also the most Islamic, and the most universal, of *all* sciences." Melvin-Koushki, "Astrology, Lettrism, Geomancy," 144. Occult sciences were understood as natural, rational, and sometimes mathematical. Melvin-Koushki, "Powers of One."

"science of the sand"). Though the specifics of the practice varied widely by time and place, it generally involved covering a board with sand or flour, drawing a series of even or odd lines, forming figures (tetragrams) on their basis, and then interpreting the chart thus formed.[121] In addition to planets and figures in the sand, numbers served as another source of occult inference. *Jafr*, which by this period referred metonymically to the science as a whole, involved the harnessing of numerical values equivalent to individual letters (*abjad*) to achieve divine insight about the future. In the fifteenth century, this "intellectual trinity" was refined and integrated into the mainstream, Islamic, mathematical tradition—a gradual occultist canon formation.[122]

Such talents had many useful applications. Siraj al-Din was a *mudarris* noted for his mastery of *ilm-i nujum* and *handasa*. At the turn of the Persian New Year (Nawroz), the amir summoned him to determine the exact day the twelfth station of the Zodiac (*burj*) would transition to the new cycle.[123] Based on this service, the amir appointed Siraj al-Din to the position of *akhund* in Bukhara—a position unrelated to the competency he had just illustrated. Just as prowess in poetry could signal excellence in other disciplines expected of the polymaths of Islam, so too could astronomy.

These occult sciences, as natural-mathematical sciences, were so intricate and demanding that many scholars did not succeed in mastering them, which perhaps explains the lower numbers of occultist scholars relative to other social roles. Lykoshin was called in for a preliminary investigation (*doznanie*) of the suicide of a Tashkent scholar who had withdrawn into solitary study before taking his own life. Scattered throughout the deceased scholar's room, Lykoshin found piles of papers and notebooks with tables of Arabic letters scrawled on them.[124] Upon finding references to an occultist work, the

---

121. Various other terms, such as *ṭarq* and *ashkāl*, were used in other Islamic territories to denote the practice, but only *raml* appears in early modern Bukharan sources. See Melvin-Koushki, "Defending Geomancy Sharaf al-Dīn Yazdī Rebuts Ibn Khaldūn's Critique of the Occult Sciences."

122. The broader field of lettrism was called *ʿilm-i ḥurūf*, although that term does not appear in Bukharan *tazkiras*. *Jafr* was often associated with Shiʿism, as it was believed that a secret book of knowledge (*Kitāb al-jafr*) was transmitted by ʿAlī down to the sixth imam, Jaʿfar al-Ṣādiq (though no such association is ever made explicit in the sources used in this study). Windfuhr, "Jafr." Letters and numbers were understood as one and the same, just as in the Hebrew and Greek traditions. Melvin-Koushki, "Astrology, Lettrism, Geomancy," 147; Melvin-Koushki, "Powers of One."

123. TsGARUz R-2678, f. 8a. The usage of *dāna* in this passage is a bit unclear, but the broader meaning is understandable. A possible translation might be: "Every year during the days of Nawruz he would prepare a new year's chart and gift it to the amir of Bukhara." As noted previously, the title *ākhūnd* was often given to a *mudarris* of the Kokaltash madrasa, though that is not specifically stated in this case.

124. Lykoshin counted 2,458,624 letters across 614,656 graphs, written in twenty-eight notebooks with twenty-eight pages in each. A completed prognosticon (*jafr-i jāmiʿ*) required over two years of seclusion to finish. Lykoshin, *Pol zhizni v Turkestane*, 267.

Russian administrator realized that the deceased had become obsessed with *jafr*. Lykoshin concluded: "he zealously worked toward his goal [of using *jafr* to predict and control his future], until overexertion brought him to a tragic denouement."[125]

Beyond the first "trinity" of astrology, lettrism, and geomancy, some scholars were adept in a second trio of arts considered even more intricate, which were sometimes termed the "occult trifecta"—*simiya*, *rimiya*, and *kimiya*.[126] *Kimiya* equated to alchemy; *simiya* could refer to a division of letter magic, alongside *jafr*, or a kind of illusionism involving the projection of the soul out of the body; and *rimiya*—like alchemy—was the practice of manipulating earthly forces to produce supernatural marvels, and was often associated with geomancy (at least in the Central Asian context).[127]

Sometime after completing his madrasa studies, Abd al-Rahman "Tamkin" was appointed *mudarris* of the Dar al-Shifa madrasa at the behest of Amir Abd al-Ahad.[128] Instead of defining his postgraduate competence by following a sufi path, Tamkin mastered the gamut of occult arts, from those acknowledged openly to the secret sciences. Tellingly, Tamkin's biographer noted that it was others who alleged that he had mastered the "occult trifecta," rather than Tamkin himself who made such a claim.[129]

Tamkin's contemporary, Muhammad Amin Hakim, combined geomancy with the medical profession.[130] The occult sciences, therefore, alongside the myriad of other pursuits considered so far, served as another competency to distinguish madrasa graduates from their competitors. Sometimes, occult training even mimicked the sufi master-disciple structure and served as an alternative or simultaneous postgraduate intellectual pursuit.[131] Anxieties

---

125. Lykoshin, *Pol zhizni v Turkestane*, 266–67.

126. Muḥtaram, Taẕkirat al-shuʿarā, f. 97a. It is unusual for these disciplines to appear in the absence of two other *īmiyā*'s, i.e., *līmiyā* and *hīmiyā*. Melvin-Koushki, "Powers of One," n. 138. A more literal translation of *ʿulūm-i s̱alās̱a-i mughayyabāt* would be "the three occult sciences," but I am so terming it here to avoid confusion with the "trinity" of occult sciences. A trifecta in place of a five-some may be specific to Central Asia.

127. Melvin-Koushki and Pickett, "Mobilizing Magic," n. 94.

128. A mid-sized madrasa of fifteen cells, constructed in the seventeenth century. Żiyāʾ, *Ẕikr-i asāmī-yi madāris*.

129. Pīrmastī, *Afżāl al-taẕkār*, f. 55a.

130. Muḥtaram, *Taẕkirat al-shuʿarā*, f. 91b–92a.

131. In a nineteenth-century petition to the Bukharan amir, one scholar wrote that it had "been 42 years since this willing servant spent three years in residence at the shrine of your ancestor, the Lion of God (*shēr-i khudā*), in Balkh, where with extreme exertion I acquired somewhat of the science of *jafr* . . . And had my teacher (*murshid*) allowed me to cease practicing it, these most satisfying results could not have been achieved." Melvin-Koushki and Pickett, "Mobilizing Magic," 277–79.

about heresies and infidelities were pervasive in Central Asia, but magic was not one of them.[132]

There were a few exceptions, however, in which some forms of magic were equated with practices seemingly forbidden in the scriptures. One *jung* manual included a brief entry condemning belief in the words of a soothsayer and astrologer as blasphemy.[133] However, the *jungs* containing practical astrology and other occult practices seem to far outnumber those condemning it. Moreover, the opinion-writer may have had in mind more popular forms of magic, rather than the refined mathematical sciences of the "occultist trinity."

Opinions such as this notwithstanding, the ulama practiced exactly the sort of folk magic the author likely had in mind, routinely and unproblematically. Lykoshin was keen on forcing all occult practices into this category, even the ones with clear scientific pedigree—a sensibility shared by his Soviet successors.[134] Indeed, "folk" magic and occult "sciences" often bled into one another.[135] Moreover, practices without any clear occultist disciplinary genealogy appear in practical notebooks used by the ulama. For instance, Qazi Mir Sayyid Qamar's *jung* included a remedy for the incessant wailing of a baby: "When a child cries a lot, write this Qur'anic verse [about the Seven Sleepers of Ephesus] and attach it to him in order to get rid of the crying."[136] On the same page another verse was noted to similarly cure shiver-inducing fevers.

If merely scrawling a few Qur'anic verses seems rather tame, later the same *qazi* included instructions for preparing a magical charm (*ta'wiz*): "Write this enchantment [i.e., a series of prescribed numbers] on a piece of paper and put it in the middle of a sheep's heart. Then take a piece of the person's cloak to serve as a piece of cloth. Then wet the cloth, roll the heart up inside of it, and place it beneath the fire. This will prepare the charm."[137]Although magical practices such as *ta'wiz* sometimes lacked the intellectual pedigree of the other occult sciences, respectable scholars practiced them all the same.

132. For more on this, see chapter 6.

133. *Agar kas-ē nazd-i fāl-bīn ū munajjim rawan[d] wa ān ḥukm kih ū mē-kunad ān-rā taṣdīq kunad, bi-sharīʿat ēn muṣaddiq kāfir bāshad. Jung-i riwāyāt* (IVANUz no. 4798). *Fiqh* references cited in this opinion draw equivalency between *fāl-bīn* and the Arabic *kāhin*. This logic is reminiscent of polemics against astrology in the Ottoman territories; attacks against the other occult sciences were far rarer. Melvin-Koushki, "Powers of One," 178.

134. Melvin-Koushki and Pickett, "Mobilizing Magic," 236–38.

135. For instance, popular fortune-telling practices at the bazaar level retained Persian vocabulary and an association with Tajiks well into the Soviet period. Privratsky, *Muslim Turkistan*, 213.

136. "Then We caused them to fall into a deep sleep for many years inside the cave." Qur'an 18:11. *Jung-i Qāżī Mīr Sayyid Qamar ṣudūr*, f. 9b.

137. *Jung-i Qāżī Mīr Sayyid Qamar*, f. 22a. Talismanic magic as performed by the ulama is also attested by Russian sources. For instance, barren women were reported to go to the local imam to prepare a charm to restore fertility. Bayram-Alibekov, "Musul'manskie sueveriia," 183.

If talismanic magic were included in the figure cited at the outset of this section, it would likely be far higher than 2 to 5 percent.[138]

The picture emerges of polymaths of Islam practicing magic along a broad spectrum, ranging from the most intricate and elite of the sciences, to folk practices not necessarily rooted in texts. A description of scapular divination illustrates that the vast majority of these forms of knowledge were understood to be Islamic—rooted in scripture, just like jurisprudence. By examining the spatial layout of colors on the left shoulder blade of an ewe, the diviner could predict whether or not a caravan would run into danger on the road. For instance, if the topmost section relating to the path of the caravan was reddish in color, the caravan was certain to fall victim to an attack. Conversely, blackness in the space dedicated to the mountains and plains was proof that the trip would be especially profitable. The scapula could also be read for predictions related to the weather, famine, and war.[139] Given the treacherous roads and long distances between cities in the region, it is not difficult to see the utility of magic such as this.

Scapular divination may seem like the folksiest of folk magic—the practice likely had roots in Mongol tradition, though no such attribution is made in the text.[140] Quite to the contrary, the author contends: "Sages have held the knowledge of scapular divination to be equal to astrology."[141] In the pages of biographical dictionaries, the "occultist trinity" was still dominant—they are absent references to scapular divinations—but this particular scholar sought to elevate it to that level. He further justified it by referencing a hadith.[142]

Like the other social roles of the ulama, occultism stood as a means specializing beyond the juridical sciences emphasized in the madrasa study circle. Just as with other forms of knowledge, this ecosystem ranged from the highly textual and intricate, to folk practices (with less textually grounded practices such as the *attar*, *maddah*, and *qalandar* serving as loose parallels for the physician, poet, and sufi shaykh, respectively). The oral cultures were

---

138. To anticipate a core argument of the next chapter, the reason "folk" magic is not mentioned in the *taẕkira* has much to do with textual genre: biographical dictionaries were produced and reproduced to glorify an elite cadre of scholars. This is why the formalized occult sciences were openly attributed to the ulama, while simpler magical remedies generally were not.

139. *Risāla dar ma'rifat-i shāna*, ff. 81a–182b.

140. Birtalan, "Ritualistic Use of Livestock Bones in the Mongolian Belief System and Customs."

141. *Ḥukamā' shinākhtan-i 'ilm-i shāna-i gōsfandān-rā bā 'ilm-i nujūm barābar dāshta-and. Risāla dar ma'rifat-i shāna*, f. 81a.

142. *Risāla dar ma'rifat-i shāna*, f. 81a. The author of this text is anonymous, but a stamp on the last page of the volume bears the date 1786/87. A short manuscript attributed to the seventeenth-century Iranian philosopher Mullā Ṣadrā references the same hadith in relation to scapular divination, so this was not necessarily an innovation of nineteenth-century Central Asia. (The Mullā Ṣadrā manuscript was once held in the Maulana Azad Library of Aligarh, India [no. 23-5], but has possibly been lost, and is now available only in a poor-quality microfilm in the Nur Library in Delhi.)

not necessarily any less sophisticated than the textual ones, and the barriers between the two poles were highly permeable. The high Persianate intellectual moved between all of them.

View from the Scholar's Notebook

The picture painted so far has mostly rested on prosopographical evidence. *Qazis* split their time between the courtroom, the sufi lodge, and the madrasa, or moved back and forth between those occupations throughout their careers. Ascetics copied famous works in new styles of calligraphy while writing fatwas on the side. Any given scholar with a madrasa education and versed in the various extracurricular and postgraduate competencies was qualified for any of these functions, with expertise in one signaling likely expertise in another to potential patrons.

This argument is further supported by another sort of writing: the scholar's notebook. In the course of the late eighteenth and nineteenth centuries a title-less genre of writing emerged often categorized as *jung*, which usually consisted of assorted excerpts and exemplary models of a predominantly legal nature. Unlike the elegant calligraphy of other manuscripts, *jung* were typically hastily scrawled, weather-beaten from use, and stuffed with various clippings from other sources. In essence, they are practical scrapbooks for judges and other legal functionaries, a unique window onto the broader world of the ulama.[143] They offer a sense of what was useful to the ulama on a daily basis and how competencies were applied in practice.

Every social role of the high Persianate intellectual is evident in one notebook. For instance, the inside cover of one *jung* specimen is filled with poetic couplets, as are the final ten pages of the book. Stuffed loosely inside the cover is a scrawled wedding prayer as well as a lithographed segment of a *ghazal*. The next insert is a Qadiri *khatm* (lit. "seal") listing the ritual prayer sequence of the sufi brotherhood, complete with instructions about when and how to perform the *khatm*. Following a prayer to the legendary figure of Khizr, the notebook includes a magic spell (*tilism*) whereby the practitioner could augur whether or not an illness would prove fatal by placing an inscribed eggshell under the pillow of the afflicted. From there the bulk of the text proceeds to outline rulings on numerous legal disputes, with heavy emphasis on the sorts of cases that would have crossed a *qazi*'s or *mufti*'s metaphorical

143. For all that the *jung* genre reveals about the social world of the ulama, it also suffers from lack of context. Presumably to render their rulings as widely applicable as possible, *jung* authors (like fatwa writers) purged their works of any references to time and place, replacing proper nouns with either "so and so" (*fulān*) or generic stand-in names such as Zayd.

desk most often—particularly marriage disputes and small financial transactions. Toward the end of the *jung* the author included prayers exalting the royal court as well as sermons to be read at the establishment of *waqfs*.[144] Other *jung* specimens are similarly wide-ranging, interspersing legal rulings with poetry, astrological diagrams, *jafr* arcana, and in one case even a recipe to make a particular kind of sweet (*halwa*).[145]

The point here is to emphasize the trend already established from the biographical dictionary genre and prove that laundry lists of accolades—such as the diverse competencies attributed to Abd al-Qadir—were not formulaic sycophancy reducible to the indulgence of his biographer. The textual residue of the many activities described in this chapter manifest in the practical notebooks scholars referenced on a daily basis. Scholars integrated the curriculum of the madrasa with a broad range of knowledge forms—both practical and esoteric—learned outside of it and distilled them all into the composite that distinguished their social group.

A Millennium of Intellectual Sedimentation

Our view of the ulama in the earliest centuries of Islam is hazy, but already by the tenth century they were polymaths. Canonical versions of the Qur'an and Hadith meant that scholars across Islamdom were mastering a common scriptural tradition. On top of the scriptures, consensus gradually emerged around Ash'ari-Ma'turidi theology (*kalam*) and four Sunni schools of law—all products of canonization processes that had crystalized by the early twelfth century. During this same early period a large-scale translation movement Islamized numerous disciplines from the Greek tradition and beyond, from rhetoric to philosophy to medicine. This ferment formed the basis for the core madrasa curriculum discussed in chapter 4. Thus the ulama would have had plenty to talk about with fellow polymaths from the "classical" age of Islam.

Yet the ulama of Central Asia were heirs to many more centuries of sedimentation than their classical forebears. New Persian literature was born in the tenth century, emerging from a synthesis of newly codified Arabic prosody conventions and pre-Islamic Iranian traditions. Early poems were composed across numerous Persian dialects (the so-called *fahlawiyat*), and still in the eleventh century most Central Asian scholars wrote in Arabic, but by the twelfth century a literary synthesis had changed the picture dramatically. New Persian literature had become an expected and unremarkable facet of intellectual life throughout much of Eurasia.

---

144. *Tetrad' s razlichnymi zapisiami*, ff. 0b–1, 54a–60a, f. V, f. 8b, ff. 29b–43a.

145. *Jung-i Qāżī Mīr Sayyid Qamar Ṣudūr*, ff. 360a, 363b.

A time-traveling scholar from the long nineteenth-century would find himself nearly at home already by the twelfth century, with several important exceptions, the most crucial being institutionalized sufism. The thirteenth century witnessed an explosion of sufi communities in various forms, with competing ideologies and corporate identities. Al-Ghazali (d. 1111) provided the intellectual scaffolding for the incorporation of sufi thinking into mainstream Islamic theology in the twelfth century, and a century later founder figures such as Shihab al-Din Suhrawardi (d. 1234) provided the organizational toolkit.[146] By the early modern period the boundaries between "scholar" and "mystic" had begun to blur; most intellectuals were both. And by the eighteenth century, even the *tariqa* as an exclusivist organizing logic had begun to break down, such that by the long nineteenth-century sufism had been thoroughly absorbed into the broader tradition.

Beyond sufism, the ulama of the long nineteenth century stood perched atop canonizations that synthesized diverse movements into the fold. Most occult sciences had pre-Islamic roots, but much of the work of theorizing them as mathematical and quintessentially Islamic took place in the fourteenth through sixteenth centuries. It was during that same period that Nastaliq, the preeminent calligraphic form of the Persian cosmopolis, was developed. These arts were standardized, reproduced, and integrated into the larger Persianate canon.

The repertoire of the polymaths of Islam of the long nineteenth century is a window into Islam itself. They were not unique in their polymathy, but they were unmatched in the sheer breadth of their eclecticism. From a modernist standpoint (e.g., that of the Jadids), the ulama often come across as unimaginative, conservative, and stuck in their ways. Some scholars have sought to combat this image by emphasizing the dynamism of their intellectual tradition. Canonization notwithstanding, every one of the intellectual traditions explored in this chapter was constantly evolving.

It is also worth emphasizing the deep consensus produced by these moments of synthesis. No scholar, no matter how erudite, was about to suggest a wholly new theology for Islam or invent a fifth school of law. This enduring stability provided a near-limitless reservoir of intellectual material for the ulama to fashion their world, justify their own influence, and shape social structures. The high Persianate intellectual was destined never to be surpassed in his eclecticism, as profound changes lurked just around the corner.[147]

---

146. Ohlander, *Sufism in an Age of Transition*.

147. In the Central Asian case, the assault on canonical consensuses was heralded by the Jadids. Khalid, *The Politics of Muslim Cultural Reform*.

Chapter 6

Between Sharia and the Beloved

Culture and Contradiction in Persianate Sunnism

If the ulama were at once mystics, jurists, occultists, poets, clerks, doctors, and musicians, how are we to assess the dominant portrayals of this social group, past and present? The Jadids and Russian administrators agreed on the fanatical nature of Turkestani mullahs, but according to British colonial officials sufis were tolerant and syncretic.[1] Poets had a reputation for drinking wine and partaking in the debauchery of princely courts, but their former classmates were known to militate against precisely that kind of activity. How could it be that these wildly disparate figures once studied together in the exact same institutions and mastered the same disciplines?

Given the pervasiveness of these contradictory stereotypes, it is small wonder that modern scholars are also tempted to retrospectively view these discrete talents, tendencies, and forms of knowledge as embodied by separate communities. After all, how could such divergent archetypes play nice together? That these diverse images seem so paradoxical says more about orientalism, politics, and genre conventions, than it does about early modern and colonial-era Bukhara.[2]

1. Ernst, "Between Orientalism and Fundamentalism," 110. This affinity for sufism as an alternative or antidote to extremism is equally true of modern U.S. and Uzbek policy, respectively.

2. Although the issue of genre figures prominently in this chapter, the role of orientalism and politics in producing these contradictory images of the ulama will remain in the background. Aside

The central thrust of this chapter is not that Bukhara was a bastion of enlightened tolerance: the ulama were intensely concerned with enforcing scripturally sound religious practice on others. Nor is it to suggest that romantic escapades were purely a literary trope without basis in lived experience: writing by the ulama was permeated with homoerotic allusions to the Beloved, and those fantasies played out in real life as well. This chapter argues that these characteristics were embodied by a single social group (and often a single individual) at the same time. In a sense, there was a grain of truth in both the "fanatical mullah" and "libertine courtier" stereotypes promoted by their respective detractors: the ulama were both at the same time, neither, and much more. The analysis presented here addresses the puzzling implications inherent in the amalgamation of so many social roles and knowledge forms into the figure of the high Persianate intellectual.

The chapter's title alludes to two sorts of tension: paradoxes of hindsight that were not necessarily perceived as such within the society in question; and apparent logical contradictions of Perso-Islamic culture emerging from the primary sources themselves, products of their own time and understood as problematic by the historical actors in question. I first address the former category: widespread belief in the everyday supernatural was for the most part compatible with scripturalist Islam, even though that imagery would seem to cut across the modern categories of "orthodoxy" and "folklore."[3] Although one can point to scripturalist versus popular tendencies within Islam, separating them into distinct categories of practice or belief fits poorly with late Persianate society.[4] At a minimum, this chapter demonstrates that there was no contradiction between these practices, to the extent that retrospective categorizations of orthodox mullahs, on the one hand, and ecstatic

---

from lingering debates over how exceptional the Russian case was, the broad insights of Edward Said's *Orientalism* have been largely absorbed by historiography on the Russian Empire. See Schimmelpenninck van der Oye, *Russian Orientalism*.

3. Throughout Islamic history, different individuals placed different emphases on the direct meaning of scriptural texts vis-à-vis other sorts of revelation (e.g., personal divine inspiration, metaphorical readings of text). There is no unproblematic way of gesturing at this split. "Orthodox," borrowed from Christianity, seems to suggest that there was a single orthodox position prescribed by a centralized church; "Sharia-minded" suggests that sufis were somehow less concerned with Islamic law; and "Salafi" (aside from being anachronistic) seems to suggest that opponents were less enamored with the example set by forebears (i.e., the literal definition of Salafism). "Scripturalist," the term preferred in this book, is admittedly not much of an improvement, as it also seems to suggest that nonscripturalists viewed the Hadith and Qur'an as dispensable, which they did not. For a critique of the concept of "folk religion," both emerging out of Soviet scholarship and otherwise, see DeWeese, "Islam and the Legacy of Sovietology," 310; McChesney, *Waqf in Central Asia*, 34; Shahrani, "Local Knowledge of Islam and Social Discourse in Afghanistan and Turkistan in the Modern Period," 164.

4. See also Robinson, "Other-Worldly and This-Worldly Islam and the Islamic Revival."

sufis and poets, on the other, ought to be jettisoned altogether. These were all social roles performed by the polymaths of Islam.

Second, I examine tensions within Islamic society during the long nineteenth century. Although no logical contradiction existed between writing fantastical stories about *jinn* on Monday and lashing someone for blasphemy on Tuesday, there was inherent tension between indulgence in wine and opium and legal rulings against precisely those activities. Like the first kind of tension (i.e., paradoxes of hindsight), the ulama did not necessarily problematize these contradictions, but they did lead to a degree of anxiety palpable in their writing. The fact that legal rulings against sodomy, for instance, coexisted comfortably with homoerotic love affairs (and not just the metaphorical kind found in poetry) had much to do with textual genre. The former were written predominantly within legal genres, while depictions of the latter appeared in poetical and mystical genres of various stripes—even though both were written by members of the same social group.

Textual conventions fundamentally shape our understanding of how people perceived and interacted with culture. This may seem like common sense, but many studies of Persianate Eurasia focus on a single type of text, which means that genre lurks silently in the background, molding the discourse of the text and its interpretation.[5] When genre is brought front and center, it is generally in literature studies, though even within that field treatments of Perso-Islamic genres are far from comprehensive.[6] However, the concept of genre is just as applicable to ostensibly historical sources as it is to ostensibly literary ones: practical documents from the chancellery and legal textbooks were every bit as subject to genre conventions as a Persian *ghazal*.[7] Considering documents, legal writing, and hagiographies as genres of literature allows us to assess what an individual was choosing

5. This is not a blanket criticism. Some of the very best studies in the field are treatments of a single genre, and there are legitimate philological advantages to comprehensively engaging a single genre of primary sources. For instance, see McChesney, *Waqf in Central Asia*; Wilde, *What Is Beyond the River?*; DeWeese, "The Masha'ikh-i Turk and the Khojagan."

6. Only the most general surveys have attempted to list the various forms of Persian writing that emerged over the centuries. Notably, many of the most distinct and recognizable genres (e.g., epics of kings, princely mirrors, various kinds of poetry) were formalized early in the history of New Persian, in the tenth and eleventh centuries. Utas, "'Genres' in Persian Literature 900–1900." There is no equivalent of Erich Auerbach's classic *Mimesis*, which contrasts representations of reality across diverse genres in the Western canon, and even fewer attempts to connect genre with social reception. A notable exception is Askari, "The Medieval Reception of Firdausī's Shāhnāma." For studies of Persian literature that engage the concept of genre, see Sharma, "Amir Khusraw and the Genre of Historical Narratives in Verse"; Losensky, *Welcoming Fighānī*; Dale, *The Garden of the Eight Paradises*.

7. On using the concept of genre for making sense of nonliterary sources that defy simple categorization, see Lenhoff, "Toward a Theory of Protogenres in Medieval Russian Letters."

when he chose to write in a given register, which in turn allows us to uncover the underlying cultural dynamics of late Persianate society—as opposed to unintentionally describing an individual genre through which that society was articulated.[8]

Such considerations of textual genre help to clarify what it meant for the high Persianate intellectual to wear so many hats simultaneously. Genres mapped loosely to the diverse social roles of Islamic scholars: most ulama were part of a sufi order and also wrote hagiographies and mystical didactic works; they were jurists and kept notebooks of legal miscellany (*jung*); they were officials in the amirate administration and drafted chancellery documents; they were also poets. It is not surprising that genre affected both the structure of a text and the worldview expressed therein. The fact that these diverse sensibilities were expressed by a single social group (and often a single individual) makes the case of the Bukharan ulama especially intriguing.[9] As will be seen, scholars might write approvingly about wine consumption in a poetical anthology and then condemn it in a legal text as a mortal sin deserving of God's punishment (*hadd*). The seeming contradiction lay not in the identity or social group of the individual scholar, but rather the possibilities opened up by the genre in question and the corresponding social context of the event in question.[10]

8. One of the most important contributions from this field is that genre should not be considered as merely classificatory, but also constitutive: "genre has come to be defined less as a means of organizing kinds of texts and more as a powerful, ideologically active, and historically changing shaper of texts, meanings, and social actions. From this perspective, genres are understood as forms of cultural knowledge that conceptually frame and mediate how we understand and typically act within various situations." Bawarshi and Reiff, *Genre*, 4. See also Frow, *Genre*, 14. Moreover, genres are fluid, historically specific categories with "multiple relational possibilities with each other, relationships that are discovered only in the process of adding members to a class." Cohen, "History and Genre," 210. In this vein, critical theorists often describe a given work as "participating" in a genre, rather than existing within it. Frow, *Genre*, 28. For this reason, the categories mustered in this chapter (e.g., the "hagiographical genre") are "rough and ready" approximations; a rigorous taxonomy of Persianate genres is certainly not attempted here.

9. Although it may seem a bit far afield, recent research on cognitive neuroscience intersects with genre theory in surprising ways. Just as different social settings are associated with different genres, scientists have shown that different contexts trigger fundamentally distinct logics of belief for explaining the world around us, seamlessly coexisting within a single individual. Van Leeuwen, "Religious Credence Is Not Factual Belief," 705. These insights from other disciplines help explain why the paradoxes of later Persianate society were not problematized; different settings and social roles were associated with different ways of perceiving and describing reality.

10. "Self-fashioning" is a concept from literature studies that overlaps with the phenomenon discussed here, especially in positing multiple "selves" for a single individual shaped by contingent social circumstances. Reiss, *Mirages of the Selfe*; Greenblatt, *Renaissance Self-Fashioning*; Kinra, *Writing Self, Writing Empire*; Gandhi, "Mughal Self-Fashioning, Indic Self-Realization." Because I tend to see broad epistemological continuity from the tenth through even early twentieth centuries, as opposed to the emergence of a new understanding of personhood coinciding with the European Renaissance,

The Everyday Supernatural

Miraculous feats were a common feature of hagiographies across many different religious traditions, and the stories told about Muhammad Ata'allah ibn Hadi Khwaja (d. 1795/96) were no exception.[11] One story reveals not only the fantastical but also what was considered ordinary:

> One day a group of friends remarked to one another that [one of the madrasa students] never took off his mosque slippers.[12] They wondered if his feet were marred by leprosy [*dagh-i barasi*] or some other ailment. One of the friends resolved that after the lesson he would steal a glance at the other student's feet. . . [When confronted,] the slipper-clad madrasa student retorted: "What business is it of yours? My footwear is my own choice." Not satisfied, the group of friends took off the student's shoes by force, revealing to their astonishment not human feet, but the hooves of a goat. The hoofed student said: "If it weren't for Hazrat-i Ustad [i.e., Ata'allah], then I would give you that which you deserve." And then he disappeared, leaving the students to run about in terror.[13]

Ata'allah was not surprised in the least to learn what had transpired, but he was furious with his pupils for violating the privacy of a fellow student.[14] He went on to order that no secret should be made of the fact that *jinn* and *pari* (separate terms for one category of otherworldly creatures) were among his apprentices.[15]

By contrast, Ata'allah's wife was warier of denizens of the unseen world (*ghayb*), and understandably so. In the Islamic tradition, *jinn* are generally held to be similar to humans in that they can be good or bad and members of various earthly religions, but different in that they have various supernatural

---

I favor different terminology to describe a similar phenomenon (e.g., "social roles" instead of "fashioning multiple selves," even though the two ideas are broadly similar).

11. The family dynasty of scholars established by Hādī Khwāja is discussed in much greater detail in the next chapter, as well as in Pickett, "Nadir Shah's Peculiar Central Asian Legacy."

12. This term refers to a kind of shoe (*khuff*, in legal texts) that can be worn during prayer, so long as it is put on during a state of purity and wiped off (hence *masḥ*, "wiping").

13. Riżawī, *Manāqib wa maqāmāt-i ʿAṭā ʾallāh*, ff. 54a–54b.

14. According to Russian sources, shaykhs were popularly believed to have the power to bend *jinn* to their will by sequestering themselves in forty days of secret prayer, subsisting only on a single date. Successfully executing this secret prayer gave the shaykh all manner of advantages, such as wealth and even super speed. Bayram-Alibekov, "Musul'manskie sueveriia," 180.

15. Riżawī, *Manāqib wa maqāmāt-i ʿAṭā ʾallāh*, f. 54b. *Jinn* and *parī*—two mythological creatures from the Arab and Iranian traditions respectively—had been amalgamated even in the earliest Persian sources, though they often remain separate species in oral traditions. Omidsalar, "Genie."

powers—which means that if one encounters the bad variety, the consequences could be dire.[16] Belief in similar supernatural creatures seems to have deep roots in Central Asia predating Islam, and in ancient times the term *pari* referred to decidedly wicked creatures.[17] It seems sensible, therefore, that when a *pari* showed up shortly after Ata'allah's death to invite his children to a special funeral feast in the unseen world, his wife was less than thrilled.[18] *Jinn* had a reputation in Central Asia for coaxing humans to feasts with nefarious ends.[19]

Two sons survived Ata'allah Khwaja—Rahmatallah and Eshan Muhammad Sharif Khwaja—and the *pari* resolved that the best way to honor the recently deceased was to invite the half-brothers to a funeral in the unseen world.[20] As an emissary, the *pari* sent Abd al-Rahman, who had been one of their grandfather's students, to invite the young scholars to their otherworldly palace. Rahmatallah immediately agreed, but Muhammad Sharif's mother remained cautious, even though she recognized the name Abd al-Rahman as one of the grandfather's *pari* disciples and knew that he would ultimately obey her son. She instructed Muhammad Sharif to tell Abd al-Rahman that he would accept the invitation to the other world, but only for the express purpose of reading the opening Surah of the Qur'an (the Fatiha). When Abd al-Rahman reappeared, he agreed that after the Fatiha at the morning prayer they would return to the human world.[21]

No sooner had Muhammad Sharif offered his consent than a dais carried by four other *jinn* miraculously appeared before him. "Sit there," commanded

---

16. Matter-of-fact belief in *jinn* as both ordinary and supernatural was a facet of Central Asian culture shared with the broader Islamic world, which is not surprising, given that their existence is established in the Qur'an. El-Zein, *Islam, Arabs, and the Intelligent World of The Jinn*. Beliefs similar to the ones described above have been attested among Russian Muslims to the north, among Pashtuns to the south, and much further afield. Frank, *Muslim Religious Institutions in Imperial Russia*, 266; Malik, "Varieties of Islamic Expression in the Mughal Province of Kabul," 13.

17. The idea of *jinn* predated the rise of Islam and was appropriated in Zoroastrian contexts following the Arab conquests (perhaps grafted on to an indigenous idea such as *parī*). Hoyland, *Arabia and the Arabs*, 145; Crone, *The Nativist Prophets of Early Islamic Iran*, 102–3. One also notes that *jinn* were portrayed as an indigenous element of Turkic belief already in al-Kāshgarī's eleventh-century work. Dankoff, "Kāšġarī on the Beliefs and Superstitions of the Turks," 74. The word existed in both Pahlavi and Sogdian (*parīg*), but the meaning was more uniformly negative than *jinn*, referring to a witch or demoness. MacKenzie, *A Concise Pahlavi Dictionary*, 65; Forrest, *Witches, Whores, and Sorcerers*, 65.

18. The word *ṭoy* is usually associated with weddings rather than funerals.

19. For instance, if the potential victim brandished an iron instrument, or uttered the name of God, then the feast might be revealed as horse dung (*polyot*). Bayram-Alibekov, "Musul'manskie sueveriia," 180.

20. On the relationship between the mortal world and those of the *jinn*, see El-Zein, *Islam, Arabs, and the Intelligent World of The Jinn*, chap. 1.

21. Riżawī, *Manāqib wa maqāmāt-i ʿAṭā ʾallāh*, ff. 54b–55a.

Abd al-Rahman, "and close your eyes." When Muhammad Sharif was permitted to open his eyes, he beheld a grand mansion in which *pari* pledged fealty to his brother Rahmatallah, the newly anointed *shaykh al-Islam.*[22] "What is this place?" Muhammad Sharif asked in wonder. Abd al-Rahman, the brothers' *pari* interlocutor, replied that this domain was known as the Garden of the Four Seasons, adding that their grandfather had once honored the *jinn* with a five-day visit. Sure enough, the *jinn* opened four doors leading to four dimensions perpetually at the peak of spring, summer, autumn, and winter, respectively.[23]

After they concluded the morning prayer on the following day, Rahmatallah instructed the *jinn* to return them to their home in the mortal world. Abd al-Rahman replied: "But so soon? Most of the great *jinn* still have not arrived to honor you. You must stay for at least a week. In another two days our kings will arrive to shower you with offerings."[24] Rahmatallah stuck to the deal struck with his younger brother, insisting that they had agreed to a single Fatiha recitation, and that the amir of Bukhara would soon begin to fret over their absence. The *jinn* insisted that they were humbly at the service of the two scions, and—after showering them with gifts—honored the agreement and returned them to their home in the mortal world.[25]

The *jinn*, as portrayed in this hagiography of Ata'allah Khwaja, were obedient acolytes to him and his family, but there was still something threatening in their otherworldliness. If it had not been for the cleverness of Muhammad Sharif's mother, the two brothers might have found themselves permanent guests at the Garden of the Four Seasons.[26] She was not surprised by the invitation to the *pari* world and was on a first-name basis with one of their number, Abd al-Rahman. The mother's apprehension was about the potential consequences of such a voyage.

The hagiographical genre is definitionally concerned with the miraculous deeds of its subject, so the preceding accounts do not by themselves prove that supernatural beings were part of the ulama's lived experience. As the previous chapter illustrated, other sorts of occult sciences were routinely

22. Raḥmatallāh's tenure in this position was cut terminally short by illness in 1807/8, leaving the mantle to be taken up by his younger brother.

23. Riżawī, *Manāqib wa maqāmāt-i ʿAṭā ʾallāh*, f. 56a.

24. *Naẓr* usually refers to a gift given from an inferior to a superior (often to the custodian of a shrine in exchange for blessing), so the *jinn* king intended to symbolically submit to Raḥmatallāh.

25. Riżawī, *Manāqib wa maqāmāt-i ʿAṭā ʾallāh*, f. 56b.

26. A separate text contains an entire section devoted to the mother of Muḥammad Sharīf (possibly, though not necessarily, the same as the one in this story, since Muḥammad Sharīf and Raḥmatallāh had different mothers), and miraculous events associated with his birth. Musayyab Bukhārī, *Kitāb-i maqāmāt-i mashā ʾikh*, f. 769a.

mastered and practiced by the ulama, as manifest across numerous textual genres. Moreover, references to *jinn* in other genres of sources suggest encounters with these sorts of supernatural beings were indeed a feature of everyday life.

Jinn are discussed matter-of-factly in many Islamic sources. Even though they generally cannot be sensed by mortals, their presence is taken for granted, and they are referenced even when their existence is incidental to the matter at hand. For instance, Hanafi law cautions not to use bones to clean up after relieving oneself because bones are food for the *jinn*.[27] This notion arose from the events surrounding the "night of the *jinn*" (*laylat al-jinn*) as recounted in several prophetic hadiths. The Prophet Muhammad was whisked from Mecca into the other world in a manner not so different from that of Ata'allah Khwaja and his descendants. After reciting the Qur'an to the *jinn*, they asked him what they should rely on for sustenance, to which the Prophet replied that they could eat any bone on which the name Allah has been mentioned, and that camel dung could serve as fodder for their otherworldly riding animals. The Prophet then instructed his followers not to use any bones for toilet-related purposes.[28] Similarly, legal texts enjoined worshippers to offer the twin salutations (*taslimatayn*) after reciting the Shahada (testimony of faith in God and the Prophet) at the end of prayer even when worshipping alone for the benefit of angels and pious *jinn* who might secretly be present.[29]

Though widely used in Central Asia, such *fiqh* texts were composed centuries earlier and are of little direct service in shedding light on the early modern and colonial-era context. However, the logic underpinning classical jurisprudence filtered into practical rulings in unexpected ways. According to Hanafi law, it is permissible to interrupt the prayer to kill troublesome scorpions and snakes. Because *jinn* had the power to take the form of animals, one medieval scholar ruled that Muslims should take care not to kill white snakes that might be visitors from the supernatural world.[30] The author of a well-known commentary on Marghinani's *al-Hidaya* rejected this view on the grounds that the Prophet Muhammad made the *jinn* swear an oath not to take the form of snakes and plague believers in their homes—and that if the *jinn* violated this agreement, Muslims were at liberty to slay them.[31]

---

27. For instance, "Do not clean yourself with dried dung or bones, for they are the sustenance of your brothers from among the *jinn*." Bābartī, *al-ʿInāya sharḥ al-hidāya*, I/347.

28. *Ṣaḥīh Muslim* IV 169.

29. Shurunbulālī, *Mukhtaṣar imdād al-fattāḥ*, 154–55.

30. Abū Jaʿfar Muḥammad ibn ʿAbdallāh al-Hinduwānī (d. 973 in Bukhara).

31. Bābartī, *al-ʿInāyat sharḥ al-hidāya*, II/171–72.

Notebooks of *jung* and legal documents reveal that *jinn* broke their oath not to shapeshift and terrorize Muslims on a regular basis—and that this was not exclusively a matter of theoretical jurisprudence.[32] Numerous entries described groups of *jinn* transforming themselves into horrific forms and proceeding to frighten a member of the Muslim community.[33] Then the opinions invariably invoked the "night of the *jinn*" when the *jinn* swore to the Prophet Muhammad not to engage in this kind of behavior. The authoring *muftis* (writers of legal opinions) then condemned them for breaking their sacred oath, pronouncing the *jinn* to be deserving of painful retribution for their actions and destined for hellfire.[34] In other words, these legal rulings appear to have been solicited at the request of the aggrieved Muslim to sanction the offending *jinn*. The otherworldly creatures were treated as legitimate targets of a legal injunction, just as real and ordinary to ulama wearing their jurist hats and writing in the legal genre as they were to ulama penning mystical texts as sufis.

If predicting hellfire for the offending *jinn* seems unsatisfactorily vague, actual fatwa documents provide a more specific remedy.[35] Following a similar scenario as that described in the *jung* entries, a band of *jinn* hooligans terrorized a woman named Sharafat Oy by manifesting in the form of snakes and various other creatures. This time the *mufti* commanded that the *jinn* cease their offending activity and repent, and if they failed to do so, it was justified to slay them. Moreover, if it turned out that those nefarious *jinn* were also infidels, then it was incumbent on Muslim leaders to order their execution even if they ceased and desisted.[36]

The images of *jinn* emerging from legal and hagiographical genres are distinct in flavor, but they similarly accept otherworldly creatures as active participants in everyday events.[37] The *jinn* of the hagiographies appear in

32. For a fuller discussion of these multi-purpose notebooks, see introduction and chapter 5.

33. "Horrific forms": *hay ʾāt-i muhība*. This case specified 658 different forms taken by the *jinn*.

34. *Riwāyāt dar khuṣūṣ-i żarar rasānīdan-i ajinna*, f. 672a. For similar cases, see *Jung fī masā ʾil al-faqīh*, f. 159a; and Ḥusaynī, *Jung-i majmū ʿa-i riwāyāt*, f. 1a. (Note that the plural *ajinna* used in the title is a false Arabic plural for *jinn* common in Central Asia.)

35. For similar examples, see also nos. 683 and 684 of Welsford and Tashev, *A Catalogue of Arabic-Script Documents from the Samarqand Museum*. The difference between what I refer to as a fatwa and the previous rulings written in *jung* is that fatwas are individual documents stamped by a *muftī*, whereas *jung* rulings were collected in a bound volume, most likely for reference. In practice, the difference is blurry, since some actual fatwa documents were pasted into *jung* to be used as models, and *jung* entries were occasionally endorsed with a *muftī*'s stamp. See introduction.

36. "If they [the *jinn*] to not repent (*tawba na namāyad*), then execution is permitted (*mubāḥ*); and if the offenders are infidels, then execution is mandatory (*lāzim*)." TsGARUz F i-126 O 1 D 1729, f. 54a.

37. Christian Novetzke conceptualizes genres as either "theographic" or "historiographic," with hagiography tending strongly toward the former. "The Theographic and the Historiographic in an Indian Sacred Life Story," 121.

much greater detail, with distinct personalities and societies. The miraculous adventures of Ata'allah Khwaja and his children in the other world are perhaps more reminiscent of the stories told about *jinn* in popular folklore as reported in Russian sources, but they are portrayed as every bit as real in legal writing—legal writing that a scholar such as Ata'allah Khwaja (who was both a *qazi-yi kalan* and *shaykh al-Islam*) would have routinely produced. Legal genres hew much closer to scripture, connecting *jinn* with events depicted in the Hadith and eschewing the colorful embellishments captured in sufi writing. There was nothing contradictory between these sources.[38] Instead, the two genres allowed the ulama to tap into a common spectrum of belief in the supernatural to different ends. Terminology in the legal genre allowed ulama acting as jurists to offer practical solutions for the population at large to combat nefarious interlopers from the other world. The hagiographical form similarly offered possibilities for enhancing the prestige of the ulama by putting them on a plane equal, or even superior, to that of the *jinn*.

Legal writing wove in other kinds of supernatural phenomena, intersecting with the various occult practices mastered by the ulama. For instance, a prayer amulet from the Samarqand Museum collection reads: "The Angel Gabriel told Muhammad that nobody who keeps this prayer about his person will experience misfortune in either of the two worlds: mankind, spirits [*jinn* and *pari*], and demons (*dew*) who inflict pain on children will all be kept at bay . . . anyone who doubts the efficacy of the prayer must be a disbeliever."[39] It is worth noting that this amulet ended up in a collection containing primarily legal documents such as fatwas and protocols of claim (*mahzar*), serving as further evidence that the ulama engaged the supernatural world from numerous registers.

Jinn thus appear as part of everyday life, associated with the supernatural and ecstatic states, to be sure, but every bit as grounded in quotidian practice as law, poetry, and other domains of the ulama. However, *jinn* possession was not the only means for high Persianate intellectuals to transcend the boundaries of sober reality.

Opium, the Not-Quite-Forbidden Substance

Were the ulama getting high in Bukhara, that sacred pillar of Islam, at least some of them? In a word: yes. This does not mean they were hypocrites. Nor

---

38. This would change: modern Islamist currents tend to reject much of the nontextual folklore associated with *jinn*. Khan, "Of Children and Jinn."

39. No. 696 in Welsford and Tashev, *A Catalogue of Arabic-Script Documents from the Samarqand Museum*, 515.

does it mean that Islamic scholars were lenient to the point of fully condoning narcotics. Once again, the onus is on us in our distant position from this society to avoid assuming tension where there was none, and to accept that incongruity between two norms was not necessarily problematic. Islamic scholars were well trained in Hanafi jurisprudence and hardly ignorant of widespread violations of Sharia, but they were simultaneously heirs to a millennium-spanning culture of recreational substance use, and most of the time they were content to live with those contradictions.[40]

Russians certainly viewed opium as one of the endemic vices in Turkestan and the substance factored into their Orientalized depiction of fanatical, lazy, pedophilic mullahs.[41] Some reports even gauged the fanaticism of the local population based on the quantity of narcotics sold.[42] The Jadids viewed it as a major social ill as well. But what do sources written by the ulama tell us about opium usage—both the social reality and attitudes toward it?

Legal sources indicate that opiates were frowned upon. To quote from a *jung* manual: "Consuming poppies and opium (*koknar u afyun*) is forbidden (*haram*), [but] through the necessity of addiction it becomes permissible. The superior opinion on this matter can be found in the collection of legal opinions [which states] that opium is *haram* because it is [by legal analogy] a kind of poison."[43] Another opinion agreed that some degree of opium use was permissible, but only to the extent necessary to stave off death; recreational use was *haram*.[44] Both *jungs* justified their positions through recourse to a commentary on al-Quduri's *al-Mukhtasar*, with the second one noting that the popular legal work's position on opium was actually ambiguous. It was not considered an intrinsic ill, but pernicious in its tendency to tempt people toward vice.[45] In other words, opium was strongly discouraged, but exceptions could be made.

---

40. There would seem to be much in common between the picture depicted here of widespread opium use in Central Asia and Iran. Matthee, *The Pursuit of Pleasure*, 115.

41. This view was shared by some Tatar ulama, one of whom warned a student bound for Bukhara "to avoid three things in Bukhara: opium, indolence in his studies, and pederasty." Frank, *Bukhara and the Muslims of Russia*, 98. A nineteenth-century Iranian observer took a similar view. Āshtiyānī, *ʿIbrat-nāma*, 111.

42. This short article connected narcotics with the Andijan uprising of 1898, the 1910 Sunni-Shia violence in Bukhara, and even the 1857 rebellion in British India: "Gashish i fanatizm," 183–84.

43. The legal category *żarūra* (more serious than *ḥāja*) is used for "necessity." *Jung-i riwāyā-i maḥżarā*, f. 30a. On the Greek etymology of *afyūn* and *taryāk*, see Matthee, *The Pursuit of Pleasure*, 97.

44. *Sbornik vypisok iz sochinenii po fikkhu i iuridicheskikh kazusov*, f. 297b–298a. The legal position in Iran was apparently much more lenient. Matthee, *The Pursuit of Pleasure*, 105.

45. The citation does not specify which commentary (*Sharḥ-i Qudūrī*) was being referenced, but one well-known (but probably not the one referenced in the *jung*) commentary on Qudūrī's *al-Mukhtaṣar* seems to take a somewhat stricter view, stating unequivocally that narcotics (*ʾakl al-banj*

Even if provisionally forbidden, opium consumption is dealt with in a rather incidental manner in certain chancellery documents. For instance, an opium den (*koknar-khana*) was the target of a Bukharan fatwa, but for the purposes of collecting taxes, not regulating consumption.[46] A tax collector agreed to temporarily accept a deposit in lieu of full payment from the owner of the opium den, but when he returned to collect the remainder the owner claimed to have already paid it (presumably to another government official). The legal opinion enjoined the opium den owner to pay up but placed no particular importance on the nature of his business.[47]

Leniency was indeed necessary. Opium was widely and openly grown in Bukhara. Mohan Lal wrote in his travelogue: "Tobacco and rice, though cultivated at Bokhara, are not so good as in Qarshi. Opium is planted here abundantly, and also mulberry trees."[48] Russian sources concurred that opium was planted in Bukhara and its environs, but clarify that much more of it was imported—especially via the route from Rustaq (now in northern Afghanistan) through Kulab, as well as from Iran via Mashhad.[49] Officials portrayed opium as an indigenous vice making inroads among Russian soldiers and settlers, but Russian rule may have indirectly facilitated the spread of opium by constructing railroads and enabling Bukhara's control over its hinterland.[50]

---

wa-l-ḥashīsh wa-l-ʾafyūn) were forbidden, with the caveat being that—unlike alcohol—they necessitate discretionary punishment (*taʿzīr*) rather than the more serious punishments for crimes against God (*ḥudūd*). Dimishqī, *al-Lubāb fī sharḥ al-kitāb*, 3/216.

46. Unlike the previous reference to *kōknār*, which likely referred to its simple meaning ("poppy") since it was paired with *afyūn*, this usage referred to a sort of opium cocktail popular in Iran and Central Asia during this period: "Of the various forms in which opium could be ingested, *kōknār* was the most addictive. *Kōknār*, which is the Persian word for the actual poppy but here refers to 'a liquor made by soaking in water the bruised capsules of the poppy after the seeds have been taken out,' was a dark brown and bitter bouillon and had been known since Antiquity." Matthee, *The Pursuit of Pleasure*, 107; Rempel', *Dalekoe i blizkoe*, 66–67.

47. TsGARUz F i-126 O 1 D 1730, f. 107a. A Russian work based on oral histories recounted during the early Soviet period mentions that night watchmen (*mīrshab*) were well aware of the profusion of opium dens, but were paid a "bribe" (*chutal'*) in order to turn a blind eye. Although the cited fatwa does not use the term *chutal'*, one wonders whether these bribes were "bribes" at all. Rempel', *Dalekoe i blizkoe*, 67.

48. Lal, *Travels in the Panjab, Afghanistan, & Turkistan, to Balk, Bokhara, and Herat*, 132.

49. "Ter'iak i 'nasha' v Bukhare," 4–5. The author further noted that the pass in this mountainous area was only open for a month and a half during the summer, which meant that Bukhara was flooded with narcotics in August. (Today, narcotics are transported along much the same route, but with fewer seasonal impediments.) On the route from Iran, see Āshtiyānī, *ʿIbrat-nāma*, 78.

50. Kulab was incorporated into Bukhara only in the 1870s under Russian protection, which likely facilitated internal trade routes. Also, opium was apparently smuggled into Turkestan via the Russian postal service with near impunity. Finally, the author noted with some puzzlement that opium usage is highest in Turkestan near the Russian border, which suggests the possibility that the narcotics trade was given a boost by the demand of Russian settlers. "Ter'iak i 'nasha' v Bukhare," 6, 10.

One estimate put the proportion of adult males in Bukhara who frequented opium dens at 40 percent.[51]

More remarkable than active cultivation or the presence of regulated opium dens is the fact that biographical dictionaries devoted to extoling Bukhara's greatest ulama did not hesitate to mention that a given scholar was a known opium addict.[52] For instance, Isa Makhdum was a prominent *mufti* and *mudarris* from Khoqand. The biographer described Isa in glowing terms, stating that he "steered many students to the very highest ranks [of the scholarly elite]." The next sentence continues that earlier in his life he fell victim to the evil passions within him (*nafs*) and gave in to the pleasures of opium, to the extent that his frame was constantly doubled over.[53] The biographer was in no way condoning Isa's poppy addiction. The author portrayed the habit as a pitiable vice, certainly, but it was not one so damning as to preclude inclusion in the ranks of the best scholars of the age. In line with the legal rulings, the biographer suggested that the substance abuse was outside of his control.[54] Like most *tazkira* entries, the entire biography for Isa was only a paragraph long, yet the author deemed opiate addiction sufficiently integral to merit inclusion.

The case of Isa Makhdum was in no way unique, either in its reference to opiates or the sympathetic attitude of his biographer. The author of a different biographical dictionary wrote that Juma-Quli Khumuli was "much of the time high as Omar Khayyam."[55] While serving as *qazi*, Khumuli was known to shout out Qur'anic passages such as, "Whomever Allah wills, He leads astray; and whomever He wills, He puts him on a straight path," or "On that Day, We shall ask Hell, 'Are you now full?' Hell will answer, 'Are there any more?' "[56] In this respect, this account would seem to support the Rus-

51. Rempel', *Dalekoe i blizkoe*, 66.

52. Russian sources corroborate this association, reporting that opium (unlike hashish) was generally a pastime of Bukharan state officials, merchants, and mullahs. "No fewer than five percent of the poor and sixty-eighty percent of the rich in Bukhara intoxicate themselves with these narcotics." "Ter'iak i 'nasha' v Bukhare," 10.

53. ʿAbdī, *Tazkirat al-shuʿarā*, ff. 126a–126b.

54. *Mard-i bēchāra qabl az āwān-i fatā bā kus̱r-i hawāyij-i khūd bi-nafs mubāshir shud*. To further make this point, the author also quoted a hadith to the effect that he who carries his own commercial goods will be free from old age. ʿAbdī, *Taẕkirat al-shuʿarā*, f. 126b.

55. *Kōknār . . . hama waqt Khayyām-ṣifat sargarm kashīdan wa khwurdan*. Wāżih, *Tuḥfat al-aḥbāb*, f. 73. This is the same Khumūlī discussed in chapter 1.

56. Qur'an 6:39, 50:30. Commentators interpreted this passage in mutually contradictory ways, but in general the foot of God was understood as a symbol of mercy, as it blocked the descent to Hell. Nasr et al., *The Study Quran*. This was probably the interpretation Khumūlī had in mind. Wāżih, *Tuḥfat al-aḥbāb*, f. 73.

sians' accusations that opium came between the ulama and their legal duties, prompting them to write incoherent, self-contradictory rulings.[57]

Khumuli understood that his addiction to opium and hashish was not above board, but his favored quotations also suggest an understanding that his behavior was not irredeemable.[58] As the biographer grudgingly conceded, Khumuli managed to produce both history and poetry through the cloud of opium smoke that enveloped his "noble life."[59] Once again, poppies are unambiguously portrayed in a negative light, albeit as an outcome dictated by the will of God. The author characterized Khumuli's affinity for narcotics as a "defect" (*illat*) rather than a personal failing. This stance aligns with the attitude encountered in the legal texts, where condemnation is tempered with recognition that self-restraint was not possible for everyone.

In other cases, even tepid disapproval was absent from descriptions of opium use. A biographer wrote that Mullah Muhammad Isa "Haran" of Uratepa acted "entirely without constraint or care" and that his mind was dominated by opium, hashish, and all manner of other intoxicants.[60] These substances did not hinder his superb understanding of his madrasa lessons. It is possible that Haran's relative youth at the time of writing mitigated Wazih's frustration with the student's constant state of intoxication.[61]

It is worth emphasizing that sources did not tie opium to any of the personas of the high Persianate intellectual in particular. Russians tended to associate opium abuse with ecstatic *qalandars*.[62] Indeed, some addict-scholars, such as Mukhtar Makhdum "Afzah," fell into this category

57. In 1911 the Russian Political Agent in Bukhara privately accused Ghiyāṣ al-Dīn Aʿlam of contradicting himself even when writing about a single issue: RGVIA F 400 O 1 D 4000, f. 11a. However, as Paolo Sartori demonstrates, Russian officials had trouble understanding that in Islamic law multiple opinions coexisted on a single issue, and oftentimes insisted that Turkestani ulama provide a single "true" ruling. Sartori, *Visions of Justice*, 252.

58. Unlike opium (*taryāk*), which appears with some frequency in sources written by ulama, the consumption of hemp (*nasha*) seems to have been a relatively rare vice and was not addressed in the legal texts I have seen. This may have been because hemp was associated with the lower classes, while opium was a pleasure of the rich. According to one Russian source, in Bukhara ten pounds of hemp (which was imported from Yarkend rather than southern Turkestan) could be purchased for the price of one pound of opium. Apparently, Russians ironically referred to hemp usage as "smoking champagne" (*kurit' shampanskoe*). "Ter'iak i 'nasha' v Bukhare," 9.

59. Wāżiḥ, *Tuḥfat al-aḥbāb*, f. 73a.

60. Muḥammad ʿĪsā inherited the unusual pen name (*takhalluṣ*) of "Hārān" from his grandfather, who had been given the moniker personally by ʿUmar Khan (1811–22) of the Ming dynasty in Khoqand, which ruled Uratepa at the time (see chapter 2). Wāżiḥ, *Tuḥfat al-aḥbāb*, ff. 237–38.

61. Wāżiḥ, *Tuḥfat al-aḥbāb*, ff. 237–38.

62. Franz Wennberg describes the Jadid and Russian view thusly: "wild-bearded illiterate pedophilic *qalandars* (stray mystics) who smoked opium, threw stones at passing trains, and called for jihad against the Russian infidels from various madrasas (higher educational institutions) and half-ruined sufi-convents in the Bukharan countryside." *An Inquiry into Bukharan Qadimism*, 5.

(*qalandar-mashrab*).[63] In the recollections of an Iranian traveler, the drug was associated with poets and *maddahs* (minstrels), as fresh-faced youths in an opium den recited from the *Shah-nama* to hedonist (*ayyash*) patrons as music played in the background.[64] Others, such as Sayyid Makhdum Bukhari "Nazmi" and Khumuli, were identified primarily by their judgeship.[65] Eshan Khwajah "Walih" was distinguished as one of the great Samarqandi descendants of the Prophet and a master of both Persian and Turkic poetry, but his eyes were also "devoid of light due to constant opium abuse."[66] Recreational poppy use was also an activity of madrasa students, such as Haran, and madrasa instructors, such as Isa Makhdum. Narcotics constituted yet another occupation in the repertoire of the ulama. Unlike other activities (such as poetry, calligraphy, or the occult), opium was not a source of praise and emulation, but nor was it sufficiently disgraceful to warrant omission.

Like many of his peers, Muhammad Salih "Nawha" was an excellent madrasa student, a fine scribe, and even better poet who happened to be addicted to opium. In his case, however, taking up the poppy was portrayed as an achievement. Previously, he had devoted himself to the pleasures of wine, until one day he "repented" of forbidden substances and turned to opium instead.[67] Before making the switch, he had become famous for the following quatrain: "In my *mazhab* [sect or school of law], if you do wine right; it's much better than turning toward opium; neither man nor woman, living or dead; whether sleeping or awake, will be drunk instead of sober."[68] After he turned to opium, he composed the following verses to take its place: "Opium is very nice, and offers a good high; it [opium] is the broom that sweeps away the cloudy day while having the benefit of a rain cloud [i.e., slaking thirst]; it [opium] is not like the earthly sun; but like the sun it rises and sets."[69]

The intersection of diverse genres allows for different interpretations of Russian accounts, which explicitly paint the opium houses as illicit hives

63. Wāżiḥ, *Tuḥfat al-aḥbāb*, f. 19.

64. This author was describing opium dens in Samarqand, then under Bukharan control. Āshtiyānī, *ʿIbrat-nāma*, 110. On *maddāḥs*, see chapter 4. On Āshtiyānī, see Eden, *Slavery and Empire in Central Asia*, chap. 3.

65. Muḥtaram, *Tazkirat al-shuʿarā*, ff. 171a–172a. The 1883 *qāżī* of Samarqand colluded with Russian customs officials to smuggle opium. Morrison, *Russian Rule in Samarkand, 1868–1910*, 261.

66. Wāżiḥ, *Tuḥfat al-aḥbāb*, f. 214–15.

67. *Ākhir al-amr az ān munkarāt tāyib gardīd wa bi-kayfiyyāt-i afyūn rāghib gardīd*. Muḥtaram, *Tazkirat al-shuʿarā*, ff. 172b–173a.

68. Muḥtaram, *Tazkirat al-shuʿarā*, ff. 172b–173a.

69. *Afyūn naghz ast kayf-i khūbī dārad; jārōb-i gham ast u naʿt-i rūyī dārad; khūrshīd-i jahān nīst walī chūn khūrshīd; ū nīz ṭulūʿī ū ghurūbī dārad*. *Rūyī*, which here means raincloud, is related to *irwāʾ*, which carries the connotation of slaking thirst. Muḥtaram, *Tazkirat al-shuʿarā*, ff. 172b–173a.

of scum and villainy. One Soviet-era writer, L. I. Rempel', wrote (based on oral testimony) that a *koknar-khana* looked just like an ordinary tea house (*chay-khana*), and like the latter was an open space viewable from the street. Locals ate pilaf, drank tea, and, yes, also drank an opium beverage. In other words, at least some of these *koknar-khanas* were ordinary tea houses where *koknar* was one of the drinks on offer.[70]

Rempel' continued his description:

> Among the fifty-or-so patrons [of a particularly well-known opium den] one could find mullahs, *muftis*, Turkic nobles, shopkeepers, and sometimes farmers, soldiers, coachmen, and gamblers. In front of every patron was a teapot . . . They would chew *chakida* [tablets produced from dried, raw opium] before eating pilaf in small portions, the size of a pea . . . After pilaf, a performer [*siyar-khwan*] recited tales of heroic deeds of champions of the faith—with unexpectedly affected speech.[71] The audience absorbed the shouts of the reciter, expressing horror, or bursting into tears. In the second half of the day, a new set of patrons appeared and the whole cycle began anew.[72]

According to this description, the tea house / opium den appears no more nefarious than a typical pub.[73] It was a space where people from diverse walks of life congregated to eat, have a drink, and be entertained. Reading against the grain of the above account, it is not so hard to imagine the likes of Mulla Muhammad Isa "Haran" or Muhammad Salih "Nawha" frequenting such a place, and without shame. After all, the madrasa was right next door, and with the tales of prophets and saints resounding through the air, one cannot characterize it as an entirely "un-Islamic" space.[74]

This is not to say that attitudes toward narcotics were not without contradiction. As with folk magic, lenient treatment of opium bridged genres of

---

70. Rempel', *Dalekoe i blizkoe*, 66–67. The Iranian traveler Āshtiyānī referred to the establishment as "opium dens" (*kōknār-khāna*), but also observed that patrons consumed tea and listened to poetry. Āshtiyānī, *'Ibrat-nāma*, 110.

71. The same author discusses the figure of the *maddāḥ* elsewhere, and by that name; sacred biography (*siyar*) was part of the repertoire of the *maddāḥ*, suggesting that these were related categories.

72. Rempel', *Dalekoe i blizkoe*, 67.

73. Rempel' himself clearly viewed opium as a social scourge in Bukhara, and it is probably not a coincidence that opium was one of the earliest targets of Soviet health campaigns in the 1920s. Latypov, "The Soviet Doctor and the Treatment of Drug Addiction." Latypov's empirical work also debunks the stereotype (dating to the pre-Soviet period) that opium abuse was specific to the native population in Central Asia.

74. Rempel' in several cases describes the location of opium dens in relation to adjacent madrasas. *Dalekoe i blizkoe*, 67. But then, in Bukhara, pretty much everything was next door to a madrasa.

writing, although here too one begins to detect internal tension. The legal sources make it clear that opium-smoking was not a practice to be emulated and only tolerated in moderation and in specific circumstances. Biographical dictionaries were also careful not to portray the use of narcotics in an actively positive light, but the poetical anthologies seemed to view it as a practice not at all out of the ordinary for the "high" (literally and figuratively) Persianate intellectual while wearing his literary hat. The authors penning these poetical *tazkiras* were also versed in Islamic law and hence could not openly condone substance usage, but these volumes were nevertheless thick with ecstatic love imagery and altered mental states. The content of the poems accompanying the short biographies in these poetical anthologies was rife with imagery of ecstasy and love for God.

The differing lens of separate genres corresponds to the social context in question. Though metaphorical, a poetical genre pregnant with the language of altered mental states anchored the lived experience of those ulama partaking in opium use in Perso-Islamic imagery. Similarly, legal genres provided the requisite tools for the scholars performing the role of a public official to ensure that opium abuse did not get out of hand. The tension between these depictions was real, but less pronounced than another substance with imagery even more pervasive in poetry—and much more ambiguous than even opium when it came to the law: wine.

Wine and Spirit-ed Revelry

For many, the Persianate cultural tradition is almost synonymous with wine, poetry, and romance. There is little debate that wine culture had deep roots in the broader region, with one wine jug from the Zagros Mountains dating back to 3500–3000 BCE.[75] The Islamic conquests did little to arrest wine consumption, though it did change attitudes toward it, and wine as a literary trope was even augmented by Islamization, as the previously independent genre of Arabic wine poetry fused with the Persian one.[76] Before the twelfth century the ubiquitous imagery of wine-soaked banquet revelry was a literal reflection of actual practice in medieval courts.[77] It was only in the following

75. McGovern, "Iranian Wine at the 'Dawn of Viniculture,'" 13.

76. Yarshater, "The Theme of Wine-Drinking and the Concept of the Beloved in Early Persian Poetry," 46.

77. Brookshaw, "Lascivious Vines, Corrupted Virgins, and Crimes of Honor." However, this imagery and practice of courtly wine revelry was alive and well in Safavid Iran. Matthee, *The Pursuit of Pleasure*, 62.

centuries that wine—as depicted in poetry—was fused with sufism, thereby taking on more exclusively metaphorical connotations.[78]

A legend about Yusuf Hamadani (d. 1141), the first of the Khwajagan community of Central Asian sufis, marks this transition in no uncertain terms: "When [Yusuf Hamadani] resolved to travel from Khurasan into Bukhara, and crossed the Amu River, all of the wine (*sharab*) in the territory of Bukhara turned to vinegar (*sirka*)."[79] Despite this miraculous feat of piety, vinegar failed to make inroads against wine's cultural status. Metaphors involving wine and the cupbearer (*saqi*) remained popular facets of Persianate culture in early modern and colonial Central Asia. For instance, Khumuli wrote in his autobiography that in his school days he had been such a tenacious student that "alacrity poured into this drunk's chalice and the antidote/opium of gentleness was mixed with harshness."[80] A hagiography described the followers of Ata'allah Khwaja visiting his grave as "crazy people drunk with desire for the chalice of eternity from service to the *shaykh al-Islam*."[81]

The Run-of-the-Mill Intoxicated Poetry of Eshan Imla

Eshan Imla (d. 1750/51) was a renowned shaykh of eighteenth-century Bukhara, and many ulama of the long nineteenth century traced their spiritual lineage through him, including Ata'allah Khwaja.[82] So respected was his mastery of jurisprudence and theology that the last Ashtarkhanid monarch of Bukhara dispatched him to debate the Sunni-Shi'a split with Nadir Shah Afshar, who at the time was laying siege to Bukhara.[83] Imla was no slouch when it came to the Islamic sciences.

What sorts of poetry might such a figure compose? Fortunately, a substantial collection of Imla's verses has survived. For instance:

> The debauched rogues (*rind*) of the world gather in our tavern (*kharabat*); desiring the wine in our cup.

78. Brookshaw, "Lascivious Vines, Corrupted Virgins, and Crimes of Honor," 92.

79. Muḥammad Nāṣir al-Bukhārī, *Tuḥfat al-zā'irīn*, 39. The Khwājagān community has been the subject of numerous studies, summarized most recently in Siddiqui, "The Medieval Khwājagān and the Early Naqshbandīyya."

80. *Bi-sāghar-i ẕihn-i ēn makhmūr hushyārī rēkht wa taryāk luṭf rā bar har qahr dar āmīkht*. Khumūlī, *Tarjuma-i ḥāl*, f. 11b.

81. Riżawī, *Manāqib wa maqāmāt-i ʿAṭā'allāh*, f. 75a–75b.

82. The significance of Imlā's tomb to Bukhara's sacred geography is discussed in chapter 2.

83. This episode is detailed in the next chapter and Pickett, "Nadir Shah's Peculiar Central Asian Legacy," 499.

> Everywhere someone sits in a ruinous place; each dawn and dusk he's at the gate of our mad court.[84]

Or:

> I'm drunk (*makhmur*), so where's the main road to the tavern (*may-khana*)?; Where's a bed for this mad heart?
> Imla was lost in a typhoon of wine; Where are the wine bearer (*saqi*), the wine, the cup, and the measure?[85]

These verses are unremarkable for the Persian literary tradition, which is saturated with references to inebriated revelry going back to the formation of New Persian.[86] And this does not prove that Imla himself engaged in any of the activities captured in these verses; it is fairly obvious that the "worldly tavern," for instance, is a metaphor for the material realm, and the wine a means to mystically transcend it. Imla's (whose poetic alias means, not coincidentally, "filling up") poetry demonstrates that even the most august jurists were not operating in a world separate from Persianate wine culture.

Colonial accounts reported that wine was strictly forbidden in the Central Asian protectorates, and there is some support in nineteenth-century legal texts for the wine-strictly-as-metaphor theory.[87] *Jungs* tended to devote less space to questions of alcohol than to opium, since the former was clearly forbidden and had been for centuries, while the latter was seen as a more complex issue.[88] A lithographed *jung* specimen duly included a section on wine but left the two pages devoted to the subject almost entirely blank. Instead, it quoted Arabic *fiqh* asserting that wine was forbidden and then proceeded to define the substance.[89]

Remarkably, sometimes these collections of legal rulings drawn from a corpus condemning wine consumption also included wine poetry (*saqi-nama*) scribbled into margins and spare pages.[90] Wine poetry scattered amid legal

84. Ṣafar-zāda, *Dīwān-i Imlā ʾ-i Bukhārāyī*, 295.

85. Ṣafar-zāda, *Dīwān-i Imlā ʾ-i Bukhārāyī*, 296.

86. Yarshater, "The Theme of Wine-Drinking and the Concept of the Beloved in Early Persian Poetry."

87. There may have been a few Jewish-operated distilleries in precolonial Khoqand. Schwarz, "Preliminary Notes on Viticulture and Winemaking in Colonial Central Asia," 240.

88. *Sbornik vypisok iz sochinenii po fikkhu i iuridicheskikh kazusov*, f. 298a. See also Matthee, "Alcohol in the Islamic Middle East," 102.

89. Ḥusam al-Dīn, *Jūng-i fatāwā wa maḥżarāt*, ff. 333a–334a.

90. *Sbornik konvoliut*, f. 221b. The poetry seems to have been written in whatever space happened to be available; there does not appear to have been any connection between the poetry and whatever

texts could be read as evidence either for or against the strictly metaphorical nature of the genre. Perhaps the figurative nature of the verses was so self-evident to the owner of the *jung* that it was safe to include in a book condemning the literal embodiment of the same imagery. It is also possible that the poetical context, along with its associated wine culture, was cognitively separate from the legal one, even though an individual scholar was at home in both social roles.

But was this wine imagery that saturated Persian poetry reducible to metaphor? Muhammad Salih "Nawha" was described as a bit of a lush before seeing the error of his ways.[91] Explicit evidence of this sort is rare, however. Even in Nawha's case, the substance he was drinking was referred to using a term with legalistic connotations—*munkarat* "forbidden things."[92] The same term is rarely found in poetical references to wine (a concept for which the Persian language is replete with synonyms), which presume metaphorical usage, even in a case like Nawha's wherein the wine imagery is explicitly confirmed as reflective of actual events. It may be that Nawha was exceptional, or it may be that the distance between the literary world depicted in power and the social reality of the ulama was less than often supposed.[93]

Russian correspondence provides further evidence of ulama pushing wine consumption beyond the allegorical. In 1919, the Russian political agent alerted his Bukharan counterpart that one Ruzi-quli Qalandar had been caught brewing wine, and suggested that he be punished according to Sharia.[94] This stands as evidence of local production of wine in Bukhara (at least by the late colonial period, and likely earlier as well), and in a context seemingly associated with the scholarly milieu.[95] Despite the radical genre differences between colonial writing and Persianate poetry, this document reinforces the picture presented in the account of Nawha: wine was unambiguously forbidden according to Islamic law (a fact emphasized even in the colonial source), but consumed and brewed nonetheless—even by ulama.

---

legal ruling it happened to border. On the *sāqī-nāma* genre, see Losensky, "Sāqi-Nāma (Book of the Cupbearer)."

91. Muḥtaram, *Tazkirat al-shuʿarā*, ff. 172b–173a.

92. The term alludes to the maxim of "commanding right and forbidding wrong," enjoined on all Muslims, and especially the *muḥtasib*, which was one of the hats worn by the ulama.

93. This judgment is shared by Matthee, "Alcohol in the Islamic Middle East," 106.

94. TsGARUz F i-126 O 2 D 685, ff. 1–2. "Wine brewing" is *vinokurenie* in the Russian document, translated as *muskirāt ṭayār kardan* in the Persian rendition.

95. Admittedly, I am assuming that Ruzi-quli is in some sense of the ulama only by virtue of his name (Qalandar/Kalendarov). Chapter 5 argues that qalandar was one among many social roles embodied by the ulama.

This tacit acceptance of wine culture—particularly the more metaphorically ambiguous imagery—gave way to condemnation in genres beyond legal writing. In 1886/87, Wazih—author of a major poetical anthology—went on the Hajj overland via Istanbul and composed a travelogue describing the experience.[96] He was less than impressed by Merv, which Russia had recently conquered (in 1884), and was already flooded with Russians, Armenians, and Jews. Wazih complained that this made living life according to Sharia difficult, since distractions such as wine and gambling were rife.[97] Once again, genre seems to play a role here: in the context of a genre emphasizing the strange and fantastical, the very same behavior that connected to local Persianate culture in the context of biographies of the ulama was condemned. Both of Wazih's works are permeated with references to wine (and even gambling, another common poetical trope), but only one of them mediated that practice through poetic metaphor.

Wine was not the only alcoholic drink appearing in historical sources: Jewish "vodka" (*peisakhovka*) and a drink called "boza" make cameo appearances as well. Boza is a malt drink fermented from corn and wheat and is popular to the present day, particularly in former Ottoman territories.[98] Jewish communities brewed a drink called *peisakhovka*, which apparently was sold to Muslims. In 1914 the Russian governor of Samarqand complained to the Bukharan government that *peisakhovka* was being transported from Shahrisabz for sale in Samarqand, where the open trade in spirits was forbidden.[99] Ironically, in this case it was the colonial power concerned with the legal implications of the alcohol industry, not Bukhara.

Although boza and *peisakhovka* consumption was not explicitly attributed to the ulama, the drink *musallas* was indeed enjoyed by some scholars.

---

96. This travelogue was apparently quite popular, as it was copied numerous times and then lithographed in Kagan (New Bukhara, the Russian settlement) in 1904.

97. Wāżiḥ used a term for "distraction" (*lahw*) that appears in legal texts in the sense of distracting one from correct religious practice. He further complained that Christian women did not cover their faces. Wāżiḥ, *Gharā ʾib al-khabar fī ʿajā ʾib al-safar*, ff. 10a–10b.

98. Boza was condemned along with arak in a *jung* legal ruling. *Sbornik vypisok iz sochinenii po fikkhu i iuridicheskikh kazusov*, ff. 297b–298a. This ruling could have been adapted from an Ottoman legal manual, though it is attested in Central Asia as well: Kılıç-Schubel, "Writing Women," 412. In Ottoman law it seems that janissaries were permitted to drink boza, but not wine and other harder beverages. Baer, *Honored by the Glory of Islam*, 118.

99. The Russian section of the document describes *peisakhovka* as "Jewish vodka"; the Persian translation describes it simply as Arak (*ʿaraq*). Apparently the name of the drink is related to "Pasah" (Passover). TsGARUz F i-126 O 2 F 163, ff. 97–98. Arak was condemned alongside boza in the aforementioned *jung* ruling (*Sbornik vypisok iz sochinenii po fikkhu i iuridicheskikh kazusov*, ff. 297b–298a). The Turkic newspaper *Tūrān* reported in 1912 that two Bukharan soldiers were lashed (*21 darra-i sharʿī taʿzīr qilinub*) for consuming arak in an Armenian shop. *Tūrān*, December 6, 1912, f. 3a.

Musallas, a kind of wine cooked until two-thirds of it has evaporated (lit. "made into three" in Arabic), was on firmer ground than boza, wine, or even opium when it came to the law.[100] Although Hanafis were divided on the lawfulness of this particular beverage, Marghinani, whose legal work, the *Hidaya*, was easily the most influential in Central Asia, ruled that it was acceptable.[101] Muhammad Hisari's memoir suggests that this drink was consumed as a more respectable substitute for the real thing (i.e., wine). In 1878/9 Hisari came down with an illness after working in the chancellery of the province of Ziya al-Din and spent several weeks recovering after consulting doctors.[102] During this respite he exchanged by courier lengthy verses with his friend Mirza Muhammad Yusuf in Samarqand. Yusuf was, according to Hisari, a celebrated poet in his own time renowned for his verse and riddle. The genre of poetry the two friends exchanged was *saqi-nama*, or "book of the cupbearer," a Persian poetical genre in which the narrator seeks relief from his hardships by repeatedly summoning the serving boy to bring him wine. Once again reality and metaphor intersected, as licit, one-third strength wine (i.e., *musallas*) lubricated Hisari's correspondence, for the aforementioned doctors had prescribed *musallas* as the perfect remedy to ease his affliction.[103]

Romancing the Beloved Today, Sexual Panic Tomorrow

In the Persian cosmopolis, wine poetry would not be complete without one additional ingredient: the Beloved, a gender-ambiguous figure serving as source of romantic and sexual desire. This figure is often male in the strictly biological sense, at least within certain poetic subgenres, but recent scholarship has challenged binary categories of gender for the early modern period and nuanced our understanding of this figure, which does not easily map to modern categories of male or female.[104] Numerous terms for describing men suitable for amorous relationships with other men circulated in the pre-

---

100. Both wine and opium were used for medicinal purposes since antiquity. Matthee, *The Pursuit of Pleasure*, 39–40, 101.

101. Haider, "Contesting Intoxication."

102. Ḥiṣārī even describes his work in the regional chancery (*khān-dabīrī*) using wine imagery (e.g., *sāghar-i shukrāna*). Ḥiṣārī, *Yāddāsht-hā*, f. 58b.

103. Ḥiṣārī, *Yāddāsht-hā*, ff. 58b–59a.

104. Brookshaw writes that in the *sāqī-nāma* genre: "It is rare that we encounter a specifically female human beloved . . . On occasion we encounter female slaves (sing. *kanīzak*, *jāriya*), although by far the most present female in the poetry is the wine herself." "Lascivious Vines, Corrupted Virgins, and Crimes of Honor," 96. Of course, there are plenty of male-female romances in Persian literature more generally (Layla and Majnun, Shirin and Farhad, etc.). Walter Andrews and Mehmet Kalpakli emphasize that a varied spectrum of genders was not exclusive to the Islamic world, but spanned the early modern world, most certainly including Europe. *The Age of Beloveds*,

modern Persianate world, many of which were not associated with effeminacy, but corresponded to life stage: young beardless men were considered separately from both women and older men.[105] The Beloved was a common feature of pre-Soviet Central Asia as well, and colonial accounts of dancing boys played a large role in the depiction of Persianate courtly culture as libertine and decadent.[106] N. A. Maev wrote in his 1875 travelogue that while being hosted by the Beg of Kitab (a city adjoining Shahrisabz) dancing boys were sent out to entertain the Russian delegation. By this point Maev had seen so many similar spectacles that his reaction was decidedly nonplussed: "Contrary to our expectation, however, we did not find anything new, nothing noteworthy."[107]

The content of local accounts is not so different from that of Maev, even though the imagery is. For instance, Muhammad Hisari wrote that upon his appointment the new governor of a Bukharan province sent two dancing boys (*shatir*, lit. "one who teases") as a gift. A high Persianate intellectual such as Hisari knew just what sort of poetic language best described these Beloveds: "From the sound of the bells on their feet [even] the nightingales of beautiful voice forgot how to lament."[108] And: "Even the cypress tree bent over in envy upon glimpsing their figures."[109] Chronicles portrayed similarly sexualized musical events, though usually in a more negative light and in combination with drunken carousing by the Turkic nobility.[110]

---

28. For an examination of how this third gender was transformed in the encounter with modernity, see Najmabadi, *Women with Mustaches and Men without Beards*.

105. Najmabadi, *Women with Mustaches and Men without Beards*, 22–23.

106. Babadzhanov, *Kokandskoe khanstvo*, sec. IV.1. Babadzhanov directly connects the dancing boys of Central Asia with *bacha-bāzī*, which is usually associated with Pashtun culture in Afghanistan and has the connotation of pederasty. Babadzhanov, *Kokandskoe khanstvo*, 570. Although I have not seen this term in a local source (and it is unclear whether Babadzhanov is citing a contemporaneous source or making an inference), based on photographs and descriptions of the practice (e.g., ankle bells [*zangūla*], Ḥiṣārī, *Yāddāsht-hā*, f. 22b), cultural continuity between these practices does indeed seem likely. There is danger in extending that continuity to binary conceptions of sexuality, which was not necessarily the case in the late Persianate period. However, it would be misleading to portray these relationships as romantic and nonexploitative just because the ulama saw it that way. For an example of a study of modern *bacha-bāzī*, see de Lind van Wijngaarden and Rani, "Male Adolescent Concubinage in Peshawar, Northwestern Pakistan."

107. Maev, *Ocherki Bukharskago khanstva*, 16–17. See also Schuyler and Grigor'ev, *Turkistan*, 132–35. A Persian source noted that the city of Urgut (located near Samarqand) was well known for its dancing boys and girls. ʿAbd al-Ghafūr-i Turkistānī, *Bayān-i dāstān*, f. 43b.

108. *Az ṣadāyi pur-nawāyi zangūla-ash bulbulān khūsh al-ḥāl rāh-i fighān farāmūsh kardī.* Ḥiṣārī, *Yāddāsht-hā*, f. 22b.

109. *Az rashk-i qāmat-i ān-hā sarw-i būstān-rā qāmat-i iqāmat kham gardīdī.* Ḥiṣārī, *Yāddāsht-hā*, f. 22a.

110. For instance, the brief reign of ʿUmar Khan was characterized by so much wine drinking and so many Beloveds that the nobility begged Amir Naṣrallāh to take the throne in 1827. *Muntakhab al-tawārīkh*, 1:419.

Young scholars who made it into the biographical dictionaries, such as Abdallah Beg Yakkabaghi, were described not only in terms of their erudition, but also in terms of their physical beauty, invoking Beloved imagery.[111] In some cases, romantic insinuations were not merely in the eye of the biographer. Mulla Gul Muhammad Biy "Afghan" (who was also a Bedil aficionado) fell so hopelessly in love with a youthful slave boy by the name of Adil Khan that "the reins of rational thought and self-control slipped from his grasp," to the point that he wished to do nothing else but gaze at the boy's visage.[112] Tragically, Adil Khan perished, which prompted the heartbroken Gul Muhammad Biy to quit his position and write poetry about his Beloved full time.[113] In this account, the Beloved is a metaphor for the divine, but it is also directly connected with an actual romance.

So far, depictions of erotic romance with the Beloved are split along the local-colonial divide, with the colonial accounts condemning a single practice romanticized by high Persianate intellectuals. But what of other genres produced by the ulama? Legal works of this period took an uncompromising stance against sodomy, as did the medieval *fiqh* texts they cited, and even certain entries from the *akhlaq* (morality) genre.[114] Consider the distance between the erotic poetry quoted above and a legal opinion about sodomy enjoining the ruler to apply discretionary punishment (*ta'zir*), such as beatings, according to the law; and that if the acts of sodomy were habitual, that the offender should be killed.[115] One particular *jung* ruling seems to implicitly recognize that homosexual romance with the Beloved was common practice in high society: "In punishing these kinds of offenses the masses (*awam*), the nobility (*ashraf*), and the noblest of the noble are on equal footing."[116]

It is critical to bear in mind that Hisari would have been fully capable of penning any of the above legal rulings; after all, he was working for a

---

111. Żiyā', *Taẕkirat al-khaṭṭāṭīn*, f. 73a. ʿAbdallāh Beg was also a deposed prince; his story is discussed in chapter 3.

112. *Zimām-i ʿaql wa shikēbā'ī az dast rafta*. Wāżiḥ, *Tuḥfat al-aḥbāb*, ff. 22–23.

113. Wāżiḥ, *Tuḥfat al-aḥbāb*, ff. 22–23.

114. From the *akhlāq* genre, Aḥmad Dānish (d. 1896/97) weighed in on appropriate kinds of sexual union, arguing that romantic passion is virtuous so long as it is contained and in accordance with the Sharia, and that the Sharia countenanced only one kind of physical penetration (i.e., heterosexual). Aḥmad Dānish, *Nawādir al-waqā'iʿ*, ff. 348a–349a.

115. This ruling is justified with reference to the story of Lot, a name etymologically related to the legal term for sodomy (*liwāṭa*). *Wa-law ʿumila ʿamalun qawmi Lūṭin, yuʿzaru bi-l-taʿzīr al-balīgh, wa-inna kāna ẕalik ʿādatan, yuqtalu*. *Jūng* (IVANUz no. 2844), f. 63b. Everett Rowson makes the important distinction that Islamic law is primarily concerned with the sexual act itself, not propensities or identities. "The Categorization of Gender and Sexual Irregularity in Medieval Arabic Vice Lists," 59.

116. *Sbornik vypisok iz sochinenii po fikkhu i iuridicheskikh kazusov*, f. 374b.

provincial governor, whose office was instructed to carry out the punishments detailed in the quoted legal opinions. Even though the tone and conclusions of the legal opinions were worlds apart from his lyrical descriptions of the very same phenomenon, samples from these disparate genres are not evidence of diametrically opposed worldviews embraced by separate social strata. Figures such as Hisari moved fluidly between both, adopting different textual strategies for different contexts.[117]

If there seems cognitive dissonance between homoerotic romance in poetry and anti-sodomy rulings in legal writing, anxiety about extramarital heterosexuality is even more pronounced—and less ambiguous across genres. In one *jung* opinion, a sufi claiming the wisdom to take on disciples gathered with his acolytes in a mosque. During the evenings, women with no licit relationship to any of the males present would mingle with them to sing, dance, and play musical instruments. Those present became so enraptured by the music that they lost themselves in it and carried on for three days straight.[118] It is not clear from the ruling whether these alleged women of ill repute were professional dancing girls of the sort described in other sources, or if this is evidence of more routine flouting of Sharia by women. The description would equally fit with ecstatic musical sufi performances (*sama, qawali*). Either way, it demonstrates both the seriousness of scripturalist Islam and the fact that the vision espoused by ulama acting as jurists was aspirational rather than descriptive of the society they lived in.

The legal genre was not exclusively a platform for articulating an austere vision of Islam. Scriptures can be deployed for myriad ends, and "scripturalism" need not be a euphemism for "misogynistic" or "draconian." Ulama writing in legal genres also used legal language to reign in excessive zeal, which is not surprising as it was often their fellow scholars who were engaging in forbidden behaviors. The *muhtasib* was the official often tasked with public enforcement of Islamic law. The opinion states that one evening a *muhtasib* gathered together a group of armed ruffians (*awbash*) and went out hunting for women potentially violating the Sharia. In their enthusiasm, they hopped a fence into the woman's quarter of a local neighborhood on the suspicion that there might be an unrelated male among them. The author of the opinion tersely remarked that this behavior was "unacceptable"—in part because in looking for an unrelated male in

117. Rowson observes a similar disconnect between genres in his study of sexuality as expressed in the Arabic *mujūn* genre (a kind of humorous belles-lettres). "The Categorization of Gender and Sexual Irregularity in Medieval Arabic Vice Lists."

118. *Jung-i riwāyāt*, ff. 440b–441a.

the women's quarters, the *muhtasib* and his cohort committed precisely the offense they were ostensibly seeking to prevent.[119]

Had the *muhtasib* and his henchmen in fact caught a couple in the act, the consequences may have been dire, or they may not have. According to a fatwa, one community dragged a local scholar named Abd al-Karim Khwaja before the local *qazi* accusing him of inappropriately spending time with an unsupervised woman.[120] The opinion recommended beating, confiscation of property, and imprisonment, but punishment could be more severe still, with adequate proof.[121] In Abd al-Karim's case, the offense was impropriety, but in the unrelated case of Mulla Nazar, a village imam, three witnesses (the requisite number to prove adultery) testified to catching him in the sexual act.[122] Mulla Nazar's eventual fate is unclear, but a British intelligence officer reported that adulterers were indeed publicly stoned to death in Bukhara from time to time.[123] Conversely, in his memoir Abd al-Ghafur Turkestani wrote about catching his uncle's wife in the act of kissing another man, but when he exposed her deception his uncle merely sought a divorce.[124]

The two sorts of tension considered in this chapter come to a head with wine and the Beloved. The fact that respected Islamic scholars policing illicit interactions between men and women sometimes drank wine and romanced young boys fits poorly with the outsider categories of orthodoxy and debauchery. It also highlights a disconnect within the society. Schuyler wrote about his travels in Turkestan: "In spite of what my friend the Mullah said about the dearth of amusements, I found that music and dancing have their votaries in Central Asia as well as elsewhere."[125] The "Mullah" acquaintance was speaking with his jurist hat on, which does not mean that he was blind to the society Schuyler witnessed—or even that the scholar himself necessarily refrained from some form of those activities. Choosing to write in either the legal or poetic genre had an impact on cultural conventions, even though neither directly represented social reality (as if any textual production can). Legal writing proscribed drink and homosexual acts, thereby implicitly recognizing their existence in practice. Poetic writing elevated wine and the Beloved to exalted metaphor and implied with varying degrees

119. *Sbornik sudebnykh postanovlenii*, f. 102a.

120. *Bi-tuhmat-i khalwat bi-ajnabiyya gardīda*. TsGARUz F i-126 O 1 D 1730, f. 49a.

121. TsGARUz F i-126 O 1 D 1730, f. 49a.

122. The three witnesses said: "We saw with our own eyes the aforementioned Mullā Nażar enter into the abode (*ḥawīlī*) of Mullā ʿAbd al-Shakūr with his wife and sleep with her and commit illicit acts (*khwāb karda kār-i nā-mashr[ū]ʿ karda*)." TsGARUz F i-126 O 1 D 1986, f. 1a.

123. "Cabul Diary from the 19th to the 22nd May 1871," Foreign Department, NAI, no. 761.

124. ʿAbd al-Ghafūr-i Turkistānī, *Bayān-i dāstān-i sarguzasht*, 34b–42a.

125. Schuyler and Grigor'ev, *Turkistan*, 131–32.

of directness that those tropes were reflective of lived practice, while maintaining an awareness of their legal prohibition. Between the seams of these idealized genres we glimpse a social milieu unselfconsciously articulating norms logically at odds with one another.

The image promoted in colonial sources and parts of the secondary literature, of scripturalist Islamic scholars striving to keep the excesses of their flock in check, is contradicted by the very sources written by that scholarly social group. As in all societies, contradictions were woven into the fabric of late Persianate Eurasia, and it is misleading to resolve those tensions by mapping genre conventions to separate social groups. We need not resolve seeming contradictions the historical actors themselves were content to live with.

This direction of argumentation does not imply that poetry and mysticism induced the ulama to be unserious about Sharia. Many polymaths of Islam married these ecstatic sensibilities with a deep commitment to the letter of Islamic law, and were more than willing to persecute those who took a more flexible view.

Scripturalism and the Discourse of Infidelity

The preceding sections might leave readers with an image of the ulama as a somewhat motley crew of magicians carousing with *jinn* while drawing poetic inspiration from drugs and alcohol. If we have to choose (which we do not), thus far the evidence might seem to weigh heavier for the "debauched princely court" stereotype than that of the "fanatically orthodox mullah."

The intention here is not to reclaim the high Persianate intellectual as some sort of enlightened Bohemian. Rather, it is to show that emphasizing contradictions between these different personas is inherently presentist: those disparate elements coexisted just fine through the end of the long nineteenth century. The ulama took scriptural orthopraxy seriously. Their repertoire contained tools for persecuting rival sects and religions and enforcing "correct" behavior—as interpreted by themselves.

At the risk of stating the obvious, Central Asia was overwhelmingly, and uncompromisingly, Hanafi.[126] In Arab lands, madrasas routinely sponsored teachers of all four Sunni *mazhabs* (schools of Islamic law), a practice that continues to the present day in Egypt and Saudi Arabia.[127] Although the

---

126. On the origins of this *mazhab's* monopoly in Central Asia, see Madelung, "The Spread of Maturidism and the Turks."

127. Makdisi, *The Rise of the Colleges Institutions of Learning in Islam and the West*, 187. From the twelfth century the Mamluks patronized all four *mazhabs* and established chief *qāżīs* for each of them. Lapidus, *Muslim Cities in the Later Middle Ages*, 136.

Ottoman Empire patronized the Hanafi *mazhab*, there was some degree of pluralism with other schools, especially Shafi'i.[128] The stance was quite different in Central Asia. One *jung* summarized the stance on non-Hanafi *mazhabs*: "If there was a situation such that a Hanafi *qazi* ruled on an issue in contradiction with the Hanafi *mazhab*, and that ruling does not originate from those capable of *ijtihad* [independent reasoning for the purpose of deriving law], the ruling from that *qazi* is invalid."[129] Crucially, the opinion quotes an Arabic *fiqh* text stating that there are none capable of *ijtihad* in the current age.[130] The logic underpinning this ruling does not technically ban the other three schools of law, but in practice forbids any kind of forum shopping between *mazhabs*. It is telling that the phrasing of the Persian-language section of the ruling specifies Hanafi as the paramount school of law, even though the citations from Arabic legal works implicitly recognize the validity of other *mazhabs*.[131] Thus, despite the existence in principle of multiple legitimate legal schools, there was less opportunity for picking and choosing between the *mazhabs* in Central Asia than elsewhere.[132]

Correct interpretation of Sharia was not a concern limited to theoretical rivalries between law schools. Judging by the volume of entries in various *jung*, blasphemy was an active issue in nineteenth-century Bukhara.[133] For instance, one *mufti* got himself into hot water by calling a farmer *kafir*, an accusation that could have consequences for the accuser if made in vain. However, the opinion exonerated the overzealous *mufti* on a linguistic technicality: *kafir* most commonly refers to blasphemer or infidel, but there is another connotation of the word's trilateral Arabic root meaning "to cover or hide." The opinion held that since the farmer covered seeds in earth, the active participle *kafir* was a legitimate term. The sophistry going on here seems fairly clear: it beggars belief that an Islamic scholar would casually

128. Peirce, *Morality Tales*, 114.

129. It is worth noting that even in systems with greater *maẕhab* pluralism—such as that of the Mamluks—individuals appointed within a given legal school were not allowed to give opinions or judgments based on a different one. Rapoport, "Royal Justice and Religious Law," 77.

130. *Sbornik vypisok iz sochinenii po fikkhu i iuridicheskikh kazusov*, f. 303b. The cited *fiqh* work is abbreviated as *Khulāsa*, likely referring to a well-known fatwa collection by Ṭahir al-Bukhārī Iftikhār al-Dīn (d. 1147/68).

131. Most legal works in the Hanafi tradition, including Marghīnānī's *Hidāya*, reference opinions by Shāfiʿī.

132. For instance, the coexistence of all four Sunni *maẕhabs* in Mamluk Egypt enabled a degree of legal flexibility. Rapoport, "Royal Justice and Religious Law," 77.

133. Unlike *jung*, *fiqh* manuals follow a consistent format even to the point of covering obsolete subjects (e.g., *walāʾ*, a system for attaching non-Arabs to Arab tribes during the initial expansion of Islam, but inactive after the eighth century). Crone, *Roman, Provincial, and Islamic Law*, 19. By contrast, *qāżīs* and *muftīs* could pick and choose which issues to copy into the *jung*. My assumption, therefore, is that greater numbers of entries stands as at least some indication of prevailing circumstances.

invoke an obscure Arabic meaning of *kafir* when amiably addressing a Muslim farmer. Although the opinion did not vindicate the *mufti*'s accusation of infidelity, it shows that some ulama were prepared to leverage their mastery of Sharia against others, even if not always successfully.[134]

There were plenty of legitimate ways one might be accused of blasphemy or infidelity—legitimate in the eyes of the ulama, that is. One ruling noted that denying one of the seven correctly transmitted readings of the Qur'an was tantamount to unbelief and should incur various punishments.[135] Another ruling stated that when a student showed open contempt for his teacher, the act was tantamount to disrespecting Islam itself, and the ruler (*padishah*) or one of his representatives was obliged to make an example of the offender to put fear in to the hearts of others who might do the same. By way of punishment (*ta'zir*), the *muhtasib* should lash the offender's bare shoulders in the public bazaar.[136]

The discourse of infidelity also provided a means of raising the stakes of legal disputes. As described in a fatwa, one Mulla Ibrahim was accused of an offense (unrelated to the matter at hand, and therefore unnamed in the fatwa) by someone named Usta Mirza. Mullah Ibrahim responded to the accusation by saying: "Come, let's go to the *qazi* and I will establish my honesty by swearing in the name of God [*bismillah*]."[137] To everyone's horror, Usta Mirza—incensed by what he perceived as flagrant dishonesty—responded: "fuck your *bismillah*."[138] According to the opinion, this statement disrespected the name of God, which made Usta Mirza an apostate (*murtadd*).[139] If this was a gambit on Ibrahim's part to nullify whatever Usta Mirza had accused him of, it was one with potentially lethal consequences. Whether or not the punishment for such an offense—potentially execution—was ever carried

134. "So long as a given person is not called an 'infidel of God', then there is no insult merely by the word '*kāfir*,' because the root word also has another meaning." *Tā shakhṣ-i mu'ayyan-rā kāfir-i Allāh na-guyad, ihānat na-mē-shawad bi-mujarrad-i kāfir guftan, zīrā kih kafara bi-ma'nāyi dīgar nīz āmada ast. Sbornik vypisok iz sochinenii po fikkhu i iuridicheskikh kazusov*, f. 373b.

135. Referring to denial of *qirā'āt sab'a-i mutawātira. Sbornik vypisok iz sochinenii po fikkhu i iuridicheskikh kazusov*, f. 374a. For additional, similarly vague accusations of blasphemy, see ibid., f. 377a.

136. *Sbornik vypisok iz sochinenii po fikkhu i iuridicheskikh kazusov*, f. 375a.

137. TsGARUz F i-126 O 1 D 1729, f. 109a.

138. At this point, the fatwa switches to Turki for the direct quotation: *bismillah ni ichida sikay* (which could be translated slightly more literally than what is quoted in the main text). Admittedly, the orthography and specific meaning at this stage of the fatwa remains elusive; but the broader intent of the document is clear. Above the blasphemous invective, the author wrote "God protect us" (*al-'iyāẕ bi-llāh*). TsGARUz F i-126 O 1 D 1729, f. 109a.

139. TsGARUz F i-126 O 1 D 1729, f. 109a.

out is impossible to know, as fatwas were merely opinions without coercive backing until decided by a *qazi* and implemented by the Turkic nobility.

The definition of blasphemy was subjective and malleable—perhaps dangerously so from the perspective of the likes of the farmer. For instance, another *jung* opinion stated that according to the Prophet's Sharia, there were only five legitimate ranks in Islam: *padishah*, *qazi*, *mufti*, *muhtasib*, and *mudarris*.[140] More important, they should sit and be honored in precisely that order, to the extent that presuming precedence (*taqaddum*) above an individual of one of these ranks was tantamount to disdain for the Sharia, which was in turn tantamount to infidelity (*kufr*).[141] The implications of this opinion are striking: public officials had expansive power to designate any given individual as either within or without the religion, at least in theory: challenging the established hierarchy was tantamount to challenging religion itself. During the medieval period Turks deployed the discourse of infidelity to combat rival theological and legal schools, such as Ash'arism or Shafi'ism respectively, but by the long nineteenth century this theological and legal diversity was a thing of the past in Central Asia.[142] Instead, the focus of *takfir* (the accusation of infidelity) shifted to narrow deviations from Hanafi doctrine and insufficient respect toward recognized authority.

The authority to invoke *takfir* was not limited to appointed positions such as the five listed above. One particular fatwa recounted an incident in which an ignorant man accused a *sayyid* (descendant of the Prophet Muhammad) of unbelief.[143] However, the tables were quickly turned, as the *mufti* ruled that accusing a pious *sayyid* (descendant of the Prophet) of unbelief was itself tantamount to infidelity. The *mufti* advised jailing the ignorant man, beating him, and also noted that his infidelity thereby nullified his marriage (since he was no longer Muslim, and it was illegal for a non-Muslim male to marry a Muslim female).[144]

---

140. It is unusual to see an etymologically Persian term (*pādishāh*) alongside these otherwise much more conventional positions of the "ideal Islamic state" (see chapter 8), as legal rulings overwhelmingly drew from Arabic (e.g., usually *amīr* or *sulṭān* instead of *pādishāh*).

141. "And each of these ranks should be seated in the aforementioned manner, and if they are made to behave in a manner counter to the aforementioned, inherent contempt (*istikhfāf*) is manifest, and contempt of Sharia is tantamount to infidelity (*kufr*)." *Jung-i riwāyāt i maḥżarā*, f. 32a. Unlike many *jung* entries, this one cited a Persian source (*Khazānat al-riwāyāt*) rather than Arabic *fiqh*. "Precedence" (*taqaddum*) is the same offence committed by the student in the previous example. *Sbornik vypisok iz sochinenii po fikkhu i iuridicheskikh kazusov*, f. 375a.

142. Madelung, "The Spread of Maturidism and the Turks," 126–29.

143. The author makes a point of spelling out the specific Turki phrasing of the slight: *bē īmān sin wa īmān-ing yoq* [orig. *īmān-ning*] ("you are without belief"). The offender was described as "of the ignorant masses": *az ʿawāmm al-nās-i jāhil-i nādān*. TsGARUz F i-126 O 1 D 1729, f. 101a.

144. TsGARUz F i-126 O 1 D 1729, f. 101a.

Despite the overwhelmingly Hanafi bent of Central Asia during this period, occasionally one observes the influence of other *mazhabs*, though not as a means of moderating scripturalist Hanafism. A letter from one Hajji Muhammad Darwish scrawled into Qazi Abd al-Wahid Sadr Sarir Balkhi's (d. 1885/6) notebook bears traces not only of the Hanbali *mazhab*, but also Wahhabism, the rise of which coincided with Darwish's pilgrimage to Mecca.[145] (Interestingly, this is the same Abd al-Wahid who was quoted in chapter 3 as reveling in the ecstatic poetry of Bedil during the candlelit gatherings of his school days.) The point of contention was pilgrimage to local sufi shrines in Central Asia, a practice ubiquitous to the present day. It seems that Darwish was not impressed by Abd al-Wahid's lenient stance toward shrine pilgrimage, which, as *qazi*, he had the power to restrict. Darwish contended that every sound school of law in the world agreed that circumambulating anything other than the House of God (i.e., the Kaaba in Mecca) was tantamount to *kufr*. He supported this point by relaying a hadith from Ibn Hanbal characterizing the practice as idolatry (*shirk*). Worshipping a shrine, Darwish continued, was a sin even more severe than the murder of Husayn at Karbala. Speaking of Husayn, he argued that there was no genuine evidence for any of the sacred pilgrimage sites attributed to Imam Husayn, and that lying about such things was cursed by the Prophet. Such acts, argued Darwish, should be punished by death.[146]

Darwish was not just railing against shrine pilgrimages generally. He wanted Abd al-Wahid to do something about their proliferation in Central Asia since the practice of erecting prayer flags (*tugh*) over shrines and attributing the graves to prophets and saints was heresy (*bid'a*).[147] Darwish then invoked the Qur'anic injunction of commanding right and forbidding wrong to urge Abd al-Wahid to do his job and demolish the shrine and burn the flags.[148] By

---

145. Wahhabi influence was marginal in Central Asia before the twentieth century, and evidence of this kind is rare. Critiques of sufi pilgrimage by reformist Muslims (Jadids) would become much more common toward the end of the nineteenth and early twentieth centuries. Abd al-Wāḥid Ṣarīr Balkhī died in 1885/86, meaning that this letter predated those debates by several decades.

146. *Jung-i ʿAbd al-Wāḥid Ṣadr Ṣarīr Balkhī*, f. 106b.

147. The Turkic origin of the term *tugh* marks the practice as specifically Central Asian (as opposed to what Darwīsh would have observed on the Hajj in Arabia) and stands out in a Persian letter otherwise thick with Arabic terms. These shrine (*mazār*) markers are common in Central Asia to the present day and usually consist of a pole marking a holy site (often a grave) topped with a ram's horns and adorned with various objects such as cloth flags and horses tails.

148. "Smite the grave, and let them send us to burn the flag, hat, bracelet, and mane of Satan, and raze that house of idolatry." *Ān qabr-rā bar ham bi-zanīd wa tugh-i shayṭān ū kulāh ū dast-band ū yāl-ish bi-firistand kih bi-sūzānīm wa ān but-khāna-rā bar-kanīd. Jung-i Abd al-Wāḥid Ṣadr Ṣarīr Balkhī*, ff. 106b–107a. On commanding right and forbidding wrong (*al-amr bi'l-maʿrūf wa al-nahy ʿan al-munkar*), see Cook, *Commanding Right and Forbidding Wrong in Islamic Thought*.

calling this act of demolition a duty of the first order (*farz*), the denial of which is considered *kufr*, Darwish was indirectly threatening Abd al-Wahid with the same sort of judgment awaiting those that erected the shrines in the first place. The letter closes by laying out the rewards for following his advice and the punishment on Judgment Day that would surely come if he failed to do so.[149]

Darwish was correct that shrine pilgrimage was ubiquitous in Bukhara, with pilgrimage sites attributed to prophets, saints, and legendary figures dotting the city. Debates over the legality of shrine visitation enjoyed a long pedigree in the region, but generally the fear was that such pilgrimages would substitute for the Hajj, and stances as uncompromising as that of Darwish were exceedingly rare.[150] The general consensus among the ulama was probably close to that articulated in the popular *Risala-i Mulla-zada*, which contained an entire section dealing with the virtues and potential pitfalls of shrine visitation. The text cautioned against incorrect practices that might equate to idolatry, but concluded that shrine visitation was a virtue (*sunnat*) when done properly, even though that author also questioned the historicity of some of the historical figures identified with different tombs.[151] Darwish would probably not have appreciated an unattributed hadith included in *Risala-i Mulla-zada* to the effect that weekly pilgrimage to the tombs of one's mother and father was equivalent to the rewards of the Hajj.[152]

Even if Darwish was in the minority when it came to pilgrimage generally, his view was more broadly accepted when it came to shrine visitation by women in particular.[153] One *jung* quoted a work of *fiqh* on the very first page saying that shrine visitation is a virtue for men but forbidden for women.[154] Juma-quli Khumuli, encountered in a previous section as an opium-addled *qazi*, clarified the stakes of this debate with a lengthy tangent on female prophethood. Khumuli was outraged that some of his opponents pointed to miracles performed by Mary, mother of Jesus, for instance, and the Queen of

149. *Dar qiyāmat aẕāb-i sakht-i muwāfiq-i farmūda-i Payghambar khwāhad shud . . . Jung-i Abd al-Wāḥid Ṣadr Ṣarīr Balkhī*, f. 106b.

150. Subtelny, *Timurids in Transition*, 193.

151. Mu'īn al-Fuqarā', *Risāla-i Mullā Zāda*, ff. 3b–8a.

152. *Ṣawāb-i hajj maqbūl yābad*. The *Risāla-i Mullā Zāda* is discussed much more extensively in chapter 2. It was written in the fifteenth century, but widely copied in the long nineteenth century, and details the major pilgrimage destinations in Bukhara.

153. The existence of debates over this question suggests that in practice women were indeed visiting shrines, though direct evidence from precolonial sources is limited.

154. *Ziyārat al-qubūr ḥasan lil-rijāl ḥarām lil-nisā'*. The quotation is attributed simply to *Nawādir*, which could refer to Abū al-Layṯ's *Kitāb al-nawādir*. *Jūng-i masā'il wa wāqi'āt*, f. 1a. The work's anonymous author included both astrological predictions and lettrist magic on the same page.

Sheba (Bilqis), as evidence for the possibility of women prophets. He offered several justifications for his position, one of which was that prophets were required to go out and mix with the public at large, an activity forbidden to women. It was similarly important for Khumuli to establish an intermediate category of miracle (*karamat*) performable not only by nonprophet figures such as Mary, but also by sufi shaykhs.[155] By this logic, he could simultaneously show why the shaykhs of his Naqshbandi order were worthy of pilgrimage by men, but not women.[156]

The vast majority of examples here are drawn from legal genres, particularly *jung* and fatwas. The intention is partly to provide a counterbalance to the ecstatic imagery emerging from the poetical and mystical genres. Bukhara's reputation in colonial sources as a bastion of strict Islamic scripturalism (an image the city-state's rulers and religious elite actively cultivated) was not entirely undeserved. It was a society in which morality police were liable to leap over the wall of your house in search of sexual transgression, and one where disrespecting the privileged could get you branded an infidel. Yet policing of moral vice and religious deviation was a trait Bukhara shared with most European societies (including Russia), and echoes from the world of wine, music, and the supernatural resound even in sources condemning those practices. Legal discourse opened up possibilities for limiting activity seen to be transgressive, and even for arbitrarily exerting power over rivals, but it was not the exclusive purview of a unified scripturalist faction of any kind. Rather, it was one more competency of the high Persianate intellectual, and the act of performing that role affected the society itself, just as the genre produced by the performance affects our view of the society.

They Contained Multitudes

It seems apropos to conclude this chapter with a story that involves a bit of romance (or at least lust), some poetry, a glass of wine (or at least its imagery), and Sharia.[157] Before moving to Bukhara to write poetry and engage in sufi activities, Abd al-Sattar "Hazini" was the imam of a local village. He

155. As opposed to *mu'jiza*, a category of miracle performable only by prophets. Fierro, "Women as Prophets in Islam," 186.

156. Khumūlī, *Tarjuma-i ḥāl*, 30a–31b.

157. Versions of this anecdote appear in two different *taẕkiras*: Sāmī, *Mir'āt al-khayāl*, ff. 179b–182a; and Pīrmastī, *Afẓāl al-taẕkār*, f. 61b–64b. Ḥazīnī is designated as a member of the Naqshbandī community in the former, and of the Kubrawiyya in the latter, but he easily could have been part of both. On "bundled *silsilas*," see DeWeese, "'Dis-Ordering' Sufism in Early Modern Central Asia."

was involved in his work and had no plans for marriage, until one day the villagers presented him with a picture of a beautiful girl taken by a Russian photographer. Hazini was immediately smitten, with "the wine of enchantment coursing through his veins," and upon inquiry learned that the girl was the daughter of a local jeweler.[158] In a rush, he committed to marry the girl without ever having laid eyes on her in the flesh. Only later did he realize the trick his friends had played on him: the Russian photo shoot had taken place many years ago and the girl was now a seventy-year-old woman. Hazini had not quite grasped the implications of photograph technology, a failing that played right into the hands of the mischievous villagers. Hazini's biographer commented on the manner in verse: "If someone has a seed of deception, he will snare many a clever hen."[159]

This anecdote drives home the themes emphasized in this chapter. Hazini was trained in Islamic law and served as the village imam, but he was also steeped in a literary culture emphasizing sexuality (both male and female) and the pleasures of intoxication (both real and metaphorical). These worlds were not separate from one another, even though they are inevitably refracted through distinct textual genres. Hazini was not at liberty to woo the jeweler's daughter outside of the confines of marriage as dictated by Hanafi law, but within the poetic genre his desire was openly articulated in a way not possible in legal writing. Individual entries about the law within a *jung* notebook, for instance, would not have openly (or humorously) celebrated Hazini's amorous advances, but those same legal texts often had Persian love poetry scribbled into the margins. The boundaries between genres of writing were not set in stone and sometimes blurred together, but the conventions of jurisprudence, poetry, magic, official documentation, and hagiography opened up different possibilities of expression for different functions acted out by a single social group.

As in all societies, there were tensions and controversies in late Persianate Eurasia. However, many of the retrospective paradoxes have much to do with a failure to appreciate the importance of textual genre both as a mediating factor on our view of the past and a constitutive tool leveraged by the ulama. It was not a society divided between devout jurists, on the one hand, and ecstatic sufis and poets, on the other. Instead, it was characterized by a single social group pulled in many directions at once, whose vision of their world varied based on context, as did the roles they played in it.

---

158. Sāmī, *Mirʾāt al-khayāl*, f. 181a.

159. *Agar dāna-i ḥīla bāshad kasī, ba dām āward murgh-i zīrak basī.* Sāmī, *Mirʾāt al-khayāl*, f. 181a.

Tales of Hazini's romantic misadventures may seem lighthearted, but it would be a mistake to think the term "intellectual" implies that activities performed by the high Persianate intellectual amounted to leisure. If one was not born into the Turkic military elite, mastering the multitudinous skills and forms of knowledge was nearly the only path to power and influence. The remainder of this book traces how seemingly esoteric competencies such as poetry and theoretical jurisprudence were translated into power.

CHAPTER 7

Opportunity from Upheaval

Scholarly Dynasties between Nadir Shah and the Bolshevik Revolution

The high Persianate intellectual in his many guises was an omnipresent figure in early modern Central Asia, just as he was in India, Afghanistan, Iran, and even further afield. However, his social currency and self-aggrandizement belied a simple truth: the armed coercive force of the state lay entirely with another group, namely the Turkic nobility. This alliance between the Turkic military and the ulama was indispensable to both parties. Without the funds of a patron, few poets would have had the opportunity to compose verses, and without a credible threat of violence a *qazi*'s ruling was unenforceable. From the other side, warriors of a nomadic background lacked the literacy and bureaucratic skills necessary to run a state, however modest, or the tools to justify their military power through the language of Islam.

This situation was not unique to Central Asia. Turks formed the military backbone of most Islamic societies in the Middle East, Eurasia, and South Asia from the ninth century to the twentieth. However, because of the proximity of the steppe zone, successive waves of nomads formed an elite stratum with lineages and tribal structures still intact—in contrast with the warrior-slave dynasties common in the Middle East.[1] In Central Asia, this arrangement dates at least as far back as the Qarakhanid dynasty (ca.

1. Crone, *Slaves on Horses*.

999–1212), and arguably from the emergence of the city of Bukhara in the fifth century, lasting until the Bolshevik conquest in 1920.[2]

How did the ulama exploit their intricate, even esoteric forms of knowledge, such as mysticism and occultism? How did these skills benefit the Turkic warrior elite and the scholars themselves? Certainly, basic literacy and mathematics were essential for administrative positions throughout the Central Asian city-states, but the seemingly less practical skills were in many ways even more crucial during crises.[3] During these moments of upheaval, Turkic rulers grasped about for scholars who had amassed prestige and authority through diverse social roles with value specific to their Perso-Islamic milieu. This chapter focuses on different crises during the even longer nineteenth century that catalyzed new "dynasties" of scholars, allowing them to entrench their descendants in the state and nonstate institutions that provided resources and authority in their world.

The emphasis on knowledge mastery as the explicit justification for scholarly authority provided fertile soil for the rise of new families into the upper rungs of the scholarly elite. Certainly, it was not uncommon for scholars to invoke descent from a particularly saintly ancestor to further justify their status. Yet even being a *sayidd* (descendant of the Prophet) was not a guarantee of high status, and it was neither necessary nor sufficient for religious authority.[4] Therefore, the ulama were relatively permeable as a social group vis-à-vis other societies, and power could not be ensured simply by virtue of lineage and descent. Rather, scholarly dynasties required constant maintenance and negotiation with temporal authorities.

To understand this dynamic, this chapter turns to two families of scholars, both of whom came into prominence as a result of the political upheaval coinciding with the Manghit dynasty's (1747–1920) rise to power. These two households provided services to the Turkic nobility that helped their patrons to justify their rule and extend it over new territories. In return, Manghit nobles provided the scholarly families with the resources necessary to perpetuate their legacy for over a century and a half. Finally, the chapter considers the new geopolitical realities precipitated by the Russian subjugation of

2. Later Sogdian society was a multilayered system consisting of Sogdian merchants and a Turkic military aristocracy. de la Vaissière, *Sogdian Traders*, 16.

3. Francis Robinson argues that the emphasis on the rational Islamic sciences in the Indian context equipped scholars for administrative positions. *The 'Ulama of Farangi Mahall and Islamic Culture in South Asia*, 53. However, the values assigned to intellectual competencies are contextual in all societies, and what is considered "practical" is inevitably dictated by social contruct, be it knowledge of Greek and Latin in the British Empire or the ability to quote Hafez in the Persianate world.

4. After all, entire villages claimed *sayyid* status: Gulshānī, *Tārīkh-i humāyūn*, f. 18b.

Bukhara in 1868 and how they led to the empowerment of a new crop of family dynasties alongside or in place of the old ones—albeit for a briefer duration, with the Bolshevik Revolution just around the corner.

The Curious Conversion of Nadir Shah Afshar

In the early twentieth century, Sadr-i Ziya, explained his matrilineal heritage:[5]

> Qazi Mirza Umid was one of ten ulama selected by Abu al-Fayz Khan [Ashtarkhanid ruler of Bukhara, 1711–47] to be part of Hadi Khwaja's retinue sent in audience to Nadir Shah Afshar at the Chahar Bakr mausoleum.[6] These ten [Bukharan Hanafi] scholars engaged in debate with ten skilled Shi'i ulama on the issue of which sect embodied the truth.[7] Mirza Umid emerged from this engagement triumphant and proved the truth of Sunnism.[8] Nadir Shah saw fit to be merciful toward Abu al-Fayz Khan [who had just surrendered Bukhara] and embraced the true Sunni sect.[9]

Why would the scion of one of the most powerful scholarly families in Bukhara make a special point of tying his lineage to a foreign invasion already fading into distant memory? And since when did Nadir Shah Afshar, the understudied eighteenth-century conqueror, "convert" to Sunnism at the hands of a people he soundly defeated?[10] By the time Ziya wrote his memoirs, over a century and a half had passed since the murder of Nadir Shah scattered his armies, and the conqueror does not loom especially large in

---

5. The next two sections relating to Hādī Khwāja's line are adapted from Pickett, "Nadir Shah's Peculiar Central Asian Legacy."

6. The Chahār Bakr *khānaqāh* and shrine complex are located only a few kilometers outside of Bukhara. See Schwarz, "From Scholars to Saints: The Bukharan Shaykhs of Ǧūybār and the Ziyārats to the Four Bakr."

7. Żiyā', *Tarjuma-i aḥwāl-i ʿAbd al-Shakūr*, ff. 116b–117a.

8. *Ḥaqqīyat-i maẕhab-i sunnat wa jamāʿat s̱ābit karda*. Żiyā', *Tarjuma-i aḥwāl-i ʿAbd al-Shakūr*, ff. 116a–117b. The transition from Iran proper as a predominantly Hanafi legal sphere to a Shi'i one was at the time of this disputation only a little over a century old, even though Sunnis and Shi'a alike venerated the House of the Prophet. Arjomand, *The Shadow of God and the Hidden Imam*, 28, 105–6.

9. Żiyā', *Tarjuma-i ḥal-i āba' wa ajdād*, ff. 116a–117b. Manghit accounts portrayed Abū al-Fayż as submitting without a fight, with an emphasis on the role of Muḥammad Ḥakīm Khan Manghit and future-ruler Raḥīm Biy Manghit as intermediaries, while Kāẓim described an actual battle in which Nadir Shah defeated the Manghit father-son duo. Kāẓim, *ʿĀlam ārā-yi Nādirī*, 790–91. Andreas Wilde suggests that this encounter was unlikely to have taken place since it was only mentioned in Kāẓim's account. *What Is Beyond the River?*, 364.

10. Nadir Shah was from a Turkmen tribe and probably raised Shi'i, though his views on religion were complex and often pragmatic. Von Kügelgen, *Legitimatsiia sredneaziatskoi dinastii Mangitov*, 233; Axworthy, *The Sword of Persia*, 34, 168; Lockhart, *Nadir Shah*, 21.

other writings of the late colonial period. Yet this particular conversion narrative bore curious resonance during Central Asia's long nineteenth century, and the story served to justify the lofty status of numerous great families of Bukhara.

This evolving conversion narrative highlights the entanglement of rising sectarian anxieties, the eclectic skill set that empowered polymaths of Islam, and the Turkic military elite. Although in previous centuries the Shi'a-Sunni split was less salient than it has often been portrayed in the literature, by the long nineteenth century those sectarian divides were hardening.[11] Voluminous work has exposed the decisive role of colonial forms of knowledge in calcifying communal boundaries, but precolonial processes (such as the collapse of the Mughal Empire and the influx of Naqshbandi-Mujaddidi missionaries) were also important.[12] Whatever the causes, this new sectarian terrain posed a retrospective problem for scholarly dynasties that owed their genesis to Nadir Shah, a figure increasingly seen as an Iranian, Shi'i ruler as the nineteenth century progressed.

This tension is put into stark relief in varying accounts of Nadir Shah's relationship with Sunnism, usually revolving in some way around the figure of Hadi Khwaja "Eshan Ustaz" (d. late eighteenth century). Although later accounts veer toward the mythological, the conversion narratives grew out of an actual encounter between Hadi Khwaja and Nadir Shah. According to an untitled, anonymous travel account written by someone apparently present for the events in question, in August 1743 Hadi Khwaja—along with a party of fellow Sunni, Central Asian ulama—set out from Bukhara to visit the Iraqi cities of Najaf and Karbala, both especially sacred in Shi'ism.[13] The travel account does not specifically say so, but he was answering an empire-wide call to assemble scholars to resolve the Sunni–Shi'i divide.[14] On the way, Hadi Khwaja visited a shrine in Mashhad that had been endowed

11. McChesney, "'Barrier of Heterodoxy?'"; Kimura, "Sunni-Shi'i Relations in the Russian Protectorate of Bukhara."

12. Cohn, "The Census, Social Structure, and Objectification in South Asia"; Pandey, *The Construction of Communalism in Colonial North India*; Werth, "From 'Pagan' Muslims to 'Baptized' Communists"; Cole, *Roots of North Indian Shīʿism in Iran and Iraq*. However, other Mujaddidī proselytizers were actively preaching tolerance. Ziad, "Traversing the Indus and the Oxus," 542. See also Pickett, "Nadir Shah's Peculiar Central Asian Legacy," 495–97.

13. Hādī-zāda, *Safar-nāma*, ff. 150b–155a. See also von Kügelgen, 242. Von Kügelgen suggests that Hādī-zāda (i.e., "son of Hādī") was none other than ʿAtāʾallāh, a figure discussed subsequently. *Legitimatsiia sredneaziatskoi dinastii Mangitov*, 242.

14. Algar, "Shi'ism and Iran in the Eighteenth Century," 330. ʿAbd Allāh ibn Ḥusayn al-Suwaydī confirms Hādī Khwāja's role in the discussions. One Mullā Umīd Ṣudūr, quite likely the same individual as Mīrzā Umīd of the opening passage of this article, also appears on the list of Central Asian scholars. Suwaydī, *Muʾtamar al-Najaf*, 40.

with Shi'i significance by the Safavid dynasty only in the previous century or so, though none of this was unusual behavior for a Sunni Muslim, especially at that early date.[15]

More remarkable is what transpired once Hadi Khwaja arrived in Iraq, parts of which were then controlled by Nadir Shah. After visiting the shrines of Adam, Moses, and Ali, located in Najaf, Hadi Khwaja entered into a religious disputation with a group of Qizilbash ulama outside of the shrine complex following the afternoon prayer.[16] The scholars debated the exigencies of religion (*zaruriyat-i din*) until the Qizilbash were persuaded to Hadi Khwaja's side, though allowances were made for those facets of their Shi'i beliefs not intrinsically at odds with Sunnism.[17] According to an Ottoman observer, it was Hadi Khwaja who was coaxed out of his stubbornly anti-Shi'a position by an Afghan colleague in attendance, but either way, Nadir Shah's position prevailed.[18] Having arrived at this accord, the next day, "the Sunni and Qizilbash mullas gathered together at the front of the tomb complex, where they wrote and sealed a document asserting that Shi'ism was within Islam."[19]

Hadi Khwaja's accord with the Qizilbash scholars makes a great deal of sense within Nadir Shah's broader efforts to secure acceptance of Shi'ism within Sunni Islam. Scholars of Iranian history have portrayed Nadir's theological efforts exclusively in relation to the Ottoman Empire. Nadir Shah exhorted the Ottoman sultan to recognize Shi'ism as the fifth juridical school (*mazhab*) of Islam, to be known as the Ja'fari school after the sixth Shi'i imam. In exchange, Shi'a would renounce certain practices particularly offensive to Sunnis, such as the ritual cursing of the first three caliphs.[20] Although Nadir Shah's primary preoccupation was indeed the Ottoman Empire, the

---

15. Robert McChesney proposes *ahl al-baytism* (people of the house [of the Prophet Muhammad]) as an alternative to "Shi'ism" to describe the reverence for the Prophet's family that cut across sectarian lines. *Waqf in Central Asia*, 34.

16. Central Asian sources often characterized all Iranian religious personages as Qizilbash, whatever their actual status—including Nadir Shah, in at least one case: AV IVR RAN, F 33 O 1 D 140. See Bashir, "The Origins and Rhetorical Evolution of the Term Qizilbāsh in Persianate Literature."

17. Lockhart, *Nadir Shah*, 233; Algar, "Shi'ism and Iran in the Eighteenth Century," 32. This encounter in Najaf was also mentioned in three of the Manghit chronicles. Von Kügelgen, *Legitimatsiia sredneaziatskoi dinastii Mangitov*, 242.

18. Algar, "Shi'ism and Iran in the Eighteenth Century," 330–31; Suwaydī, *Mu'tamar al-Najaf*, 40–44.

19. Hādī-zāda, *Safar-nāma*, f. 152b. The signed document is included in a published collection of Afsharid documents; Hādī Khwāja's name is apparently not among the discernable seals, but several of his colleagues attested by Suwaydī indeed appear. Nawā'ī, *Nādir Shāh wa bāzmāndagānash*, 339.

20. Nadir hoped that securing such an accord with the Ottomans would at once deprive them of a convenient casus belli for waging war against Iran and cast him as a defender of Shi'ism. Toward the end of his reign, after many battles with the Ottomans, Nadir abandoned his calls for a Ja'farī *mazhab*. Tucker, "Nadir Shah and the Ja'fari Madhhab Reconsidered."

Sunni ulama who actually signed off on his agenda (such as Hadi Khwaja and colleagues, but also a delegation of Afghans) overwhelmingly hailed from territories he had conquered.[21] The text of the Najaf accord signed by Hadi Khwaja's delegation explicitly cedes Nadir Shah final authority in punishing anyone throughout his empire who failed to abide by the agreement and continued to persecute Shi'a.[22] Thus the Council of Najaf bore importance as a tool not only of diplomacy but also of imperial integration.

These efforts ultimately came to naught, but Hadi Khwaja's role in justifying them proved extremely lucrative. After Friday prayer in Kufa with his new Qizilbash colleagues, Hadi Khwaja proceeded to Karbala where he visited the shrine of Husayn and was honored with a personal audience with the shah. According to Hadi Khwaja's account, Nadir Shah showered him with unprecedented hospitality while they drank tea together. More concretely, whoever transcribed the travelogue scribbled in the margin that Hadi Khwaja was given 6,000 rupees, and all of his fellow Bukharan companions were given 2,000.[23] At the end of the account, the author further added in the margins that in December 1744 Hadi Khwaja was appointed military judge (*qazi-yi askari*) of Bukhara—the first step in his family's dominance of the city-state's highest religious posts.[24]

This terse travelogue stands as our earliest account of Hadi Khwaja's relationship with Nadir Shah. That it is an eyewitness account and fits with our understanding of Nadir Shah's theological ambitions is indicative of authenticity. However, later, substantially altered versions of the encounter between Nadir Shah and Hadi Khwaja are no less revealing of the event's symbolic importance for the fortunes of scholarly dynasties in subsequent decades.

Certain changes in the depiction of this debate are present in Muhammad Sharif's *Taj al-tawarikh*, a chronicle commissioned by Amir Haydar Manghit in ca. 1800. The most important change is the lack of compromise or conciliation with Shi'ism: Sunni victory is total. In this version, the Qizilbash Mulla Bashi made a fool of himself through the spurious deployment of the Hadith, and Nadir Shah was fully convinced of his treachery.[25] Nadir Shah went on to issue a decree that all should recognize the rightness of the Sunni path,

---

21. The composition of the scholars in attendance partly explains why the Ottomans had so little interest in it. Algar, "Shi'ism and Iran in the Eighteenth Century," 332.

22. Nawā'ī, *Nādir Shāh wa bāzmāndagānash*, 338–39.

23. Hādī-zāda, *Safar-nāma*, f. 153 marginalia and f. 154a. The rupees Nadir Shah was handing out in Iraq presumably originated from his famous sack and pillage of Delhi in 1739.

24. Hādī-zāda, *Safar-nāma*, f. 155a, marginalia.

25. The Mulla Bashi was the highest religious authority under the Safavids. Sefatgol, "From Dār al-Salṭana-yi Iṣfahān to Dār al-Khilāfa-yi Ṭihrān," 76–77.

which prevailed from the foundation of Islam until the perversions of Shah Isma'il (the founding Safavid ruler, r. 1501–24). Nonetheless, many of the details resemble those of the briefer travelogue: the disputation also takes place in Najaf, though in this version Nadir Shah himself is present, having summoned scholars from all corners of his empire to determine the true *mazhab*.[26] The *Taj al-tawarikh* also makes special note of the rewards (including Indian rupees) handed out to the victorious Sunni ulama. The text does not mention Hadi Khwaja specifically, but it does single out one "Hazrat-i Eshan Ustad" as particularly deserving of recompense.[27] Although this was a fairly common title of ulama in Central Asia, it was one used in other texts to refer to Hadi Khwaja.[28]

Most later accounts preserve the climactic Sunni–Shi'a debate with Nadir Shah as arbiter but shift the encounter to an earlier date and the location to the Chahar Bakr shrine outside of Bukhara. According to Muhammad Hakim Khan's Khoqand-centric *Muntakhab al-tawarikh*, composed in the 1840s, after Nadir Shah crossed the Oxus he camped his massive army at Chahar Bakr, which left the militarily weak Abu al-Fayz Khan (r. 1711–47) at a loss. Conferring with his advisers, Abu al-Fayz determined to greet Nadir graciously and—after fruitlessly dispatching several ambassadors (*elchi*)—sent a wise sufi named Eshan Imla to meet the Iranian shah.[29] Impressed, Nadir treated the Eshan with great honor, and as a result of their discussions of religion, Nadir Shah repented and forsook the Shi'i *mazhab* in favor of Sunnism. Thanks to Eshan Imla's intervention, Bukhara was compensated for its military subjugation with a theological victory.[30] Instead of appearing as an arbiter above the religious disputes, as in previous versions, here Nadir Shah's personal conversion to Sunnism is emphasized—although, fitting with previous versions, in this one Nadir Shah rewarded the scholar handsomely with an assortment of jewels. In contrast with the characterization of Hadi Khwaja in the *Safar-nama*, the author is careful to clarify that Eshan

26. Naqī, *Tāj al-tawārīkh*, ff. 308b–310, f. 310, and f. 312. Nadir Shah convened the debate in order to "expose the correct path and legal school" and to "eliminate doubt and dissention." Naqī, *Tāj al-tawārīkh*, ff. 307b–308b.

27. Naqī, *Tāj al-tawārīkh*, f. 311b.

28. Musayyab Bukhārī, *Kitāb-i maqāmāt-i mashāyikh*, f. 676b.

29. Ḥakīm Khan, *Muntakhab al-tawārīkh* vol. 1, 344. Muḥammad Yaʿqūb Bukhārī, who was the twelfth son of the second Manghit ruler, Dāniyāl Ataliq (r. 1759–85), referenced a delegation of ulama and Turkic nobles (*umarāʾ*) sent to Chahār Bakr, but emphasized the role of Manghit dynasty founder Raḥīm Khan (r. 1747–59) and did not mention any theological debates. Muḥammad Yaʿqūb, *Risāla*, f. 2b–3b. Another account puts Ēshān Imlā at the Chahār Bakr parlay but mentions no conversion. *Ẓikr-i tārīkh-i Abū al-Fayż Khān*, f. 266a.

30. By contrast, in the *Safar-nāma-i Qāżī Hādī Khwāja* it is the Bukharan scholar who performs a religious service for Nadir.

Imla had no use for the trappings of temporal power and immediately gave the jewels away to his servant.[31] Following the Eshan's intervention, Abu al-Fayz was able to secure peace with Nadir.

As this narrative evolved over the nineteenth century, the emphasis on conversion became more pronounced, as did the agency of Hadi Khwaja. The act of conversion simultaneously assimilated elements increasingly understood to be outside the fold (Shi'ism) and sacralized a new community of scholars (Hadi Khwaja and his descendants).[32] Ziya's account of the event (quoted at the start of this section), composed in the early twentieth century, combined elements of the *Safar-nama*, the *Taj al-tawarikh*, and the *Muntakhab al-tawarikh*. In this newest version, Nadir Shah crossed into the Bukharan Oasis not to conquer, but for the express purpose of visiting the Naqshbandi shrine at Chahar Bakr. He sent a letter to Abu al-Fayz boasting that: "seizing this city would be incredibly easy for me. My only pretension in coming here is to visit (*ziyara*) Hazrat Eshan Imla."[33] Ziya asserted that Nadir Shah was secretly a Sunni all along, which is why he wanted to meet Eshan Imla in the first place.[34]

Later in his history, Ziya inserts into the narrative ten ulama alongside Eshan Imla in the audience with Nadir Shah at Chahar Bakr, with Hadi Khwaja foremost among them. As in the *Safar-nama* and *Taj al-tawarikh*, we find a theological debate between Sunni and Shi'i scholars, though this time taking place in Chahar Bakr, just as in *Muntakhab al-tawarikh*. Rather than serving to legitimate Nadir Shah's theological agenda uniting the Sunni and Shi'i sects, in this version (as in the *Taj al-tawarikh*) the Sunni victory is absolute, with the Bukharan scholars convincing the Shi'a of the ultimate truth of Sunnism. Ultimately, Ziya contradicted his own assertion of Nadir's secret Sunnism by claiming that Nadir Shah also embraced the Sunni *mazhab* as a result of this religious debate.[35]

The evolution of this conversion narrative over the course of the long nineteenth century reveals both the lasting impact of the Afsharid imperial project and mounting sectarian tensions. Nadir Shah's empire facilitated exchange, including between scholars, and his theological ambitions left a

31. That servant (*kafsh bardār*, lit. "shoe carrier"), Muḥammad Sharīf, used the wealth to become a scholar in his own right and eventually built an eponymously named madrasa where Muḥammad Ḥakīm Khan, the chronicle's author, studied. Ḥakīm Khan, *Muntakhab al-tawārīkh*, 1: 345.

32. DeWeese, *Islamization and Native Religion in the Golden Horde*, 6, 11; Viswanathan, *Outside the Fold*, xi.

33. Żiyā', *Nawādir-i żiyā'īya*, f. 37a. Żiyā' also mentions Nadir Shah's royal gift to Ēshan Imlā and the subsequent founding of the Muḥammad Sharīf madrasa—where żiyā''s father, ʿAbd al-Shakūr, taught for a time—on that largesse. Żiyā', *Tarjuma-i aḥwāl-i ʿAbd al-Shakūr*, 103b.

34. Żiyā', *Nawādir-i żiyā'īya*, f. 37b.

35. Żiyā', *Tarjuma-i aḥwāl-i ʿAbd al-Shakūr*, ff. 38a–39b and ff. 116b–117a.

lasting imprint on the memory of families of ulama in the region. What originated as his attempt to integrate Shi'ism into the Sunni fold morphed over time into his own conversion to Sunnism as facilitated by the Bukharan ulama, which transformed the memory of his initial patronage into an asset rather than a liability. That memory was not just an idle story; it empowered Hadi Khwaja's family in particular for over a century.

Nadir Shah and the Genesis of Hadi Khwaja's Family Dynasty

Hadi Khwaja likely performed a theological service for Nadir Shah, but the memory of that service changed radically over the long nineteenth century as the Sunni-Hanafi gaze toward Shi'ism became increasingly strained. Hadi Khwaja, along with a cadre of peers, morphed from Afsharid servants into champions of Hanafi Islam, fulfilling the role of mythological ancestor sacralizing a discreet community of descendants.[36] Here I demonstrate that this memory proved a powerful force, as Hadi Khwaja's new scholarly dynasty perpetuated itself to the Bolshevik Revolution in 1917. Piecemeal genealogies and hagiographies connected Hadi Khwaja's ancestors to that foundational conversion event, as well as to the Prophet and numerous saintly figures.

Hadi Khwaja "Eshan Ustaz" was most likely a scholar of some prestige before the events described above, but no reference is made to influential ranks held by prominent forebears, so it is impossible to know for sure.[37] However, the social, material, and political benefits that emerged from putting his religious expertise at the service of Nadir Shah allowed him to perpetuate a family dynasty on his own merit. Following the execution of Nizam al-Din Husayni in 1785, Hadi Khwaja was elevated to his deceased colleague's recently vacated chief judgeship (*qazi-yi kalan*) and was appointed *shaykh al-Islam*, *mudarris/akhund* of the prestigious Kokaltash madrasa, and personal tutor of Shah-Murad Manghit (r. 1785–1800).[38]

---

36. Other scholars (ten, in most accounts) tapped into the memory of Nadir Shah's conversion as well, and some of those scholars initiated family dynasties of their own. For instance, Mīrzā Umīd (mentioned in the introductory quote in this chapter) and his descendants were rewarded handsomely: Mīrzā Umīd was appointed *qāżī*, his son Ṣābir-jān personally tutored one of Amir Ḥaydar's sons, another son—Mīrzā Sharīf—became a famous *muftī*, and his grandson Karāmatallāh continued the tradition of princely tutoring. Żiyāʾ *Tarjuma-i aḥwāl-i ʿAbd al-Shakūr*, ff. 117a–b, 119a–b.

37. However, a major section of Mīr Musayyab Bukhārī's work traces Hādī Khwāja's ancestry to the Prophet. Musayyab Bukhārī, *Kitāb-i maqāmāt-i mashāʾikh*, ff. 6a–8b. Also, Suwaydī lists him first among the Central Asian delegates to Najaf, and with the title *al-ʿalāma* (learned scholar) and *baḥr al-ʿilm* (ocean of knowledge). *Muʾtamar al-Najaf*, 40.

38. Żiyāʾ, *Nawādir-i żiyāʾīya*, 43, 45b. *Ākhūnd* was an honorific title given to the *mudarris* of the Kokaltash madrasa; it also had the more general meaning of teacher. Niẓām al-Dīn Khwāja Ḥusaynī (d. 1785/86) was the first *qāżī-yi kalān* appointed by the founding Manghit ruler, Raḥīm Khan (r.

Hadi Khwaja's son, Muhammad Ata'allah (d. 1795–96) became a force in his own right, certainly in no small part due to the fact that his father managed to pass on all three of his major positions: *shaykh al-Islam*, *qazi-yi kalan*, and *mudarris* of Kokaltash.[39] Not only was he connected to the new crop of elite scholars embroiled in the rise of the Manghit dynasty through his father, he was also a disciple of Muhammad Siddiq, a member of the Naqshbandiyya-Mujaddidiyya who emigrated from India and rose to the top of the Dahbidi community.[40]

Ata'allah was inducted into that order by Eshan Imla, whose role in the Nadir Shah conversion legend eclipsed that of Hadi Khwaja in some accounts.[41] Suggestively, Eshan Imla's legacy does not seem to extend much past his lifetime, and the sources do not speak of any heirs to his legacy from his family. By contrast, hagiographical sources make much of Ata'allah taking up Eshan Imla's *spiritual* legacy. One such source states that when Ata'allah was fifteen years old, his father, Hadi Khwaja, entrusted him over to Eshan Imla, stating: "Muhammad Ata'allah is your servant [*ghulam*]." To this, Imla responded: "Ata'allah is my child." Ata'allah was thus symbolically adopted into the genealogy of Eshan Imla, who was also held to have participated in the legendary conversion of Nadir Shah.

Just as Hadi Khwaja had passed on his authority to his offspring, Ata'allah ensured that the family's prestige lived on in future generations.[42] Ata'allah's son Rahmatallah was appointed *ra'is* (aka *muhtasib*, morality enforcer), then *mudarris*, and ultimately succeeded his father as *shaykh al-Islam*. Fittingly, one of the madrasas in which Rahmatallah taught was none other than Damulla Muhammad Sharif—the institution that had been endowed by Eshan Imla's follower using the treasure given by Nadir Shah.[43] He also tapped into the memory of the conversion narrative from another direction by marrying

---

1747–59). He was allegedly one of the "ten scholars" who converted Nadir Shah to Sunnism (as against the "seven" reported by Suwaydī in Najaf), but that service did not save him when Shah Murad Manghit found him guilty of corruption and impious behavior. Żiyā', *Nawādir-i żiyā'īya*, 39b.

39. Documents bear ʿAṭā'allāh's *shaykh al-Islām* seal from at least 1788/89. Welsford and Tashev, *A Catalogue of Arabic-Script Documents from the Samarqand Museum*, 56.

40. Musayyab Bukhārī, *Kitāb-i maqāmāt-i mashāyikh*, ff. 640a—41b, 676b. On Muḥammad Siddīq, see Babadzhanov, "On the History of the Naqshbandiya Mujaddidiya in Central Mawara'nnahr in the Late 18th and Early 19th Centuries," 395–96.

41. Musayyab Bukhārī, *Kitāb-i maqāmāt-i mashāyikh*, f. 676b; Rizawī, *Manāqib wa maqāmāt-i ʿAṭā'allāh*, f. 3.

42. Memory of ʿAṭā'allāh was also perpetuated through the sanctification of his tomb, which (along with that of his father) was reported as a pilgrimage destination in an early twentieth-century Tatar pamphlet. Muʿaẓī, *Tārīkh-i Bukhārā wa-tarjumat al-ʿulamā'*, 17.

43. Musayyab Bukhārī, *Kitāb-i maqāmāt-i mashāyikh*, ff. 729b–730a; Rizawī, *Manāqib wa maqāmāt-i ʿAṭā'allāh*, f. 64.

the daughter of one of the attested participants in the Council of Najaf.[44] Rahmatallah's promising career was cut terminally short by some variety of plague in 1807/8, but not before the Turkic-scholarly alliance was cemented with a marriage between Rahmatallah and one of Shah Murad's daughters.[45]

Rahmatallah's untimely demise did not, however, spell the end of Hadi Khwaja's legacy, as Ata'allah's other son, Eshan Sharif Khwaja, inherited all of the positions held by his forebears: *qazi-yi kalan, shaykh al-Islam, mudarris/akhund* of Kokaltash madrasa, and personal tutor of the amir, in this case Nasrallah (r. 1827–60), who appointed him at the astonishingly young age of thirty-five.[46] Ziya noted the poetic symmetry between the Manghit dynasty and Hadi Khwaja's line thusly: "These three renowned members of the ulama of a single hue (*bi-yak-rang*) and of a single repose (*bi-yak-qarar*) were in the respective ages of three powerful shahs appointed to great ranks and mighty titles."[47]

Hadi Khwaja's prestige continued to elevate his descendants even after Eshan Sharif Khwaja's death. Eshan Sharif Khwaja's son, Buzurg Khwaja, served Amir Muzaffar (r. 1860–85) in the most serious way possible by taking up arms and joining the Bukharan military resistance against the Russian Empire, which was ultimately quashed in 1868. He was rewarded for his service with the rank of *sadr* (an honorary title) and the position of *muhtasib*. Another son, Fayzallah Khwaja, served as military *mufti* (*mufti-yi askari*, legal opinion writer for the military) and was granted the rank of *sudur* (another honorific).[48]

As with Nadir Shah's conquest, the Russian subjugation of Bukhara altered the political landscape, once again creating new opportunities for new families of scholars. As Stéphane Dudoignon demonstrates, the Russian-enabled Bukharan conquest of the mountainous eastern provinces resulted in the influx of scholars from territories such as Kulab. The presence of these new competitors, particularly the descendants of Ibn Bayza Khatlani, allowed the

---

44. Raḥmatallāh married the daughter of Ṣadr al-Din Khwaja. Musayyab Bukhārī, *Kitāb-i maqāmāt-i mashāʾikh*, f. 725a. Ṣadr al-Din was the son of Padishah Khwaja, whose presence at Najaf is attested by Suwaydī. *Muʾtamar al-Najaf*, 40.

45. Riżawī, *Manāqib wa maqāmāt-i ʿAṭāʾallāh*, f. 49. The plague was referred to as *al-wabāʾ al-ʿām*. Marjānī, *Wafiyyat al-aslāf*, f. 139b. Based on document evidence, Raḥmatallāh was legally active since at least 1799/1800. Welsford and Tashev, *A Catalogue of Arabic-Script Documents from the Samarqand Museum*, 68–69.

46. Ēshān Sharīf Khwāja was legally active from at least 1818/19, as military judge (*qāżī-yi ʿaskar*) from 1820/21, and *qāẓī-yi kalān* from 1826/27, with a last document reference from 1841. Welsford and Tashev, *A Catalogue of Arabic-Script Documents from the Samarqand Museum*, 78.

47. Ṣadr-i Żiyāʾ, *Nawādir-i żiyāʾīya*, ff. 45b–46a.

48. Ṣadr-i Żiyāʾ, *Nawādir-i żiyāʾīya*, ff. 48b–49a and f. 49.

amir greater leverage over more established lineages such as that of Hadi Khwaja.[49] Until the Bolshevik conquest of Bukhara in 1920, the Bukharan amirs tended to rotate the position *qazi-yi kalan* (chief judge) between the descendants of Ibn Bayza Khatlani (the Kulabi faction) and Ziya's Bukharan faction of ulama—the latter of which was separate from that of Hadi Khwaja, but similarly rooted in Bukhara. In this context the relinquishment of Hadi Khwaja's family hold on Bukhara's top positions open to the ulama is understandable. However, it is worth noting that Ziya's maternal grandfather, Sabir-jan, was one of Hadi Khwaja's students, so the two lines were intertwined in terms of intellectual pedigree.[50]

Even if the top judicial positions were dominated by other families of ulama during the colonial period, Hadi Khwaja's successors were hardly left out in the cold. The seal of a third, perhaps younger son of Eshan Sharif Khwaja, Muhammad Alim Khwaja, turned up on court documents he stamped as a *qazi* in Charjuy and Qarshi during the 1880s, having attained the honorary rank of *sudur*.[51] Likewise, Abd Allah Khwaja "Tahsin" carried on the tradition of his uncle (several steps removed) Fayz Allah Khwaja by holding the post of *mufti-yi askari* during the reign of Abd al-Ahad Khan Manghit (r. 1885–1911), though he was descended from Hadi Khwaja via Rahmatallah's line rather than Eshan Sharif Khwaja.[52] He was also employed on the *qazi* circuit, serving as judge in the provinces of Wabkand and Waghanza, and was honored with the rank of *uraq*—as well as sudur and sadr—during the course of his career.[53]

If one considers Hadi Khwaja's intellectual and patronage ties more expansively, his legacy remained vibrant well into the colonial period. Although his last direct descendant to hold the top judicial post appears to have been his grandson, Eshan Sharif Khwaja, one of Hadi Khwaja's students—Damulla Inayatallah Khwaja "Qazi-yi Kalan Taht-i Minari" ("Chief Judge Beneath the Minaret")—rose to the position of *qazi-yi kalan* under Nasrallah and had assumed the full suite of top posts (*shaykh al-Islam*, *mudarris/akhund* of Kokaltash madrasa) by the reign of Amir Muzaffar (r. 1860–85).[54] Like his predecessors, he cemented his political alliance with the ruler by personally

49. Dudoignon, "Faction Struggles among the Bukharan Ulama."

50. Żiyā', *Tarjuma-i aḥwāl-i 'Abd al-Shakūr*, f. 116b.

51. Welsford and Tashev, *A Catalogue of Arabic-Script Documents from the Samarqand Museum*, 128, 140–42.

52. Żiyā', *Tażkār-i ash'ār*, 289–90; Pīrmastī, *Afżāl al-tażkār*, ff. 51a–b.

53. Muḥtaram, *Tażkirat al-shu'arā*, f. 96b; Pīrmastī, *Afżāl al-tażkār*, ff. 51a–b.

54. Welsford and Tashev, *A Catalogue of Arabic-Script Documents from the Samarqand Museum*, 48; Żiyā', *Nawādir-i żiyā'īya*, f. 43a. However, another source puts 'Ināyatallāh's death at 1856/57, before the reign of Amir Muẓaffar. Muḥammad Nāṣir al-Bukhārī, *Tuḥfat al-zā'irīn*, 98.

tutoring Amir Muzaffar.[55] Inayatallah's son, Muhammad Parsa also served as a princely tutor, and rose to the rank of military *qazi*, but not the chief judgeship.[56] Muhammad Parsa's son, and Inayatallah's grandson, however, rose to the highest positions of *shaykh al-Islam* and *qazi-yi kalan* in the final days of the Bukharan protectorate, thus placing the top religious positions back in the orbit of Hadi Khwaja's intellectual lineage.[57]

Hadi Khwaja's line—both intellectual and familial—truly did constitute a dynasty, passing on spiritual authority like a baton for well over a century. As with other family dynasties, genealogies and hagiographies emphasized his family's descent from the Prophet and individual achievements. The legendary conversion of Nadir Shah served as one further pillar buttressing the family's authority, anchoring the lineage to a particular place (the Chahar Bakr shrine outside of Bukhara, by the conversion narrative's final incarnation), and burnishing its Sunni-Hanafi credentials in an age when sectarian boundaries between Sunni and Shi'a were sharpening. All of Hadi Khwaja's successors accessed this foundational event through the production and reproduction of texts, which genealogically connected later members of the scholarly dynasty to their forebears, collapsing chronology just as the narrative itself collapsed geography.

Abd al-Hayy's Samarqandi Line

Just as Nadir Shah's conquest of Central Asia and the Manghit dynasty's subsequent rise to power ushered in a new cast of scholarly characters in Bukhara, a similar reshuffling is evident in Samarqand, the amirate's second most important city. Aside from Bukhara, Samarqand was the only city to enjoy sufficient size and prestige to merit its own *qazi-yi kalan* and *shaykh al-Islam* (positions often held by the same individual), and unlike city-states such as Hisar and Shahrisabz, Bukhara was usually successful in enforcing its political claim on Samarqand.[58] In an arena slightly more removed from the

55. Żiyā', *Nawādir-i żiyā'īya*, f. 48b.

56. This is the same figure mentioned in chapter 3, having served as an ambassador to the Ottoman Empire.

57. Muḥammad Baqā Khwāja held the post of *qāżī-yi kalān* from 1908 until a rival line wrested control of the chief judgeship from him in 1913. He was then awarded the position of *shaykh al-Islām* as a consolation prize. Żiyā, *The Personal History of a Bukharan Intellectual*, 298–99. Muḥammad Baqā had at least two influential sons as well, one of whom handwrote a history of Bukhara in 1927: Hāmid ibn Qāḍī Baqā Khwāja, *Tanzīl al-amthāl fī żikr bayān al-aḥwāl.*

58. Amir Ḥaydar (r. 1800–1826) lost control of the city numerous times during his reign. In 1842 Bukhara conquered Khoqand and installed its own *qażī-yi kalān* in the city, only to be ejected three months later.

capital, Abd al-Hayy Khwaja (l. 1755/56–1827/28) was able to secure a legacy every bit as enduring as that of Hadi Khwaja.[59]

Few details have come down to us concerning Abd al-Hayy's father, Mawlawi Abu al-Khayr. However, given that Samarqand lay in ruins during the early part of the eighteenth century, pickings would have been slim no matter how ambitious Abu al-Khayr was.[60] Abd al-Hayy's break came slightly later than Hadi Khwaja's. The first *qazi-yi kalan* under the Manghits, Nizam al-Din Husayni (d. 1785/86)—mentioned in the previous section for having been executed for alleged religious transgressions—managed to install his own relatives and supporters in the positions of *shaykh al-Islam* and *qazi-yi kalan* in Samarqand.[61] Bukhara's hold on Samarqand during the tenure of these two judicial figures was tenuous, however. During the reign of Daniyal Ataliq (r. 1759–85) the rival Yuz dynasty of Uratepa at one point conquered the city (along with a number of other important population centers in the surrounding region) and captured Daniyal's brother, who had been serving as governor of Samarqand. Daniyal's son and successor, Shah-Murad (r. 1785–1800), realized that he needed someone both loyal and locally rooted in the top position available to religious scholars to ensure control over the ulama of Samarqand. Though details are sparse, it seems that Abd al-Hayy found himself out of work in Samarqand due to paralysis from the waist down, but was nevertheless able to find favor in the amir's personal entourage.[62] According to an account written by his son, Mir Salman Samarqandi, Shah-Murad appointed Abd al-Hayy to the posts of *shaykh al-Islam* and *qazi-yi kalan* of Samarqand after being impressed by the scholar's legal acumen.[63]

In 1796/97 Abd al-Hayy was afforded the chance to validate the amir's vote of confidence, and in a much more direct fashion than Hadi Khwaja's theological efforts. The Manghit dynasty's archrival, the Keneges tribe,

---

59. There is confusing slippage in the sources between ʿAbd al-Ḥayy and Abū al-Ḥayy for this individual, with some sources using both names in different instances. However, his seal in official documents reads "ʿAbd," which is the variant I use here.

60. By the time "Nādir Shāh invaded the city in 1740, only about one thousand families lodged at the fort. It took the entire second half of the eighteenth century to rebuild Samarqand." Sela, *The Legendary Biographies of Tamerlane*, 126.

61. Żiyāʾ, *Nawādir-i żiyāʾīya*, f. 39b. His supporters were: Shihāb al-Dīn Aḥrārī and Maḥmūd Khwāja Ḥusaynī, who were described as *qarībān*. Żiyāʾ, *Nawādir-i żiyāʾīya*, f. 39b.

62. Żiyāʾ, *Taẕkirat al-khaṭṭāṭīn*, f. 86b; Żiyāʾ, *Ẕikr-i chand nafar-i ʿulamāʾ*, f. 154b.

63. Salmān Samarqandī, *Tafṣīl wa bayān-i dawlat-i jamāʿat-i Manghit*, ff. 177b–178a. (The specifics of this anecdote are elaborated in the next chapter to elucidate the authority claims being made by the monarch and the ulama, respectively.) ʿAbd al-Ḥayy soon gained the nickname "Qāḍī-yi Kalān-i Shall" ("The Paralyzed Chief Judge"). Salmān Samarqandī, *Tafṣīl wa bayān-i dawlat-i jamāʿat-i Manghit*, f. 178a.

sent troops from its capital in Shahrisabz to the mountains separating that city from Samarqand and occupied the fortress of Qaratepa.[64] Shah-Murad ordered his military to lay siege to the fortress, but after two days Qaratepa still had not fallen, and—making matters worse—it became known that reinforcements were marching from Shahrisabz. Fearing loss of prestige, and likely the fall of Samarqand itself under threat from such a strategic position, the Bukharan amir ordered every able-bodied man in Samarqand capable of riding or at least holding a sword to march on the fortress. Although the business of war was generally left to the Turkic nobility, in these dire straits Abd al-Hayy heeded his patron's call and commanded his madrasa students to join the assault. These added troops tipped the scales and Bukhara carried the day.[65]

After having his tenure renewed under the next amir, Abd al-Hayy successfully passed the position of *qazi-yi kalan* to his son, Abu Sa'id Khwaja, who played an even more pivotal role in lending his scholarly authority to the service of the amir.[66] The Manghit dynasty generally enjoyed a remarkably smooth series of accessions to the Bukharan throne, but one notable exception to this trend was Nasrallah's succession struggle in 1827. Following the death of Amir Haydar (r. 1800–1826), his son Husayn Tore took advantage of his presence in Bukhara—and his brothers' absence, serving as governors in the various provinces—to seize the throne.[67] Husayn Tore perished only three months after his enthronement (apparently from an illness), and his brother Umar Khan took his place, but immediately earned great unpopularity by losing himself to vice and drink. Perhaps even more tellingly, Umar Khan was portrayed as having ceased paying attention to the counsel of his supporters. In avoiding a similar mistake, Nasrallah brought Abd al-Hayy's Samarqandi line back into the picture.

Just when Nasrallah found his ambitions for the Bukharan throne blocked, the governor of Samarqand along with Abu Sa'id Khwaja ibn Abd al-Hayy sent a letter inviting the aspiring ruler to the region's former capital. Nasrallah moved his army from Qarshi to Samarqand, where he was greeted with great enthusiasm and proclaimed sultan above the Heavenly Stone

64. On the Keneges dynasty of Shahrisabz, see Pickett, "Written into Submission."

65. Khumūlī was himself a madrasa student in Samarqand and was an eyewitness to the battle, which he described in vivid detail. Khumūlī, *Tārīkh*, ff. 274a–276a.

66. ʿAbd al-Ḥayy's *qāḍī al-qużāt* (synonymous with *qāḍī-yi kalān*) seal is found on an endowment document as late as 1817/18. Welsford and Tashev, *A Catalogue of Arabic-Script Documents from the Samarqand Museum*, 271–72.

67. Though Ḥusayn Töre was generally remembered in a positive light by chroniclers, at least one scholar wrote that Naṣrallāh was always the favored successor. Salmān Samarqandī, *Tafṣīl wa bayān-i dawlat-i jamāʿat-i Manghit*, ff. 167b–168a; Ḥakīm Khan, *Muntakhab al-tawārīkh*, 1:417.

(Kok-Tash).[68] His time as a rebel was short-lived, as Nasrallah wasted little time in marching on Bukhara, removing Umar Khan from power, and exiling him.[69] Nasrallah owed his very throne to Abu Sa'id Khwaja and rewarded the scholar handsomely for his support, appointing him to the post of *qazi-yi kalan*, which he held at least into the late 1840s.[70] Abu Sa'id's younger brother, Mir Salman, was given the post of *mufti* of Samarqand, as well as *mudarris* of the Tilla-kari madrasa.[71]

Abu Sa'id Khwaja's children reaped the benefits of their father's loyalty, and the family dynasty of Abd al-Hayy soon reached far beyond the borders of Samarqand itself. In 1842 Nasrallah achieved a string of victories that culminated in the capture of the city of Khoqand, capital of one of the most powerful rival city-states. Nasrallah then proceeded to put Khoqand's ruler and some members of his family to death and installed a Manghit governor in his place.[72] Khoqand was a city of sufficient prestige and size that it merited its own *qazi-yi kalan*, a distinction it apparently shared only with Bukhara and Samarqand, and Nasrallah selected Abu Tahir Khwaja Samarqandi (son of Abu Sa'id Khwaja, son of Abd al-Hayy) for the job.[73]

Nasrallah's approach proved a bit heavy-handed three months later when the Khoqandis rose up and ejected Abu Tahir along with the governor. This setback did not spell the end of Abu Tahir's career, however. As of 1849, he was serving as *mufti* of Samarqand, and after his father's death inherited the position of Samarqand's *qazi-yi kalan*.[74] Then following the city's conquest by

---

68. Salmān Samarqandī *Tafṣīl wa bayān-i dawlat-i jamā 'at-i Manghit*, f. 167b; Muḥammad Ya'qūb Bukhārī, *Risāla*, ff. 20a–20b. Although the stone was believed in the eighteenth and nineteenth centuries to have been Timur's coronation stone, Ron Sela holds this legend to be an "invented tradition" originating in the eighteenth century to legitimate rivals to Bukhara. "The 'Heavenly Stone' (Kök Tash) of Samarqand."

69. Salmān Samarqandī, *Tafṣīl wa bayān-i dawlat-i jamā 'at-i Manghit*, ff. 172a–172b.

70. Abū Sa'īd Khwāja's *qāżī al-qużāt* seal appears on legal documents until at least May–June 1849. Welsford and Tashev, *A Catalogue of Arabic-Script Documents from the Samarqand Museum*, 286. The sources are contradictory as to whether Abū Sa'īd Khwāja held the post of *qāżī-yi kalān* in Samarqand prior to Naṣrallāh's succession or was later appointed by him, as another source asserts. It does seem clear, however, that at this time the post of *shaykh al-Islām* was held by another individual—Mu'min Khwāja, who was also the uncle of the chronicler Muḥammad Ḥakīm Khan (*Muntakhab al-tawārīkh*, 1:422)—despite the fact that Abū Sa'īd's father, Abū al-Hayy, apparently managed to hold both posts simultaneously. Żiyā', *Zikr-i chand nafar-i 'ulamā'*, f. 155b.

71. Salmān Samarqandī, *Tafṣīl wa bayān-i dawlat-i jamā 'at-i Manghit*, f. 178b.

72. Salmān Samarqandī, *Tafṣīl wa bayān-i dawlat-i jamā 'at-i Manghit*, ff. 173a–174b.

73. Żiyā', *Nawādir-i żiyā 'īya*, f. 45b. This is the same Abū Ṭāhir Khwāja who wrote the *Samarīyya* in the 1830s, a description of pilgrimage sites in Samarqand. Semenov, ed., *Sobranie vostochnykh rukopisei Akademii Nauk Uzbekskoi SSR* vol. 1, 306–7.

74. His *muftī-yi Samarqand* seal appears on the same declaration of sale as Abū Sa'īd Khwāja's *qāżī al-qużāt* seal, suggesting that in later years the father-son duo worked as a team. Welsford and Tashev, *A Catalogue of Arabic-Script Documents from the Samarqand Museum*, 286.

Russia, he continued to serve as *qazi* in various Bukharan provinces during the tenure of Nasrallah's successor, Amir Muzaffar (r. 1860–85).[75]

Abu Tahir was not the only of Abd al-Hayy's grandchildren forced to relocate in the face of military upheaval. Abu al-Hayy Sudur was also forced to flee his family's ancestral home in Samarqand when it was annexed by the Russian Empire in 1868.[76] Although the position of *qazi* was retained under Russian rule, and some scholars appearing in Bukharan sources elected to stay and serve in such a capacity, the position of *qazi-yi kalan* and all the associated perks were abolished.[77] Perhaps realizing what he stood to lose, Abu al-Hayy Sudur was listed among the ulama who took up arms to resist the Russian advance, and was greeted with great honor by Amir Muzaffar.[78] Though he never rose to the heights of *qazi-yi kalan* like his brother, cousin, and grandfather, he was appointed *qazi* of several provinces, including Shahrisabz. Ironically, the latter was under Bukharan control only because Russia conquered the competitor city-state in 1870 and then turned it over to Bukhara.[79]

Several of Abd al-Hayy ibn Abu al-Khayr's great-grandchildren rose to prominence in the final decades of the Bukharan protectorate, but Abd al-Samad ibn Abu al-Hayy Sudur ibn Ma'sum Khwaja ibn Abd al-Hayy's (d. ca. 1920) career perhaps serves as the most appropriate epitaph for the family dynasty.[80] Abd al-Samad was described by his biographer as an exceptionally talented calligrapher and jurist who, despite his youth, was appointed *qazi* of several important provinces close to Bukhara, such as Ghijduwan and Charjuy, and eventually rose to the powerful post of *ra'is* of Bukhara. From there, his career took a downhill turn. During the Russian Civil War, Abd al-Samad, along with several of his colleagues, was captured by the Bolsheviks and executed in the town of Baljuwan, located in the mountainous province of Khatlan.[81]

---

75. Salmān Samarqandī, *Tafṣīl wa bayān-i dawlat-i jamā ʿat-i Manghit*, f. 178b.

76. Abū al-Hayy Ṣudūr was descended from his namesake via a different son: Maʿṣūm Khwāja ibn Abū al-Hayy.

77. Morrison, *Russian Rule in Samarkand, 1868–1910*, 250–53. For instance, ʿAbd al-Jabbār Ūrgūtī, who was also renowned calligrapher and formerly a *mudarris* in Bukhara, served as a *qāżī* under Russian rule. Żiyāʾ, *Tadẕhkār-i ash ʿār*, 294.

78. Żiyāʾ, *Nawādir-i żiyā ʾīya*, f. 49a.

79. Aside from Shahrisabz, Abū al-Ḥayy Ṣudūr served as *qāżī* in Qarshi, Ghijduwān, and Ḥisār. Legal documents attest his presence in Qarshi in November-December 1885. Welsford and Tashev, *A Catalogue of Arabic-Script Documents from the Samarqand Museum*, 135.

80. ʿAbdallāh Khwāja ibn Abū al-Hayy Ṣudūr (d. 1905/06) was a well-known calligrapher, served as a provincial *qāżī*, and was a personal friend of Żiyāʾ as was his brother Ạbū Ṭāhir Khwāja. Żiyāʾ, *Ẕikr-i chand nafar-i ʿulamā*, f. 124b, 155b.

81. Żiyāʾ, *Taẕkirat al-khaṭṭāṭīn*, f. 86b.

As with Hadi Khwaja's family, turbulent political circumstances rendered Abd al-Hayy ibn Abu al-Khayr's services to the Turkic nobility urgent and essential, which allowed him to help establish a new status quo and secure the fortunes of his descendants for over a century. Both scholarly dynasties managed to weather Bukhara's total defeat by Russia in 1868, but for other families that same event marked the beginning of their ascent.

Patronage Networks and Family Dynasties in the Colonial Period

The Russian subjugation of Bukhara created new opportunities not just for the newly integrated scholars from the Kuhistan, but also for those riding their coattails. The dynamic of the factions dueling for the top judicial posts during the protectorate period has been well illustrated by Dudoignon.[82] Here I focus on some of the families who found advancement in more modest positions, often obtained through services to scholarly families above them, or to less powerful Turkic provincial nobility.

Russian military backing made the amirs far less dependent on the ulama than they had been historically, which gave them greater leeway to play different families of scholars against one another, which in turn meant more frequent turnover.[83] In the decades preceding the Russian conquest, scholars such as Abd al-Hayy wielded sufficient clout to make positions like the *qazi*-ship all but hereditary, but protectorate-era rulers could hire and fire with greater impunity.[84] Moreover, the radical geopolitical reconfiguration in Central Asia and northern Afghanistan led to an influx of émigrés from many provinces beyond Kulab (a mountainous province in the Kuhistan), so there was greater competition for choice positions. Although these lineages tended to last only two or three generations, cut short by the Bolshevik conquest in 1920, the intention here is to emphasize the deep power shifts that spilled into the middling ranks of the ulama rather than the dynastic longevity illustrated in the previous cases.

Abd al-Wahid Sarir Balkhi (l. ca. 1790/91–1885/86) originated from a village in eastern Khurasan called Sancharak, some fifty kilometers from Sar-i Pul and one hundred from Balkh.[85] Although the city-states of Khurasan were for most intents and purposes independent when Abd al-Wahid journeyed

82. Dudoignon, "Faction Struggles among the Bukharan Ulama."

83. Khalid, "Society and Politics in Bukhara, 1868–1920."

84. Even the protectorate-era amirs, however, had to take local interests into account: Wilde, "Creating the Façade of a Despotic State: On Āqsaqāls in Late 19th-Century Bukhara."

85. Żiyā', *Tażkirat al-khaṭṭāṭīn*, f. 84a. It is worth noting that Wāżiḥ, writing decades earlier, cites ʿAbd al-Wāḥid's *nisbat* (geographic appellation) as Khulmī rather than Balkhī. Wāżiḥ, *Tuḥfat*

to Bukhara for madrasa study, following Dost Muhammad's conquest of Balkh in 1848–50 the region was gradually becoming a hinterland to Kabul, having previously been a more formidable cultural center.[86] In Bukhara Abd al-Wahid found ready patronage support at the hands of the amir and through his alliance with the Ibn Bayza Kulabi lineage, upon which Amir Muzaffar increasingly came to rely after the province was integrated into Bukhara following the Russian conquest.[87]

We last encountered Abd al-Wahid in chapter 3 reciting Persian poetry in his madrasa after hours, and indeed his diverse competencies very much epitomized a polymath of Islam. Although Abd al-Wahid did not directly leverage his reputed mastery of the Islamic hard sciences to find prestige, the way Hadi Khwaja had, he managed to transform his other, more artistic skills into temporal power. Beyond the aesthetic pleasures of Persian poetry, it often served a political function in the form of the eulogy (*madh*), poetic verse praising an important figure.[88] One poetic biographical dictionary notes that Abd al-Wahid wrote verses in praise of Sadr al-Din Khatlani, the *qazi-yi kalan* appointed by Amir Muzaffar, as well his grandson Badr al-Din (l. 1836–1908), who was then serving as *muhtasib/ra'is* of Bukhara, and who would later also serve as the *qazi-yi kalan* from 1889–1908. Both were of the powerful Kulabi line of Ibn Bayza.[89]

Abd al-Wahid was at least as well known for his calligraphy as his poetry and appears in both varieties of *tazkiras*. He was descended from Saqi Muhammad Sanchariki, who innovated a famous style of calligraphy that became popular in Bukhara, and who followed Subhan Quli Khan (r. 1680–1702) to Bukhara to serve as a *mufti* when the khan conquered the city from Balkh during a succession struggle.[90] Though Abd al-Wahid was too young to have ever personally studied under the master calligrapher, Ziya counted this as

---

al-aḥbāb, f. 121a. This is probably because by the time Żiyā' was writing, the city-state of Khulm had ceased to exist for half a century.

86. Arash Khazeni has argued that environmental changes—particularly endemic cholera outbreaks—transitioned Balkh from an urban center at the beginning of the nineteenth century to a backwater half a century later. "The City of Balkh and the Central Eurasian Caravan Trade in the Early Nineteenth Century." Bukhara was also commonly reported to be disease-ridden, so environmental reasons can only partially explain the region's apparent decline as a cultural and economic center.

87. "When the Khatlan province came to be annexed to the Emirate of Bukhara in 1876, the mullahs and *ṭalabas* from Kulab began to enjoy stronger weight in the political balance among the Bukharan clergy." Before that they had been more closely tied to the city-state of Khoqand. Dudoignon, "Faction Struggles among the Bukharan Ulama," 77.

88. On the role of poetry in advancing scholarly careers, see also McChesney, "Earning a Living."

89. Muḥtaram, *Tażkirat al-shuʿarā*, f. 123a.

90. Żiyā', *Tażkirat al-khaṭṭāṭīn*, f. 83a.

an advantage at it allowed Abd al-Wahid the space to innovate and improve on Saqi's style.[91] This talent earned him the personal notice of the amirs, and Nasrallah (r. 1827–60) commissioned him to scribe a commentary on Islamic law.[92]

Abd al-Wahid's skills in the arts were not purely of a recreational nature; they were also tools for securing the attention and patronage of powerful individuals within both the Turkic and scholarly hierarchies. He went on to employ an entirely different type of knowledge serving as a *mudarris* as well as *qazi* in at least four different provinces, including Ghijduwan, where he died in 1885/86.[93]

The evidence that his services rendered directly led to these appointments is circumstantial but telling. Abd al-Wahid was a recent immigrant to Bukhara in need of sponsors. As a consequence of shifting geopolitical formations, Sadr al-Din Khatlani had recently arrived in the city of Bukhara and lacked a local network but as *qazi-yi kalan*, he had considerable patronage to offer. It appears that the *qazi-yi kalan* at times had the power to appoint regional *qazis*, and at the very least exerted influence over the amir's decision.[94] Ziya wrote that Rahim Khan (r. 1747–59) delegated the power to hire and fire *qazis* to the ill-fated *qazi-yi kalan*, Nizam al-Din.[95] Students who failed to attach themselves to the chief judge and pay their dues, which was the custom of the time, found themselves cut off from patronage.[96]

Abd al-Wahid's status may have been beneath that of Sadr al-Din Khatlani, but he had considerable resources at his disposal and those close to him did quite well for themselves. His son-in-law, Taj al-Din Balkhi "Aslam" (d. 1910/11), was a fellow immigrant from eastern Khurasan and gained renown as a poet, *qazi*, *mudarris*, and *mufti* in the city of Bukhara.[97] For one

91. Żiyā', *Taẕkirat al-khaṭṭāṭīn*, f. 84a.

92. Wāżiḥ, *Tuḥfat al-aḥbāb*, f. 121. As argued in chapter 5, the ulama were so uniformly eclectic that excellence in one area (such as calligraphy) could lead to promotion in an unrelated field (such as jurisprudence).

93. ʿAbd al-Wāḥid's biographers were careful to note his self-imposed spiritual austerity and simple dress despite his considerable wealth, which he put to use financing his pilgrimage to Mecca via Istanbul. Wāżiḥ, *Tuḥfat al-aḥbāb*, f. 121; Pīrmastī, *Afżāl al-taẕkār*, f. 98b. He also likely used his wealth to collect books, as his library was rumored to contain over 2,000 volumes. żiyā', *Taẕkirat al-khaṭṭāṭīn*, f. 84b.

94. This only applies, of course, to the territories actually controlled by Bukhara to any significant degree at any given time.

95. Żiyā', *Nawādir-i żiyā'īya*, f. 39a–39b.

96. Decades later, ʿAbd al-Rasūl "Tājir" (d. 1914/15), who appeared in chapter 4 as a merchant-cum-scholar, made the mistake of slighting the reigning Kulabi *qāżī-yi kalān*, Badr al-Dīn, and consequently he was not only blacklisted from appropriate religious positions, but his merchant interests suffered as well. Muḥtaram, *Taẕkirat al-shuʿarā*, f. 95a.

97. Muḥtaram, *Taẕkirat al-shuʿarā*, ff. 88b–89a.

of his students, Azizallah "Qadari," the primary sources offer much more direct evidence for a narrow Balkh network under Abd al-Wahid's patronage. Azizallah obtained his position as *ra'is/muhtasib* of Ghijduvan as a direct result of his service (*khizmat*) to Abd al-Wahid, which he in turn secured through their common Balkh heritage (*balkhi-gi*).[98]

The family dynasty that consistently served as a counterbalance to the Kulabi one, referred to by Dudoignon as the "Bukharan faction," cultivated its own set of patron-client relationships. Abd al-Karim "Shatir" served in many mid-level administrative positions (e.g., alms collector [*zakat-chi*]), under Nasrallah (r. 1827–60). When Abd al-Shakur "Ayyat" 's fortunes began to rise under the next amir, Abd al-Karim offered his daughter's hand in marriage, and witnessed his own elevation as a result as he was appointed *qazi* of Kamat and subsequently Qarakol.

Ziya, Abd al-Shakur's son and author of the source referenced here, made it exceedingly clear both that this constituted a substantial social promotion (*taraqqi*) and that the spillover of good fortune lasted only as long as the patron was in favor. When Abd al-Shakur was removed from his tenure as *qazi-yi kalan* in favor of the Kulabi faction, Abd al-Karim's own disappointment followed. He had been hoping to be awarded the rank of Sudur but was forced to settle for a madrasa teaching position. Nevertheless, the so-called Bukharan faction would move in and out of the top positions until the last days of the Bukharan amirate, so Abd al-Karim's sons would have their own opportunities. One of his sons was appointed *qazi* in Khayrabad and a second was training to do the same under Ziya, though his life was cut short by the revolution while he was still young.[99]

Knowledge into Power

At first glance, the peculiar skill set of the polymaths of Islam would appear rather removed from power politics and practical concerns, seemingly split between leisure activities (poetry, calligraphy, music), mysticism, and theoretical jurisprudence. True, judges applied Sharia law on a daily basis, but doing so required only a small fraction of the Hadith study, Qur'anical exegesis, and legal theory emphasized in their training. Yet Persianate society had a logic and power dynamic all its own, which rendered exactly those talents indispensable for the temporal authorities. Some rulers,

98. Muḥtaram, *Taẕkirat al-shu'arā*, f. 150b.

99. Żiyā', *Ẕikr-i chand nafar-i 'ulamā'*, ff. 124b–125a.

such as Nadir Shah, had theological ambitions impossible to achieve without the expertise and support of the ulama. Others depended on the social mobilization offered by prominent ulama, which in turn depended on respect and loyalty within the educational system. More artistic talents, such as poetry, played a role in burnishing a noble's legitimacy and legacy.

Once the Turkic military elite granted influence to a scholar, it compounded on itself and was not so easily rescinded. The power accorded to the top judicial positions allowed the scholar to amass further the very skills that had prompted the noble to reward the scholar in the first place, which manifested in scholarly family dynasties. None of the family dynasties traced in this chapter produced any single text identifying their family tree as such. Rather, the connections have been cobbled together from a multitude of sources across a wide range of genres—which makes the enduring imprint these families left all the more remarkable. An outline of these potent kinship networks emerges organically from the social institutions they permeated, even though they were never consciously objectified as such.

The Turkic nobility needed the ulama for bureaucratic tasks and religious legitimacy, but their need was particularly acute during periods of political upheaval, and with the rise of new configurations of political-military authority went new sets of scholarly families as well. Islamic scholars were no strangers to the halls of power, but nor were they its direct representatives. The next chapter continues to examine the interplay between Islamic knowledge and power, bringing into focus the ulama's complicated understanding of their sphere of moral authority vis-à-vis that of the prince.

Chapter 8

The Sovereign and the Sage

The Precarious, Paradoxical Relationship between the Ulama and Temporal Power

When the eighth-century Abbasid monarch al-Mansur demanded that Abu Hanifa put his considerable juridical knowledge to practical use as a *qazi* (judge), the latter insisted that he was not cut out for the position.[1] "You lie," rejoined the caliph at this affront. Thinking fast, Abu Hanifa replied: "Verily, the Commander of the Faithful himself has declared me unworthy by ascribing dishonesty to me, for if I am a liar then I am not fit for the post of *qazi*."[2] Whatever the historicity of this anecdote, it illustrates an underlying tension between the demands of the state and a morality emphasizing austerity and freedom from both material and political concerns. Though legends differ as to whether Abu Hanifa ultimately resisted the lure of political influence and material comfort to the end of his life, his pious suffering in the caliph's dungeon and righteous struggle are universally valorized by his biographers.[3] Abu Hanifa's student Abu Yusuf followed a rather different path, enthusiastically taking on the mantle of *qazi*

1. Abu Hanifa is credited as the founder of the Hanafi school of jurisprudence (*mazhab*), which has been dominant in Anatolia, Central Asia, and India since the Seljuk era.

2. Ẕahabī, *Manāqib al-Imām Abī Ḥanīfa*, 26.

3. One tradition relayed by Ẕahabī depicts Abu Hanifa eventually submitting to the caliph and serving as *qāżī*, dying three days later and adjudicating only a single case. Most accounts agree that he maintained his distance from politics. Ẕahabī, *Manāqib al-Imām Abī Ḥanīfa*, 27.

and advocating forcefully for the legitimacy of the Abbasid state.[4] These two archetypes epitomize a tension in Islam still palpable in Central Asia during the long nineteenth century.

However, much of the historiography would seem to imply that the specter of Abu Hanifa, reminding the ulama of their independent moral authority, had already faded from memory by this period. The Soviet historiographical model conceived of the ulama as the religious branch of government, the clerical arm of the same exploitative class.[5] Similarly, scholarship on the ulama in colonial Turkestan has depicted them as quickly reconciling themselves to Russian rule and endorsing it as a "house of Islam."[6] Although many of the Jadids (Islamic modernists) emerged from the ranks of the madrasa-trained elite, they too viewed the ulama as lackeys of the old order.[7] Conversely, some modern scholars have described the Hanafi ulama as "quietist" in that they were content to stay out of politics, so long as they continued to play a prominent role in religious life.[8]

These contrasting images pose an interpretive dilemma. Soviet scholarship was correct that the ulama permeated all levels of government, so this social group as a whole was not "quietist" in the Abu Hanifa sense of being above state politics. Moreover, scholarship on Bukhara during the Russian protectorate period portrays the ulama as not at all quietist, actively inciting religious riots in opposition to the amir.[9] How, then, are we to understand the ulama's relationship with state power?

Political quietism means choosing not to oppose the state, while simultaneously suggesting that the social group in question would have good reason to do precisely that. After all, one would not characterize the Russian colonial bureaucracy as "quietist" for doing its job and staying out of politics. Rather, the term "quietism" entails separateness from, and even moral or ideological opposition to, the state. Although the term is generally used to

---

4. Zaman, *Religion and Politics Under the Early ʿAbbāsids*, 101.

5. For example, Muminov, *Istoriia Uzbekskoi SSR*, 117. More recent Uzbek scholarship has nuanced this picture to portray the ulama not only as government officials but also as a sort of bridge between the upper and lower strata of society. Alimova, *Istoriia Uzbekistana*, 74–75.

6. Komatsu, "Dār al-Islām Under Russian Rule as Understood by Turkestani Muslim Intellectuals"; Crews, *For Prophet and Tsar*, 263–64.

7. Khalid, *The Politics of Muslim Cultural Reform*, 104.

8. For instance, Adeeb Khalid writes that in the face of Russian aggression "the ulama fell back on a long tradition of quietism well articulated in the local Hanafi tradition." *Islam after Communism*, 38. Muhammad Qasim Zaman argues that a quietist stance had already become mainstream by the Abbasid period, and across *maẕhabs*. *Religion and Politics Under the Early ʿAbbāsids*, 78. For a discussion of the term's use in late Central Asia history, see Sartori, "Towards a History of the Muslims' Soviet Union," 330–31.

9. Becker, *Russia's Protectorates in Central Asia*, 160–61; Wennberg, *On the Edge*, 66.

refer to ulama who elected not to challenge the state in the Russian and Soviet contexts, Abu Hanifa's brand of quietism was an act of defiance. With such a range of meanings, the term is perhaps inadequate for engaging the question of the ulama's relationship with state power.

A broad argument advanced in this book—that the ulama stood as a unified social group with an eclectic range of competencies—only thickens the plot. If ascetic sufis constituted a social group separate from the jurists, then one could imagine that a cave-dwelling mystic's attitude toward the state might differ fundamentally from that of the legal clerk serving it.[10] But because the polymaths of Islam moved between those vocations and beyond, the contradictory picture conveyed by the idea of "quietism" must be indicative of a deeper ideological tension.

This chapter argues that by the long nineteenth century the ulama stood as a pillar of the state, limited though that state was. Islamic scholars systematically deployed their diverse Persianate skill set and leveraged Islamic knowledge on behalf of the Turkic nobility.[11] Nevertheless, the ulama still envisioned the state as an Islamic state, and they carefully guarded their moral prerogative to speak for the religion both groups agreed had a total monopoly on politics and social life. Although in certain instances evidence exists of this most important of prerogatives—the authority to legitimately speak for religion—shifting in favor of the Turkic military elite, the ulama cultivated a spirit of moral independence and superiority to the state.

This moral distance between the ulama and the Turkic nobility was not a contrast between religious authority and secular state authority.[12] "Temporal" is used here as a shorthand term for referring to anything not explicitly tied to the textual, madrasa-rooted tradition of learning, but it does not mean nonreligious.[13] Scholars have recently demonstrated that in the aftermath of the Mongol conquests, monarchs in the Islamic world increasingly styled themselves as sacred kings, embodying scholarly, mystical, and millenarian

10. Conversely, the same logic holds for the specter of radical "eshanism," a holdover trope from the Russian campaigns in the Caucasus, where sufis were associated with anti-colonial resistance. Knysh, "Sufism as an Explanatory Paradigm."

11. As discussed in chapters 1 and 4, this study conceptualizes the ulama and Turkic nobility in terms of distinct logics of power: one rooted in the madrasa and Islamic knowledge, and the other in lineage and tribal standing (i.e., the steppe tradition).

12. Although religion existed as a concept within the Islamic tradition (*dīn* vs. *dunyā*), it is often difficult to separate the nonreligious in any modern, secular sense (see chapter 1). See also Rapoport, "Royal Justice and Religious Law," 75.

13. Moshe Halbertal's understanding of a "text-centered community" is helpful for making this distinction: *People of the Book*, 6–8.

authority.[14] This tradition of divine kingship was still alive and well in Central Asia's long nineteenth century.[15]

The Turkic military establishment certainly did not see itself as secular, but the fact that both social groups were Muslims who portrayed themselves and their world predominantly through the prism of Islam did not ameliorate the core dispute over who speaks for religion and by which means.[16] Despite their common grounding in Islamic discourse and symbols, and despite the substantial overlap and fluidity between the two social groups in practice (at least in one direction), the ulama and Turkic nobility owed their social advancement to fundamentally distinct logics of power, which accounts for the enduring tension in their alliance of convenience.[17]

Ultimately, the governor of a province or the local garrison commander was appointed to that position because of his lineage and tribal standing—even though that did not make his status in any way "secular," and even though some of the Turkic nobility (especially the monarchs) justified their position based on religious erudition as well. The extent to which the Turkic nobility was successful in appropriating both logics of power, or superseding the alternative one, was the extent to which the ulama were no longer necessary. In other words, the ulama's claim to independent religious authority was not only an intellectual issue: it was an existential one.

Islamic scholars waged this struggle through subtle turns of phrases and selective invocations of the canon.[18] At times, scholars openly defied the will of the monarch. More frequently, they served the monarch, while taking care

---

14. Brack, "Mediating Sacred Kingship"; Moin, *The Millennial Sovereign*; Balabanlilar, "Lords of the Auspicious Conjunction."

15. Ziad, "Traversing the Indus and the Oxus," 553. At the very least, we can observe that titles such as "Lord of the Auspicious Conjunction" (*Ṣāḥib-Qirān*) were in wide circulation among Central Asian monarchs (e.g., attributed to Naṣrallāh in the Manghit case [*Jung-i Qāḍī Mīr Sayyid Qamar Ṣudūr*, f. 175b], or to numerous members of the Qongrat dynasty [Munis, *Firdaws al-Iqbāl*.]) What is less clear is the extent to which claiming this title was perfunctory by the nineteenth century, or if it still entailed rigorous astrological and occult justification (as in the Timurid, Mughal, and Safavid cases).

16. Even the native courts artificially separated out by the colonial regime as based on "custom" (*ʿādat*) rather than Sharia stubbornly continued to deploy terms and concepts drawn from Islamic law. Sartori, "The Birth of a Custom."

17. Individuals of Turkic origins could acquire Perso-Islamic knowledge and move into the ranks of the ulama, but no amount of learning could enable someone of non-Turkic origins to join the Turkic nobility. See chapter 4.

18. This inversion of authority roles between philosopher-king and philosopher-scholar has instructive parallels in the Roman Empire: "The philosopher, whose presence in pedagogical capacity is 'supposed' to help legitimise the emperor, might well subtly subvert his authority, for those who have the ear to hear. Power is not unilateral here: the equivocations and ambivalences of language allow the speaker or writer to open and close various alternative readings, to allow for multiple responses from different sources." Whitmarsh, "Reading Power in Roman Greece," 195.

to portray themselves as sage mentors and tutors of the Turkic nobility. The ulama conceded and even bolstered the monarch's claims of divine sanction but did so while simultaneously asserting their own role as mediators of that sanctity. Their writing often served the immediate end of underwriting the authority of their temporal patrons, while also asserting the independent authority of religion, and their own role as custodians and truest interpreters of religion. The ulama's success in this regard had everything to do with their mastery of the intersecting array of competencies and knowledge forms.

Imagining the Ideal Islamic State

In broad strokes, the ulama had a specific blueprint in mind when it came to how a proper Islamic state ought to be run, who should govern, and even what administrative roles should buttress it. These core features emerged within the first few centuries of Islam and were largely consistent across schools of law. This scaffolding evolved over time, incorporating pre-Islamic ideas of Persian kingship, adding a mystical dimension, and coexisting with myriad official positions of Turkic origin.[19] Yet that centuries-old schematic of an ideal Sharia-based state lurked in the background, copied and recopied in legal manuals, and subtly influencing—though not determining—governmental practices. This is why figures like the *qazi* and *mufti* (writer of legal opinions) appear in nearly any study of Islam, worldwide. It is also why powerful figures outside of the legal canon—such as the *yasawul* or *udaychi* (both Turkic military ranks) in the Central Asian case—are so frequently invisible in the sanitized texts written by the ulama, and why those terms did not, for the most part, travel beyond the region.

Counterintuitively, this Islamic state was effectively beyond the reach of the monarch supposedly perched at its apex, and endured as a textually inscribed, aspirational edifice that survived Mongol and Russian conquests. The ulama had evolved independently from the state and were not dependent on it in the same way that other elite groups were, such as the Zoroastrian clergy that preceded them or the Turkic nobility.[20] This afforded the

---

19. Ideas of justice and kingship with pre-Islamic Persian origins, but effectively Islamized, survived in *akhlāq* manuals. Alam, *The Languages of Political Islam*; Subtelny, "A Late Medieval Persian Summa on Ethics." Turkic positions existing alongside the more generic Islamic ones (e.g., *qāżī*) are reflected both in schematic texts and in chancery documents. An example of the former is Badīʿ-Dīvān, *Madzhmaʿ al-arḳām*.

20. Patricia Crone argues that there is something peculiar about early Islamic society in its production of an elite class fiercely defensive of its moral distance from the state. Crone, *Slaves on Horses*, 63, 75. By contrast, the Sasanian Empire was buttressed by an agrarian service aristocracy with the shah as its ideological core. Payne, "Cosmology and the Expansion of the Iranian Empire, 502–628

ulama moral independence from temporal authorities that set them apart. Even a millennium later, Islamic ideals antithetical to the state very much lived on in the form of an insistence on superior moral authority and independent mediation of religion.

Multiple genres of political writing refracted subtly differing visions of the Islamic state. Theological texts in the core madrasa curriculum inculcated the ideal of the Imamate, which was theoretically supposed to be coterminous with the state (though almost never was in practice).[21] The "mirrors for princes" (*akhlaq*) genre had roots in pre-Islamic Iran, was almost immediately adapted for an Islamic context, and was ubiquitous by the medieval period.[22] In principle, *akhlaq* texts indeed posited an absolutist model of the state, with the universe revolving around the monarch.[23] Even so, and even despite the pre-Islamic origins of this sensibility, the *akhlaq* genre was not hermetically sealed from more explicitly legalistic genres, which subordinated the monarch to divine law. Nasir al-Din Tusi's foundational thirteenth-century work emphasized that virtuous government was synonymous with the Imamate, and later entries into the genre similarly insisted that a just ruler should not make a ruling without first consulting with the ulama.[24]

Legal treatises on government are less common than mirrors for princes, but those that do exist tend to make more explicit the primacy of the ulama.[25] As a legal treatise explicitly theorizing the state, Fazlallah ibn Ruzbihan Khunji's *Suluk al-muluk* ("Conduct of Kings"), stands as a rare exception. Although this work was composed in Bukhara, there is no reason to think it was especially influential in the long nineteenth century, and it was less so than *akhlaq* writing.[26] Nevertheless, Khunji's work is worth briefly considering because it built on legalistic models of government that preceded it, and

---

CE." This also differentiated Islamic states from the Russian Empire, where the aristocracy earned merit in tandem with the tsar's pleasure. Wortman, *Scenarios of Power*.

21. Messick, *Sharīʿa Scripts*, 10.

22. Subtelny, "A Late Medieval Persian Summa on Ethics"; O'Hanlon, "Kingdom, Household and Body History, Gender and Imperial Service under Akbar." Sasanian mirrors were translated into Arabic already in the Umayyad period, incorporating Islamic figures and motifs, but were later more common in Persian. Marlow, *Counsel for Kings*.

23. Subtelny, "A Late Medieval Persian Summa on Ethics," 605.

24. Ṭūsī, *The Nasirean Ethics*, 227, 230; Kāshifiī, *Akhlāq-i muḥsinī*, chap. 38.

25. The most famous Arabic treatise on government is ʿAlī ibn Muḥammad Māwardī's *al-Ahkām al-sultāniyya*, which, along with several other works, is discussed in Calder, "Friday Prayer and the Juristic Theory of Government."

26. *Sulūk al-mulūk* was copied into the nineteenth century (e.g., IVANUz, no. 2621), but the surviving copies of *akhlāq* texts (both that of Ṭūsī and later works building on his) are far greater in number. Of relevance is the fact that Khunjī himself adhered to the Shafi'i school of law, whereas Central Asia was predominantly Hanafi—though theory of government was not a major point of contention between the schools, and Khunjī drew on Hanafi scholarship as well, having fled from Iran

its core tenets (e.g., the role of the *qazi*) are reflected even in seemingly unrelated genres (e.g., poetical anthologies). Moreover, Khunji's model stands as an "outer boundary" for the absolutist state: Khunji is remembered as diehard statist, and yet even his work implicitly subordinates the monarch to the Sharia and its interpreters.[27]

Early jurists held that the "great imam" of the Islamic community (as opposed to the local imam, or prayer leader of a mosque) was to be elected and deposed by the ulama, and execute God's law (as interpreted by the ulama).[28] By contrast, Khunji asserted the sultan's right to the imamship of the community through conquest, and subsequent religious appointments in the realm were delegated only by the sultan/imam.[29] Khunji then envisioned a centralized administration emanating down from the sultan, who appointed a *shaykh al-Islam* to monitor all religious instruction, as well as *qazis* and *muhtasibs* (public morality enforcers) all of whom he had the right to depose at will.[30] Interpretations of *Suluk al-muluk* as a tool for the dominance of the military elite over the ulama, therefore, can be grounded in substantial evidence.

Yet even in defending the power of the prince over matters of religion, Khunji explicitly elevated the ulama above their patrons. Having just asserted the sultan's right to the imamate by conquest, Khunji continued: "The ulama have said that it is necessary to obey the imam and sultan in all things that he commands and forbids, whether he is just or unjust—*so long as it is not contrary to the Sharia.*"[31] That caveat carries profound implications. The Sharia's status as something separate from and above the monarch is perhaps obvious, and has been emphasized by scholars of Islam in other contexts.[32] Nevertheless, in the context of Central Asia, where the monarchy is often characterized as despotic and absolutist, this point is worth reemphasizing.[33] If

to Bukhara. Khunjī's work was also known in the Mughal court but was rejected for its intolerance and inflexibility. Alam, *The Languages of Political Islam*, 69.

27. Melvin-Koushki, "Khunji, Fazl Allah b. Ruzbihan (1455–1521)"; Lambton, *State and Government in Medieval Islam*, chap. 11; Haarmann, "Yeomanly Arrogance and Righteous Rule: Faḍl Allāh Ibn Rūzbihān Khunjī and the Mamluks of Egypt."

28. Crone, *God's Rule*, 277.

29. Lambton, *State and Government in Medieval Islam*, 180. Khunjī, *Sulūk al-mulūk*, 82.

30. Khunjī, *Sulūk al-mulūk*, 93, 162, 179.

31. *Wa ʿulamāʾ gufta-and: wājib ast ṭāʿat-i imām wa sulṭān dar har chi amr wa nahy kunad mā-dām ki mukhālif-i sharʿ nabāshad, khwāh ʿādil k-hwāh jāʾir.* Khunjī, *Sulūk al-mulūk*, 82; emphasis added. Note that Khunjī did not seem to place much importance on the personal conduct of the sultan; his rule was what was important. Elsewhere Khunjī wrote that the sultan who takes the imamate by conquest has the right to rule even if he is "immoral and ignorant" (*fāsiq wa jāhil*). Khunjī, 82.

32. Crone, *God's Rule*, chap. 17; Hallaq, *The Impossible State*.

33. See discussion in Pickett, "Written into Submission," 832.

we can glimpse the specter of Abu Hanifa even in Khunji's political thought, then perhaps even those ulama serving in the amirate administration were not the mere cogs in a wheel they have sometimes been portrayed.

Khunji was clear that the sultan's role was to enforce the law not to create it. The sultan was subordinate to the Sharia, which raised obvious questions about who was to interpret that law. Drawing from the same script as his predecessors, Khunji deployed numerous anecdotes in which the Rightly Guided Caliphs deferred to the ulama on matters of religion, a sentiment shared in *akhlaq* texts. Similarly, he prescribed that after the sultan (a term Khunji used interchangeably with *padishah*) appointed a *shaykh al-Islam*, that appointee should be afforded complete deference.[34]

Thus the ideal Islamic state theorized in Khunji's more legalistic writing converges with that posited in mirrors for princes: both genres emphasize the power of the monarch while also explicitly or implicitly mandating his subordination to divine law, often at least implying that it was the ulama who interpreted that law. In both cases, this normative ambiguity was productive, masking potential power struggle by aggressively portraying the supremacy of the monarch and that of the ulama as compatible. In both genres, the etymologically Turkic titles of the nobility were elided almost entirely, since they did not fit comfortably within the idealized Islamic state modeled on the early caliphates.

It is clear from chancery documents that reality departed dramatically from this imagined ideal. Turkic positions specific to Central Asia were often the most powerful roles in the amirate, and the amir's personal retinue intervened in every sphere of government, including the ostensibly separate domain of the Sharia court.[35] Yet the deep roots of the Islamic state as an imagined ideal continued to influence the ulama's relationship with temporal power through the Bolshevik Revolution. Turkic state positions such as the *qushbegi* and *ataliq* stood as a potent reminder that Sharia was hardly the only relevant variable in this dynamic, but those roles were nevertheless layered on top of the ones modeled in legal treatises and taken for granted in other genres.[36] So long as that dominant paradigm was in force, eliminating positions such as *qazi* and *mufti* was effectively not an option for the ruler.

---

34. Khunjī, *Sulūk al-mulūk*, 88, 95.

35. Sartori, "The Evolution of Third-Party Mediation in Sharīʿa Courts in 19th- and Early 20th-Century Central Asia"; Sartori, *Visions of Justice*, chap. 1.

36. The *Majmaʿ al-arqām*, a 1798 Bukharan administrative manual, covers most of the Khunjī's Islamic positions, as well as many others. Badīʿ-Dīvān, *Madzhmaʿ al-arḳām*, 92–93. For a discussion of this work, focusing primarily on the rank of *qushbegi*, see Bregel, *The Administration of Bukhara Under the Manghïts and Some Tashkent Manuscripts*.

The logic underpinning Khunji's analysis provided Islamic scholars with an independent moral universe, separate from the will of the monarch. The reason that scholars such as Khunji felt the need to expound a normative vision of the Islamic state had much to do with the divergence of actual power dynamics from that model in practice. Even though Khunji certainly cherished the alliance of convenience with the Turkic nobility as a means to an end, his work can also be read as a challenge to temporal authority—or at least as an injunction for those authorities to safeguard the ulama's prerogative to speak for religion.

This same dynamic explains important dimensions of the ulama's relationship to the Turkic nobility in Central Asia during the long nineteenth century. The friction of an idealized Islamic state grafted onto a much more complex reality helps us understand both why Islamic scholars were such loyal allies to the Turkic nobility so much of the time, and why at other times they performed bold acts of defiance, drawing on a script many centuries in the making.

Perso-Islamic Knowledge as a Weapon of the Turkic Nobility

The ideal Islamic state modeled in Khunji's writing is reflected in the everyday legal practice of high Persianate intellectuals. Already by Khunji's time in the sixteenth century, the Abbasid caliphs of Baghdad were a distant memory, and there was a substantial textual basis for the explicit endorsement of temporal authority. I now turn to fatwas and entries in *jung* collections to bring back into focus precisely what those directly controlling the horses and cannons got out of the bargain in their aggressive courtship of the ulama.[37]

Unlike their predecessors, the "new Uzbek" dynasties that emerged from the rubble of Nadir Shah's short-lived empire in the mid-eighteenth century could not boast Chinggisid descent. This did not prevent them from invoking Mongol legitimacy, sometimes in new and creative ways, but the new amirates were nevertheless more dependent on Islam to justify their rule than their predecessors.[38] Although the sorts of documents considered here are very much part of an Islamic tradition stretching back over a millennium,

37. *Jung* refers to scholarly scrapbooks of extremely diverse contents, but generally focusing on juridical issues. For more on this, see the introduction and chapter 5.

38. See, for instance, Sela, *Ritual and Authority in Central Asia*. The earliest Manghit rulers also experimented with keeping puppet Chingissid khans on the throne, and Amir Ḥaydar (r. 1800–1827) could also boast matrilineal descent from Chinggis Khan. Salmān Samarqandī, *Tafṣīl wa bayān-i dawlat-i jamā ʿat-i Manghit*, ff. 161–161b, 164a. On the increasing importance of Islamic discourse to Central Asian rulers, see von Kügelgen, *Legitimatsiia sredneaziatskoi dinastii Mangitov*.

they took on new importance at this particular juncture—especially prior to the Russian conquest, when the coercive authority of the Manghit state was (counterintuitively) weaker.[39]

A letter copied into Qazi Mir Sayyid Qamar's *jung* demonstrates the ability of the ulama to turn a war of conquest into a righteous one on behalf of the Turkic nobility.[40] Bukhara only sporadically exerted meaningful control over the turbulent neighborhood of Turkic dynasties in the region. Shahrisabz, in particular, stood as a serious contender for regional supremacy during the 1840s and 1850s when this *jung* was written. The *jung* contains a copy of a letter addressed to Iskandar Wali-nima, governor of Shahrisabz, and written by Khalifa Muhammad, instructor of the Juybar madrasa.[41] Khalifa Muhammad pursued a three-fold strategy in this letter, taking advantage of a range of scholarly competencies: reason, jurisprudence, and mystical authority.

After lavishing praise on the ruling Bukharan amir, Nasrallah Khan (r. 1827–60), Khalifa Muhammad reminded Iskandar Wali-nima that Bukhara had subordinated his ancestors and rewarded them handsomely for their subsequent loyalty.[42] Then he quoted Khwaja Ahrar, a famous fifteenth-century Naqshbandi shaykh, on the virtues of a just, Sharia-abiding king, and the danger of infidelity (*kufran*) for those who oppose him. For the likes of Iskandar Wali-nima, Khalifa Muhammad continued, there were but two paths: submission and the path of peace, or continued opposition and the path of war.[43]

As if the threat of a holy war was not enough, Khalifa Muhammad topped off the letter by intimating that Iskandar Wali-nima's recalcitrance would lead him to a similar fate to that of the erstwhile monarch of Khoqand. Khalifa Muhammad alleged that Muhammad Ali, erstwhile monarch of Khoqand (r.

39. This is because after the Russian conquest of 1868, the Turkic nobility could count on Russian military backing, which made them relatively less beholden to the ulama. See Khalid, "Society and Politics in Bukhara, 1868–1920."

40. Sayyid Qamar's notebook illustrates the eclectic world of a polymath of Islam, with attestations of shrine pilgrimage, enchantments, astronomical/astrological essays, and a wide variety of juridical notes. *Jung-i Qāżī Mīr Sayyid Qamar Ṣudūr*.

41. The term *ḥākim* can also mean "ruler," but since it is contrasted with the Bukharan "Sultan and Commander of the Faithful [*Amīr al-Mū ʾminīn*]," in this instance it implies a subordinate status for Shahrisabz (from the perspective of Bukhara). Iskandar Wālī-niʿmā's alleged status as a governor of Bukhara is belied by Khalīfa Muḥammad's reference within the same letter to a request for permission to visit Shahrisabz as the Bukharan emissary. For a more detailed discussion of the sovereign claims of Bukhara vis-à-vis Shahrisabz, see Pickett, "Written into Submission."

42. *Jung-i Qāżī Mīr Sayyid Qamar Ṣudūr*, f. 142b.

43. *Rāh-i dū ṭarīqa hast: yā ṭarīqa-i muṣāliḥa, yā ṭarīqa-i muḥāriba*. *Jung-i Qāżī Mīr Sayyid Qamar Ṣudūr*, f. 142b. Khwāja Aḥrār was an apt reference, given his tremendous political clout among Timurid rulers in Central Asia. See Aḥrār, *The Letters of Khwāja ʿUbayd Allāh Aḥrār and His Associates*.

1822–41), married the wife of his father and denied the holy word of the Qur'an.[44] His execution at the hands of Nasrallah was not only necessary but enjoined by God.[45] Despite having implicitly just threatened a Sunni ruler with an apostate's death, Khalifa Muhammad followed his anecdote with an assertion that stately politics (*maslahat-i mulk*) were beyond him—all he could hope to do for Iskandar Wali-nima was convey the wisdom of a prophetic hadith to the effect that one who dies without recognizing the imam of his time dies an ignorant death.[46]

Sayyid Qamar included more general legal opinions in his notebook of similar value to a ruler facing frequent challenges to his authority. One such opinion ruled that if a just, Muslim ruler has inherited his kingdom from his forefathers, only to have his domain violated militarily by another, waging war against such an enemy is permitted (*mubah*), even if the usurping forces are Muslim as well.[47] Moreover, killing the transgressors (*mufsidin*) merits great reward, as does seizing their property. Funeral prayers for slain rebels were not deemed permissible. Finally, the opinion doomed collaborators to the same fate, and anyone asserting the religious legitimacy of the rebels was to be considered an infidel (*kafir*).[48] This opinion pointed to the alleged transgressions of the opponent—martyring innocent Muslims, enslaving them, and taking their property—as the source of justification. These are common outcomes of war, and the ulama provided the necessary legalese for placing a Sunni opponent on the same plane as a Buddhist, Shi'i, or Christian one (the more common *kafir* enemies in early modern Central Asia).

---

44. Some Bukharan chronicles remember Muḥammad ʿAlī Khoqandī in a similarly negative light, vaguely asserting that he failed to promote Islam among his people. Salmān Samarqandī, *Tafṣīl wa bayān*, f. 172b. Khoqand chronicles, unsurprisingly, portray Naṣrallāh as the villain and the death of Muḥammad ʿAlī (as well as his heir and mother, who were also executed) as martyrdom (*shahādat*). ʿAważ Muḥammad, *Tuḥfat al-tawārīkh khānī*, ff. 230b–231a.

45. "Since Muḥammad ʿAlī of Khoqand rejected the word of the Qur'an (*munkar-i naṣṣ-i Qurʾān gashta*), and has married the wife of his father, and on top of that has committed limitless transgressions; thus the killing of that deviant (*qatl-i ān mufsid*), along with his brothers and entourage, has become a sacred duty (*farż*); and if [the ruler of Bukhara] were not to kill him and his kin, that would be tantamount to shirking his sacred duty." *Jung-i Qāżī Mīr Sayyid Qamar Ṣudūr*, f. 142b.

46. *Jung-i Qāżī Mīr Sayyid Qamar Ṣudūr*, f. 142b. Khalīfa Muḥammad referenced a "famous" hadith to the effect that "he who dies without recognizing the Imam of his time dies a pagan death [i.e., death of the Jāhiliyya]." *Jung-i Qāżī Mīr Sayyid Qamar ṣudūr*, f. 142b. No hadith exists of precisely the wording employed by the author, though there are several that convey a similar idea and with some key words in common. See Ṣaḥīḥ al-Bukhārī: 7054 or Ṣaḥīḥ Muslim: 1848. Khalīfa Muḥammad's usage of the term "imam" fits with that of Khunjī, which holds the sultan to effectively be the acting imam of the community. Khunjī, *Sulūk al-mulūk*, 82.

47. The usurper forces deserving death are referred to as "a group from the army of Islam" (*jamʿī az sipāh-i Islām*) who "violate" (*tajāwuz namūda*) the domain of the rightful ruler. *Jung-i Qāżī Mīr Sayyid Qamar Ṣudūr*, f. 81b.

48. *Jung-i Qāżī Mīr Sayyid Qamar Ṣudūr*, f. 81b.

Islam has a long history of conceptualizing the suppression of rebellions in religious terms and fatwas invariably closed with at least one Arabic quotation from a classic text of jurisprudence.[49] The active engagement of the ulama with the classic texts through the production of commentaries and—as in this case—legal opinions afforded the tradition dynamism to react to the circumstances of the moment.[50] Though Bukhara eventually emerged as a regional force under Russian protection, in much of the eighteenth century and in the first part of the nineteenth century numerous serious competitors were present. Having worked so hard to establish Bukhara as a timeless beacon of Islam, Manghit rulers enjoyed greater credibility being equated with the "caliph" referenced in fatwas, which drew on the religious terminology of the first centuries of Islam when the aspirational category was a bit closer to reality.[51]

Such letters and legal opinions provided not only a justification for geopolitical expansion, but also a defense mechanism in the face of defeat. At the low point of Amir Haydar's reign, sometime after 1818, Bukhara suffered the loss of Samarqand at the hands of rebels, as well as embarrassing defeats by Shahrisabz and Khoqand.[52] Just when it seemed matters could not get any worse, the khanate of Khiva invaded as well, pillaging the surrounding provinces and setting fire to one of the city's gates. According to one chronicler, the fighting was so savage that for decades after one could recognize a resident of the deserts surrounding Bukhara by the absence of a single ear, the other having been cut off by the invading Khorezmians.[53] In this context, the author of a different anthology of legal rulings endowed the invasion with Islamic significance in a manner similar to that of the opinion reproduced in Sayyid Qamar's notebook.[54] The issue in question was the custody of women

49. The rhetoric of jihad was often deployed as a moral weapon against political rebellion, but such opponents were usually considered to have been in a category separate from non-Muslim adversaries. Bonner, *Jihad in Islamic History*, 11. Also, it is important to bear in mind that the endurance of the term "jihad" over time and geography masked constantly shifting meanings and practices. Syed, "Between Jihād and History."

50. An individual scholar could invoke examples from a vast array of texts, but it was the form of the opinion that lent it authority: "rather than see [Islamic legal] theory as producing doctrine, theory might be more properly assigned the role of validating doctrine." Jackson, "Fiction and Formalism," 195.

51. Although Shibani Khan (r. 1500–1510) briefly claimed the title of caliph, the Manghit rulers left that designation for the Ottoman sultan, though they did refer to themselves routinely as *Amīr al-Mu'minīn* ("Commander of the Faithful"). Von Kügelgen, *Legitimatsiia sredneaziatskoi dinastii Mangitov*, 45.

52. Muḥammad Ya'qūb Bukhārī, *Risāla*, ff. 15a–15b.

53. Ḥakīm Khan, *Muntakhab al-tawārīkh* vol. 1, 408–9. On the rivalry between Khiva and Bukhara, see Pickett, "Enemies beyond the Red Sands."

54. Although fatwas as preserved in *jung* collections endeavor to strip a case of proper nouns so as to endow the ruling with a sense of timelessness and generalizability, occasionally the names of

and children abducted by the Khorezmians and given respectively to new husbands and fathers in Khiva, but who later managed to escape and make it back to Bukhara. After denouncing the violations perpetrated by the enemy soldiers, the Bukharan scholar ruled that the forced marriages were invalid and that the victims should revert to their original Bukharan marriage.[55] The ulama could not turn back the clock to offer military victory to the Turkic nobility, but they could play a part in salving the wounds of defeat.

Another ruling in the same collection addressed the fact that during the crisis some residents of Bukhara were less than loyal in the face of the probable victory of Khiva. According to the opinion's premise, a certain sufi acolyte had been attending a Bukharan shaykh, but during the invasion joined with the Khorezmian army and followed it back to Khiva. Sufi communities frequently allied themselves with Turkic rulers, but their organizational structures transcended political boundaries, so this ostensible betrayal was no crime from the perspective of Islamic law. Instead, the opinion focused on the sufi's alleged heresy, claiming that he turned to innovations (*bida*) and began spreading heretical ideas among the simple folk, implying a Shi'i connection, and by emphasizing the Sunni orthodoxy of his former shaykh. After the sufi moved his family to Khiva, he was alleged to have continued sending heretical literature into Bukhara, which included verses falsely attributed to the Qur'an. The opinion denounced the sufi's actions and demanded that he be forced to repent through beating and imprisonment.[56]

Whatever the underlying motives of these legal opinions, their political utility for the Turkic nobility cannot be ignored. Instead of legitimate competitors, the enemies of Bukhara became enemies of religion, "those who wage war against God and His Messenger and endeavor to work corruption on earth," meriting divinely ordained capital punishment.[57] The ulama were empowering their Turkic sponsors to move against perceived enemies. It is not difficult to see how beneficial such a ruling could be for the Turkic nobility; instead of one thug fighting another thug, the monarch becomes a holy avenger. Such a move was also empowering for the ulama because by elevating the offense to the religious domain, they also placed it within their own moral jurisdiction.

---

places and persons remain intact, such as the references to Khorezm in these cases. No details specifically tie the opinion to the invasion of the early nineteenth century, but given the timing of the collection's composition, there are few other possibilities.

55. *Sbornik vypisok iz sochinenii po fikkhu i iuridicheskikh kazusov*, f. 390b.

56. *Sbornik vypisok iz sochinenii po fikkhu i iuridicheskikh kazusov*, f. 22a.

57. Q 5:32–33. Most of the preceding legal opinions reference the Qur'anic idea of *fasad fī al-arż*, which warrants the divine *ḥadd* punishment.

Ceding Islamic Authority to the Prince

In addition to serving the Turkic nobility, the ulama were complicit in ceding elements of their authority to their patrons. In certain respects, this had long been the case in Islamic history. During the medieval period, the ulama shared judicial authority with the military elite, who ran parallel legal courts (*mazalim*).[58] Turkic rulers of Central Asia did not avail themselves of *mazalim*, as did their Qajar neighbors, nor did they succeed in fully bureaucratizing the ulama, as did their Ottoman ones, but they did exert increasingly tight control over the Sharia court system within their domains.[59] The ulama in some cases actively justified the encroachment on their jurisdiction by their Turkic patrons. As emphasized previously, the difference between the Turkic nobility and the ulama was predicated on distinct logics of power, and members of the former—notably several of the Manghit amirs—crossed into the latter by justifying their authority in terms of their own learnedness in Islam. Theoretically, if the ulama were to fully accept that the amir was a paragon not only of Turkic authority but also of Islamic learning, then the Manghits would have succeeded in seizing the mantle of "God's caliph" where the Umayyads failed.[60] The ulama did not go quite so far as to accept the amir as their leading member, but movement in that direction—even beyond what Khunji was willing to allow—is evident in the examples that follow.

The *qazi* section of one *jung* opened with an Arabic passage from a popular collection of fatwas to the effect that the sultan has the right to simultaneously serve as a judge.[61] The next page included a similar ruling from a

58. In some cases this was tantamount to direct infringement on the prerogatives of the ulama. Coulson, *A History of Islamic Law*, 123. However, these *maẓālim* tribunals were not always competitor institutions. Bulliet, *The Patricians of Nishapur*, 26. In the Mamluk case, at least, it seems the *maẓālim* courts involved *qāżīs* alongside the rulers; the difference between *maẓālim* and a *qāżī* courts was simply jurisdictional (as opposed to informal law vs. Sharia). Rapoport, "Royal Justice and Religious Law," 81.

59. Sartori, "The Evolution of Third-Party Mediation in Sharīʿa Courts in 19th- and Early 20th-Century Central Asia." Although they pursued a different strategy than the Manghits did, the Qajar case similarly illustrates the gradual encroachment of temporal authority on legal matters. Schneider, "Religious and State Jurisdiction during Nāṣir Al-Dīn Shāh's Reign." Meanwhile, the Ottoman ulama evolved into a branch of the military elite, cogs in the wheel of a systematized bureaucracy unparalleled anywhere else in the Islamic world. Atçıl, *Scholars and Sultans in the Early Modern Ottoman Empire*, 5.

60. The Umayyad caliphs (661–750) claimed the right to adjudicate Islamic law and dictate the correct interpretation of religion, but their early Abbasid successors ultimately lost this prerogative to the ulama. See Crone and Hinds, *God's Caliph*.

61. *Fatāwā-yi kāfūrīya*, a compilation of Hanafi fatwas by Muḥammad b. Ḥājjī Muḥammad b. al-Ḥasan al- Samarqandī.

separate source that acknowledged the controversy over this very point, but held that the correct opinion confirmed the sultan's right to give legal rulings.[62] Similar sections of other *jung* emphasized that the *qazi* should follow the will of the monarch—even an unjust or infidel one—in all matters except those that explicitly contradict the revealed text.[63]

These rulings are drawn from legal works written centuries earlier. Yet the fact that these passages were deemed worthy of copying indicates that the issues detailed therein were of pressing concern in this time and place. Notably, they serve as evidence of an expansion of princely authority viewed as legitimate by the ulama. With regard to the monarch's ability to serve as *qazi*, Khunji was ambivalent on the matter. He recounted two Hanafi opinions on the issue, one in favor and one against, and interjected his own opinion that it is dishonorable (*wafi nist*) for a sultan to appoint himself as *qazi*.[64] Central Asian positions favored several centuries later were even more statist than those of Khunji, since they were seemingly more amenable to the monarch embodying numerous kinds of authority at once.

A fatwa from sometime in the late eighteenth or early nineteenth century used similar logic to justify the ruler's interference in legal affairs.[65] The actual point of dispute was over the ability of a *qazi* to continue prosecution of a matter beyond the statute of limitations (i.e., after an "Islamic legal era of thirty years").[66] The *mufti* came down heavily on the side of the temporal authorities, charging the *qazi* in question to stand down and obey the order. Then the *mufti* took a step further and broadened the point, writing: "All judges appointed by the sovereign (obeyed by all the world) are enjoined to take heed and submit to this order."[67] This ruling advanced the Turkic nobility's ability to intervene in judicial affairs, and it was endorsed with eight

62. *Jung* (IVANUz no. 8412), f. 202a–202b. The second *fiqh* source is identified only as *Jawāhir*, likely referring to *Jawāhir-i akhlāṭī* by the seventeenth-eighteenth-century Ottoman jurist Burhān al-Dīn Ibrāhīm ibn Abī Bakr ibn Muḥammad ibn Ḥusayn al-Akhlāṭī. It is worth noting that also that this particular *jung* seems to originate from Khorezm, not Bukhara, based on a Turkic inscription dating it to 1921/22.

63. *Jung-i maḥżar wa riwāyāt*, f. 37b.

64. Khunjī also directly refuted the logical transitive argument, that if a sultan appointed a *qāżī* then his authority trumped that of his appointee: "It would be faulty to say that [the sultan's judicial ruling] is valid because the *qāżī* derives his authority from the sultan and accepts his rulings and that it would be impossible for the *qāżī's* ruling to be valid and the sultan's invalid." Khunjī, *Sulūk al-mulūk*, 128.

65. TsGARUz F i-126 O 1 D 1730, f. 99. One of the seals on the fatwa appears to be dated 1192 hijri (i.e., 1778/79 CE), which is rather early for the Qushbegi collection (i-126).

66. *Baʿd az qarn-i sharʿī ki sī sāl ast*. I am uncertain where this idea of a thirty-year Sharia era comes from, and have not seen it explained, or even referenced, elsewhere.

67. TsGARUz F i-126 O 1 D 1730, f. 99.

separate *mufti* seals. It is not as though there was any separation between church and state, either real or aspirational, but there was a millennium-old understanding that the ulama were the best-qualified stratum of society to adjudicate Sharia. Fatwas such as this one shifted that balance.

It is important not to lose sight of the core logic underpinning even statist legal opinions characterizing the sultan as the "shadow of God" (*zill allah*). The fatwa did not authorize the sultan to intervene in legal affairs because of any intrinsic quality he possessed. Rather, the underlying logic was that his judgment happened to be the correct one according to the Sharia in this particular instance. For example, this fatwa opened with a dramatic assertion of royal privilege: "Submission and obedience from the judges, governors, and masses and to both the shah and his eminent deputy is necessary (*wajib u lazim*)—in matters that accord with the Sharia—and disobedience in such matters is against the Sharia."[68] Khunji emphasized this point as well: the prince's will is paramount in all things, but only so long as it is in conformity with Islamic law. Even so, such a caveat mattered little if the sovereign himself was recognized as the paramount authority in deciding *what* was "in accordance with the Sharia."

A *jung* opinion regarding the soundness of fatwas follows similar logic. The opinion validated a proclamation by the monarch (*padishah-i Islam*) that *qazis* and *muftis* under his jurisdiction should follow only sound legal opinions and avoid weak ones that are out of circulation.[69] This obvious point seems superfluous and is not of direct relevance to the actual substance of the opinion, which deals with the unlawful selling of endowment lands—an act implied to have been justified by some unscrupulous *mufti*'s faulty legal reasoning. The true stakes of the opinion are clarified in the closing lines: "Carrying out these weak opinions against the order of the monarch is tantamount to sin (in view of the conditions relating to this case) even though the implementer of these weak opinions was a judge of the country and knowledgeable [in religion]."[70]

Once again, the core logic in this opinion is not fundamentally distinct from that of legal-political theorists of previous eras. Here too the prince is not correct because he is the prince. Rather, the prince is correct because his position happens to be closer to the fundamental truth of Sharia. Nevertheless, the focus of the opinion is on the person of the monarch, whose

68. TsGARUz F i-126 O 1 D 1730, f. 99.

69. *Jung-i masāʾil-i fiqhiyya*, f. 373b. The phrasing for avoiding weak, out-of-circulation opinions is *az riwāyāt-i żaʿīfa-i ghayr-i maʿmūla ijtināb nimāyand*. This opinion is also copied into a separate *jung*: *Sbornik vypisok iz sochinenii po fikkhu i iuridicheskikh kazusov*, f. 303a-b.

70. *Jung-i masāʾil-i fiqhiyya*, f. 373b.

judgment is portrayed as superior to that of the ulama, at least in this case. The author of the opinion implicitly drew attention to the fact that the showdown was between the shah and the ulama by using the word *alim* (Arabic singular of ulama) to characterize the purveyor of weak opinions. In this instance, the monarch is portrayed as the arbiter over what is a weak opinion and what is a sound opinion, even though the *jung* author complicit in that judgment was himself a member of the ulama.

It seems clear, then, that in certain instances the ulama elevated the monarch to a position of exercising both logics of authority: that of the Turkic nobility and that of the ulama. These stand as instances where the ulama explicitly and consciously ceded to the ruler priority in interpreting correct Islamic practice, or at least came close to doing so. Such legal positions provided ideological scaffolding for the expanding role of the Turkic nobility into legal matters. The Turkic elite had already inserted themselves into the world of Islamic law through parallel institutions of third-party mediation in Islamic courts, which duplicated or subordinated the role of the *qazi*.[71] In part thanks to legal opinions such as those in the preceding examples, it seems that ideology was beginning to catch up with reality. Nonetheless, the Manghit Amir was still not quite God's caliph, and in many other instances the ulama continued to safeguard their own right to interpret religion.

The Ulama's Moral Distance from Temporal Power

Thus far the discussion seems to support a view of the ulama in lockstep with the Turkic nobility, and at times Islamic scholars seemed to be rendering their claims to moral authority obsolete.[72] Indeed, the Manghit chroniclers even took pains to portray their sovereigns as members of the ulama in their own right, emphasizing in particular Shah-Murad and Haydar's piety and erudition, which also justified some of the encroachments into religious authority exposed in the previous section. Although the ulama welcomed expressions of piety from the monarchs, they still positioned themselves as

71. See Sartori, "The Evolution of Third-Party Mediation in Sharīʿa Courts in 19th- and Early 20th-Century Central Asia"; Sartori, *Visions of Justice*, chap. 1; Khalid, "Society and Politics in Bukhara, 1868–1920."

72. This situation was not unique to Central Asia. Even in Qajar Iran, where the Shi'i ulama had arguably the most independent power base, scholars almost uniformly backed the Shah until the Constitutionalist period, and most of them through the 1960s. Arjomand, *The Turban for the Crown*, 177.

mediators of that piety—as illustrated by this anecdote about Abd al-Hayy Samarqandi:

> There was a certain madrasa student who studied both under Abd al-Hayy and Amir Shah-Murad. During a lesson about an issue related to punishment [*mujazat*], the amir was overcome with doubt. Shah-Murad solicited a solution to the issue from many ulama of the realm, but none was forthcoming. Finally, the student informed Shah-Murad he had studied the same lesson under his other teacher, Abd al-Hayy, who was able to successfully resolve it. Sure enough, Abd al-Hayy provided a satisfactory answer to the jurisprudential conundrum without hesitation, and without even reviewing any texts.[73]

On the one hand, this passage has the Manghit monarch personally instructing students in religion—effectively performing the role both of ruler and *mudarris*, one of the core social roles of the ulama. On the other hand, the text unambiguously portrays Shah-Murad as subordinate to the independent truth of Islamic law, and the ulama as better able to interpret that truth. Shah-Murad is an authoritative teacher in relation to the young madrasa student (*talib-i ilm*), but in relation to Abd al-Hayy the monarch becomes the student. So impressed was Shah-Murad that he appointed Abd al-Hayy to a prestigious madrasas in Samarqand on the spot.[74]

Thus close examination of the sources reveals the limits to which the ulama were willing to equate their own religious authority to that of their Turkic patrons. The ulama rarely asserted their moral supremacy ostentatiously, preferring instead to couch their pretensions indirectly in subtext, as necessitated by the power imbalance between them and the Turkic nobility. Their success in doing so was fundamentally wound up in their mastery of the Perso-Islamic canon, which provided them with the tools necessary for serving the prince while also undermining him. Just as their livelihoods were intertwined with their alliance with the Turkic military elite, the ulama continued to emphasize their moral distance and independence from those very same forces, as well as their own superiority in spiritual matters.

Examples of this dynamic are evident across diverse genres. The fatwas in Sayyid Qamar's *jung* consistently justified the ruler's right to suppress rebellions in religious terms, yet in doing so those same rulings occasionally revealed alternatives. For instance, one legal note condemned an imam

---

73. Salmān Samarqandī, *Tafṣīl wa bayān*, f. 178a.

74. Salmān Samarqandī, *Tafṣīl wa bayān*, f. 178a. See chapter 7 on the long-term impact of this promotion on ʿAbd al-Ḥayy's family dynasty.

who justified rebellion against the legitimate ruler (*padishah-i Islam*) based on interpretations of the Qur'an and Hadith.[75] Ironically, this is the inverse of the dynamic depicted earlier. In this case, an Islamic ruler is condemned for invoking scripture to justify war against a fellow Muslim ruler, the exact same maneuver valorized when the tables were turned. In both cases, it was the ulama who adjudicated whether such a textual invocation was legitimate or illegitimate. Implicitly, because ulama appear on both sides of this divide, the fatwa recognized that the ulama's first loyalty was to a moral edifice far greater than any individual ruler.

Moreover, the ulama invoked this higher power to exert authority over the Turkic nobility. One fatwa held that if a mosque community failed to cough up the imam's salary, "it would be incumbent upon the ruling authorities to seize remuneration and hand it over to the imam."[76] Evidence such as this carries the same limitations inherent in any study relying on fatwas: it was merely an opinion, which could be countered with competing fatwas, and we rarely know for certain whether it was carried out in practice.[77] Nevertheless, the core logic underpinning this opinion was clear: the stakes were divine favor and access to heaven, which rested on the ulama's ability to navigate Islamic texts.[78]

Just as the ulama deployed their eclectic skill set to advance the interests of the monarch, they also used it to extract something in return. Another ruling from a *jung* stated that if a ruler appointed a *qazi* and *muhtasib* (the same person in this case) to a given village, but state coffers were insufficient to pay him a salary, then the sovereign was obliged to make the village pay the salary out of pocket.[79] One can see how this judgment was likely appealing to both the ulama and the Turkic nobility, but it constituted an independent demand asserted by the ulama over the ruler.

In other legal opinions the tension between these two poles of authority comes more explicitly to the fore. In one such instance, an individual had willed a *waqf* (endowment) in full accordance with Islamic law and stipulated that his descendants should serve as custodians (*mutawalli*) of the *waqf* in perpetuity. However, after the endowment had taken effect, the amir designated a new family as custodians of the *waqf*. The *mufti* ruled on the side

75. *Jung-i Qāżī Mīr Sayyid Qamar Ṣudūr*, f. 273b.

76. TsGARUz F i-126 O 1 D 1729, f. 52a.

77. On the theoretical ramifications of working with fatwas generally, see Masud, Messick, and Powers, "Muftis, Fatwas, and Islamic Legal Interpretation."

78. "Because of that [i.e., coercing the congregation to pay the imam], [the rulers] become deserving of divine reward (*s̱awāb*) and entrance to paradise." TsGARUz F i-126 O 1 D 1729, f. 52a.

79. *Jung-i masā'il-i fiqhiyya*, f. 375a.

of the wishes of the endower, stating that the ruler's decision was incorrect. Interestingly, even in this moment when an ordinary *mufti* contradicted the will of the ruler, the author still deployed the same language as his peers to glorify the Turkic monarch, referring to the ruler as the caliph of the age of rank equal to the sun.[80] Implicitly, the Sharia and its scholarly interpreters hailed from a plane loftier still.

In practice, the ulama most often abetted the Turkic elite's exercise of coercive authority, but their rhetoric at times placed them in its path. One opinion contained in a *jung* addressed such coercion directly, citing a situation in which the amir's henchmen were extracting agreements (*uqud*) from the population by holding either their property or their lives hostage.[81] The *mufti* opined that all such agreements and transactions were null and void (*batil*).[82] Again, this does not mean that the ulama served as a check against temporal authority in practice. But it does illustrate that the Turkic nobility often appeared as villains in the worldview of high Persianate intellectuals—to be respected, but only insofar as their behavior was in accordance with Sharia.

In addition to asserting their independent mediation of religious law within the state, in other instances the ulama depict themselves as quietist in the more common sense of the term—implicitly critiquing temporal power by eschewing politics entirely. This sort of moral distance between the ulama and temporal authority manifests most prominently in genres such as biographical dictionaries and sufi hagiographies. Nasrallah Khan's accession to the throne in 1827 was fraught with turbulence and upon securing his position he appointed his younger brothers Zubaydallah and Ubaydallah as joint governors in the province of Narzum on the banks of the Amu River—a form of exile designed to ensure that they would not pose a threat to him. Karamatallah ibn Sabir-jan ibn Mirza Umid had been serving as the young princes' tutor and Nasrallah asked the scholar whether he would go with them to Narzum or not, implicitly expecting him to remain in Bukhara. Karamatallah replied: "During the reign of your illustrious father

80. *Dar-ēn mas'ala kih 'Azīz amlāk-i kaẓā-yē khūd-rā wāqif-i lāzim-i shar'ī karda ast bar maṣraf-i kaẓā; bi-sharī'at, chūn 'ālī-haẓrat-i muta'ālī-martabat khūrshīd-manzalat, kih khalīfa-i 'asr and, farmūda and kih Khālid akbar ū asann ū aqrab awwalan ēn awlā* [likely *awwal-i awlād-i*] *ēn 'Azīz* [referring to the endowed] *ast mutawwalī shar'ī-yi ēn wāqif bāshad. Dar-ēn-ṣūrat ēn ḥukm az ān-'ālī-haẓrat nā-durust bāshad. Jung-i riwāyāt i maḥẓarā*, f. 203a. In many *jung* entries, such as this one, but unlike an actual fatwa document, no final answer is offered to the posed question (i.e. *nā-durust bāshad bi-sharā'iṭ-ihi yā nē*?). However, fatwa questions are nearly always answered in the affirmative.

81. The specific wording could refer exclusively to the property being held hostage; both meanings support the broader point here. Ḥusaynī, *Jung-i majmū'a-i riwāyāt*, f. 173a.

82. In this case the fatwa in question was pasted into the *jung* in the original (as opposed to copied into the notebook). Ḥusaynī, *Jung-i majmū'a-i riwāyāt*, f. 173a.

I was entrusted with the upbringing of these two children and that training has yet to be completed. I will remain in their service until I see it through." Though the defiant response angered Nasrallah, he nevertheless appointed Karamatallah *qazi* of Narzum and sent him on his way along with the two princes.[83]

If the moral standing of Karamatallah vis-à-vis the khan was not driven home by his initial disobedience, it would be by subsequent events. After six months Nasrallah affected a permanent solution to any potential succession crisis by executing Zubaydallah and Ubaydallah, and then throwing Karamatallah into prison. One day, while Karamatallah was languishing in captivity, Nasrallah went to visit one of the many shrines in Bukhara, per his daily morning routine. Suddenly, an old man sitting by the side of the road shouted, "Hey amir, stop for a moment. I would have words with you." Nasrallah replied that he was going to the shrine to pray and offer charity to the needy. Hearing this, the old man guffawed and scoffed at the irony of performing such deeds across the street from the home of none other than Sabirjan, whom Nasrallah's father, Haydar (r. 1800–1826) had treated with such deference and esteem, but whose son, Karamatallah, Nasrallah had so abused. The old man railed that Karamatallah had been thrown in among common thieves and murderers despite having committed no action contrary to Islamic law.[84] "On the Day of Judgment, what will you say? Today you are a snake and the other an ant, but tomorrow it is you who will be the ant and all those who you have aggrieved the snakes."[85]

Just as in the legal opinions, here the Sharia is held up as an authority fundamentally above that of the monarch. As if to ensure that there was no ambiguity about who's duty included safeguarding Islamic law, the old man added one final comment in his appeal to Nasrallah: "It is only on account of fear that the ulama have so far failed to speak truth to this abuse of your offspring and wake you from the drunken excess brought by worldly extravagance." The story ended with total victory for the ulama as Nasrallah broke down into tears and appointed Karamatallah *qazi* of Kamat in front of stunned onlookers.[86]

---

83. Żiyā', *Ẕikr-i chand nafar-i 'ulamā'*, f. 119a.

84. *Bidūn-i jarīma-i shar'īa*. Żiyā', *Ẕikr-i chand nafar-i 'ulamā'*, f. 119b.

85. Żiyā', *Ẕikr-i chand nafar-i 'ulamā'*, f. 120a. Ants appear both in the Qur'an and Hadith as righteous servants of God who should not be killed (e.g., Q 27:18), which probably influenced the old man's metaphor.

86. Karāmatallāh's luck did not hold for very long: he died of tuberculosis (*sil*) a year later. Żiyā', *Ẕikr-i chand nafar-i 'ulamā'*, ff. 120a–121b.

Sufi writing is rife with similar accounts valorizing defiance of the khan. When the governor of Namangan demanded that Hazrat Akhund Mulla Irnazar (d. 1797/98) serve as the town judge, the scholar responded by simply packing up and leaving for Shahrisabz.[87] Although the author describing Irnazar was himself a *qazi*, in his view the post was only deemed an honor if accepted out of the scholar's free will. No direct reference is made to the Abu Hanifa parable, but the situation is so similar that the story may well be a direct reference to those events. When the governor summoned Irnazar to honor him with the post, the scholar humbly protested that he was not sufficiently versed in *qazi* matters and did not possess the requisite piety for carrying out such an important function. Despite this refusal, the governor through coercion and violation (*bi-kurh u ta'addi*) shackled a free man with the weight of the judgeship, tempting him to become a slave to the greedy part of his soul (*banda-i nafs-i ammara*).[88]

The language deployed by the author is striking in that it suggests that public positions such as *qazi* and service to the prince contained no intrinsic merit and were considered pernicious when enacted contrary to the will of the ulama. Once in Shahrisabz, Irnazar went on to teach in a madrasa under the patronage of the local dynasty but on his terms.[89] The circumstances in Shahrisabz differed little from those in Namangan except with regard to who was subservient to whom; in Shahrisabz, he found the local dynasts to be more suitably deferential to the ulama's role in interpreting religion.

Sufi Khwaja (d. 1823/24) offers an even starker example of pious disobedience and the valorization of moral distance from the prince. Although his biographer does not fault other scholars mentioned for accepting royal appointments, Sufi Khwaja was considered especially virtuous for avoiding the trappings of wealth and power, maintaining himself instead on alms. Eventually his piety and erudition reached the ears of the amir (probably

87. Īrnaẓar did not choose Shahrisabz at random; he was actively recruited by its ruling dynasty, which was vying with Bukhara for regional dominance. Khumūlī (author of the source and Īrnaẓar's student) justified the flight by citing a hadith to the effect that it was permissible to flee in extenuating circumstances: "Fleeing from the intolerable is from the traditions of the normative practices of the messengers [i.e., prophets]" (*al-firār mimmā lā yuṭāq min sunan al-mursalīn*). However, this tradition does not appear in the sound Hadith, and was dismissed by one scholar of spurious hadiths (ʿAlī al-Qārī [d. 1605/06]), who said that the notion that the Prophet Muhammad "fled" was tantamount to unbelief. The eighteenth-century compiler further noted that the exodus from Mecca (*hijra*) was not a "flight," but rather a divine command. Jarrāḥī, *Kashf al-khafāʾ*, 85 (no. 1823). This hadith is referenced in Munis's history of the Qongrat dynasty in Khiva as well: *Firdaws al-Iqbāl*, 228.

88. Sufi philosophy popular during this period posited that the soul (*nafs*) consisted of three aspects: the greedy, tempting soul (*ammāra*); the blaming, censoring soul (*lawwāma*); and the inspired soul (*mulham*).

89. Khumūlī, *Tarjuma-i ḥāl*, ff. 15b–17a.

Amir Haydar), who then summoned Sufi Khwaja to the royal court with the intention of appointing him to a position such as *mudarris*. Sufi Khwaja refused to even show up at the royal court.[90]

Undeterred, the amir enlisted Sufi Khwaja's brother to persuade him of the virtues of princely service. In preparation for their confrontation, the brother reviewed Hadith, *tafsir* (Qur'anic exegesis), and legal manuals regarding the virtues of submission to a just and righteous ruler.[91] There was no attempt to convince Sufi Khwaja of the amir's divine kingship, or embodiment of neo-Platonic justice. Instead, Sufi Khwaja listened quietly with head bowed while his brother appealed first to reason, then flattery, and then even rough language, but he would not budge. His brother accused him of madness (*diwanagi*), with which Sufi Khwaja agreed, but asserted that it was through this madness that he mastered the science of certain belief (*ilm-i yaqin*). This response impressed his brother and settled the matter.[92]

Sufi Khwaja was not a crazy hermit; he was trained in the same suite of competencies as all polymaths of Islam. He was not even opposed to teaching in a madrasa—a role he was performing when the amir sought him out. Juma-quli Khumuli, the author of this account, wrote that he lived in a wooden mosque with five or six cells, where he worked tirelessly teaching his three students.[93] Rather, Sufi Khwaja eschewed the corrupting influence of the state in favor of something loftier and purer—just as had Abu Hanifa.

Humble Servants, Above the State

The picture that has emerged in this chapter is one of a reluctant, self-righteous, sometimes disgruntled scholarly elite that was nevertheless intimately entwined with the Turkic nobility. The ulama served the state, but that did not mean that the monarch was the center of their moral world. Increasingly they seemed to accept the pretensions of learned members of the Turkic nobility to engage in matters of learning and religion, but for the most part the ulama stopped short of ceding their position as independent—and superior—mediators of religion.

90. Khumūlī, *Tarjuma-i hāl*, f. 41b and f. 42a.

91. *Bāb-i iṭā ʿat-i ulū al-amr* [*sic*; likely intended to be *wulāt al-amr* ("those vested with authority")] *wa inqiyād-i ḥukkām*. Khumūlī, *Tarjuma-i hāl*, f. 42b.

92. At first, one of the brothers suspected Sūfī Khwāja was arrogant and feared that the appointment would put him in the presence of those wiser than he. So the brother engineered a thinly veiled test in Islamic law, which Sūfī Khwāja passed with flying colors and awed everyone in attendance Khumūlī, *Tarjuma-i hāl*, f. 42b–44a.

93. Khumūlī, *Tarjuma-i hāl*, f. 42b.

Was this paradoxical relationship at all consequential in the region's broader historical trajectory? Although it would be a mistake to overemphasize this factor as determinative, the ulama's peculiar distance from state authority might inform our understanding of the ease with which Russia crippled the Turkic nobility, and—conversely—the difficulties faced by Soviet officials tasked with liquidating the ulama and extirpating Islamic culture. The Turkic nobility was eliminated as a governing elite following the Russian conquest, but the ulama were not displaced alongside their former patrons.[94] Rather, the Turkestani ulama continued to run the native judiciary under the Russian administration. Their prestige was diminished somewhat, and their duties bureaucratized, but the ulama remained an influential social stratum. By contrast, Turkic elite were not drafted into the Russian army (Turkestani Muslims were not permitted to serve at all), and did not rise through the ranks of colonial Turkestani society on the explicit basis of their lineage.[95] The Perso-Islamic logic of power still carried some currency even in directly ruled Central Asia, but the steppe tradition did not.

Within the protectorates the alliance of convenience between the ulama and Turkic nobility persisted until 1920, but in the years immediately after the Bolshevik conquest the ulama followed the pattern already set by their colleagues in Russian Turkestan by continuing to run the Sharia courts through 1928.[96] Moreover, many of the Jadids who ran the short-lived Bukharan People's Soviet Republic (1920–24) were ulama in terms of their educational background (even if they did not identify as such) and deeply invested in Islamic modernist projects.[97] It is true that the Russian nobility and the tsarist bureaucracy embraced the opportunities from the upheaval of revolution, so perhaps there is less to the specter of Abu Hanifa than meets the eye. However, when a Russian general switched sides and became a Bolshevik, the logic underpinning his power changed along with it.[98] What had formerly been a major asset—noble lineage—suddenly became an obstacle to

---

94. On the Russian liquidation of the Turkestani landed gentry (*amlāk-dār*), see Morrison, *Russian Rule in Samarkand*, chap. 3. Paolo Sartori has challenged the extent to which this actually entailed an expropriation of the Turkic nobility's land, so many of these Turkic nobles may have retained their estates, but they were in any case never integrated into the Russian imperial administration. Sartori, *Visions of Justice*, chap. 3.

95. Rather, deposed princes tended to live out their days under house arrest. See, for instance, Beisembiev, "Unknown Dynasty."

96. Sartori, "What Went Wrong? The Failure of Soviet Policy on Sharīʿa Courts in Turkestan, 1917–1923."

97. Khalid, "The Bukharan People's Soviet Republic in the Light of Muslim Sources"; Khalid, *The Politics of Muslim Cultural Reform*, 98–99.

98. Mayzel, *Generals and Revolutionaries*, 187.

advancement, even if not an insurmountable one. Islamic scholars, by contrast, were still Islamic scholars, even under Russian and early Soviet rule. The ulama as a social elite were separable from the dynastic elite they served.

This ideological separateness from the Turkic nobility meant that the ulama could continue writing fatwas in the 1920s USSR, but it also meant that once the Soviets marshaled enough strength to wage an all out war on religion in the late 1920s and 1930s, they faced a challenge much greater in Central Asia than elsewhere in the Soviet Union.[99] In Russia, the Orthodox clergy was crippled by the liquidation of the landed nobility during the Civil War. In Central Asia, the ulama had already done without the support of the Turkic elite in Turkestan proper for half a century. Removing the amir and Turkic elite did nothing to diminish the moral authority of the ulama, who had never fully relinquished their independent claim on religious knowledge and social order. The scale of resistance the Soviets encountered during unveiling campaigns in the 1920s and 1930s is suggestive of the continued influence of an elite with claims to authority antithetical to those of the Soviets and morally independent of the vanquished Turkic nobility.[100]

Other reasons also existed to resist massive social change imposed from without, and by itself the specter of Abu Hanifa hardly explains Central Asian resistance to Sovietization. Nevertheless, for those who did resist, the presence of a powerful social group articulating a language of resistance certainly did not hurt. Ultimately, however, it did not change the outcome.

---

99. Agitation of Central Asian women as a "surrogate proletariat" has received treatment in at least three monographs. Massell, *The Surrogate Proletariat*; Northrop, *Veiled Empire*; Kamp, *The New Woman in Uzbekistan*.

100. Massell, *The Surrogate Proletariat*, 72.

Conclusion

United in Eclecticism

An Islamic scholar was a jack-of-all-trades, a renaissance man who answered to no one but God. He was a canny operator, putting his considerable talents in the direct service of temporal authorities, to whom he owed his influence and fortune. He was a wandering holy fool, a beggar unafraid to speak truth to the most powerful forces of the realm. He was an occultist who used magic to serve that very same political elite, predicting victory in battle and even miraculously ensuring a favorable outcome. He was a humble madrasa instructor, traveling from city-state to city-state in search of patronage, ranging as far as his very particular Persianate skill set would take him. He was a littérateur, reveling in the romance of wine and homoerotic love poetry. He was a fiery preacher who meted out punishment for those same indulgences. He was a self-made man, justifying his authority only through his deft deployment of Islamic knowledge. He was the privileged scion of a family dynasty, rising to prominence only thanks to the accumulated material wealth bequeathed by his forefathers.

In the final analysis, does a crew this motley really constitute a coherent social group? For all of their eclecticism, and for all their seeming paradoxes, these polymaths of Islam were united by a common madrasa education (which accounted for at least a decade of their lives), mastery of a canon of texts, and shared regional networks. Their curriculum went far beyond the grammar and logic emphasized in the madrasa. Even mastering substantive Islamic law from medieval Arabic texts was necessary, but not sufficient, to distinguish a high Persianate intellectual from his many, many competitors. Most of the ulama—especially those who rose to the top—studied a plethora of collateral disciplines: poetry, mysticism, astronomy, calligraphy, medicine, trade, and more. Secondary scholarship often pairs these forms of knowledge with discrete communities, differentiating scholars, poets, sufis, and physicians into distinct social groups, with the sufi-ulama dichotomy especially pronounced. However, these were not separate groups with separate corporate identities. Rather, they were discrete social roles performed by a single social group. Their integrated knowledge base allowed them to mix and match social functions with impunity.

The "Persianate" part of the high Persianate intellectual moniker helps account for their integration as a single social group and situates them in the longue durée of Islamic history. Like their successors in the long nineteenth century, the ulama of the earliest centuries of Islam were also polymaths. Having translated, synthesized, and Islamized a wide range of Greek texts by the tenth century, these pioneering scholars mastered grammar, rhetoric, mathematics, law, theology, and astronomy—and their textual production remained essential many centuries later.

Yet those ulama were not yet Persianate polymaths. The Persian cosmopolis emerged in the eleventh century as a derivation and expansion of Islamic high culture more broadly, incorporating its core Arabic texts and building upon them with an emergent Persian corpus of literature. Over the centuries, this high cultural complex picked up new disciplines like a snowball rolling down a hill, from poetry to occult sciences to sufism of various stripes. These new Persianate social roles and forms of knowledge not only coexisted symbiotically with the Arabic canon that informed them, but also with a Turkic vernacular sphere that interacted with the Persianate in an analogous fashion. Many of the individual scholars in Bukhara could just as accurately be dubbed "high Turkic(icate) intellectuals," though the Persian cosmopolitan sphere was much more pronounced in Bukhara relative to its more thoroughly vernacularized Khorezmian and Ottoman neighbors.

Even though the ulama produced these texts under this common Perso-Islamic rubric, the differences between the textual genres they performed were nevertheless significant and consequential. Indeed, the many roles of the ulama are often imagined as constituting separate social groups in part because they align so closely with textual genres, many of which articulate worldviews seemingly in tension with one another. The ulama depicted their society differently depending on whether they chose to write a sufi hagiography, for instance, or a legal text. Most of these scholars were capable of moving between different genres as circumstances dictated—a point driven home by practical legal notebooks (*jung*), which contained sufi litanies, occult diagrams, love poems, legal excerpts, and medical remedies, all jotted within the margins of a single volume. When an individual performed the role of a jurist, he consulted medieval Arabic manuals to produce an opinion condemning wine consumption—a position appropriate for that setting. When he wrote poetry, however, wine was a source of celebration—and not exclusively as a metaphor for intoxicated love of God. Different social roles called for different genres, but this did not entail professional specialization. The contradictions that inevitably cropped up in the face of such polymathy led to some degree of anxiety, but far less than one might think, and the ulama were mostly content to live with the tension most of the time.

Unity in eclecticism—this seeming paradox helps explain how a social group could share so much in common across such a large sweep of territory with tremendous political stratification. If the Perso-Islamic cosmopolis was enduring and expansive, geopolitical realities on the ground were anything but. Nadir Shah Afshar's (r. 1736–47) invasions left wide swathes of Eurasia in a state of political fragmentation, ushering in a long nineteenth century of competing city-states. The advance of European empires incorporated those city-states as protectorates and princely states, hardening the political divisions within the Persianate cultural sphere—most spectacularly with the Russian conquest of Bukhara in 1868. The fact that the cosmopolis weathered colonial dominance and even prospered is a testament to its enduring resilience.

Turkic dynasts are not the central protagonists of this book, but high culture is impossible without financing, and the ulama cannot be understood separately from their patrons. Chronologically sandwiched between Nadir Shah's conquest in 1740 and the Russian conquest of 1868, the Manghit dynasty that ruled Bukhara until 1920 never held a candle to its predecessors in terms of raw geopolitical might: Timur's empire it was not. Even so, the city-state-cum-protectorate of Bukhara rose above its competitors in the cultural arena, and against exactly this inauspicious backdrop. During the reign of the Manghit dynasty at least 64 new madrasas were constructed—far more than any other city in the region could boast in total. This put Bukhara's 200 madrasas on the same scale as Istanbul, capital of the most powerful empire in the Islamic world. This outsized educational infrastructure provided the resources necessary for the ulama to enshrine their city within the Perso-Islamic tradition. Manuscripts connected Bukhara to Persian epic literature, such as the *Shah-nama*, and then integrated that narrative with Islamic history and sacred geography.

These touchstones were in no way unique to Bukhara; in fact, imagined universality was entirely the point. Common symbols and narratives anchored Bukhara within the much larger Persianate sphere. Buttressed by mythologization and tangible institutional investment, Bukhara's allure extended most strongly into Khurasan, the Farghana Valley, and the mountainous region to the east (the Kuhistan)—but also to the Muslim areas of the Russian Empire, western China, and northern India. Elsewhere, rulers constructed Persianate spheres of their own, employing many of the same strategies as the patricians of Bukhara. Together, these "little Persianate spheres" of human exchange empowered a much larger cultural zone of texts, ideas, and sacred geography stretching from the Balkans to Bengal. This is what made the ulama of Bukhara so much larger than the dynasty that offered them patronage.

Nevertheless, that patronage was essential. The ulama were but one pillar of the patriciate and were every bit as dependent on the Turkic nobility in practice as they imagined themselves to be morally independent of it in principle. The many talents of the high Persianate intellectual were essential for the Turkic nobility, just as patronage and material resources were essential for the scholars. Services the ulama rendered to the Turkic military elite allowed them to establish family dynasties that spanned centuries.

In investing in this alliance with Islamic scholars, the Turkic nobility got their money's worth. At first glance, the specific talents of the ulama may seem academic or even esoteric, but they were indispensable within their home environment. Mystical poetry, calligraphy, and theoretical law were not merely pursuits of leisure: there were political stakes to these forms of knowledge and a material side to this story as well. The ulama were products of education, and education cost money. Numerous competitor city-states invested in infrastructure related to religion and learning, especially madrasas and sufi lodges. Cultural-religious infrastructure attracted Islamic scholars, who staffed the city-states' administrations and lent them prestige. With the wave of a pen, the ulama could justify territorial conquest in terms of cosmological struggle between good and evil, ensure the outcome of the battle through occult intervention, and describe the victory through metaphors from Persian epics. On a more quotidian basis, the intellectual class was needed to perform marriages and lead prayers, which invariably included an affirmation of loyalty to the ruler. They were also the paper-pushers staffing the amirate bureaucracy.

This did not mean that the relationship between the scholarly elite and the Turkic nobility was without friction. Ultimately, theirs was an alliance of convenience. Even though most ulama loyally served the Turkic military, they did not cede their prerogative to independently speak for religion. Even as the ulama constantly deployed their skill set on behalf of their patrons, they jealously guarded their moral independence from the state. The Russian colonial regime liquidated the Turkic landowning class beyond the Bukharan protectorate's borders, but the ulama carried on without them.

The picture emerging from this research is one of cultural efflorescence before a twentieth-century eclipse. It was not the first such efflorescence, but it was quite possibly the last of its kind. Whether or not it held a candle to other cultural high points in Islamic history is beside the point, because the products of those previous epochs did not simply disappear: Bukhara of the long nineteenth century incorporated and built on that legacy. The polymaths of Islam stood on the shoulders of giants, and they knew it. Yet if they expected their successors to pay it forward, they were to be sorely disappointed. The names appearing throughout this book remain obscure precisely because what came next was a radical repudiation of the Persian cosmopolis. The last ulama of Bukhara went out with a bang but went out nonetheless.

Epilogue

Efflorescence before the Eclipse

Throughout this book, I frequently underscored continuity with the long run of Islamic history even into the early twentieth century, illustrating the ways the ulama perpetuated a Perso-Islamic legacy stretching back over a thousand years. Of course, a great deal had changed as well, much more than the ulama would have liked to admit.[1] Yet nothing could compare with the disruption that would be unleashed by the Bolshevik Revolution in 1917 and subsequent conquest of Bukhara in 1920. Indeed, it is difficult to point to another part of the Islamic world where the rupture was anywhere near the scale experienced in the Soviet Union. This contrast is all the more striking given the transformative impact of the twentieth century elsewhere in the Islamic world. In Turkey, the ulama as a social group were forever changed by Ataturk's modernization program.[2] Yet in Central Asia thousands upon thousands of them were repressed in the 1930s or executed, and those that survived were Sovietized.[3] In Afghanistan the state set up min-

1. As argued in this book, Bukhara was not the timeless beacon of Islam the ulama imagined it to be, nor did the state resemble the ideal Islamic polity they modeled on the early caliphate. Even what it meant to be a scholar had expanded dramatically.

2. The same was true in Iran under Reza Shah. Keshavarzian, "Turban or Hat, Seminarian or Soldier."

3. By Shoshanna Keller's estimates, 14,000 religious functionaries were repressed in Uzbekistan during the 1920s and 1930s, which was upward of 70 percent of the clerical population. *To Moscow,*

istries to manage *waqf* (endowments). The Soviet government expropriated them wholesale. In Iran, poets innovated modern literary forms. In Soviet Uzbekistan, Persian was effectively expunged from public life, and in Soviet Tajikistan it was expressed through the Cyrillic alphabet (after a brief stint in Latin script) and confined to literature departments and quasi-underground study circles.[4] Transformations elsewhere were not on the same scale of magnitude, even if similar in kind.[5]

The Communist Party of the Soviet Union did not eliminate Islam, and by the Brezhnev period it was no longer even attempting to do so.[6] There were still ulama under Soviet rule, both state-sponsored and unofficial, some of whom could trace intellectual roots to the pre-Soviet period.[7] There were still mosques and madrasas in operation, albeit in far fewer numbers. No state-directed campaign can eliminate a thousand-year-old legacy overnight. Yet the endurance of key terms such as "ulama" and "madrasa" disguise meaningful transformations in the very nature of those concepts. The murk shrouding the still understudied pre-Soviet period can make the persistence of any religious practice in the face of sustained assault appear as the survival of tradition, rather than an evolution or the creation of something new. This epilogue considers the Soviet-era implications: What did the Perso-Islamic cosmopolis look like in Central Asia after Sovietization?

As with any such question, the answer depends on where you look. The Soviet rupture was particularly pronounced from the perspective of the ulama, for it was specifically Persianate Islam and elite culture that either disappeared or was altered beyond recognition. The world of the madrasa was hit much harder by the Soviet transformation than rural shrine culture. As emphasized in previous chapters, there is inherent danger in thinking in terms of "high" or "elite" culture as distinct from "local" or "popular" culture. The two were poles of an integrated spectrum, and one was not

---

Not Mecca, 241. That is more than twice the number of the entire student population of pre-Soviet Bukhara, by some estimates.

4. Partial exceptions to this trend include Tajik-medium schools within the Uzbek SSR and a number of Tajik publications that continued to be disseminated in Soviet Uzbekistan (along with separately categorized Judeo-Tajik publications). As Stéphane Dudoignon shows, even the literary study circles that reemerged in the post–World War II period drew on Soviet orientalist scholarship. Dudoignon, "Sur Le 'Mail Des Rhapsodes.'"

5. For the "similar in kind" argument, see Khalid, "Central Asia between the Ottoman and the Soviet Worlds." An analogous argument has been forwarded about the Soviet Union more generally. Kotkin, "Modern Times"; Kalinovsky, *Laboratory of Socialist Development*.

6. Tasar, *Soviet and Muslim*, chap. 6. One notes that nations too were originally intended to eventually disappear, but that goal also receded to the background in the post-Stalin era.

7. Following World War II, there emerged a narrower class of Soviet religious scholars. Yo'ldoshxo'jaev and Qayumova, *O'zbekiston ulamolari*.

any more sophisticated or intricate than the other. It was institutionalized Islam—madrasas, canonical texts, ulama—that was transformed most profoundly, and the more localized, popular practices that carried on beneath the Soviet radar.[8]

Paradoxically, the displacement of the ulama created new space for local flavors of Islam generally sanitized out of premodern cosmopolitan texts. Even if sufi communities largely ceased to exist in an organized form, local shrines continued to function and carried on textual traditions of the pre-Soviet world through oral retellings and unofficial publications.[9] In nineteenth-century Bukhara, even the imams of local mosques were expected to have a basic madrasa education, but with the Soviet purges targeting exactly the sorts of ulama capable of imposing a degree of uniformity on the periphery, new religious authorities lacking a formal education emerged to fill the void. There was a gendered dimension to this shift, as female ulama—often obscured in nineteenth-century sources—had less competition.[10] With the upper strata sidelined, and their institutional base of support eliminated, religious practices that had already been present suddenly had more space to operate, as did formerly marginalized practitioners.

Yet even these important areas of continuity operated in a radically transformed environment. Oral testimony about the anti-religion campaigns of the 1920s and 1930s in Uzbekistan collected by Marianne Kamp illustrates this point: "There was always a mosque in the village, but at that time, people did not go there to recite. People were told they were not allowed in there, and the mosque was made into a storehouse . . . The village had a mullah. There was no place that a mullah would be left in peace, so he [led people in prayer] in secret."[11] Before 1920, a madrasa education was one of the most effective levers of upward mobility. After 1930, Central Asians continued to practice Islam for reasons of piety, and in substantial numbers, but in doing so they created liabilities for themselves rather than opportunities.

---

8. Paolo Sartori conceptualizes this phenomenon as "agrarian religion." Sartori, "Of Saints, Shrines, and Tractors: Untangling the Meaning of Islam in Soviet Central Asia." In fact, "official vs. unofficial" too is a heuristic, as the two spheres were intimately intertwined: Tasar, *Soviet and Muslim*, chap. 6.

9. Oral traditions collected at Khorezmian shrines by Soviet ethnographers, and Turkic texts written during the Soviet period, were sometimes nearly word-for-word reproductions of pre-Soviet narratives. Sartori, "Of Saints, Shrines, and Tractors: Untangling the Meaning of Islam in Soviet Central Asia." Memories of sufi descent groups also survived in some communities. DeWeese, "Re-Envisioning the History of Sufi Communities in Central Asia," 55–56.

10. Krämer, *Geistliche Autorität und islamische Gesellschaft im Wandel*. These were the *otins* and *bībī khalīfas* discussed in chapter 4.

11. The specific prayer this quote refers to was the *janāza* funerary prayer. Kamp, "Where Did the Mullahs Go?," 515–16.

Old scholarly families reinvented themselves as devoted communists but had to be careful about how they invoked their past.[12]

No one described this world turned upside down better than Mubashar al-Tarazi, a Bukhara-trained scholar who saw the writing on the wall and fled Central Asia for Egypt after the Bolshevik conquest. His Persian verse, published in exile, reads:

> Oh son, I must write now to inform you of the mosques and schools,
> All of which are under orders for destruction and closure in Bukhara, Khoqand, and Tashkent,
> Some of them have been made into Red Communist Tea Houses for the sake of leading astray the masses.[13]

Moreover, the radically changed institutional landscape of Central Asia indirectly influenced practices even outside the orbit of official Soviet Islam. Discreet elements of urban Persianate culture explored throughout this book, from poetry to sufi miracles, disappeared from the sanctioned public sphere but survived in the rural context of a collective farm.[14] Scholarly traditions from the pre-revolutionary period carried on in the privacy of the home, but the significance of banishment from the public sphere and halls of power should not be understated. Ulama of the Soviet period self-consciously invoked continuity with their polymathic forebears, but that insistence belied a tradition that had changed a great deal.

Plenty of examples of Islamic practice in opposition to the state exist, such as rural sufi shaykhs miraculously teleporting between locales to avoid the NKVD (secret police).[15] But for many Central Asians the fate of Islam was more mundane. Having liquidated the religious elite and reconstituted them (in far smaller numbers) as state bureaucrats, Islam was Sovietized as a component of the national cultures of the Central Asian republics; it was not necessarily understood to be in opposition to the state.[16] Although the Jadids

---

12. According to Flora Roberts, many former ulama in Khujand managed to thrive in the Soviet system by emphasizing their participation in the struggle against Basmachi, just as fighting in the Civil War was central to early party cadres elsewhere in the USSR. Roberts, "Old Elites under Communism," 74–76.

13. Ṭarāzī, *Maṣnawī-i yādigār-i zindān*, 127. Al-Ṭarāzī wrote in the reformist journals *al-Iṣlāḥ* and *Āyina* before emigrating.

14. Dudoignon, "From Revival to Mutation"; Frank, *Gulag Miracles*.

15. Dudoignon, "From Revival to Mutation," 61–62. My own interviews have also revealed instances of Persian calligraphy and poetry being maintained under the Soviet radar in Bukhara.

16. Khalid, *Islam after Communism*, chap. 4. Sartori deploys the term "Muslimness" to account for the connections between unofficial observance carried out under the radar (such as the kind Dudoi-

(Islamic modernists) were vastly outnumbered by their ulama counterparts during the time period covered by my research, their alliance with the Bolsheviks allowed them to implement key elements of their vision backed by the full force of the state.[17] Soviet Uzbeks still self-identified as Muslim but, by the mid-twentieth century, for many that meant celebrating Muslim weddings, circumcisions, and national holidays. The ulama were not around to object, at least not in the same form nor in the same numbers.[18] Islam-as-heritage survived in various guises, but Islam-as-hegemonic-discourse did not.

As with any historical narrative, whether one emphasizes rupture or continuity depends on the question asked, along with the dominant assumptions of one's audience. Soviet scholarship portrayed the revolution as a radical break with the past, and—relative to that narrative—continuity was considerably greater than official Marxist histories would like to admit. After all, the founder of the Soviet Central Asian muftiate came from an old family of Tashkent ulama and presided over the reopening of the Mir-i Arab madrasa in Bukhara in 1944.[19] Conversely, some Cold War–era scholarship emphasized continuity, wistfully magnifying the importance of nonstate Islam as a form of resistance to the Soviet regime.[20] During the Soviet period, the narrative of covert sufi brotherhoods fit the paradigm of state oppression versus popular resistance in the broader historiography of the Soviet Union, and after 1991 the same paradigm abetted a revised understanding of the Soviet period as a mere interregnum for the newly independent nations to overcome.[21] Underground Islam also provided a convenient explanation for the few modern Islamist movements that emerged in post-Soviet Central Asia, despite the fact that many of the new "Islamists" of the late and post-Soviet period were themselves products of the Soviet experience, even from the margins.[22]

---

gnon reveals) as well as Khalid's "Islam as national culture" model. Sartori, "Towards a History of the Muslims' Soviet Union," 320–22.

17. This was true until the late 1930s, when the Jadids were executed almost to a man. Their imprint on the newly minted Soviet Uzbek culture remained, however. Khalid, *Making Uzbekistan*.

18. On the afterlife of ulama in Soviet orientalist establishments, see Babadjanov, "'Ulama' v Sovetskom Institute vostokovedeniia."

19. Tasar, *Soviet and Muslim*, 48–56. Theological disputes from the pre-Revolutionary period even continued to play out within the circumscribed domain of the official Soviet Islamic establishment. Sartori and Babajanov, "Being Soviet, Muslim, Modernist, and Fundamentalist in 1950s Central Asia."

20. Lacking firsthand or archival access to Soviet Central Asia, Western scholars were eager to take paranoid Soviet reports of underground Islamic resistance at face value. For instance, Bennigsen and Wimbush, *Mystics and Commissars*.

21. Starr, "Rediscovering Central Asia," is an example of this tendancy to write off the Soviet period.

22. Olcott, "Roots of Radical Islam in Central Asia," 8–10; Ro'i, *Islam in the Soviet Union*, 714–15. The Hizb ut-Tahrir, however, is no Muslim Brotherhood. On nonstate Islamist circles in the late Soviet period, see Tasar, *Soviet and Muslim*, 361.

In my view, this is cause for specificity: Rupture where? Continuity for whom? Imagine for a moment that instead of being magically whisked to the Garden of the Four Seasons in the land of the *jinn* (see chapter 6), Muhammad Sharif Khwaja was teleported back in time to the thirteenth century. To be sure, it would take some time for him to find his bearings. Sufi brotherhoods would be novel and operating on very different principles than he was used to. The occult sciences he had mastered would have yet to be fully brought into the Islamic fold, and his knowledge of Turkic vernacular literature would have seemed quite mysterious. Yet, with some modification, many of Muhammad Sharif's other talents would have been transferable—Hanafi law, Persian poetry, rhetoric—and the time-traveling scholar would probably have eventually landed on his feet.

The same cannot be said if Muhammad Sharif were to teleport forward in time a mere century and a half to 1950. He might find that his many vintage talents could earn him respect in private study circles.[23] But if he were to attempt to obtain gainful employment at the newly reopened Mir-i Arab madrasa, or in any way access the sort of institutionalized authority his family enjoyed in nineteenth-century Bukhara, he would likely have found himself in jail. The forms of knowledge Muhammad Sharif had spent decades mastering had no place in communist society, and he lacked the one talent that was truly indispensable, even for the Soviet ulama: speaking Bolshevik.[24]

Thus the argument for high cultural rupture does not rest merely on the fact that there were far fewer ulama, far fewer madrasas, and far fewer sufi lodges, as al-Tarazi lamented. The Persian cosmopolis serves as a tool for understanding why conceiving of the new Soviet religious elite as "ulama," seamlessly picking up the torch from their forebears, obscures important changes in the very nature of that social group, and over a breathtakingly short period of time. This book conceptualizes Persianate culture as inseparable from Islam. By contrast, studies that emphasize continuity across the pre-Soviet and Soviet ulama implicitly take a position in defining what properly constitutes "Islam," one that posits Persianate culture as a separable

23. At least some of these circles emphasized curriculums similar to those of the nineteenth-century madrasa. For instance, Muḥammad-jān Hindūstānī's study circle in 1980s Tajikistan integrated Persian literature and the "core" disciplines (e.g., syntax, logic). Muḥammad-jān Hindūstānī's study circle has received significant attention, though it is unclear how exceptional or widespread his retro-style study-circle actually was. Tasar, *Soviet and Muslim*, 353.

24. Soviet studies have recently engaged the question of how subjectivities were shaped in relation to the state irrespective of personal conviction. Kotkin, *Magnetic Mountain*, chap. 5; Yurchak, *Everything Was Forever, Until It Was No More*. Muslims were not separate from this phenomenon, and the importance of institutions like the Spiritual Administration of the Muslims of Central Asia and Kazakhstan (SADUM) must be judged in comparison to Komsomol or the Communist Party.

additive. If the story of Soviet Islam is one of continuity, and that continuity lies in Hadith study and Islamic law, but not in poetry or occult sciences, then the former are tacitly taken to be essential elements of the religion, and the latter dispensable.[25]

Even if many facets of cultural and social life in Soviet Central Asia might still be meaningfully described as "Islamic," they were certainly no longer Persianate—at least not in the sense of a transregional cosmopolis.[26] Instead of a beacon of Islam, centered within the Persian cosmopolis, the city of Bukhara calcified into a museum city meant to showcase Uzbek national heritage. In Tajikistan, classical Persian poetry was a formidable asset for new Soviet elite.[27] However, the process of Sovietizing Persian into Tajik robbed literary production of its power even elsewhere within the USSR, let alone the vast Persianate space formerly connecting the Ottoman Balkans to the Mughal Deccan.[28] In a structural sense, Tajik litterateurs had more in common with Ukrainian poets than with their own ancestors.

Whereas the Persianate sphere's abrupt historical emergence remains mysterious, its equally sudden displacement is better understood.[29] The development of modern ideas about the connection between ethnicity, language, homeland, and so on has been extensively researched.[30] To make a long story short, in the first several decades of the twentieth century the Persian

25. This argument against a scripturalist understanding of "authentic" Islam is also made in Sartori, "Of Saints, Shrines, and Tractors: Untangling the Meaning of Islam in Soviet Central Asia." See also Ahmed, *What Is Islam?*, 32, 62 passim. However, Bukharan ulama who fled to Afghanistan found that their broader Persianate skill set remained intact for a few more decades. Shahrani, "Pining for Bukhara in Afghanistan: Poetics and Politics of Exilic Identity and Emotion."

26. As explained in chapter 1, I map the term "Persianate" to Sheldon Pollock's concept of "cosmopolis," which was formulated in contrast with national literary formations. This usage coexists with other scholarly definitions of "Persianate," some of which would encompass twentieth-century national offshoots.

27. Kalinovsky, *Laboratory of Socialist Development*, chap. 2.

28. That said, Tajik literature in translation could be an asset as representative national socialist-realist literature at Soviet Writer's Union conferences. Hodgkin, "Revolutionary Springtimes," 293. And the shared Persianate legacy played a role in showcasing Uzbekistan to Iran in the 1940s as a culturally similar model of economic development, and Tajikistan to Afghanistan and India during the Brezhnev era. Pickett, "Soviet Civilization through a Persian Lens"; Kalinovsky, *Laboratory of Socialist Development*, 203–6.

29. The notion of the Persianate being displaced has recently been challenged, or at least complicated. For instance, Mana Kia and Afshin Marashi contend that conceiving the Persianate as a premodern paradigm capitulates to modernist assumptions of rationality ("premodernity began as a construct of modernity seeking to outline itself"). Kia and Marashi, "Introduction," 381. This is an important point, but it is also worth remembering that ideas imagined to be categorically "modern" had teeth, backed by state coercion worldwide.

30. See, for instance, Marashi, *Nationalizing Iran*; Khalid, *Making Uzbekistan*; Hirsch, *Empire of Nations*; Pollock, *The Language of the Gods in the World of Men*, chap. 14.

language was divested from a multiethnic, transregional, cosmopolitan high culture and associated exclusively with the newly minted Tajik ethnicity in Soviet Central Asia, and separately with the Iranian and Afghan nations.[31] Certain elements of that heritage were reimagined as Uzbek or Azerbaijani, sometimes in direct conflict with Tajik claims, but all of it was apportioned into a specifically national framework.[32] Not everyone embraced these modernist categories, but this was the direction of change and the paradigm underwritten by the state.

What, then, is a high Persianate intellectual absent Persianate high culture? There were points of continuity, even in the reopened Soviet madrasas; the new Soviet ulama read some of the same religious texts, such as Marghinani's *Hidaya*.[33] Yet this emphasis implicitly valuates Arabic-medium scripture and law (taught in the new national language of Uzbek rather than Persian) as indispensably Islamic, but jurisprudence was only one small part of the high Persianate intellectual's repertoire. Persian literature (transliterated into a new alphabet) was now the purview of the Soviet Tajik cultural elite in the newly built capital of Dushanbe/Stalinabad. Sufi practice was once again separate from state-educated establishment ulama, in stark contrast with the long nineteenth century.[34] Calligraphy was gone from the public sphere, along with the Arabic script.[35] Occult sciences were dubbed "superstition" and also actively suppressed.[36] Islamic medicine (*tibb*) was also lost, and the word *tabib* was demoted to refer to folk healers.

"Islamic resurgence" or "revival" is a phrase frequently associated with post-Soviet Central Asia. Both terms entail a chronological hiatus separating

31. Tavakoli-Targhi, "Early Persianate Modernity"; Pickett, "Soviet Civilization through a Persian Lens."

32. Moreover, the Persianate past was reconstituted and objectified as "heritage" in the USSR and elsewhere. Hodgkin, "Classical Persian Canons of the Revolutionary Press," 187.

33. On the new Soviet madrasa in Central Asia, see Tasar, "The Official Madrasas of Soviet Uzbekistan."

34. Sartori and Babajanov, "Being Soviet, Muslim, Modernist, and Fundamentalist in 1950s Central Asia," 140 passim. The Babakhanov family, who ran the Central Asian muftiate, owed its prestige in part to sufi connections (like most ulama). But, within the Soviet system, they strove to distance themselves from those roots, emphasizing instead their scripturalist bona fides, and actively repressed surviving sufi legacies understood as "unofficial Islam." Tasar, *Soviet and Muslim*, 49, 299; DeWeese, "Re-Envisioning the History of Sufi Communities in Central Asia," 53–54.

35. Some individuals continued to read and write in the Arabic script, not only in Central Asia but even as far away as Leningrad. A manuscript of the *Samarīya* (a Samarqand pilgrimage guide discussed in chapter 2) was copied in 1957, scribed into a quad-ruled Russian notebook. Abū Ṭāhir Khwājah, *Samarīya*, f. 174. Arabic script was occasionally used in correspondence between public officials, even in the post-Stalinist period: Sartori and Babajanov, "Being Soviet, Muslim, Modernist, and Fundamentalist in 1950s Central Asia."

36. Melvin-Koushki and Pickett, "Mobilizing Magic," 236–38.

a single phenomenon. Yet religion and culture in the former Soviet Union were profoundly transformed by the twentieth century. Previously, Islamic scholars could cross the Amu River into Balkh without experiencing any cultural disjuncture, and roamed far beyond that without leaving an integrated cultural continuum. Now the Soviet legacy dividing them is every bit as powerful as the supposed shared ethnicity between Afghan Uzbeks and Uzbekistani Uzbeks, or Afghan Tajiks and Tajikistani Tajiks, or the common adherence to Hanafi Islam. Even where one cannot point to the Soviet legacy as formative in modern Central Asian culture and religion, the origins are just as often from abroad rather than pre-Soviet "tradition."[37]

The long nineteenth century remains an important context for understanding the Soviet aftermath, but contextualization need not entail direct chains of cultural-religious transmission, and the premodern dynamic of the period must first be understood on its own terms.[38] At the very least, in terms of the subject matter of this book—institutionalized Islam of the madrasas, elite Persianate literary culture, organized sufism, esoteric learning—Sovietization was the end of a way of life and understood as such. The polymaths of Islam are gone and excavating their world from the rubble of Soviet empire and tangled webs of nationalist narrative entails a daunting leap of imagination. The perilous traverse is a worthwhile one.

---

37. The Hizb ut-Tahrir originating in Palestine; or the South Asian Tablighi Jamaat.

38. For a broader defense of the importance of the pre-Soviet period for understanding Soviet Islam, see Sartori, "Towards a History of the Muslims' Soviet Union," 324.

Bibliography

Unpublished Primary Sources

Archival Sources

Archive of Foreign Policy of the Russian Empire (Arkhiv vneshnei politiki Rossiiskoi Imperii), Moscow

F 147 O 486 D 49, ff. 3a–4b: "Zapiska po voprosu o rasshirenii deistviia russkogo suda v Bukharskom khanstve"

Archive of the Orientalists of the Russian Academy of Sciences (Arkhiv vostokovedov Instituta vostochnykh rukopisei RAN), Saint Petersburg

F 33 O 1 D 140: "Fragmenty iz istorii Srednei Azii ot o epokhe Nadir-shakha i Abdully-khana"
F 33 O 1 D 149: "Zhizneopisanie Abdully-beka, odnogo iz pridvornykh Bukharskogo emira Mozaffara"
F33 O1 D 218: Kuhn, "Predislovia/soobshcheniia o Iskanderkul'skoi eksp., mirzi Abdurrakhmane, tseli i khode issledovaniia"

National Archive of India, Delhi

"Narrative of a journey through Toorkistan made by Futteh Muhummid by order of Major H. B. Edwardes, C. B. Commissioner and Superintendent Peshawar Division," Foreign Department, Consultation 28 December 1855, no. 48
"Cabul Diary from the 19th to the 22nd May 1871," Foreign Department, no. 761
"The Amir's proceedings in Wakhan and Shighnan," National Archives of India, Foreign Department, Pros. May 1884, nos. 286–92

Russian State Archive of Early Acts (Rossiiskii gosudarstvennyi arkhiv drevnikh aktov), Moscow

F 1385 O 1 D 652: "Pis'mo Turkestanskogo general-gubernatora k emiru Bukharskomu o zakliuchenii mira"

Russian State Historical Archive (Rossiiskii gosudarstvennyi istoricheskii arkhiv), Saint Petersburg

F 1396 O 1 D 342, ff. 138–51: "Madrasy . . . v gorode Samarkanda"
F 821 O 6 D 612: "Svod statisticheskikh svedenii o sostoianii glavneishikh musul'manskikh uchrezhdenii Turkestanskago kraia: K 1-omu Ianvaria 1900 goda"

Russian State Military-Historical Archive (Rossiiskii gosudarstvennyi voenno-istoricheskii archiv), Moscow

F 400 O 1 D 1936: "O polozhenii v Egipete vykhodtsev iz Srednei Azii"
F 400 O 1 D 3914: "O polozhenii del v Bukhare"
F 400 O 1 D 4000: "O brozhenii bukharskago dukhovenstva napravlennom protiv russkago vliianiia"
F 483 O 1 D 132
F 1396 O 2 D 2088: "Perepiska s nachal'nikom Askhabadskogo otriada"
F 1141 O 1 D 102: "Pokazaniia Russkikh plennykh vozvrashchennykh iz Bukhary"

State Archive of Uzbekistan (Tsentral'nyi archiv Respubliki Uzbekistana), Tashkent

F i-126 O 1 D 1160: Catalog "Avtobiografiia emirskogo predstaviteli"
F i-126 O 1 D 1293: Catalog "Pasport, vydannyi indiiskim kniazom Nizam Mulk bukharskomu poddannomu Mavlavi Alauddinu Bukhari na vozvrashchenie v Bukharu"
F i-126 O 1 D 1729: Catalog "Makhzar i rivaiat, zaverennye v kantseliarii kazi"
F i-126 O 1 D 1730: Catalog "Makhzar i rivaiat, zaverennye v kantseliarii kazi"
F i-126 O 1 D 1953: Catalog "Khodataistva kazi-kalana pered emirom o naznachenii na dolzhnosti muedaina, shaikha, imama"
F i-126 O 2 F 163
F i-126 O 2 D 685
F i-126 O 2 D 6100
F i-126 O 2 D 6172
F i-323 O 1 D 127
F i-323 O 1 D 396
R-2678: "Soobshcheniia o prepodavateliakh bukharskikh medrese"

Manuscript Sources

Al-Biruni Institute of Oriental Studies, Academy of Sciences of the Republic of Uzbekistan (Institut vostokovedeniia imeni Abu Raikhana Beruni Akademii nauk Respubliki Uzbekistana), Tashkent

ʿAbdī, ʿAbdallāh Khwājah. *Tazkirat al-shuʿarā-yi ʿAbdallāh Khwājah ʿAbdī.* IVANUz no. 64.

Aḥmad Dānish, Aḥmad ibn Nāṣir al-Ṣiddīqī al-Bukhārī Aḥmad-i Kalla. *Nawādir al-waqāʾiʿ*. IVANUz no. 2095.

ʿĀlim, Mullā Mīrzā. *Dar bayān-i rāh-i ḥajj*. IVANUz no. 9379/III.

Baltaev, Abdallāh. *Khiva esdaliklari*. IVANUz no. 11645.

Bayānī, Muḥammad Yūsuf. *Shajara-i Khwārazmshāhī*. IVANUz no. 9596.

Hādī-zāda. *Safar-nāma-i Qāżī Hādī Khwāja az Bukhārā ba Ērān*. IVANUz no. 5255/XVIII.

Hāmid ibn Qāżī Baqā Khwāja. *Tanzīl al-amṣāl fī ẕikr bayān al-aḥwāl*. IVANUz no. 602.

Ḥishmat, Sayyid Mīr Ṣiddīq Töre. *Taẕkirat al-shuʿarāʾ-i Ḥishmat*. IVANUz no. 2728.

Ḥusam al-Dīn Ṣudūr Muftī, Mullā. *Jūng-i fatāwā wa maḥżarāt 1325* (lithograph). IVANUz no. 6354.

Ḥusaynī, Ḥabīballah ibn Jalāl al-. *Jung-i majmūʿa-i riwāyāt*. IVANUz no. 2802.

Jung. IVANUz no. 2844.

Jung. IVANUz no. 8412.

Jung-i ʿAbdallāh Balkhī Kātib. IVANUz no. 3211.

Jung-i ʿAbd al-Wāḥid Ṣadr Ṣarīr Balkhī. IVANUz no. 2260.

Jung-i maḥżar wa riwāyāt. IVANUz no. 9767.

Jung fī masāʾil al-faqīh. IVANUz no. 8885/III.

Jung-i masāʾil-i fiqhiyya. IVANUz no. 6029.

Jūng-i masāʾil wa wāqiʿāt. IVANUz no. 8887.

Jung-i riwāyāt-i maḥżarā. IVANUz no. 2719/II.

Jung-i riwāyāt. IVANUz no. 4798.

Jung-i Qāżī Mīr Sayyid Qamar Ṣudūr. IVANUz no. 2588.

Khumūlī, Qāżī Jumʿa-qulī ibn Ṣūfī Taghāy Turk al-Samarqandī. *Dīwān-i Khumūlī*, IVANUz no. 345.

——. *Tārīkh-i Khumūlī*, IVANUz no. 37.

Muḥammad Nāṣir al-Bukhārī, Sayyid. *Hādī al-zāʾirīn*. IVANUz no. 2193.

Muḥammad Ṭāhir ibn Muḥammad Ṭayyib Khwārazmī. *Taẕkira-i Ṭāhir Ēshān (Silsila-i Khwājagān-i Naqshbandiyya)*. IVANUz no. 855/I.

Muḥtaram, Ḥājjī Niʿmatallāh. *Taẕkirat al-shuʿarā-yi Muḥtaram*. IVANUz no. 2252/II.

Mujaddidī, Muḥammad Maẓhar. *Manāqib al-ahmadiyya wa-maqāmāt al-saʿīdiyya*. IVANUz no. 2933/II.

Muʿīn al-Fuqarāʾ, Aḥmad ibn Muḥammad. *Risāla-i Mullā-zāda*. IVANUz no. 3396/I.

Naqī, Muḥammad Sharīf ibn Muḥammad. *Tāj al-tawārīkh*. IVANUz no. 2092.

Pīrmastī, Afżāl al-Harawī. *Ażfāl al-taẕkār fī ẕikr al-shuʿarāʾ wa al-ashʿār*. IVANUz no. 2303.

Risāla dar maʿrifat-i shāna. IVANUz no. 415/IV.

Riwāyāt dar khuṣūṣ-i żarar rasānīdan-i ajinna. IVANUz no. 3211/X.

Sharʿī, Ḥājjī ʿAbd al-ʿAẓīm. *Taẕkirat al-shuʿarā-yi ʿAbd al-ʿAẓīm Sharʿī*. IVANUz no. 3396/III.

Siddīq, Mīr Muḥammad. *Zhizneopisanie bukharskogo uchennogo sheikha* (Untitled biography of Muḥammad ʿAṭāʾallāh Khwā). IVANUz no. 79/XII.

Walī-allāh ibn al-Shaykh ʿAbd al-Raḥīm. *al-Qawl al-jamīl fī bayān sawāʾ al-sabīl*. IVANUz no. 500/XXIII.

Wāżiḥ, Qārī Raḥmatallāh ibn ʿĀshūr Muḥammad al-Bukhārī. *Gharāʾib al-khabar fī ʿajāʾib al-safar*, ms., IVANUz no. 2106.

Żiyāʾ, Sharīf-jān Makhdūm Ṣadr-i. *Nawādir-i żiyāʾīya*. IVANUz no. 1304/II.

——. *Taẕkirat al-Khaṭṭāṭīn-i Mīrzā Muḥammad Sharīf "Żiyāʾ,"* ms. IVANUz no. 1304/III.

——. *Tarjuma-i aḥwāl-i Qāżī ʿAbd al-Shakūr*. IVANUz no. 1304/IV.

——. *Ẕikr-i asāmī-yi madāris-i dākhila-ʾi Bukhārā-i Sharīf*. IVANUz no. 2193/XIII.
——. *Ẕikr-i awāʾil-i Bukhārā*. IVANUz no. 2193.
——. *Ẕikr-i chand nafar-i ʿulamāʾ-i mutabaḥḥir-i nāmdār wa fużalāʾ-i mutafarrid-i ṣāhib-i iʿtibār*. IVANUz no. 1304/IV.

British Library, London

Bulghārī, Muḥammad Karīm al-. *Sabab-i taqwiyat al-taḥṣīl wa najāt-i taṣnīʿ al-waqt*. BL no. Or. 11042.

G. Ibragimov Institute of Language, Literature, and Art (Institut iazyka, literatury i iskusstva imeni G. Ibragimova Akademii nauk Respubliki Tatarstan), Tatarstan Academy of Sciences, Kazan

Ziyārāt-i Bukhārā. IIaLI AN RT no. 1003.

Institute of Oriental Manuscripts of the Russian Academy of Sciences (Sankt-Peterburgskii filial instituta vostokovedenii, Rossiiskoi akademii nauk: Institut vostochnykh rukopisei), Saint Petersburg

ʿAważ Muḥammad. Mullā. *Tuḥfat al-tawārīkh khānī*. IVR RAN no. C 440.
Biografiia sheikhov Naqshbandiia i Mudzhadddidiia (Untitled). IVR RAN C 2019-2.
Muḥammad Yaʿqūb Bukhārī. *Risāla-i Muḥammad Yaʿqūb Bukhārī*. IVR RAN no. C 1934.
Saʿādatallāh. *Luṭf-i buzūrg*. IVR RAN no. B 1932.
Salmān Samarqandī, Mīr. *Tafṣīl wa bayān-i dawlat-i jamāʿat-i Manghit az zamān-i Raḥīm Khān*. IVR RAN no. 667.
Sāmī, ʿAbd al-ʿAẓīm Muḥammad Munshī, *Mirʾāt al-khayāl*. IVR RAN no. C 1943.
Żikr-i tārīkh-i Abū al-Fayż Khān. IVR RAN no. C 667.

Manuscripts and Rare Books section of Kazan State University (Nauchnoi biblioteki imeni N.I. Lobachevskogo Kazanskogo gosudarstvennogo universiteta, Otdel rukopisei i redkikh knig), Kazan

Marjānī, Shihāb al-Dīn. *Wafiyyat al-aslāf wa-taḥiyyāt al-akhlāf*, vol. 6. NBKGU no. 615ar.

National Library of Tajikistan (Natsional'naia biblioteka Tadzhikistana), Dushanbe

Abū Ṭāhir Khwājah. *Samarīya*. NBT no. 655.

Oriental Department of the Scientific Library of Saint Petersburg State University (Vostochnyi otdel nauchnoi biblioteki imeni Gor'kogo SPbGU), Saint Petersburg

Musayyab Bukhārī, Mīr. *Kitāb-i maqāmāt-i mashāyikh*. NBSPGU no. 854.

Rare Books Collection of the National Library of Russia (Otdel redkikh knig Rossiiskoi natsional'noi bilbioteka), Saint Petersburg

ʿAbd al-Ghafūr Turkistānī. *Bayān-i dāstān-i sarguzasht-i ʿAbd al-Ghafūr Turkistānī.* OR RNB no. Khanykov 53.
Kuhn, OR RNB F 940 (Kun), no. 144.
Kuhn, OR RNB F 940 (Kun), no. 150.
Riżawī, Abū al-Barakāt al-mulaqqab bi-Pādishāh ʿAzīz Khwāja Mirghānī. *Manāqib wa maqāmāt-i Sayyid Muḥammad ʿAṭā ʾallāh Shaykh al-Islām.* OR RNB no. P.n.s. 200.
Sbornik sudebnykh postanovlenii (Untitled). OR RNB no. F 924 D 624.
Sbornik vypisok iz sochinenii po fikkhu i iuridicheskikh kazusov (Untitled). OR RNB no. F 924 D 558.
Sbornik konvoliut (Untitled). OR RNB no. F 924 D 568.
Tetrad' s razlichnymi zapisiami (Untitled). OR RNB F 924 no. 561.

Rudaki Institute of Institute of Language, Literature, Oriental and Written Heritage, Academy of Sciences of the Repulbic of Tajikistan (Institut iazyka, literatury, vostokovedeniia i pis'mennogo naslediia imeni Rudaki Akademii nauk Tadzhikistana), Dushanbe

Gulshanī, Muḥammad Ṣādiq. *Tārīkh-i humāyūn.* IVANTaj no. 2968.
Ḥiṣārī, Mīrzā Bābā bin Dāmullā Ṣafar Muḥammad. *Yāddāsht-hā.* IVANTaj no. 1428/1.
——. *Tarjuma-i ḥāl-i Qāżī Jum ʿa-qulī Khumūlī,* ms. IVANTaj no. 294
——. *Tuḥfat al-aḥbāb fī tazkirat al-aṣḥāb.* IVANTaj no. 483.

Newspapers

Bukhārā-yi sharīf (Bukhara, 1912)
Raḥamīm (Farghana, 1910)
Tūrān (Bukhara, 1912)

Published Primary Sources

ʿAbd al-Muʾmin ibn Sayyid Akrām. *Ażwāʾ ʿalā tārīkh Tūrān.* n.p., ca. 1975.
ʿAbdī, *Tazkirat al-shu ʿarā.* Edited by S. Siddikov. Dushanbe: Izd-vo "Donish," 1983.
Abū Ṭāhir ibn Abī Saʿid Samarqandī. *Samariyya.* Tehran: Dānish, 1952.
Aḥrār, ʿUbayd Allāh ibn Maḥmūd. *The Letters of Khwāja ʿUbayd Allāh Aḥrār and His Associates.* Edited by Jo-Ann Gross and A. Urunbaev. Leiden: Brill, 2002.
Āshtiyānī, Mīrzā Maḥmūd Taqī ʿImād al-Daftarī. *ʿIbrat-nāma (Khāṭirātī az dawrān-i pas az jang-hā-yi Harāt ū Marw).* Edited by Ḥusayn ʿImādī Āshtiyānī. Tehran: Nąshr-i Markaz, 2003.
ʿAynī, Ṣadr al-Dīn. *Bukhārā inqilābīning tāʾrīkhī.* Edited by Shizuo Shimada and Sharifa Tosheva. Central Eurasian Research Series 4. Tokyo: University of Tokyo, 2010.
——. *Yāddāsht-hā.* Dushanbe: Sarredaksiiai ilmii ensiklopediaii millii tojik, 2009.

Bābur, Ẓahīr al-Dī Muḥammad. *Bābur-Nāma (Waqāyi'): Critical Edition Based on Four Chaghatay Texts with Introduction and Notes.* Translated by Eiji Mano. Kyoto: Shokado, 1995.

Badī'- Dīvān, Mīrzā. *Madzhma' Al-Arḳām ("predpisaniia Fiska") (Priemy dokumentatsii v Bukhare XVIII v.).* Translated by A.B. Vil'danova. Pamiatniki Pis'mennosti Vostoka, LIV. Moscow: Izd-vo "Nauka," Glav. red. vost. lit., 1981.

Bābartī, Muḥammad ibn Muḥammad Akmal al-Dīn al-Rūmī al-. *al-'Ināya sharḥ al-hidāya.* Dār al-Fikr, n.d.

Bakrān, Muḥammad ibn Najīb. *Jahān-nāma.* Edited by Muḥammad Amīn Riyāḥī. Tehran: Intishārāt-i Kitābkhāna-i Ibn Sīnā, 1962.

Ba'uniyyah, A'ishah al-. *The Principles of Sufism.* Translated by Th. Emil Homerin. New York: Library of Arabic Literature, 2014.

Bayram-Alibekov, Teymur-bek. "Musul'manskie sueveriia." *Kaspii* (1892) in *Turkestanskii sbornik* 475 (no. 900).

Daryaee, Touraj, ed. *Šahrestānīhā ī Ērānšahr.* Costa Mesa, CA: Mazda Publishers, 2002.

Dimishqī, 'Abd al-Ghanī ibn Ṭālib ibn Ḥamāda ibn Ibrāhīm al-Ghanīmī al-. *al-Lubāb fī sharḥ al-kitāb.* Edited by Muḥammad Muḥyī al-Dīn 'Abd al-Ḥamīd. Beirut: al-Maktaba al-'Ilmiyya, n.d.

Durkilī al-Tūnī, Naḏīr al-. *Muslim Culture in Russia and Central Asia: Die Islamgelehrten Daghestans und ihre arabischen Werke.* Edited by Michael Kemper and Amri R Šichsaidov. Berlin: Klaus Schwarz, 2004.

Durgeli, Nazir al-. *Uslada umov v biografiiakh dagestanskikh uchenykh (Nuzkhat al-azkhān fī tarādzhim "ulamā" Dāgistān): Dagestanskie uchenye X–XX vv. i ikh sochineniia.* Edited by A.R. Shikhsaidov, Michael Kemper, and Alfrid Kashafovich Bustanov. Moscow: Izdatel'skii dom Mardzhani, 2012.

Dzhakhan-name (Kniga o mire). Edited by Iu. E. Borshchevskii. Moscow: Izdatel'stvo vostochnoi literatury, 1960.

Fazil Khan, Hafiz Muḥammad. *The Uzbek Emirates of Bukhara & Khulum in the Early 19th Century as described in an Indian Travelogue: Tarikh-i-Manazil-i-Bukhara (1812).* Transated by Iqtidar Husain Siddiqui. Patna: Khuda Bakhsh Oriental Public Library, 1999.

Fażlī, Muhammad Yaḥyā al-. *Tarjimat wālidī al-Shaykh Muḥammad Ibrāhīm al-Fażlī al-Khutanī al-Madanī.* Riyadh: Fihrisat Maktabat al-Malik Fahd al-Waṭaniyya Asnā' al-Nashr, 1993.

Ferdowsi, Abu'l-Qasem. *The Shahnameh*, vol. 2. Edited by Djalal Khaleghi-Motlagh. Costa Mesa, CA: Mazda Publishers, 1990.

Fūfalzā'ī, 'Azīz al-Dīn Wakīlī. *Tīmūr Shāh Durrānī: [bā sharḥ-i tamām-i guzārish-i zindagānī-i Siyāsī, idārī, 'irfānī, 'umrānī, adabī wa ijtimā-i].* Ṭab'-i 2. Anjuman-i Tarīkh. Kabul: Anjuman-i Tarīkh-i Afghānistān, 1346 [1927/28].

——. *Durrat al-Zamān: Tārīkh-i Shāh Zamān*, 1337 [1928/29].

"Gashish i fanatizm." *Turkestanskii kur'er*, no. 9 (1910) in *Turkestanskii sbornik* 533 (no. 3193).

Ḥakīm Khān, Muḥammad. *Muntakhab al-tawārīkh.* Tokyo: Mu'assasa-i Muṭāla'āt-i Farhang-hā va Zabān-hā-yi Āsiyā wa Ifrīqā, 2009.

Ḥudūd al-'alam. Edited by Abū al-Sharaf Jarbādhaqānī. Kabul University, 1362/1943f.

Hudud al-Alam. The Regions of the World: A Persian Geography. Translated by Vladimir Minorsky. London: 1937.

Ḥusaynī, Aṣīl al-Dīn al-. *Risāla-i mazārāt-i Harāt: Maqṣad al-iqbāl al-sulṭāniyya*. Edited by Fikrī Saljūqī. 3 vols. Kabul: Bunyād-i Farhang-i Īrān 1967.

Ṭarāzī, Mubashar al-Husaynī al-. *Maṡnawī-i yādigār-i zindān yā āyīna-i jahān wa risāla-i ijmāl al-kalām fī sīrat al-imām*. Edited by ʿAlī bin Ḥusayn bin ʿAlī. Cairo: 1986.

Ibn Balkhī. *Fārs-nāma*. Edited by Guy Le Strange and Reynold A. Nicholson. Tehran: Intishārāt-i Asāṭīr, 2007.

Ibn Baṭṭūṭa. *Riḥlat Ibn Baṭṭūṭah al-musammāh tuḥfat al-nuẓẓār fī gharā'ib al-amsṣār wa-ʿajaā'ib al-asfaār*, 2nd edition. Egypt: Maṭṭbaʿat al-Taqaddum, 1322 [1904/5].

Ijāzat al-Imām Muḥammad Zāhid al-Kawṡarī li-l-Shaykh Muḥammad Ibrāhʿim al-Khutanī. Edited by Muḥammad ibn ʿAbdallāh Āl Rashīd. Amman: Dār al-Fatḥ li-l-Dirāsāt wa-l-Nashr, 2012.

Isfandiyār, Bahā' al-Dīn Muḥammad ibn Ḥasan ibn. *Tārīkh-i Ṭabaristān*. Edited by Muḥammad Ramażānī. Tabaristan: Kitāb'khāna-i Khāwar, 2007.

Jarrāḥī, Ismāʿīl ibn Muḥammad al-ʿAjlūnī al-. *Kashf al-khafā' wa muzīl al-ilbās ʿammā ishtahara min al-aḥādīth ʿalā alsina al-nās* 85 (no. 1823). Cairo: Maktabat al-Qudsī, 1351 [1932/33].

Kāshifiī, *Akhlāq-i muḥsinī* (lithograph). Lucknow: Nawal Kishor, 1377 [1957/58].

Kaykāwus ibn Iskandar ibn Qābūs. *Kitāb-i naṣḥīḥat-nāma: Qābūs-nāma*. Edited by Amīn Ābd al-Majīd Badawī. Tehran: Ibn Sīnā, 1956.

Kāẓim, Muḥammad. *ʿĀlam ārā-yi Nādirī*. Tehran: Kitābfurūshī-i Zavvār, 1985.

Kerenskii, O. M. "Nashi uchebnyia zavedeniia: Medrese Turkestanskago kraia." *Zhurnal ministerstva narodnago prosveshcheniia* no. 11 in *Turkestanskii sbornik* no. 418. Tashkent, 1892.

Khunjī, Fażl Allāh ibn Rūzbahān Iṣfahānī. *Sulūk al-mulūk*. Edited by Muḥammad ʿAlī Muwaḥḥid. Tehran: Khwārazmī, 1362.

Lal, Mohan. *Travels in the Panjab, Afghanistan, & Turkistan, to Balk, Bokhara, and Herat; A Visit to Great Britain and Germany*. London: William H. Allen & Co., 1846.

Lykoshin, N. S. *Pol zhizni v Turkestane: Ocherki byta tuzemnago naseleniia*. Petrograd: Sklad T-va "V.A. Berezovskii," 1916.

Maḥmūd ibn Walī. *Tārīkh baḥr al-asrār fī manāqib al-akhyār*. Kabul: Akādīmī-yi ʿUlūm-i Afghānistān, 1981.

Malīḥā Samarqandī. *Taẕkira-i muẕākir al-aṣḥāb (yā taẕkira al-shuʿarā-yi Malīḥā-yi Samarqandī)*. Edited by Kamal al-Din S. Aini. Dushanbe: Sifārat-i Jumhūrī-yi Islāmī-yi Īrān dar Tājīkistān, 1385.

Maev, N. A. *Ocherki Bukharskago khanstva*. Tashkent, 1875.

Masʿūdī, Abu al-Ḥasan. *Murūj al-ẕahab wa-ma ʿādin al-jawhar*, vol. 5. Edited by Charles Pellat. Beirut: al-Jāmiʿa al-Lubnāniyya, 1965.

Meiendorf, Baron Yegor Fiodorovich. *Journey of the Russian Mission from Orenbourg to Bokhara*. Spectator Press, 1840.

Muʿallimī, Abdallah ibn ʿAbd al-Raḥman ibn ʿAbd al-Rahīm al-. *Aʿlām al-Makayyain min al-qarn al-tāsiʿa ʿilā al-qarn al-rābiʿa ʿashar al-hijrī*, vol. 1. Mecca: Mu'assasat al-Farqān lil-Turāth al-Islamī Farʿ Mu'assasat Makka al-Mukarrama wa al-Madīna al-Munawwara, 2000.

Muʿaẕī, Muḥammad ʿĀrif al-. *Tārīkh-i Bukhārā wa-tarjumat al-ʿulamā' (Tārīkh-i Muʿaziyya)*. Orenburg, Russia: Dīn u Ma'īshat, 1908.

Muḥammad Nāṣir al-Bukhārī, Sayyid. *Tuḥfat al-zāʾirīn* (lithograph). New Bukhara, 1910.

Muʿīn al-Fuqarā, Aḥmad ibn Maḥmūd. *Tārīkh-i Mullā-zāda; dar ẕikr-i mazārāt-i Bukhārā*. Edited by Aḥmad Gulchīn Maʿānī. Tehran: Kitābkhāna-yi Ibn Sīnā, 1960.

Muḥammad Qāsim Amīn Turkistānī. *al-Iʿlām li-baʿż rijālāt Turkistān*. Mecca: Fihrist Maktabat al-Malik Fahd al-Waṭaniyya ʾAsnāʾ al-Nashr, 2008.

Munis, Shir Muhammad Mirab. *Firdaws al-Iqbāl: History of Khorezm*. Translated by Yuri Bregel. Leiden: Brill, 1988.

Muṭribī Samarqandī, Sulṭān Muḥammad. *Taẕkirat al-shuʿarāʾ*. Edited by Aṣghar Jānfadā and ʿAlī Rafīʿī ʿAlā Marwdasthī. Tehran: Āyina-i Mīrāṡ, 1999.

Nalivkin, V.P. *Tuzemtsy, ran'she i teper'*. Tashkent: Turk t-va Pechatnago Dela, 1913.

Narshakhī, Abū Bakr Muḥammad ibn Jaʿfar. *Tārīkh-i Bukhārā*. Translated by Abū Naṣr Aḥmad al-Qubāwī. Tehran: Bunyād-i Farhang-i Ērān, 1972.

——. *The History of Bukhara*. Translated by Richard Nelson Frye. Cambridge, MA: Mediaeval Academy of America, 1954.

Nawāʾī, ʿAbd al-Ḥusayn, ed. *Nādir Shāh wa bāzmāndagānash hamrāh bā nāmaʾhā-yi sulṭānatī wa asnād-i siyāsī wa idārī*. Tehran: Intishārāt-i Zarīn, 1990.

Nawāʾī, Mīr ʿAlī Shīr. *Muḥākamat al-lughatayn*. Translated by Robert Devereux. Leiden: Brill, 1966.

Olsuf'ev, A. A., and V. P. Panaev. *Po Zakaspiiskoi voennoi zheleznoi doroge*. St. Petersburg: Ripol Klassik, 1899.

Ostroumov, N. "Narodnoe obrazovanie: Madrasy v Turkestanskom krae." *Zhurnal ministerstva narodnago prosveshcheniia* no. 10 (1906) in *Turkestanskii sbornik* 418.

Rempel', Lazar' Izrailevich. *Dalekoe i blizkoe: Bukharskie zapisi—stranitsy zhizni, byta, stroitel'nogo dela, remesla i iskusstva Staroi Bukhary*. Tashkent: Izd-vo Literatury I iskusstva imeni Gafura Gulama, 1981.

Ṣafar-zāda, Ḥabīb, ed. *Dīwān-i Imlāʾ-i Bukhārāyī*. Tehran: Intishārāt-i Bayn al-Milalī al-Hadī, 2009.

Samʿānī, ʿAbd al-Karīm al-. *al-ʾAnsāb*, vol. 10. Hyderabad: Dāʾirat al-Maʿārif al-ʿUṡmāniyya, 1962.

Schuyler, Eugene, and Vasilii Vasil'evich Grigor'ev. *Turkistan: Notes of a Journey in Russian Turkistan, Khokand, Bukhara, and Kuldja*. Scribner, Armstrong & Company, 1877.

Shurunbulālī, Ḥasan ibn ʿAmmār ibn ʿAlī al-. *Mukhtaṣar imdād al-fattāḥ marāqī fallāḥ: sharḥ nūr al-ʾīżāḥ wa-najāt al-ʾarwāḥ*. Edited by Bashshār Bakrī ʿUrābī. Damascus: Dār Qubāʿa, 1423 [2002/3].

Subḥān Quli Khan. *A Turkic Medical Treatise from Islamic Central Asia: A Critical Edition of a Seventeenth-Century Chagatay Work by Subḥān Qulï Khan*. Edited by László Károly. Brill's Inner Asian Library, volume 32. Leiden : Brill, 2015.

"Ter'iak i 'nasha' v Bukhare." *Turkestanskii kur'er*, nos. 155, 157, 160 (1910) in *Turkestanskii sbornik* 543 (no. 3194).

Suwaydī, ʿAbd Allāh ibn Ḥusayn. *Muʾtamar al-Najaf*. Egypt: al-Maṭbaʿa al-Salafiyya, 1973.

Ṭūsī, Naṣīr al-Dīn Muḥammad ibn Muḥammad. *The Nasirean Ethics*. Translated by G. M. Wickens. London: G. Allen & Unwin, 1965.

Vambery, Armenius. *Travels in Central Asia; Being the Account of a Journey from Teheran Across the Turkoman Desert on the Eastern Shore of the Caspian to Khiva, Bokhara, and Samarcand*. New York: Harper & Brothers, 1865.

Xuanzang, and Bianji. *The Great Tang Dynasty Record of the Western Regions*. Translated by Rongxi Li. Berkeley, Calif: Numata Center for Buddhist Translation & Rese, 1997.

Yāqūt ibn ʿAbd Allāh al-Ḥamawī *Muʾjam al-buldān*, vols. 1, 4. Beirut: Dār Ṣādir lil-Ṭibāʿa wa-l-Nashr, 1955.

Yumgī, Shāh ʿAbdallāh Badakhshī. *Armaghān-i Badakhshān*. Edited by Maḥmūd Afshārīzadī. Tehran: Bunyād-i Mawqūfāt-i Duktur Maḥmūd Afshār, 2006.

Ẕahabī, Abū ʿAbdallāh Muḥammad ibn ʾAḥmad ibn ʿUs̱mān al-. *Manāqib al-Imām Abī Ḥanīfa wa Ṣāḥibayhi Abī Yūsif wa Muḥammad ibn al-Ḥasan*. Edited by Muḥammad Zāhid al- Kawtharī and ʾAbū al-Wafāʾ al-Afghānī. Beirut: Lajnat Iḥyāʾ al-Maʿārif al-Nuʿmāniyya, 1419 [1998/99].

Zakarīyāʾ al-Qazwīnī. *As̱ār al-bilād wa-akhbār al- ʿibād*. Beirut: Dār Ṣādir, 1960.

Zamakhsharī, Abū al-Qāsim al-. *Rabīʿ al- ʾabrār*, vol. 1. Beirut: Muʾassasat al-ʿAʿlamī, 1412 [1991/2].

Żīyāʾ, Sharīf Jān Makhdūm Ṣadr. *Taẕkār-i ashʿār*. Edited by Shakuri Bukhārāʾī. Tehran: Soroush Press, 2001.

Published Secondary Works

Abdukholiqov, F., E. Rtveladze, A. Razzaqov, K. Rahimov, A. Hakimov, B. Abdukhalimov, A. Mansurov, A. Mannonov, and N. Muhamedov. *Architectural Epigraphy of Uzbekistan: Bukhara—Part 1*. Tashkent: Uzbekistan Today, 2016.

Abdurasulov, Ulfatbek. "'And the Išān's Consciousness Flew Out of His Head': On the Authority of Holy Men in Khorezm." Indiana University Press, forthcoming.

——. "Ot Arabshakhidov k Kungradam: Dinamika i politicheskii landshaft Khorezma v period pravleniia dvukh dinastii." *O'zbekiston tarixi*, February 2013, 17–32.

Adshead, Samuel Adrian M. "World History and Central Asia: Time, Place and People." In *Central Asia in World History*, 3–26. London: Macmillan, 1993.

Ahmed, Asad Q. *The Religious Elite of the Early Islamic Ḥijāz: Five Prosopographical Case Studies*. Oxford: Unit for Prosopographical Research, 2011.

Ahmed, Shahab. *What Is Islam?: The Importance of Being Islamic*. Princeton: Princeton University Press, 2015.

Ahmed, Shahab, and Nenad Filipovic. "The Sultan's Syllabus: A Curriculum for the Ottoman Imperial Medreses Prescribed in a Fermān of Qānūnī I Süleymān, Dated 973 (1565)." *Studia Islamica* 98/99 (January 1, 2004): 183–218.

Akgündüz, Murat. *Osmanlı medreseleri XIX. Asır*. Istanbul: Beyan Yayınları, 2004.

Alam, Muzaffar. *The Languages of Political Islam*. London: Hurst & Company, 2004.

Alavi, Seema. *Muslim Cosmopolitanism in the Age of Empire*. Cambridge, MA: Harvard University Press, 2015.

Algar, Hamid. "Shi'ism and Iran in the Eighteenth Century." In *Shi'ism*, edited by Paul Luft and Colin Turner, 1:325–40. New York: Routledge, 2008.

Alimova, D.A., ed. *Istoriia Uzbekistana (XVI–pervaia polovina XIX veka)*. Tashkent: Izd-vo "Fan" Akademii nauk Respubliki Uzbekistan, 2012.

Allsen, Thomas T. *Culture and Conquest in Mongol Eurasia*. Cambridge Studies in Islamic Civilization. Cambridge: Cambridge University Press, 2001.

——. *The Royal Hunt in Eurasian History*. Philadelphia: University of Pennsylvania Press, 2006.

Allworth, Edward. *The Modern Uzbeks: From the Fourteenth Century to the Present—A Cultural History*. Stanford: Hoover Press, 1990.

Amanat, Abbas. "Remembering the Persianate." In *The Persianate World: Rethinking a Shared Sphere*, edited by Abbas Amanat and Assef Ashraf, 15–62. Leiden: Brill, 2018.

Amin, Shahid. *Conquest and Community: The Afterlife of Warrior Saint Ghazi Miyan*. New Delhi: Orient BlackSwan, 2015.

Amster, Ellen J. *Medicine and the Saints: Science, Islam, and the Colonial Encounter in Morocco, 1877–1956*. Austin, TX: University of Texas Press, 2013.

Andrews, Walter, and Mehmet Kalpakli. *The Age of Beloveds: Love and the Beloved in Early-Modern Ottoman and European Society and Culture*. Durham, NC: Duke University Press, 2005.

Antrim, Zayde. *Routes and Realms: The Power of Place in the Early Islamic World*. New York: Oxford University Press, 2012.

Anzali, Ata. *Mysticism in Iran: The Safavid Roots of a Modern Concept*. Columbia: University of South Carolina Press, 2017.

Arjomand, Said Amir. "The Salience of Political Ethic in the Spread of Persianate Islam." *Journal of Persianate Studies* 1, no. 1 (2008): 5–29.

——. *The Shadow of God and the Hidden Imam: Religion, Political Order, and Societal Change in Shi'ite Iran from the Beginning to 1890*. Chicago:University of Chicago Press, 2010.

——. *The Turban for the Crown: The Islamic Revolution in Iran*. New York: Oxford University Press, 1989.

Asad, Talal. *Genealogies of Religion: Discipline and Reasons of Power in Christianity and Islam*. Baltimore: Johns Hopkins University Press, 1993.

Asanova, Galina, and Martin Dow. "The Ṣarrāfān Baths in Bukhara." *Iran* 39 (2001): 187–205.

Ashraf, Assef. "From Khan to Shah: State, Society, and Forming the Ties That Made Qajar Iran." PhD diss., Yale University, 2016.

Askari, Nasrin. "The Medieval Reception of Firdausī's Shāhnāma: The Ardashīr Cycle as a Mirror for Princes." PhD diss., University of Toronto, 2013.

Atçıl, Abdurrahman. *Scholars and Sultans in the Early Modern Ottoman Empire*. Cambridge: Cambridge University Press, 2018.

Auerbach, Erich. *Mimesis: The Representation of Reality in Western Literature*. Princeton: Princeton University Press, 1953.

Axworthy, Michael. "The Awkwardness of Nader Shah: History, Military-History, and Eighteenth-Century Iran." In *Crisis, Collapse, Militarism and Civil War: The History and Historiography of 18th Century Iran*, edited by Michael Axworthy, 43–59. New York: Oxford University Press, 2018.

——. *The Sword of Persia: Nader Shah, from Tribal Warrior to Conquering Tyrant*. London: I. B. Tauris, 2009.

Azad, Arezou. *Sacred Landscape in Medieval Afghanistan: Revisiting the Faḍ'il-i Balkh*. Oxford Oriental Monographs. Oxford: Oxford University Press, 2013.

Babadjanov, Bakhtiyar. "'Ulama' v Sovetskom Institute vostokovedeniia." In *Istoriia i istoriki Uzbekistana v XX veke*, edited by D. A. Alimova, 301–48. Tashkent: Izd-vo "Navroʿz," 2014.

——. "On the History of the Naqshbandiya Mujaddidiya in Central Mawaraʿnnahr in the Late 18th and Early 19th Centuries." In *Muslim Culture in Russia and Central Asia from the 18th to the Early 20th Centuries*, edited by Anke von Kügelgen, Michael Kemper, and Allen Frank, 385–413. Berlin: Klaus Schwartz, 1998.

——. *Kokandskoe khanstvo: Vlast', politika, religiia*. Tokyo—Tashkent: NIHU Program Islamic Area Studies Center at the University of Tokyo (TIAS); Institut Vostokovedeniia Akademii Nauk Respubliki Uzbekistan, 2010.

Baer, Marc David. *Honored by the Glory of Islam: Conversion and Conquest in Ottoman Europe*. New York: Oxford University Press, 2011.

Balabanlilar, Lisa. "Lords of the Auspicious Conjunction: Turco-Mongol Imperial Identity on the Subcontinent." *Journal of World History* 18, no. 1 (March 2007): 1–39.

Balkin, J. M., and Sanford Levinson. "Legal Canons: An Introduction." In *Legal Canons*, 3–44. New York: New York University Press, 2000.

Baltacı, Cahid. *XV–XVI. Asırlarda Osmanlı medreseleri*. Istanbul: İrfan Matbaası, 1976.

Barthold, V. V. *Four Studies on the History of Central Asia*. Translated by T. Minorsky. Leiden: Brill, 1956.

Bashir, Shahzad. "On Islamic Time: Rethinking Chronology in the Historiography of Muslim Societies." *History and Theory* 53, no. 4 (December 2014): 519–44.

——. "The Origins and Rhetorical Evolution of the Term Qizilbāsh in Persianate Literature." *Journal of the Economic and Social History of the Orient*, no. 57 (2014): 364–91.

——. *Sufi Bodies: Religion and Society in Medieval Islam*. New York: Columbia University Press, 2011.

Bawarshi, Anis S., and Mary Jo Reiff. *Genre: An Introduction to History, Theory, Research, and Pedagogy*. Fort Collins, CO: Parlor Press, 2010.

Bayly, C. A. *Empire and Information: Intelligence Gathering and Social Communication in India, 1780–1870*. Cambridge: Cambridge University Press, 1996.

Bayly, Susan. "The Limits of Islamic Expansion in South India." In *Islam and Indian Regions*, edited by Anna Libera Dallapriccola and Stephanie Zingel-Avé Lallemant, 453–90. Stuttgart: Franz Steiner Verlag, 1993.

Beben, Daniel. "The Legendary Biographies of Nāṣir-i Khusraw: Memory and Textualization in Early Modern Persian Ismāʿīlism." PhD diss., Indiana University, 2015.

Becker, Seymour. *Russia's Protectorates in Central Asia: Bukhara and Khiva, 1865–1924*. Cambridge, MA: Harvard University Press, 1968.

Beecroft, Alexander. *An Ecology of World Literature: From Antiquity to the Present Day*. New York: Verso, 2015.

——. *Authorship and Cultural Identity in Early Greece and China: Patterns of Literary Circulation*. Cambridge: Cambridge University Press, 2010.

Behrens-Abouseif, Doris. "The Image of the Physician in Arab Biographies of the Post-Classical Age." *Der Islam* 66 (1989): 331–43.

Beisembiev, T. K. "Farghana's Contacts with India in the 18th and 19th Centuries (According to the Khokand Chronicles)." *Journal of Asian History* 28, no. 2 (1994): 124–35.

——. "Unknown Dynasty: The Rulers of Shahrisabz in the 18th and 19th Centuries." *Journal of Central Asia* 15, no. 1 (July 1992): 20–22.

——. "Farhang-i wāzhigān wa iṣṭilāḥāt-i dīwānī/tārīkhī dar nigāshta-hā-yi far-āwardī," 2008. Unpublished manuscript.

Bellér-Hann, Ildikó. *Community Matters in Xinjiang 1880–1949: Towards a Historical Anthropology of the Uyghur*. Leiden: Brill, 2008.

Bennigsen, Alexandre, and S. Enders Wimbush. *Mystics and Commissars: Sufism in the Soviet Union*. Berkeley: University of California Press, 1986.

Binbaș, İlker Evrim. *Intellectual Networks in Timurid Iran: Sharaf al-Dīn ʾAlī Yazdī and the Islamicate Republic of Letters*. New York: Cambridge University Press, 2016.

Birtalan, Ágnes. "Ritualistic Use of Livestock Bones in the Mongolian Belief System and Customs." In *Proceedings of the 45th Permanent International Altaistic Conference (PIAC) Budapest, Hungary, June23–28, 2002*, edited by Alice Sárközi and Attila Rákos, 34–62. Altaica Budapestinensia, MMII. Budapest, 2003.

Bodrogligeti, András J. E. "Notes on the Turkish Literature at the Mameluke Court." *Acta Orientalia Academiae Scientiarum Hungaricae* 14, no. 3 (1962): 273–82.

Bonner, Michael. *Jihad in Islamic History: Doctrines and Practice*. Princeton: Princeton University Press, 2006.

Boratav, P. N. "Maddāḥ." In *Encyclopaedia of Islam*, 2nd ed. Edited by P. Bearman, Th. Bianquis, C. E. Bosworth, E. van Donzel, and W. P. Heinrichs. http://dx.doi.org/10.1163/1573-3912_islam_SIM_4728.

Bosworth, C. E. *The Ghaznavids: Their Empire in Afghanistan and Eastern Iran 994–1040*. Edinburgh: Edinburgh University Press, 1963.

——. "Raʾīs." In *Encyclopaedia of Islam*, 2nd ed. Edited by P. Bearman, Th. Bianquis, C. E. Bosworth, E. van Donzel, and W. P. Heinrichs. http://dx.doi.org/10.1163/1573-3912_islam_COM_0904.

——. "Ziyarids." In *Encyclopædia Iranica*. http://www.iranicaonline.org/articles/ziyarids.

Brack, Jonathan Z. "Mediating Sacred Kingship: Conversion and Sovereignty in Mongol Iran." PhD diss., University of Michigan, 2016.

Bregel, Yuri. "The New Uzbek States: Bukhara, Khiva and Khoqand c. 1750–1886." In *The Cambridge History of Inner Asia: The Chinggisid Age*, edited by Nicola Di Cosmo, Allen J. Frank, and P. Golden, 392–410. Cambridge: Cambridge University Press, 2009.

——. "Uzbeks, Qazaqs and Turkmens." In *The Cambridge History of Inner Asia: The Chinggisid Age*, 221–36. Cambridge: Cambridge University Press, 2009.

——. *An Historical Atlas of Central Asia*. Leiden: Brill, 2003.

——. "Abuʿl-Khayrids." In *Encyclopædia Iranica*. http://www.iranicaonline.org/articles/abul-khayrids-dynasty.

——. "Bukhara iii. After the Mongol Invasion." *Encyclopædia Iranica*. http://www.iranicaonline.org/articles/bukhara-iii.

——. "The Role of Central Asia in the History of the Muslim East." Occasional Paper 20. Institute of Asian and African Affairs, The Hebrew University of Jerusalem, 1980.

——. *The Administration of Bukhara under the Manghïts and Some Tashkent Manuscripts*. Papers on Inner Asia, no. 3. Bloomington: Indiana University, Research Institute for Inner Asian Studies, 2000.

Brockopp, Jonathan E. *Muhammad's Heirs: The Rise of Muslim Scholarly Communities, 622–950*. Cambridge: Cambridge University Press, 2017.

Brookshaw, Dominic Parviz. "Lascivious Vines, Corrupted Virgins, and Crimes of Honor: Variations on the Wine Production Myth as Narrated in Early Persian Poetry." *Iranian Studies* 47, no. 1 (September 23, 2013): 87–129.

Brophy, David. "Taranchis, Kashgaris, and the 'Uyghur Question' in Soviet Central Asia." *Inner Asia* 7, no. 2 (2005): 163–84.

——. *Uyghur Nation: Reform and Revolution on the Russia-China Frontier*. Cambridge, MA: Harvard University Press, 2016.

Brower, Daniel R. "Russian Roads to Mecca: Religious Tolerance and Muslim Pilgrimage in the Russian Empire." *Slavic Review* 53, no. 3 (Autumn 1996): 567–84.

——. *Turkestan and the Fate of the Russian Empire*. New York: RoutledgeCurzon, 2003.

Brown, Jonathan. *The Canonization of Al-Bukhārī and Muslim: The Formation and Function of the Sunnī Ḥadīth Canon*. Islamic History and Civilization, vol. 69. Leiden : Brill, 2007.

Bulliet, Richard W. "Islamic Reformation or 'Big Crunch'? A Review Essay." *Harvard Middle Eastern and Islamic Review* 8 (2009): 7–18.

——. *Islam: The View from the Edge*. New York: Columbia University Press, 1995.

——. *The Patricians of Nishapur: A Study in Medieval Islamic Social History*. Cambridge, MA: Harvard University Press, 1972.

Burbank, Jane, Mark Von Hagen, and Anatoly Remnev, eds. *Russian Empire: Space, People, Power, 1700–1930*. Bloomington: Indiana University Press, 2007.

Burton, Antoinette, ed. *After the Imperial Turn: Thinking with and through the Nation*. Durham, NC: Duke University Press, 2003.

Burton, Audrey. "Relations between the Khanate of Bukhara and Ottoman Turkey, 1558–1702." *International Journal of Turkish Studies* 5, no. 1–2 (1990): 83–103.

Burton, Audrey. *The Bukharans: A Dynastic, Diplomatic and Commercial History, 1550–1702*. New York: St. Martin's Press, 1997.

Cahen, C., M. Talbi, R. Mantran, A. K. S. Lambton, and A. S. Bazmee Ansari. "Ḥisba." In *Encyclopaedia of Islam*, 2nd ed. Edited by P. Bearman, Th. Bianquis, C. E. Bosworth, E. van Donzel, and W. P. Heinrichs. http://dx.doi.org/10.1163/1573-3912_islam_COM_0293.

Calder, Norman. "Friday Prayer and the Juristic Theory of Government: Sarakhsī, Shīrāzī, Māwardī." *Bulletin of the School of Oriental and African Studies, University of London* 49, no. 1 (January 1986): 35–47.

Can, Lale. *Spiritual Subjects: Central Asian Pilgrims and the Ottoman Hajj at the End of Empire*. Stanford: Stanford University Press, 2020.

Canfield, Robert L. "Introduction: The Turko-Persian Tradition." In *Turko-Persia in Historical Perspective*, edited by Robert L Canfield, 1–34. Cambridge: Cambridge University Press, 1991.

Casanova, Pascale. *The World Republic of Letters*. Translated by M. B. DeBevoise. Cambridge, MA: Harvard University Press, 2004.

Chamanara, Sohrab. *Kitāb-i muqaddas-i Ērānīyān, Shāh'nāma-i Firdawsī*. Los Angeles: Ketab Corp, 2014.

Chamberlain, Michael. *Knowledge and Social Practice in Medieval Damascus, 1190–1350*. New York: Cambridge University Press, 1994.

Christian, David. "Inner Eurasia as a Unit of World History." *Journal of World History* 5, no. 2 (1994): 173–211.

Cohen, Ralph. "History and Genre." *New Literary History* 17, no. 2 (Winter 1986): 203–18.

Cohn, Bernard S. "The Census, Social Structure, and Objectification in South Asia." In *Colonialism and Its Forms of Knowledge: The British in India*, 224–54. Princeton Studies in Culture/Power/History. Princeton: Princeton University Press, 1996.

Cole, Juan. *Roots of North Indian Shīʿism in Iran and Iraq: Religion and State in Awadh, 1722–1859*. Berkeley: University of California Press, 1989.

Cook, Michael. "Pharaonic History in Medieval Egypt." *Studia Islamica* 57 (January 1983): 67–103.

Cook, Michael. *Ancient Religions, Modern Politics: The Islamic Case in Comparative Perspective*. Princeton: Princeton University Press, 2014.

——. *Commanding Right and Forbidding Wrong in Islamic Thought*. Cambridge: Cambridge University Press, 2004.

Cooperson, Michael. "'Arabs' and 'Iranians': The Uses of Ethnicity in the Early Abbasid Period." In *Islamic Cultures, Islamic Contexts. Essays in Honor of Professor Patricia Crone*, 364–87. Leiden: Brill, 2015.

Cornwall, Owen. "Alexander and the Persian Cosmopolis, 1000–1500." PhD diss., Columbia University, 2015.

Coulson, N. J. *A History of Islamic Law*. Edinburgh: Edinburgh University Press, 1964.

Coupe, Laurence. *Myth*. 2nd ed. The New Critical Idiom. New York: Routledge, 2009.

Crews, Robert D. *For Prophet and Tsar: Islam and Empire in Russia and Central Asia*. Cambridge, MA: Harvard University Press, 2006.

Crone, Patricia. "The Significance of Wooden Weapons in Al-Mukhtār's Revolt and the ʾAbbasid Revolution." In *From Arabian Tribes to Islamic Empire: Army, State and Society in the Near East c.600–850*, 174–87. Aldershot: Ashgate Variorum, 2008.

——. *God's Rule: Government and Islam*. New York: Columbia University Press, 2004.

——. *Pre-Industrial Societies: Anatomy of the Pre-Modern World*. Oxford: Oneworld Publications, 1989.

——. *Roman, Provincial, and Islamic Law: The Origins of the Islamic Patronate*. Cambridge: Cambridge University Press, 1987.

——. *Slaves on Horses: The Evolution of the Islamic Polity*. London: Cambridge University Press, 1980.

——. *The Nativist Prophets of Early Islamic Iran: Rural Revolt and Local Zoroastrianism*. New York: Cambridge University Press, 2012.

Crone, Patricia, and Martin Hinds. *God's Caliph: Religious Authority in the First Centuries of Islam*. New York: Cambridge University Press, 2003.

Csirkés, Ferenc Péter. "'Chaghatay Oration, Ottoman Eloquence, Qizilbash Rhetoric': Turkic Literature in Ṣafavid Persia." PhD diss., University of Chicago, 2016.

Dabashi, Hamid. *The World of Persian Literary Humanism*. Cambridge, MA: Harvard University Press, 2012.

Dağyeli, Jeanine. *"Gott liebt das Handwerk": Moral, Identität und religiöse Legitimierung in der mittelasiatischen Handwerks-risāla*. Wiesbaden: Reichert, 2011.

Dale, Stephen Frederic. *Indian Merchants and Eurasian Trade, 1600–1750*. Cambridge Studies in Islamic Civilization. Cambridge: Cambridge University Press, 1994.

——. *The Garden of the Eight Paradises: Babur and the Culture of Empire in Central Asia, Afghanistan and India (1483–1530)*. Leiden: Brill, 2004.

Dankoff, Robert. "Kāšġarī on the Beliefs and Superstitions of the Turks." *Journal of the American Oriental Society* 95, no. 1 (January 1975): 68–80.

Davis, Dick. "Religion in the Shahnameh." *Iranian Studies* 48, no. 3 (May 4, 2015): 337–48.

de la Vaissière, Étienne. "Sogdiana iii. History and Archeology." *Encyclopædia* Iranica, 2011. http://www.iranicaonline.org/articles/sogdiana-iii-history-and-archeology.

——. *Sogdian Traders: A History*. Translated by James Ward. Leiden: Brill, 2005.

DeWeese, Devin. "Atā'īya Order." In *Encyclopædia Iranica*. http://www.iranicaonline.org/articles/ataiya-order-a-branch-of-the-yasaviya-sufi-brotherhood-especially-active-in-karazm-from-the-8th-14th-century.

——. "The Descendants of Sayyid Ata and the Rank of Naqīb in Central Asia." *Journal of the American Oriental Society* 115, no. 4 (December 1995): 612–34.

——. " 'Dis-Ordering' Sufism in Early Modern Central Asia: Suggestions for Rethinking the Sources and Social Structures of Sufi History in the 18th and 19th Centuries." In *History and Culture of Central Asia*, edited by Bakhtiyar Babadjanov and Kawahara Yayoi, 259–79. Tokyo: University of Tokyo Press, 2012.

——. "Foreword." In *Sobranie fetv po obosnovaniiu zikra dzhakhr i sama'*, edited by A. K. Muminov, 9–15. Pamiatniki po istorii i kul'ture Tsentral'noi Azii. Almaty: Daik-Press, 2008.

——. "Islam and the Legacy of Sovietology: A Review Essay on Yaacov Ro'i's Islam in the Soviet Union." *Journal of Islamic Studies* 13, no. 3 (September 1, 2002): 298–330.

——. *Islamization and Native Religion in the Golden Horde: Baba Tükles and Conversion to Islam in Historical and Epic Tradition*. University Park: Pennsylvania State University Press, 1994.

——. "The Masha'ikh-i Turk and the Khojagan: Rethinking the Links between the Yasavi and Naqshbandi Sufi Traditions." *Journal of Islamic Studies* 7, no. 2 (1996): 180–207.

——. "Muslim Medical Culture in Modern Central Asia: A Brief Note on Manuscript Sources from the Sixteenth to Twentieth Centuries." *Central Asian Survey* 32, no. 1 (2013): 3–18.

——. "Organizational Patterns and Developments within Sufi Communities." In *The Wiley Blackwell History of Islam*, edited by Armando Salvatore, 329–50. Hoboken, NJ: Wiley-Blackwell, 2018.

——. "Re-Envisioning the History of Sufi Communities in Central Asia: Continuity and Adaptation in Sources and Social Frameworks, 16th–20th Centuries." In *Sufism in Central Asia: New Perspectives on Sufi Traditions, 15th–21st Centuries*, edited by Devin DeWeese and Jo-Ann Gross, 21–74. Leiden: Brill, 2018.

——. "Sacred History for a Central Asian Town: Saints, Shrines, and Legends of Origin in Histories of Sayrām, 18th–19th Centuries." *Revue des mondes musulmans et de la Méditerranée*, July 2000, 245–95.

Dickson, Martin B. "Uzbek Dynastic Theory in the Sixteenth Century." In *Trudy XXV-ogo mezhdunarodnogo kongressa vostokovedov*, 208–16. Moscow, 1960.

Doumani, Beshara. *Rediscovering Palestine: Merchants and Peasants in Jabal Nablus, 1700–1900*. Berkeley: University of California Press, 1995.

Dudney, Arthur Dale. "A Desire for Meaning: Ḳhān-i Ārzū's Philology and the Place of India in the Eighteenth-Century Persianate World." PhD diss., Columbia University, 2013.

Dudoignon, Stéphane A. "Faction Struggles among the Bukharan Ulama during the Colonial, the Revolutionary and the Early Soviet Periods (1826–1929): A Paradigm for History Writing?" In *Muslim Societies: Historical and Comparative Aspects*, edited by Sato Tsugitaka, 62–96. London: RoutledgeCurzon, 2004.

——. "From Revival to Mutation: The Religious Personnel of Islam in Tajikistan, from de-Stalinization to Independence (1955–91)." *Central Asian Survey* 30, no. 1 (2011): 53–80.

——. "Sur Le 'Mail des Rhapsodes': Sociabilités traditionnelles, groupes de statut, ethnies minoritaires en Asie Centrale soviétique." *Asiatische studien/Études asiatiques* 2 (2009): 273–321.

Durgeli, Nazir al-. *Uslada umov v biografiiakh dagestanskikh uchenykh (Nuzkhat al-azkhān fī tarādzhim "ulamā" Dāgistān): Dagestanskie uchenye X–XX vv. i ikh sochineniia*. Edited by A. R. Shikhsaidov, Michael Kemper, and Alfrid Kashafovich Bustanov. Moscow: Izdatel'skii dom Mardzhani, 2012.

Durkilī al-Tūnī, Naḏīr al-. *Muslim Culture in Russia and Central Asia: Die Islamgelehrten Daghestans und ihre arabischen Werke*. Edited by Michael Kemper and Amri R Šichsaidov. Berlin: Klaus Schwarz, 2004.

Eaton, Richard Maxwell, and Phillip B. Wagoner. "The Persian Cosmopolis (900–1900) and the Sanskrit Cosmopolis (400–1400)." In *The Persianate World: Rethinking a Shared Sphere*, edited by Abbas Amanat and Assef Ashraf, 63–83. Leiden: Brill, 2018.

——. *Power, Memory, Architecture: Contested Sites on India's Deccan Plateau, 1300–1600*. New Delhi: Oxford University Press, 2014.

——. *The Rise of Islam and the Bengal Frontier, 1204–1760*. Berkeley: University of California Press, 1996.

——. *Sufis of Bijapur, 1300–1700: Social Roles of Sufis in Medieval India*. Princeton Princeton University Press, 1978.

——. Eckman, János. "The Mamluk-Kipchak Literature." *Central Asiatic Journal* 8, no. 4 (1963): 304–19.

Eden, Jeff. *Slavery and Empire in Central Asia*. Cambridge: Cambridge University Press, 2018.

Edwards, Catharine, and Greg Woolf. "Cosmopolis: Rome as World City." In *Rome the Cosmopolis*, edited by Catharine Edwards and Greg Woolf, 1–20. Cambridge: Cambridge University Press, 2006.

Eickelman, Dale F. "The Art of Memory: Islamic Education and Its Social Reproduction." *Comparative Studies in Society and History* 20, no. 4 (October 1978): 485–516.

El-Zein, Amira. *Islam, Arabs, and the Intelligent World of The Jinn*. Syracuse: Syracuse University Press, 2009.

Elliott, Mark C. *The Manchu Way: The Eight Banners and Ethnic Identity in Late Imperial China*. Stanford: Stanford University Press, 2001.

Erdal, Marcel. *A Grammar of Old Turkic*. Leiden: Brill, 2004

——. "The Turkish Yarkand Documents." *Bulletin of the School of Oriental and African Studies, University of London* 47, no. 2 (1984): 260–301.

Erkinov, Aftandil. "Islamskii institut maddakhov- propovednikov v Turkestanskom krae: Ideologizatsiia russkoi administratsiei repertuara ikh propovedei." In *Ars Islamica: In Honor of Stanislav Mikhailovich Prozorov*, edited by Mikhail B. Piotrovsky and Alikber K. Alikberov, 746–97. Moscow: Nauka—Vostochnaia Literatura, 2016.

——. "Persian-Chaghatay Bilingualism in the Intellectual Circles of Central Asia during the 15th–18th Centuries (the Case of Poetical Anthologies, Bayāz)." *International Journal of Central Asian Studies* 12 (2008): 57–82.

Ernst, Carl W. "Between Orientalism and Fundamentalism: Problematizing the Teaching of Sufism." In *Teaching Islam*, edited by Brannon Wheeler, 108–23. New York: Oxford University Press, 2002.

——. "The Limits of Universalism in Islamic Thought: The Case of Indian Religions." *The Muslim World* 101 (January 2011): 1–19.

Ernst, Carl, and Bruce B. Lawrence. "What Is a Sufi Order?" In *Sufism: Critical Concepts in Islamic Studies*, edited by Lloyd Ridgeon, 1:231–49. New York: Routledge, 2008.

Ernst, Carl W., and Tony Stewart. "Syncretism." In *South Asian Folklore: An Encyclopedia*, edited by Peter J. Claus, Sarah Diamond, and Margaret Ann Mills, 586–88. New York: Routledge, 2002.

Fabian, Johannes. *Out of Our Minds: Reason and Madness in the Exploration of Central Africa*. Berkeley: University of California Press, 2000.

Faruqui, Munis Daniyal. *Princes of the Mughal Empire, 1504–1719*. Cambridge: Cambridge University Press, 2012.

Fathi, Habiba. "Otines: The Unknown Women Clerics of Central Asian Islam." *Central Asian Survey* 16, no. 1 (March 1, 1997): 27–43.

Fawzīya Turkistānī. *al-Qurrāʿ fī Turkistān*. Jeddah: al-Hayʾa al-ʿĀlamiyya lil-Kitāb wa-l-Sunna, 2015.

Fierro, Maribel. "Women as Prophets in Islam." In *Writing the Feminine: Women in Arab Sources*, edited by Manuela Marín and Randi Deguilhem, 183–98. New York: I. B. Tauris, 2002.

Fletcher, J. "V.A. Aleksandrov on Russo-Ch'ing Relations in the Seventeenth Century: Critique and Résumé." *Kritika* 7, no. 3 (1971): 138–70.

Flood, Finbarr Barry. *Objects of Translation: Material Culture and Medieval "Hindu-Muslim" Encounter*. Princeton: Princeton University Press, 2009.

Ford, Graeme. "The Uses of Persian in Imperial China: The Translation Practices of the Great Ming." In *The Persianate World: Rethinking a Shared Sphere*, edited by Abbas Amanat and Assef Ashraf, 15–62. Leiden: Brill, 2018.

Forrest, K. Mendoza. *Witches, Whores, and Sorcerers: The Concept of Evil in Early Iran*. Austin: University of Texas Press, 2011.

Fowden, Garth. *Empire to Commonwealth: Consequences of Monotheism in Late Antiquity*. Princeton: Princeton University Press, 1993.

Frank, Allen J. "A Month among the Qazaqs in the Emirate of Bukhara: Observations on Islamic Knowledge in a Nomadic Environment." In *Explorations in the Social History of Modern Central Asia (19th–Early 20th Century)*, edited by Paolo Sartori, 247–66. Leiden: Brill, 2013.

——. *Bukhara and the Muslims of Russia: Sufism, Education, and the Paradox of Islamic Prestige*. Leiden: Brill, 2012.

——. *Gulag Miracles: Sufis and Stalinist Repression in Kazakhstan*. Vienna: Verlag der Österreichischen Akademie der Wissenschaften, 2019.

——. *Muslim Religious Institutions in Imperial Russia: The Islamic World of Novouzensk District and the Kazakh Inner Horde, 1780–1910*. Leiden: Brill, 2001.

Frembgen, Jürgen Wasim. "Divine Madness and Cultural Otherness: Diwānas and Faqīrs in Northern Pakistan." In *Islam in South Asia*, edited by David Taylor, 1:238–52. South Asian Islam in Historical and Cultural Context. London: Routledge, 2011.

Frow, John. *Genre: The New Critical Idiom*. New York: Routledge, 2006.

Fuchs, Juan Carlos Estenssoro. *Del paganismo a la santidad: La incorporación de los indios del Perú al catolicismo, 1532–1750*. Translated by Gabriela Ramos. Lima: IFEA Instituto Francés de Estudios Andinos, 2003.

Gandhi, Supriya. "Mughal Self-Fashioning, Indic Self-Realization: Dārā Shikoh and Persian Textual Cultures in Early Modern South Asia." PhD diss., Harvard University, 2011.

Gangler, Anette, Heinz Gaube, and Attilio Petruccioli. *Bukhara, the Eastern Dome of Islam: Urban Development, Urban Space, Architecture and Population*. London: Edition Axel Menges, 2004.

Gibb, H.A.R. *The Arab Conquests in Central Asia*. London: The Royal Asiatic Society, 1923.

Golden, Peter. *Nomads and Sedentary Societies in Medieval Eurasia*. Essays on Global and Comparative History. Washington, DC: American Historical Association, 1998.

Grafton, Anthony, and Lisa Jardine. *From Humanism to the Humanities*. Cambridge, MA: Harvard University Press, 1986.

Green, Nile. *Bombay Islam: The Religious Economy of the West Indian Ocean, 1840–1915*. Cambridge: Cambridge University Press, 2011.

——. "Introduction: The Frontiers of the Persianate World (ca. 800–1900)." In *The Persianate World: The Frontiers of a Eurasian Lingua Franca*, edited by Nile Green, 1–74. Oakland: University of California Press, 2019.

——. *Making Space: Sufis and Settlers in Early Modern India*. OUP India, 2012.

——. "Perspectives from the Peripheries." *Journal of Persianate Studies* 8, no. 1 (August 24, 2015): 1–22.

——. "Rethinking the 'Middle East' after the Oceanic Turn." *Comparative Studies of South Asia, Africa and the Middle East* 34, no. 3 (2014): 556–64.

——. *Terrains of Exchange: Religious Economies of Global Islam*. Oxford: Oxford University Press, 2015.

——. "Transgressions of a Holy Fool: A Majzub in Colonial India." In *Islam in South Asia in Practice*, edited by Barbara Daly Metcalf, 173–86. New Delhi: Permanent Black, 2009.

Greenblatt, Stephen. *Renaissance Self-Fashioning: From More to Shakespeare*. Chicago: University of Chicago Press, 1980.

Griffith, Sidney Harrison. *The Bible in Arabic: The Scriptures of the People of the Book in the Language of Islam*. Jews, Christians, and Muslims from the Ancient to the Modern World. Princeton: Princeton University Press, 2013.

Gross, Jo-Ann. "The Naqshbandīya Connection: From Central Asia to India and Back (16th—19th Centuries)." In *India and Central Asia: Commerce and Culture, 1500–1800*, edited by Scott Levi, 232–59. New Delhi: Oxford University Press, 2007.

Grousset, Professor René. *The Empire of the Steppes: A History of Central Asia*. New Brunswick, NJ: Rutgers University Press, 1970.

Gupta, Narayani. *Delhi between Two Empires, 1803–1931: Society, Government and Urban Growth*. Delhi: Oxford University Press, 1981.

Haarmann, Ulrich W. "Yeomanly Arrogance and Righteous Rule: Faḍl Allāh Ibn Rūzbihān Khunjī and the Mamluks of Egypt." In *Iran and Iranian Studies: Essays in Honor of Iraj Afshar*, edited by Kambiz Eslami, 109–24. Princeton, NJ: Zagros, 1998.

Haider, Najam. "Contesting Intoxication: Early Juristic Debates over the Lawfulness of Alcoholic Beverages." *Islamic Law and Society* 20, no. 1–2 (January 1, 2013): 48–89.

Ḥakham, Simon. *The Musā-Nāma of R. Shim'on Ḥakham*. Edited by Herbert H. Paper. Judeo-Iranian Text Series, no. 1. Cincinnati: Hebrew Union College Press, 1986.

Halbertal, Moshe. *People of the Book: Canon, Meaning, and Authority*. Cambridge, MA: Harvard University Press, 1997.

Hall, Bruce Stewart, and Charles C. Stewart. "The Historic 'Core Curriculum' and the Book Market in Islamic West Africa." In *The Trans-Saharan Book Trade: Manuscript Culture, Arabic Literacy and Intellectual History in Muslim Africa*, edited by Graziano Krätli and Ghislaine Lydon, 109–74. Leiden: Brill, 2011.

Hallaq, Wael B. "Takhrij and the Construction of Juristic Authority." In *Studies in Islamic Legal Theory*, edited by Bernard G. Weiss, 317–36. Leiden: Brill, 2002.

——. *The Impossible State: Islam, Politics, and Modernity's Moral Predicament*. New York: Columbia University Press, 2013.

Hanaoka, Mimi. *Authority and Identity in Medieval Islamic Historiography: Persian Histories from the Peripheries*. New York: Cambridge University Press, 2016.

Hanaway, William L. "Eskandar Nāma." In *Encyclopædia Iranica*. http://www.iranicaonline.org/articles/eskandar-nama.

Hanks, William F. *Converting Words: Maya in the Age of the Cross*. The Anthropology of Christianity 6. Berkeley: University of California Press, 2010.

Hanley, Will. "Grieving Cosmopolitanism in Middle East Studies." *History Compass* 6, no. 5 (September 1, 2008): 1346–67.

Hasan, Mushirul. *From Pluralism to Separatism: Qasbas in Colonial Awadh*. The Mushirul Hasan Omnibus. New Delhi: Oxford University Press, 2004.

Hermansen, Marcia K., and Bruce B. Lawrence. "Indo-Persian Tazkiras as Memorative Communications." In *Beyond Turk and Hindu: Rethinking Religious Identities in Islamicate South Asia*, edited by David Gilmartin and Bruce B. Lawrence, 149–75. Gainesville: University Press of Florida, 2000.

Hirsch, Francine. *Empire of Nations: Ethnographic Knowledge & the Making of the Soviet Union*. Ithaca, NY: Cornell University Press, 2005.

Hobsbawm, Eric, and Terence Ranger, eds. *The Invention of Tradition*. Cambridge University Press, 2012.

Hodgkin, Samuel. "Classical Persian Canons of the Revolutionary Press: Abū al-Qāsim Lāhūtī's Circles in Istanbul and Moscow." In *Persian Literature and Modernity: Production and Reception*, edited by Hamid Rezaei Yazdi and Arshavez Mozafari, 185–211. New York: Routledge, 2019.

———. "Revolutionary Springtimes: Reading Soviet Persian-Tajik Poetry, from Ghazal to Lyric." In *Iranian Languages and Literatures of Central Asia*, edited by Matteo de Chiara and Evelin Grassi, 273–305. Paris: Association Pour l'Avancement des Études Iraniennes, 2015.

Hodgson, Marshall G. S. *The Venture of Islam: The Expansion of Islam in the Middle Periods*, vol. 2. Chicago: University of Chicago Press, 1974.

Holzwarth, Wolfgang. "Bukharan Armies and Uzbek Military Power, 1670–1870: Coping with the Legacy of a Nomadic Conquest." In *Nomad Military Power in Iran and Adjacent Areas in the Islamic Period*, 273–354. Wiesbaden: Dr. Ludwig Reichert Verlag, 2015.

———. "The Uzbek State as Reflected in Eighteenth Century Bukharan Sources." In *Nomaden und sesshafte—Fragen, methoden, ergebnisse*, edited by Wolfgang Holzwarth and Thomas Herzog, 93–129. Halle: Teil 2, 2004.

Hoyland, Robert G. *Arabia and the Arabs: From the Bronze Age to the Coming of Islam*. New York: Routledge, 2001.

Humphreys, R. Stephen. *Islamic History: A Framework for Inquiry*. Princeton: Princeton University Press, 1991.

Isogai, Ken'ichi. "Seven Fatwa Documents from Early 20th Century Samarqand: The Function of Mufti in the Judicial Proceedings Adopted at Central Asian Islamic Court." *Annals of Japan Association for Middle East Studies* 27, no. 1 (July 2011): 259–82.

Ivanov, P. P. "Kul'turnaia zhizn' narodov Srednei Azii v XVIII–pervoi polovine XIX v." In *Ocherki po istorii Srednei Azii (XVI–seredina XVX v.)*, 214–25. Moscow: Izd-vo Vostochnoi Literatury, 1958.

Jackson, Sherman A. "Fiction and Formalism: Toward a Functional Analysis of Uṣūl al-Fiqh." In *Studies in Islamic Legal Theory*, edited by Bernard G. Weiss, 177–200. Leiden: Brill, 2002.

Jafri, Saiyid Zaheer Husain. "*Madrasa* and *Khānaqāh*, or *Madrasa* in *Khānaqāh*? Education and Sufi Establishments in Northern India." In *Islamic Education, Diversity and National Identity: Dīnī Madāris in India Post 9/11*, edited by Jan-Peter Hartung and Helmut Reifeld, 73–103. New Delhi: SAGE, 2006.

James, Boris. "Uses and Values of the Term Kurd in Arabic Medieval Literary Sources." In *Seminar at the American University of Beirut (AUB) Center for Arab and Middle Eastern Studies (CAMES)*. Beirut, 2006.

Jones, Linda G. *The Power of Oratory in the Medieval Muslim World*. New York: Cambridge University Press, 2012.

Jumanazar, Abdusattor. *Buxoro ta'lim tizimi tarikhi*. Tashkent: Akademnashr, 2017.

Kalinovsky, Artemy M. *Laboratory of Socialist Development: Cold War Politics and Decolonization in Soviet Tajikistan*. Ithaca: Cornell University Press, 2018.

Kamp, Marianne. "Where Did the Mullahs Go? Oral Histories from Rural Uzbekistan." *Die Welt Des Islams* 50 (2010): 503–31.

——. *The New Woman in Uzbekistan: Islam, Modernity, and Unveiling Under Communism*. Jackson School Publications in International Studies. Seattle: University of Washington Press, 2006.

Kane, Eileen. *Russian Hajj: Empire and the Pilgrimage to Mecca*. Ithaca, NY: Cornell University Press, 2015.

Karamustafa, Ahmet T. *God's Unruly Friends: Dervish Groups in the Islamic Later Middle Period, 1200–1550*. London: Oneworld, 2006.

Karpat, Kemal H. *Ottoman Population, 1830–1914: Demographic and Social Characteristics*. Madison: University of Wisconsin Press, 1985.

Keller, Shoshana. *To Moscow, Not Mecca: The Soviet Campaign Against Islam in Central Asia, 1917–1941*. Westport, CT: Praeger, 2001.

Kerimova, A. A. *Govor tadzhikov Bukhary*. Moscow: Izd-vo Vostochnoi Literatury, 1959.

Keshavarzian, Arang. "Turban or Hat, Seminarian or Soldier: State Building and Clergy Building in Reza Shah's Iran." *Journal of Church and State* 45, no. 1 (Winter 2003): 81–112.

Keshavmurthy, Prashant. *Persian Authorship and Canonicity in Late Mughal Delhi: Building an Ark*. New York: Routledge, 2016.

Khalfin, N.A. *Rossiia i Bukharskii emirat na zapadnom Pamire*. Moscow: Nauka, 1975.

Khalid, Adeeb. "The Bukharan People's Soviet Republic in the Light of Muslim Sources." *Die Welt Des Islams* 50, no. 3 (December 2010): 335–61.

——. "Central Asia between the Ottoman and the Soviet Worlds." *Kritika: Explorations in Russian and Eurasian History* 12, no. 2 (2011): 451–76.

——. "Society and Politics in Bukhara, 1868–1920." *Central Asian Survey* 19, no. 3 (2000): 364–93.

——. *Islam after Communism: Religion and Politics in Central Asia*. Berkeley: University of California Press, 2007.

——. *Making Uzbekistan: Nation, Empire, and Revolution in the Early USSR*. Ithaca: Cornell University Press, 2015.

——. *The Politics of Muslim Cultural Reform: Jadidism in Central Asia*. Berkeley: University of California Press, 1998.

Khan, Mawlānā Muḥammad ʿAbd al-Salām. *Madrasa-i ʿālīya-i Rāmpūr: Ēk tārīkhī darsgāh*. Rampur: Rāmpūr Reẓā Library, 2002.

Khan, Naveeda. "Of Children and Jinn: An Inquiry into an Unexpected Friendship during Uncertain Times." *Cultural Anthropology* 21, no. 2 (2006): 234–64.

Khan, Pasha Mohamad. "The Broken Spell: The Romance Genre in Late Mughal India." PhD diss., Columbia University, 2013.

Khan, Sarfraz. *Muslim Reformist Political Thought: Revivalists, Modernists and Free Will*. New York: Routledge, 2013.

Khanykov, N. "Opisanie Bukharskogo khanstva." In *Istoriia Srednei Azii*, edited by A. I. Buldakov, S. A. Shumov, and A. R. Andreev, 202–27. Moscow: Evrolints—Russkaia Panorama, 2003.

Khazeni, Arash. "The City of Balkh and the Central Eurasian Caravan Trade in the Early Nineteenth Century." *Comparative Studies of South Asia, Africa and the Middle East* 30, no. 3 (2010): 463–72.

Kia, Mana. "Indian Friends, Iranian Selves, Persianate Modern." *Comparative Studies of South Asia, Africa and the Middle East* 36, no. 3 (January 1, 2016): 398–417.

——. *Persianate Selves: Memories of Place and Origin Before Nationalism*. Stanford: Stanford University Press, 2020.

Kia, Mana, and Afshin Marashi. "Introduction: After the Persianate." *Comparative Studies of South Asia, Africa and the Middle East* 36, no. 3 (December 1, 2016): 379–83.

Kimura, Satoru. "Sunni-Shi'i Relations in the Russian Protectorate of Bukhara, as Perceived by the Local 'Ulama.'" In *Asiatic Russia: Imperial Power in Regional and International Contexts*, edited by Tomohiko Uyama, 189–215. London: Routledge, 2011.

Kinra, Rajeev. *Writing Self, Writing Empire: Chandar Bhan Brahman and the Cultural World of the Indo-Persian State Secretary*. Oakland: University of California Press, 2015.

Kılıç-Schubel, Nurten. "Writing Women: Women's Poetry and Literary Networks in Nineteenth-Century Central Asia." In *Horizons of the World: Festschrift for İsenbike Togan*, 405–40. Istanbul: İthaki, 2011.

Knysh, Alexander. "Sufism as an Explanatory Paradigm: The Issue of the Motivations of Sufi Resistance Movements in Western and Russian Scholarship." *Die Welt Des Islams*, New Series, 42, no. 2 (January 1, 2002): 139–73.

——. *Islamic Mysticism: A Short History*. Leiden: Brill, 2000.

Komatsu, Hisao. "Dār al-Islām Under Russian Rule as Understood by Turkestani Muslim Intellectuals." In *Empire, Islam, and Politics in Central Eurasia*, edited by Tomohiko Uyama. Sopporo, Japan: Slavic-Eurasian Research Center, 2007.

Kotkin, Stephen. "Modern Times: The Soviet Union and the Interwar Conjuncture." *Kritika: Explorations in Russian and Eurasian History* 2, no. 1 (2001): 111–64.

——. "Mongol Commonwealth?: Exchange and Governance across the Post-Mongol Space." *Kritika: Explorations in Russian and Eurasian History* 8, no. 3 (2007): 487–531.

——. *Magnetic Mountain: Stalinism as a Civilization*. Berkeley: University of California Press, 1997.

Kowalski, Tadeusz. "The Turks in the Shāh-Nāma." In *The Turks in the Early Islamic World*, edited by C. Edmund Bosworth, 121–34. The Formation of the Classical Islamic World 9. Burlington, VT: Ashgate Variorum, 2007.

Krämer, Annette. *Geistliche Autorität und islamische Gesellschaft im Wandel: Studien über Frauenälteste (otin und xalfa) im unabhängigen Usbekistan*. Berlin: Klaus Schwarz, 2002.

Kügelgen, Anke von. "Rastsvet Nakshbandiia-Mudzhaddidiia v Srednei Transoksanii s XVIII–do nachala XIX vv.: Opyt detektivnogo rassledovaniia." In *Sufism v Tsentral'noi Azii*, edited by A.A. Khismatulin, 275–330. St. Petersburg: Filologicheskii Fakul'tet Sankt-Peterburskogo Gosudarstvennogo Universiteta, 2001.

——. *Legitimatsiia sredneaziatskoi dinastii Mangitov v proizvedeniiakh ikh istorikov, XVIII–XIX vv*. Almaty: Daik-Press, 2004.

——. "Bukhara Viii. Historiography of the Khanate, 1500–1920." In *Encyclopædia Iranica*. http://www.iranicaonline.org/articles/bukhara-viii.

Kumar, Sunil. *The Emergence of the Delhi Sultanate*. New Delhi: Permanent Black, 2007.

Lambton, Ann K. S. *State and Government in Medieval Islam: An Introduction to the Study of Islamic Political Theory: The Jurists*. New York: Oxford University Press, 1981.

Lapidus, Ira M. *Muslim Cities in the Later Middle Ages*. Cambridge: Cambridge University Press, 1984.

Latypov, Alisher B. "The Soviet Doctor and the Treatment of Drug Addiction: 'A Difficult and Most Ungracious Task.'" *Harm Reduction Journal* 8 (December 30, 2011). https://doi.org/10.1186/1477-7517-8-32.

Lazard, Gilbert. "The Dialectology of Judeo-Persian." In *Pādyāvand*, edited by Amnon Netzer, 33–59. Costa Mesa, CA: Mazda Publishers, 1996.

Lee, Jonathan L. *The "Ancient Supremacy": Bukhara, Afghanistan and the Battle for Balkh, 1731–1901*. Leiden: Brill, 1996.

Lee, Joo-Yup. "The Historical Meaning of the Term Turk and the Nature of the Turkic Identity of the Chinggisid and Timurid Elites in Post-Mongol Central Asia." *Central Asiatic Journal* 59, no. 1–2 (2016): 101–32.

——. *Qazaqlïq, or Ambitious Brigandage, and the Formation of the Qazaqs*. Leiden: Brill, 2015.

Lenhoff, Gail. "Toward a Theory of Protogenres in Medieval Russian Letters." *The Russian Review* 43, no. 1 (1984): 31–54.

Levi, Scott, and Ron Sela, eds. *Islamic Central Asia: An Anthology of Historical Sources*. Bloomington: Indiana University Press, 2010.

Levi, Scott, ed. *India and Central Asia: Commerce and Culture, 1500–1800*. New Delhi: Oxford University Press, 2007.

——. "The Ferghana Valley at the Crossroads of World History: The Rise of Khoqand, 1709–1822." *Journal of Global History* 2, no. 2 (2007): 213–32.

——. *The Indian Diaspora in Central Asia and Its Trade, 1550–1900*. Leiden: Brill, 2002.

——. *The Rise and Fall of Khoqand, 1709–1876: Central Asia in the Early Modern World*. Pittsburgh: University of Pittsburgh Press, 2017.

Liechti, Stacy. "Books, Book Endowments, and Communities of Knowledge in the Bukharan Khanate." PhD diss., New York University, 2008.

Lind van Wijngaarden, Jan Willem de, and Bushra Rani. "Male Adolescent Concubinage in Peshawar, Northwestern Pakistan." *Culture, Health & Sexuality* 13, no. 9 (October 2011): 1061–72.

Livshits, V. A., ed. *Sogdiiskie dokumenty s gory Mug: Iuridicheskie dokumenty i pis'ma*, vol. 2. Moskva: Izd-vo Vostochnoi Literatury, 1962.

Lockhart, L. *Nadir Shah: A Critical Study Based Mainly Upon Contemporary Sources*. London: Luzac & Co., 1938.

Losensky, Paul. "Sāqi-Nāma (Book of the Cupbearer)." In *Encyclopædia Iranica*. http://www.iranicaonline.org/articles/saqi-nama-book.

——. *Welcoming Fighānī: Imitation and Poetic Individuality in the Safavid-Mughal Ghazal*. Costa Mesa, CA: Mazda Publishers, 1998.

Lur'e [Lurje], Pavel Borisovich. "Istoriko-lingvisticheskii analiz sogdiiskoi toponimii." PhD diss., Sankt-Peterburgskii Filial Instituta Vostokovedeniia RAN, 2004.

Lydon, Ghislaine. *On Trans-Saharan Trails: Islamic Law, Trade Networks, and Cross-Cultural Exchange in Nineteenth-Century Western Africa*. Cambridge: Cambridge University Press, 2009.

MacKenzie, D. N. *A Concise Pahlavi Dictionary*. London: Oxford University Press, 1971.

Madelung, Wilferd. "The Spread of Maturidism and the Turks." In *Religious Schools and Sects in Medieval Islam*, 109–68. London: Variorum Reprints, 1985.

Makdisi, George. *The Rise of the Colleges: Institutions of Learning in Islam and the West*. Edinburgh: Edinburgh University Press, 1981.

Malik, S. Jamal. "Varieties of Islamic Expression in the Mughal Province of Kabul." In *Islam and Indian Regions*, edited by Anna Libera Dallapriccola and Stephanie Zingel-Avé Lallemant, 7–30. Stuttgart: Franz Steiner, 1993.

Marashi, Afshin. *Nationalizing Iran: Culture, Power, and the State, 1870–1940*. Seattle: University of Washington Press, 2008.

Marlow, L. *Counsel for Kings: Wisdom and Politics in Tenth-Century Iran*. Volume I: *The Nasihat al-Muluk of Pseudo-Mawardi: Contexts and Themes*. Edinburgh: Edinburgh University Press, 2016.

Massell, Gregory J. *The Surrogate Proletariat: Moslem Women and Revolutionary Strategies in Soviet Central Asia, 1919–1929*. Princeton: Princeton University Press, 1974.

Masud, Muhammad Khalid, Brinkley Messick, and David S. Powers. "Muftis, Fatwas, and Islamic Legal Interpretation." In *Islamic Legal Interpretation: Muftis and Their Fatwas*, edited by Muhammad Khalid Masud, Brinkley Messick, and David Powers, 3–32. Cambridge, MA: Harvard University Press, 1996.

Matthee, Rudi. *The Pursuit of Pleasure: Drugs and Stimulants in Iranian History, 1500–1900*. Princeton: Princeton University Press, 2009.

——. "Alcohol in the Islamic Middle East: Ambivalence and Ambiguity." *Past & Present* 222, no. 9 (2014): 100–125.

Mayzel, Matitiahu. *Generals and Revolutionaries: The Russian General Staff during the Revolution. A Study in the Transformation of Military Elite*. Osnabrück: Biblio-Verlag, 1978.

McChesney, Robert D. "The Amirs of Muslim Central Asia in the XVIIth Century." *Journal of the Economic and Social History of the Orient* 26, no. 1 (1983): 33–70.

——. " 'Barrier of Heterodoxy?': Rethinking the Ties Between Iran and Central Asia in the 17th Century." In *Safavid Persia: The History and Politics of an Islamic Society*, edited by Charles Melville, 231–67. London: I.B. Tauris, 1996.

——. "Central Asia's Place in the Middle East: Some Historical Considerations." In *Central Asia Meets the Middle East*, edited by David Menashri, 25–51. London: Frank Cass, 1998.

——. "The Chinggisid Restoration in Central Asia: 1500–1785." In *The Cambridge History of Inner Asia: The Chinggisid Age*, edited by Allen Frank, Nicola Di Cosmo, and Peter Golden, 277–302. Cambridge: Cambridge University Press, 2009.

——. "Earning a Living: Promoting Islamic Culture in the Sixteenth and Seventeenth Centuries." In *Afghanistan's Islam: From Conversion to the Taliban*, edited by Nile Green, 89–104. Oakland: University of California Press, 2016.

——. "Economic and Social Aspects of the Public Architecture of Bukhara in the 1560's and 1570's." *Islamic Art* 2 (1987): 217–42.

——. "The 'Rerforms' of Bāqī Muḥammad Khān." *Central Asiatic Journal* 24, no. 1/2 (1980): 69–84.

——. *Waqf in Central Asia: Four Hundred Years in the History of a Muslim Shrine, 1480–1889*. Princeton: Princeton University Press, 1991.

——. "Waḳf, Central Asia." In *Encyclopaedia of Islam*, 2nd ed. Edited by P. Bearman, Th. Bianquis, C. E. Bosworth, E. van Donzel, and W. P. Heinrichs. http://dx.doi.org/10.1163/1573-3912_islam_COM_1333.

McGovern, Patrick E. "Iranian Wine at the 'Dawn of Viniculture.'" In *Wine Culture in Iran and Neighbouring Countries*, edited by Bert G. Fragner, Ralph Kauz, and Florian Schwarz, 11–21. Vienna: Veröffentlichungen zur Iranistik, 2014.

Mehrabadi, Mitra. *Tārīkh-i silsila-i Ziyārī (History of the Ziyarid Dynasty)*. Mashhad: Dunyā-yi Kitāb, 1995.

Melvin-Koushki, Matthew, and James Pickett. "Mobilizing Magic: Occultism in Central Asia and the Continuity of High Persianate Culture under Russian Rule." *Studia Islamica* 111, no. 2 (November 2016): 231–84.

Melvin-Koushki, Matthew. "Astrology, Lettrism, Geomancy: The Occult-Scientific Methods of Post-Mongol Islamicate Imperialism." *Medieval History Journal* 19, no. 1 (March 2016): 142–50.

——. "How to Rule the World: Occult-Scientific Manuals of the Early Modern Persian Cosmopolis." *Journal of Persianate Studies* 11, no. 2 (January 28, 2019): 140–54.

——. "In Defense of Geomancy: Šaraf al-Dīn Yazdī Rebuts Ibn Ḫaldūn's Critique of the Occult Sciences." *Arabica* 64, no. 3–4 (September 2017): 346–403.

——. "Khunji, Fazl Allah b. Ruzbihan (1455–1521)." In *The Princeton Encyclopedia of Islamic Political Thought*. Edited by Gerhard Bowering, Patricia Crone, Wadad Kadi, Devin J. Stewart, Muhammad Qasim Zaman, and Mahan Mirza, 297–98. Princeton: Princeton University Press, 2012.

——. "Persianate Geomancy from Ṭūsī to the Millennium: A Preliminary Survey." In *Occult Sciences in Premodern Islamic Culture*. Beirut: Orient-Institut Beirut, 2017.

——. "Powers of One: The Mathematicalization of the Occult Sciences in the High Persianate Tradition." *Intellectual History of the Islamicate World* 5, no. 1–2 (January 1, 2017): 127–99.

Messick, Brinkley Morris. "Islamic Texts: The Anthropologist as Reader." In *Islamic Studies in the Twenty-First Century*, edited by L. Buskens and A. van Sandwijk, 29–46. Amsterdam: Amsterdam University Press, 2016.

——. *The Calligraphic State: Textual Domination and History in a Muslim Society*. Comparative Studies on Muslim Societies 16. Berkeley: University of California, 1993.

——. *Sharīʿa Scripts: A Historical Anthropology*. New York: Columbia University Press, 2018.

Metcalf, Barbara Daly. *Islamic Revival in British India: Deoband, 1860–1900*. New York: Oxford University Press, 2004.

Meyer, James H. *Turks Across Empires: Marketing Muslim Identity in the Russian-Ottoman Borderlands, 1856–1914*. New York: Oxford University Press, 2014.

Mirbabaev, Abdullodzhon. *Istoriia madrasa Tadzhikistana*. 2 vols. Dushanbe: Meros, Akademiia Nauk Respubliki Tadzhikistana, 1994.

Moin, A. Azfar. *The Millennial Sovereign: Sacred Kingship and Sainthood in Islam*. New York: Columbia University Press, 2013.

Morony, Michael G. *Iraq after the Muslim Conquest*. Princeton: Princeton University Press, 1984.

Morrison, Alexander. *Russian Rule in Samarkand, 1868–1910: A Comparison with British India*. Oxford: Oxford University Press, 2008.

Mottahedeh, Roy Parviz. "Review of The Patricians of Nishapur: A Study in Medieval Islamic Social History by R.W. Bulliet." *Journal of the American Oriental Society* 95, no. 3 (September 1975): 491–95.

——. *The Mantle of the Prophet*. London: Oneworld Publications, 2008.

Muminov, I.M., ed. *Istoriia Uzbekskoi SSR*. Tashkent: Izd-vo "Fan" Uzbekskoi SSR, 1974.

Musawi, Muhsin J. al-. *The Medieval Islamic Republic of Letters: Arabic Knowledge Construction*. Notre Dame, IN: University of Notre Dame Press, 2015.

Muzio, Ciro Lo. "An Archaeological Outline of the Bukhara Oasis." *Journal of Inner Asian Art and Archaeology* 4 (2009): 43–68.

Nair, Shankar. "Sufism as Medium and Method of Translation: Mughal Translations of Hindu Texts Reconsidered." *Studies in Religion/Sciences Religieuses* 43, no. 3 (2014): 390–410.

Najmabadi, Afsaneh. *Women with Mustaches and Men without Beards: Gender and Sexual Anxieties of Iranian Modernity*. Berkeley: University of California Press, 2005.

Nasr, Seyyed Hossein, Caner K. Dagli, Maria Massi Dakake, Joseph E. B. Lumbard, and Mohammed Rustom, eds. *The Study Quran: A New Translation and Commentary*. New York: HarperOne, 2015.

Ngom, Fallou. *Muslims beyond the Arab World: The Odyssey of ʿAjamī and the Murīdiyya*. Religion, Culture, and History. New York: Oxford University Press, 2016.

Northrop, Douglas Taylor. *Veiled Empire: Gender & Power in Stalinist Central Asia*. Ithaca, NY: Cornell University Press, 2004.

Novetzke, Christian Lee. "The Theographic and the Historiographic in an Indian Sacred Life Story." In *Time, History and the Religious Imaginary in South Asia*, edited by Anne Murphy, 115–32. Abingdon: Routledge, 2011.

O'Hanlon, Rosalind. "Kingdom, Household and Body History, Gender and Imperial Service under Akbar." *Modern Asian Studies* 41, no. 5 (2007): 889–923.

Obolensky, Dimitri. *The Byzantine Commonwealth: Eastern Europe, 500–1453*. New York: Praeger, 1971.

Ohlander, Erik. *Sufism in an Age of Transition: ʿUmar al-Suhrawardī and the Rise of the Islamic Mystical Brotherhoods*. Leiden: Brill, 2008.

Ohtsuka, Kazuo. "Magic." In *The Oxford Encyclopedia of Philosophy, Science, and Technology in Islam*, edited by Salim Ayduz, 502–4. New York: Oxford University Press, 2014.

Olcott, Martha Brill. "Roots of Radical Islam in Central Asia." *Carnegie Endowment for International Peace*, January 17, 2007. http://carnegieendowment.org/2007/01/17/roots-of-radical-islam-in-central-asia/hazo.

Omidsalar, Mahmoud. "Genie." In *Encyclopædia Iranica*. http://www.iranicaonline.org/articles/genie-.

Pandey, Gyanendra. *The Construction of Communalism in Colonial North India*. Delhi: Oxford University Press, 1990.

Papas, Alexandre. *Thus Spake the Dervish: Sufism, Language, and the Religious Margins in Central Asia, 1400–1900*. Leiden: Brill, 2019.

Paul, Jürgen. "The Histories of Samarqand." *Studia Iranica* 22 (1993): 69–92.

Payne, Richard. "Cosmology and the Expansion of the Iranian Empire, 502–628 CE." *Past & Present* 220, no. 1 (August 1, 2013): 3–33.

——. "The Making of Turan: The Fall and Transformation of the Iranian East in Late Antiquity." *Journal of Late Antiquity* 9, no. 1 (June 1, 2016): 4–41.

Peirce, Leslie. *Morality Tales: Law and Gender in the Court of Aintab*. Berkeley: University of California Press, 2003.

Pelló, Stefano. "Drowned in the Sea of Mercy: The Textual Identification of Hindu Persian Poets from Shi'i Lucknow in the Taẕkira of Bhagwān Dās 'Hindī.'" In *Religious Interactions in Mughal India*, edited by Vasudha Dalmia and Munis D. Faruqui, 135–58. Oxford University Press, 2014.

Péri, Benedek. "Notes on the Literary-Linguistic Term 'Čaġatay': Evaluating the Evidence Supplied by Native Sources." Edited by Alice Sárközi and Attila Rákos. *Altaica Budapestinensia MMII*, Proceedings of the 45th Permanent International Altaisitic Conference (PIAC) Budapest, Hungary, June 23–28, 2003, 248–55.

Perry, John R. "New Persian: Expansion, Standardization, and Inclusivity." In *Literacy in the Persianate World: Writing and the Social Order*, edited by Brian Spooner and William L. Hanaway, 70–94. Philadelphia: University of Pennsylvania Museum of Archaeology and Anthropology, 2012.

——. "Šāh-nāma v. Arabic Words." *Encylopedia Iranica*, 2005. http://www.iranicaonline.org/articles/sah-nama-v-arabic-words.

Petrov, N.P. "Bukharskii mukhtasib v nachale XX veka." *Problemy vostokovedeniia*, no. 1 (1959): 139–42.

Petry, Carl F. *The Civilian Elite of Cairo in the Later Middle Ages*. Princeton: Princeton University Press, 1981.

Pickett, James. "Categorically Misleading, Dialectically Misconceived: Language Textbooks and Pedagogic Participation in Central Asian Nation-Building Projects." *Central Asian Survey* 36, no. 4 (December 2017): 555–74.

——. "The Darker Side of Mobility: Refugees, Hostages, and Political Prisoners in Persianate Asia." In *Asia Inside Out*, vol. 3. Cambridge: Harvard University Press, 2019.

——. "Enemies beyond the Red Sands: The Bukhara-Khiva Dynamic as Mediated by Textual Genre." *Journal of Persianate Studies* 9, no. 2 (October 2016): 158–82.

——. "Nadir Shah's Peculiar Central Asian Legacy: Empire, Conversion Narratives, and the Rise of New Scholarly Dynasties." *International Journal of Middle East Studies* 48, no. 3 (July 2016): 491–510.

——. "The Persianate Sphere during the Age of Empires: Islamic Scholars and Networks of Exchange in Central Asia 1747–1917." PhD diss., Princeton University, 2015.

——. "Soviet Civilization through a Persian Lens: Iranian Intellectuals, Cultural Diplomacy and Socialist Modernity 1941–55." *Iranian Studies* 48, no. 5 (September 3, 2015): 805–26.

——. "Written into Submission: Reassessing Sovereignty through a Forgotten Eurasian Dynasty." *American Historical Review* 123, no. 3 (June 2018): 817–45.

Pickett, James, and Paolo Sartori. "From the Archetypical Archive to Cultures of Documentation." *Journal of the Economic and Social History of the Orient* 62, no. 5–6 (2019): 773–98.

Pollock, Sheldon, Homi K. Bhabha, Carol Breckenridge, and Dipesh Chakrabarty. "Cosmopolitanisms." *Public Culture* 12, no. 3 (2000): 577–89.

Pollock, Sheldon. "Introduction." In *Forms of Knowledge in Early Modern Asia: Explorations in the Intellectual History of India and Tibet, 1500–1800*, edited by Sheldon I. Pollock, 1–16. Durham, NC: Duke University Press, 2011.

——. *The Language of the Gods in the World of Men: Sanskrit, Culture, and Power in Premodern India*. Berkeley: University of California Press, 2006.

Pourshariati, Parvaneh. *Decline and Fall of the Sasanian Empire: The Sasanian-Parthian Confederacy and the Arab Conquest of Iran*. London: I. B. Tauris, 2008.

Privratsky, Bruce G. *Muslim Turkistan: Kazak Religion and Collective Memory*. Richmond, Surrey: Curzon Press, 2001.

Rafeq, Abdul-Karim. "Relations between the Syrian 'Ulamā' and the Ottoman State in the Eighteenth Century." *Oriente Moderno* 18, no. 79 (1999): 67–95.

Rapoport, Yossef. "Royal Justice and Religious Law: Siyāsah and Shariʿah under the Mamluks." *Mamluk Studies Review* 16 (2012): 71–102.

Reichmuth, Philipp. "Semantic Modeling of Islamic Legal Documents: A Study on Central Asian Endowment Deeds." PhD diss., Martin-Luther-Universität Halle (Saale), 2010.

Reiss, Timothy J. *Mirages of the Selfe: Patterns of Personhood in Ancient and Early Modern Europe*. Stanford: Stanford University Press, 2002.

Ricci, Ronit. *Islam Translated: Literature, Conversion, and the Arabic Cosmopolis of South and Southeast Asia*. Chicago: University of Chicago Press, 2011.

Roberts, Flora J. "Old Elites Under Communism: Soviet Rule in Leninobod." PhD diss., University of Chicago, 2016.

Robinson, Francis. "Other-Worldly and This-Worldly Islam and the Islamic Revival: A Memorial Lecture for Wilfred Cantwell Smith." *Journal of the Royal Asiatic Society* 14, no. 1 (April 2004): 47–58.

——. *The 'Ulama of Farangi Mahall and Islamic Culture in South Asia*. New Delhi: Permanent Black, 2001.

Ro'i, Yaacov. *Islam in the Soviet Union: From the Second World War to Gorbachev*. New York: Columbia University Press, 2000.

Rowson, Everett. "The Categorization of Gender and Sexual Irregularity in Medieval Arabic Vice Lists." In *Body Guards: The Cultural Politics of Gender Ambiguity*, edited by Julia Epstein and Kristina Straub, 45–72. Minneapolis: University of Minnesota Press, 2003.

Sahadeo, Jeff. *Russian Colonial Society in Tashkent: 1865–1923*. Bloomington: Indiana University Press, 2007.

Sahner, Christian C. "From Augustine to Islam: Translation and History in the Arabic Orosius." *Speculum* 88, no. 4 (October 2013): 905–31.

Sartori, Paolo. "The Birth of a Custom: Nomads, Sharīʿa Courts and Established Practices in the Tashkent Province, ca. 1868–1919." *Islamic Law and Society* 18, 3–4 (2011): 293–326.

——. "The Evolution of Third-Party Mediation in Sharīʿa Courts in 19th– and Early 20th-Century Central Asia." *Journal of the Economic and Social History of the Orient* 54 (2011): 311–52.

——. "Of Saints, Shrines, and Tractors: Untangling the Meaning of Islam in Soviet Central Asia." *Journal of Islamic Studies*, February 2019, 1–40.

——. "On Madrasas, Legitimation, and Islamic Revival in 19th-Century Khorezm: Some Preliminary Observations." *Eurasian Studies* 14, no. 1–2 (2016): 98–134.

——. "Seeing Like a Khanate: On Archives, Cultures of Documentation, and Nineteenth-Century Khwarāzm." *Journal of Persianate Studies* 9, no. 2 (October 28, 2016): 228–57.

——. "Towards a History of the Muslims' Soviet Union: A View from Central Asia." *Die Welt Des Islams* 50 (2010): 315–34.

——. *Visions of Justice: Sharīʿa and Cultural Change in Russian Central Asia*. Leiden: Brill, 2016.

——. "What Went Wrong? The Failure of Soviet Policy on Sharīʿa Courts in Turkestan, 1917–1923." *Die Welt Des Islams* 50 (2010): 397–434.

Sartori, Paolo, and Bakhtiyar Babajanov. "Being Soviet, Muslim, Modernist, and Fundamentalist in 1950s Central Asia." *Journal of the Economic and Social History of the Orient* 62, no. 1 (December 6, 2019): 108–65.

Savant, Sarah Bowen. *The New Muslims of Post-Conquest Iran: Tradition, Memory, and Conversion*. Cambridge : Cambridge University Press, 2013.

Schimmelpenninck van der Oye, David. *Russian Orientalism: Asia in the Russian Mind from Peter the Great to the Emigration*. New Haven: Yale University Press, 2010.

Schneider, Irene. "Religious and State Jurisdiction during Nāṣir Al-Dīn Shāh's Reign." In *Religion and Society in Qajar Iran*, edited by Robert Gleave, 84–110. New York: Routledge, 2009.

Schwartz, Kevin L. "The Curious Case of Carnatic: The Last Nawab of Arcot (d. 1855) and Persian Literary Culture." *Indian Economic and Social History Review* 53, no. 4 (2016): 533–60.

——. "The Local Lives of a Transregional Poet: ʿAbd al-Qāder Bidel and the Writing of Persianate Literary History." *Journal of Persianate Studies* 9 (2016): 83–106.

Schwarz, Florian. "From Scholars to Saints: The Bukharan Shaykhs of Čūybār and the Ziyārats to the Four Bakr." In *Iz Istorii Kul'turnogo Naslediia Bukhary: Sbornik Statei*, vol. 6. Bukhara: Uzbekistan, 1998.

——. "Politische Krise und kulturelle Transformation im mongolenzeitlichen Iran." In *Krise und Transformation*, edited by Arnold Suppan and Sigrid Jalkotzy-Deger, 169–78. Vienna, 2012.

——. "Preliminary Notes on Viticulture and Winemaking in Colonial Central Asia." In *Wine Culture in Iran and Neighbouring Countries*, edited by Bert G. Fragner, Ralph Kauz, and Florian Schwarz, 239–49. Vienna: Veröffentlichungen zur Iranistik, 2014.

Shanazarova, Aziza. "A Female Saint in Muslim Polemics: Aghā-Yi Buzurg and Her Legacy in Early Modern Central Asia." PhD diss., Indiana University, 2019.

Sefatgol, Mansur. "From Dār al-Salṭana-yi Iṣfahān to Dār al-Khilāfa-yi Ṭihrān." In *Religion and Society in Qajar Iran*, edited by Robert Gleave, 71–83. New York: Routledge, 2009.

Sela, Ron. *The Legendary Biographies of Tamerlane: Islam and Heroic Apocrypha in Central Asia*. Cambridge: Cambridge University Press, 2011.

——. "The 'Heavenly Stone' (Kök Tash) of Samarqand: A Rebels' Narrative Transformed." *Journal of the Royal Asiatic Society* 17, no. 1 (2007): 21–32.

——. *Ritual and Authority in Central Asia: The Khan's Inauguration Ceremony*. Papers on Inner Asia, no. 37. Bloomington: Indiana University, Research Institute for Inner Asian Studies, 2003.

Semenov, S. S., ed. *Sobranie vostochnykh rukopisei Akademii Nauk Uzbekskoi SSR*, vol. 1. Tashkent: Izd-vo Akademii nauk UzSSR, 1952.

Shahrani, M. Nazif. "Local Knowledge of Islam and Social Discourse in Afghanistan and Turkistan in the Modern Period." In *Turko-Persia in Historical Perspective*, edited by Robert L. Canfield, 161–88. Cambridge: Cambridge University Press, 1991.

——. "Pining for Bukhara in Afghanistan: Poetics and Politics of Exilic Identity and Emotion." In *Türkistan'da Yenilik Hareketleri ve Ihtilaller, 1900–1924: Osman Hoca Anısına Incelemeler / Reform Movements and Revolutions in Turkistan, 1900–1924: Studies in Honour of Osman Khoja*, edited by Timur Kocaoğlu. Haarlem: SOTA, 2001.

Sharma, Sunil. "Amir Khusraw and the Genre of Historical Narratives in Verse." *Comparative Studies of South Asia, Africa and the Middle East* 22, no. 1 & 2 (2002): 112–18.

Shohat, Ella. "The Invention of Judeo-Arabic: Nation, Partition and the Linguistic Imaginary." *Interventions* 19, no. 2 (2017): 153–200.

Shukurov, Muhammadjon. *Khurāsān ast īn jā: ma'nawīyat, zabān wa ihyā-yi millī-yi tājikān*. Dushanbe: Oli Somon, 1997.

Siddiqui, Ali Gibran. "The Medieval Khwājagān and the Early Naqshbandīyya." In *Oxford Research Encyclopedia of Asian History*. Edited by David Ludden. Oxford: Oxford University Press, 2018. http://asianhistory.oxfordre.com/view/10.1093/acrefore/9780190277727.001.0001/acrefore-9780190277727-e-286.

Sims-Williams, Nicholas, and Frantz Grenet. "The Sogdian Inscriptions of Kultobe." *Shygys* 2006 (2007): 95–111.

Sims-Williams, Nicholas. *Bactrian Documents from Northern Afghanistan, I: Legal and Economic Documents*, vol. 1. Oxford: Oxford University Press, 2012.

Skjærvø, Prods O. "Eastern Iranian Epic Traditions I: Siyāvaš and Kunāla." In *Mír Curad: Studies in Honor of Calvert Watkins*, edited by J. Jasanoff, H.C. Melchert, and L. Oliver, 645–58. Innsbruck: Innsbr. Beitr. z. Sprachwiss., 1998.

Smail, Daniel Lord, and Shryock Andrew. "History and the 'Pre'History and the 'Pre.'" *American Historical Review* 118, no. 3 (June 1, 2013): 709–37.

Sokrovishcha vostochnykh rukopisei Instituta Vostokovedeniia imeni Abu Raikhana Biruni Akademii Nauk Respubliki Uzbekistan. Tashkent: UNESCO, 2012.

Solov'eva, O. A. *Liki vlasti blagorodnoi Bukhary*. St. Petersburg: Rossiiskaia Akademiia Nauk, Muzei Antropologii i Etnografii im. Petra Velikogo (Kunstkamera), 2002.

Sourdel, D. "Dār al-'Ilm." In *Encyclopaedia of Islam*, 2nd ed. Edited by P. Bearman, Th. Bianquis, C. E. Bosworth, E. van Donzel, and W. P. Heinrichs. http://dx.doi.org/10.1163/1573-3912_islam_SIM_1702.

Spooner, Brian. "Epilogue: The Persianate Millennium." In *The Persianate World: The Frontiers of a Eurasian Lingua Franca*, edited by Nile Green, 301–16. Oakland: University of California Press, 2019.

Starr, S. Frederick. *Lost Enlightenment: Central Asia's Golden Age from the Arab Conquest to Tamerlane*. Princeton University Press, 2013.

——. "Rediscovering Central Asia." *Wilson Quarterly* (Summer 2009): 33–43.

Stilt, Kristen. *Islamic Law in Action: Authority, Discretion, and Everyday Experiences in Mamluk Egypt*. New York: Oxford University Press, 2012.

Storey, C.A. *Persidskaia literatura: Bio-bibliograficheskii obzor*. Translated by Yuri Bregel, vol. 2. Moscow: Glavnaia Redaktsiia Vostochnoi Literatury, 1972.

Subrahmanyam, Sanjay. "Iranians Abroad: Intra-Asian Elite Migration and Early Modern State Formation." *Journal of Asian Studies* 51, no. 2 (1992): 340–63. https://doi.org/10.2307/2058032.

——. *Courtly Encounters: Translating Courtliness and Violence in Early Modern Eurasia*. London: Harvard University Press, 2012.

Subtelny, Maria Eva. "Art and Politics in Early 16th Century Central Asia." *Central Asiatic Journal* 27, no. 1–2 (1983): 121–48.

——. "A Late Medieval Persian Summa on Ethics: Kashifi's Akhlāq-i Muḥsinī." *Iranian Studies* 36, no. 4 (2003): 601–14.

——. "The Making of Bukhārā-yi Sharīf: Scholars, Books and Libraries in Medieval Bukhara (The Library of Khwāja Muḥammad Pārsā)." In *Studies on Central Asian history in honor of Yuri Bregel*, 79–111. Bloomington: Research Institute for Inner Asian Studies, Indiana University, 2001.

——. "The Symbiosis of Turk and Tajik." In *Central Asia in Historical Perspective*, edited by Beatrice Forbes Manz, 45–61. Oxford: Westview Press, 1994.

——. *Timurids in Transition: Turko-Persian Politics and Acculturation in Medieval Iran*. Leiden: Brill, 2007.

Sukhareva, O. A. *Bukhara XIX–nachalo XX v*. Moscow: Izd-vo "Nauka," 1966.

——. *Kvartal'naia obshchina pozdnefeodal'nogo goroda Bukhary*. Moscow: Izd-vo "Nauka," 1976.

Sultonova, Gulchekhra. "Trade Relations between Bukhara and Yarkend Khanates in the 16–Earlier 17 Centuries." *Bulletin of IICAS*, International Institute for Central Asian Studies, 11 (2010): 40–48.

Syed, Amir. "Between Jihād and History: Re-Conceptualizing the Islamic Revolutions of West Africa." In *The Handbook of Islam in Africa*, edited by Fallou Ngom, Mustapha Kurfi, and Toyin Falola. New York: Palgrave Macmillan, forthcoming.

Taffazoli, A. "Arabic Language II. Iranian Loanwords." In *Encyclopædia Iranica*, 2:231–33, 1986. http://www.iranicaonline.org/articles/arabic-ii.

Tasar, Eren. "The Official Madrasas of Soviet Uzbekistan." *Journal of the Economic and Social History of the Orient* 59, no. 1–2 (February 11, 2016): 265–302.

——. *Soviet and Muslim: The Institutionalization of Islam in Central Asia*. Oxford University Press, 2017.

Tavakoli-Targhi, Mohamad. "Early Persianate Modernity." In *Forms of Knowledge in Early Modern Asia: Explorations in the Intellectual History of India and Tibet, 1500–1800*, edited by Sheldon Pollock, 257–87. Durham, NC: Duke University Press, 2011.

——. *Refashioning Iran: Orientalism, Occidentalism, and Historiography*. London: Palgrave Macmillan, 2001.

Thum, Rian. *The Sacred Routes of Uyghur History*. Cambridge, MA: Harvard University Press, 2014.

Too, Yun Lee. "Introduction." In *Pedagogy and Power: Rhetorics of Classical Learning*, edited by Yun Lee Too and Niall Livingstone, 1–15. Cambridge: Cambridge University Press, 2007.

Trepavlov, Vadim V. *The Formation and Early History of the Manghït Yurt*. Papers on Inner Asia 35. Bloomington: Indiana University Research Institute for Inner Asian Studies, 2001.

Truschke, Audrey. *Culture of Encounters: Sanskrit at the Mughal Court*. New York: Columbia University Press, 2016.

Tsereteli, George V. "The Influence of the Tajik Language on the Vocalism of Central Asian Arabic Dialects." *Bulletin of the School of Oriental and African Studies* 33, no. 1 (1970): 167–70.

Tucker, Ernest. "Nadir Shah and the Ja'fari Madhhab Reconsidered." *Iranian Studies* 27, no. 1/4 (1994): 163–79.

Tuna, Mustafa. *Imperial Russia's Muslims: Islam, Empire and European Modernity, 1788–1914*. Cambridge: Cambridge University Press, 2015.

Utas, Bo. " 'Genres' in Persian Literature 900–1900." In *Literary Genres: An Intercultural Approach*, 199–241. Literary History: Towards a Global Perspective 2. New York: Walter de Gruyter, 2006.

Van Leeuwen, Neil. "Religious Credence Is Not Factual Belief." *Cognition* 133, no. 3 (December 2014): 698–715.

Venuti, Lawrence. *The Translator's Invisibility: A History of Translation*. New York: Routledge, 1995.

Verboven, Koenraad, Myriam Carlier, and Jan Dumolyn. "A Short Manual to the Art of Prosopography." In *Prosopography Approaches and Applications: A Handbook*, edited by K. S. B. Keats-Rohan, 35–70. Prosopographica et Genealogica 13. Oxford: Occasional Publications UPR, 2007.

Viswanathan, Gauri. *Outside the Fold: Conversion, Modernity, and Belief*. Princeton: Princeton University Press, 1998.

Vohidov, Šodmon, and Aftandil Erkinov. "Le fihrist (catalogue) de la bibliothèque de Ṣadr-i Żiyâ." Translated by Maria Szuppe and Alié Akimova. *Cahiers d'Asie centrale* 7 (July 1999): 141–73.

Warikoo, K. "Central Asia and Kashmir: A Study in Political, Commercial and Cultural Contacts during the 19th and Early 20th Centuries." *Central Asian Survey* 7, no. 1 (January 1988): 63–83.

Weismann, Itzchak. *The Naqshbandiyya: Orthodoxy and Activism in a Worldwide Sufi Tradition*. London: Routledge, 2007.

Welsford, Thomas. *Four Types of Loyalty in Early Modern Central Asia: The Tūqāy-Tīmūrid Takeover of Greater Mā Warā al-Nahr, 1598–1605*. Leiden: Brill, 2013.

Welsford, Thomas, and Nouryaghdi Tashev, eds. *A Catalogue of Arabic-Script Documents from the Samarqand Museum*. Samarqand—Istanbul: International Institute for Central Asian Studies, 2012.

Wennberg, Franz. *An Inquiry into Bukharan Qadimism: Mirza Salim-Bik*. Berlin: Klaus Schwarz, 2002.

——. *On the Edge: The Concept of Progress in Bukhara during the Rule of the Later Manghits*. Uppsala, Sweden: Uppsala University Press, 2013.

Wensinck, A. J. "al-Khaḍir." In *Encyclopaedia of Islam*, 2nd ed. Edited by P. Bearman, Th. Bianquis, C. E. Bosworth, E. van Donzel, and W. P. Heinrichs. http://dx.doi.org/10.1163/1573-3912_islam_COM_0483.

Werth, Paul W. "From 'Pagan' Muslims to 'Baptized' Communists: Religious Conversion and Ethnic Particularity in Russia's Eastern Provinces." *Comparative Studies in Society and History* 42, no. 3 (July 1, 2000): 497–523.

Wheeler, Brannon. *Mecca and Eden: Ritual, Relics, and Territory in Islam*. Chicago: University of Chicago Press, 2006.

Whitmarsh, Tim. "Reading Power in Roman Greece: The Paideia of Dio Chrysostum." In *Pedagogy and Power: Rhetorics of Classical Learning*, edited by Yun

Lee Too and Niall Livingstone, 192–213. Cambridge: Cambridge University Press, 2007.

Wilde, Andreas. "Creating the Façade of a Despotic State: On Āqsaqāls in Late 19th-Century Bukhara." In *Explorations in the Social History of Modern Central Asia (19th–Early 20th Century)*, edited by Paolo Sartori, 267–98. Leiden: Brill, 2013.

——. *What Is Beyond the River? Power, Authority and Social Order in Eighteenth and Nineteenth-Century Transoxania*. Vienna: Verlag der Österreichischen Akademie der Wissenschaften, 2016.

Williams, Alan. "The Continuum of 'Sacred Language' from High to Low Speech in the Middle Iranian (Pahlavi) Zoroastrian Tradition." In *Religion, Language, and Power*, edited by Nile Green and Mary Searle-Chatterjee, 123–42. London: Routledge, 2008.

——. *The Zoroastrian Myth of Migration from Iran and Settlement in the Indian Diaspora: Text, Translation and Analysis of the 16th Century Qesse-Ye Sanjān "The Story of Sanjan."* Leiden: Brill, 2009.

Windfuhr, Gernot. "Jafr." In *Encyclopedia Iranica*. http://www.iranicaonline.org/articles/jafr.

Wortman, Richard. *Scenarios of Power: Myth and Ceremony in Russian Monarchy: From Peter the Great to the Abdication of Nicholas II*. Princeton: Princeton: University Press, 2006.

Yarshater, E. "The Theme of Wine-Drinking and the Concept of the Beloved in Early Persian Poetry." *Studia Islamica* 13 (1960): 43–53.

Yazıcı, Tahsin. "Ḳalandar." In *Encyclopaedia of Islam*, 2nd ed. Edited by P. Bearman, Th. Bianquis, C. E. Bosworth, E. van Donzel, and W. P. Heinrichs. https://referenceworks.brillonline.com/entries/encyclopaedia-of-islam-2/kalandar-SIM_3810.

Yo'ldoshxo'jaev, Haydarxon, and Irodaxon Qayumova. *O'zbekiston ulamolari*. Tashkent: O'zbekiston Musulmonlari Idorasi, 2015.

Yurchak, Alexei. *Everything Was Forever, until It Was No More: The Last Soviet Generation*. Princeton: Princeton University Press, 2005.

Zaman, Muhammad Qasim. *Religion and Politics under the Early ʿAbbāsids: The Emergence of the Proto-Sunni Elite*. Leiden: Brill, 1997.

Ziad, Waleed. "From Yarkand to Sindh via Kabul: The Rise of Naqshbandi-Mujaddidi Sufi Networks in the Eighteenth and Nineteenth Centuries." In *The Persianate World: Rethinking a Shared Sphere*, edited by Abbas Amanat and Assef Ashraf, 125–68. Leiden: Brill, 2019.

——. "Traversing the Indus and the Oxus: Trans-Regional Islamic Revival in the Age of Political Fragmentation and the 'Great Game' 1747–1880." PhD diss., Yale University, 2017.

Zilfi, Madeline C. *The Politics of Piety: The Ottoman Ulema in the Postclassical Age (1600–1800)*. Minneapolis: Bibliotheca Islamica, 1988.

Zutshi, Chitralekha. *Kashmir's Contested Pasts: Narratives, Sacred Geographies, and the Historical Imagination*. New Delhi: Oxford University Press, 2014

Index

Page numbers in *italics* indicate illustrations, tables, and charts. Authored works are generally found under the name of the author.

Abd al-Ahad (amir), 53, 54, 60n83, 81, 103, 147, 155, 207
Abd al-Alim al-Qazani, 132
Abd al-Ghafur Turkestani, 15n47, 124–25n125, 186
Abd al-Hayy Khwaja ibn Abu al-Khayr, 208–13
Abd al-Hayy Samarqandi, 235
Abd al-Karim Khwaja, 186
Abd al-Karim Shakir, 216
Abd al-Mumin, 100n10, 103n18
Abd al-Qadir "Bedil." *See* Bedil
Abd al-Qadir "Sawda be Pul" "Pishak-baz," 149–50
Abd al-Rahman, 10, 100, 105, 166–67
Abd al-Rasul "Tajir," 108, 215n96
Abd al-Samad ibn Abu al-Hayy Sudur ibn Ma'sum Khwaja ibn Abd al-Hayy, 212
Abd al-Shakur "Ayyat," 108, 143–44, 203n33, 216
Abd al-Wahid Sadr Sarir Balkhi, 77n12, 117, 191–92, 213–16
Abd al-Zahir Makhdum Bukhari, 150
Abd Allah Khwaja "Tahsin," 207
Abdallah al-Dihlawi (Ghulam Ali Shah), 137
Abdallah Beg Udaychi, 99–103
Abdallah Beg Yakkabaghi, 104, 184
Abdallah Damullam, 87n61
Abdallah Fazil Bukhara'i, 80n23
Abdallah Khan, 52n48, 83, 120
Abdi, 75n6, 141
Abdurasulov, Ulfat, 142n68
Abu al-Fayz Khan, 198, 202–3
Abu al-Layth, 192n54
Abu al-Nizam, 147n91
Abu al-Nizam Rahmatallah, 147
Abu Hanifa, 69, 218–20, 225, 239, 241, 242
Abu Hurayra, 150n100
Abu Rahir Khwaja Samarqandi, 211–12
Abu Sa'id Khwaja, 79n21
Abu Sa'id Khwaja ibn Abd al-Hayy, 210–11
Abu Tahir Khwaja, 69n128
Abu Yusuf, 218–19
Abu'l-Khayr, Mawlawi, 209
adabiyat, 22n18
Adil Khan, 184
Afghanistan: Bukhara and, 20, 76–80, 95; contradictory cultural impulses in, 172, 183n106; eclectic knowledge of ulama and, 140; geopolitics of region and, 6, 9, 10, 12; scholarly dynasties and, 196, 213; Sovietization of Central Asia and, 248–49, 254n25, 254n28, 256; Turkic nobility and, 103, 105, 117n86
Ahmad, Shahab, 27n43
Ahmad Makhdum, 139
akhlaq (mirrors for princes) genre, 223
Akram Khan Tora, Sayyid, 103n18
Al-Mas'udi, 24n27
Ala al-Din Bukhari, Mawlawi, 92
Alam, Muzaffar, 23n22
alcohol consumption, 161, 163, 175, 177–82, 186–87
Alexander the Great, 12, 26n34, 45n12, 68
Altishahr, 86–88
Amanat, Abbas, 23n22
Amir Kulal, 118
Andkhoy, 78–79
apothecaries, 151–53
Arcot, 71n132
Arsi, 138–39
Asad, Talal, 23
Asbat ibn Ilyasa al-Bukhari, 59n81
Ash'ari-Ma'turidi theology, 145, 159
Ashtarkhanids, 7, 9, 10, 44, 48, 80, 198
Asil al-Din al-Husayni, 79–80n23

Asrar Khwaja Urguti "Muftaqir," 135
astronomy and astrology, 153, 154, 155
Ata, Sayyid, 83n37
Ataturk, 248
Ata'allah ibn Hadi Khwaja, Muhammad, 113, 165–68, 170, 178, 199n13, 205
Attar, *Conference of the Birds,* 116n83
attars (perfumers-apothecaries), 151–53, 157
Auerbach, Erich, 163n6
authority: Islamic authority of prince, 224–25, 231–34; knowledge base of scholars, relationship to, 197, 216–17; of state / sovereign (*see* state / sovereign and ulama)
Avicenna (Ibn Sina), 150n107
Ayni, Sadriddin, 31n59, 110n49, 110n51, 114n70
Azizallah "Qadari," 216

Babadzhanov, Bakhtiyar, 183n106
Babakhanov family, 255n34
Babur and *Babur-nama,* 29n48
Badakhshan, 53, 75, 81–82, 94
Badakhshi, Muhammad Nasir, 79n22
Badr al-Din, 214
Baha al-Din Naqshband, 130, 136
Bahram Chubin, 65
Bajur, 94
Bakharzi shrine complex, Bukhara, 48n28
Imam Bakir Hamid, 58
Bakran, Muhammad, 46n19
Balkh: Bukhara, mythologization of, 45, 46, 48, 59n79, 67n112, 69; Bukhara as network center, 75, 76, 77n11, 78, 83, 94; eclecticism of ulama knowledge and, 155n131; geopolitical backdrop, 6, 214n86; scholarly dynasties and, 214, 216
Balkhi, Izzatallah Khwaja, 78
Balkhi', Abdallah, 55n59
Balkin, J. M., 22n19
The Ballad of Sanjan, 35
Baltacı, Cahid, 50n43
Baqi, Mawlana, 83
Bard al-Din "Raja," 143–44
Barthold, V. V., 44n7
Mulla Bashi, 201
Bashir, Shahzad, 132n23
Bayram Ali Khan, 104–5
Bedil (Abd al-Qadir), 87, 94n104, 107–8, 116n83, 117, 127, 159
Beecroft, Alexander, 20n8, 22n17, 26n39
Behrens-Abouseif, Doris, 151n111
Bellér-Hann, Ildikó, 86n57
Beloved, gender-ambiguous figure of, 182–83
al-Beruni, 33n71
Bibi Khalifa, 121, 122
Bijapur, 129, 131n17
Bilqis (Queen of Sheba), 192–93
biographical dictionaries, 14
al-Biruni, 128
Bolshevik Revolution (1919), 7, 17, 88n67, 212, 241–42, 248
Bosworth, C. E., 24n27, 46n19
boza (alcoholic drink), 181–82
Bregel, Yuri, 34n75
Brookshaw, Dominic Parviz, 182–83n104
Buddhism, 65, 66–67n112, 228
Bukhara, 42–97; as "Abode of Knowledge" *(Dar al-Ilm),* 43, 49, 65, 97; curriculum in, 110n49; geographic centering of study on, 1, 3–7, *5*; geopolitical backdrop, 9, 10–11; historical background, 45–48; as "little Persianate sphere" of human exchange, 74, 75; "little Persianate spheres" beyond orbit of, 88–95; madrasas in, 48–54, *51*; mosques, 61–63, 142; *muhtasib* of, 143–44; mythologization project, 42–45, 54, 61, 69–74; nonstate transregional network, as pole of, 75–82, *77*; outer ring of "little Persianate sphere" of, 82–88; Persian epic literature and, 64–70; political weakness of, 44; Prophet Muhammad and Companions, associations with, 56–57, 60n86, 64; *qazi-yi kalan* (chief judge) of, 144; relics, tombs, and shrines, 57–64, *61*, *62*; rivals to, 96; Russian subjugation of (1868), 11n26, 48, 52, 88, 206–7, 245; sacred history, sacred geography, and sacred sites, 54–64; social history, applying concept of cosmopolis to, 73–75; Turkic nobles fleeing to, 105–6. *See also specific sites*
Bukhara the Noble, 42
Bukharan ulama. *See* Islamic scholars of Central Asia
al-Bukhari, Sayyid Muhammad Nasir, 59
al-Bulghari, Muhammad Karim, 116–17
Bulliet, Richard, 98n1, 128n2
Buzurg Khwaja, 206

calligraphers, scholars as, 145–49, 214, 255
Canfield, Robert, 31n55
Chaghatay, 26n37, 30n51, 65n107, 74n4, 89
Chahar Bakr, 6, 198, 202–3, 208
Chinggis (Genghis) Khan, 9, 54, 226

Christians/Christianity, 35, 150–51, 228
contradictory cultural impulses, 161–95; apparent problem of, 161–63, 170–71, 193–95; everyday supernatural, belief in, 162, 165–70; opium use, 163, 170–77; romance, homoeroticism, and sexual panic, 162, 163, 171, 182–87; scripturalism, tolerance, and blasphemy/infidelity, 161, 162n3, 187–93; text/genre and, 163–64, 168–70, 194; wine, spirits, and revelry, 161, 163, 175, 177–82, 186–87
Cornwall, Owen, 30n54
cosmopolis, concept of, 19–22, 73–74. *See also* culture of Turko-Persian cosmopolis
Crone, Patricia, 24n27, 222n20
Csirkés, Ferenc Péter, 26n35
culture of Turko-Persian cosmopolis, 18–41; Arabic and Persianate language and culture, relationship between, 23–27; canon of literature of, 22–23, 24–25; cosmopolis paradigm for, 19–22; Islam and, 22–27, 35–37; non-Islamic concepts, Islamic expression of, 35–39; origins and continuity with Iranian civilization, 28–29; political implications of, 34–40; reconceptualizing, 18–19; secular versus sacred, concept of, 23, 24, 27n43; Turkic ethnicity, identity, and literary culture, 29–34

Dabashi, Hamid, 23n22
dad-khwah, 100
Dagestan, 86
Damla Mirak A'lam, 105
Damulla Hasan Akhund, 120
Damulla Inayatallah Khwaja, 58
Danish, Ahmad, 184n114
Daniyal Ataliq Manghit, 202n29, 209
Dars-i Nizami curriculum, 112, 113
Darwaz, 68n121, 82n34
Darwish, Hajji Muhammad, 191–92
darwishes, 138, 139–40
decline paradigm, 52
Delhi, 4, 73, 76, 91, 93, 95, 201n23
DeWeese, Devin, 25n32, 151n109
al-Din, Jamal and Qawwam, 77–78
Diwan-begi madrasa, Bukhara, 119
doctors, 149–53
Dost Muhammad, 214
Dudoignon, Stéphane, 206, 213, 251–52n16
Durrani Empire, 7, 9, 79–80
Dushanbe/Stalinabad, 82n33, 255
dynasties of Islamic scholars, 196–217; Abd al-Hayy Khwaja, 208–13; Abd al-Karim Shakir, 216; Abd al-Wahid Sadr Sarir Balkhi, 213–16; Hadi Khwaja, 198–208; interdependence of Turkic military elite and, 196–97, 199, 208, 213, 216–17; knowledge base and authority of scholars, relationship between, 197, 216–17; Sovietization of, 251

Eaton, Richard Maxwell, 23n23, 24n24, 130, 131n17
eclectic intellectual range of ulama, 127–60, 243; in Islamic history, 128–30; *jung* evidencing, 158–59; medicine, 149–53; occultists, 153–58; poetry and calligraphy, 145–49; polymaths, Islamic scholars as, 1, 14, 127, 128, 159–60; public administration *(muhtasib, mufti, qazi, mirza, mudarris),* 141–45; sufism, as spectrum of activities, 130–41 (*see also* sufis and sufism)
education: Bukhara, madrasas in, 48–54, *51*; co-educational primary schools, 12–122; core requirements for ulama status, 119; curriculum, textbooks, and reading lists, 109–17, 119; diplomas *(ijaza),* 112, 115–16, 117–18, 120n101; institutions of (madrasas), 119–20; law, study of, 111–12, 114–15; *maddahs,* 123–26; madrasa knowledge system, 109–22, 126; Persian culture in, 116–17; private tutoring, 123; Samarqand 1909 Russian report on madrasas in, 110n49, 111n53, 112, 114n70; scholasticism/humanism and, 110n50; social background and mobility of students, 120–21; Sovietization, effects of, 249–50, 251, 253n23, 255; sufism, tutelage in, 79n21, 80n23, 83, 117–18
elites, non-scholarly. *See* Turkic nobility
Ernst, Carl W., 35n76
Eshan Khwajah "Walih," 175
Eshan Muhammad Sharif Khwaja, 166–68, 206, 207

Fa'iz (Mirza Shah), 108–9
al-Farabi, 128
Farghana Valley, 6–7, 80–81, 82, 83, 84, 85, 86, 87, 95, 246
fatwa texts: contradictory cultural impulses and, 169n35, 190; eclectic knowledge base of scholars and, 135, 143n72, 158n143; *jung* and, 15; state/sovereign and ulama, relationship between, 226, 229–33, 235–36, 237n80, 237n82

Fayzallah Khwaja, 206, 207
Fazil Khan, Hafiz Muhammad, 149n99
Fazl Ahmad Ma'sum, 94n104
Fazl Diwana-i Katib-i Shikast-nawis, 107–8
Fenin, Captain, 49n36, 49n39
Ferdowsi, *Shah-nama,* 22–23, 24–25, 27n41, 28, 65–69, 71, 74, 116, 246
fiqh texts, 156n133, 168, 188n133
Frank, Allen, 32n65, 49n36, 52n48, 84, 111n55

Geertz, Clifford, 23n24
gender. *See* women
gender-ambiguous figure of the Beloved, 182–83
Genghis (Chinggis) Khan, 9, 54, 226
genres and genre theory, 14–15, 163–64, 168–70, 194
geomancy, 153–54, 155
Ghalib, Mirza Asadallah Beg, 31
al-Ghazali, 60, 160
Ghijduwan, 6, 76n9, 87, 212, 215
Ghulam Ali Shah (Abdallah al-Dihlawi), 137
Ghunjar, Muhammad ibn Ahmad, 59n81, 60n84
Golden, Peter, 103n18
Grafton, Anthony, 110n50
Green, Nile, 3n2, 23n22
Gross, Jo-Ann, 93n95
Gul Muhammad Biy, 184
Gulshani, Muhammad, *Tarikh-i humayun,* 49, 50, 52n45, 56, 63–64, 68, 81n28
"gunpowder empires," 7, 10
Guzar, 100n10, 110n49

Habiballah (sufi), 63
Habiballah "Zuhuri" (physician), 151
Hadi Khwaja "Eshan Ustaz," 64, 112n58, 198–208
Hafez, 116, 124, 151
Hajj, 27, 83n40, 88, 89, 109n45, 124, 133, 140, 181, 191, 192
Hajji Muhammad Husayn Khan, 105
Hajji Sayyid Ahmad Khwaja Samarqandi "'Ajzi," 109n45
Hallaq, Wael, 31n57, 113n69
Hamadani, Yusuf, 59, 178
Hamid Beg Eshik Aqabashi ibn Amjad Qilich Ali Biy, 105–6
Hanafi school of jurisprudence: Abu Hanifa credited as founder of, 218n1; Bukhara, as network center, 74, 78, 86n53, 91, 92, 94, 96; Bukhara, mythologization of, 47, 58, 60; eclectic nature of ulama knowledge and, 194; education of Turkic nobility and, 112, 114; on opium and alcohol use, 171, 182; public roles of ulama and, 145; scholarly dynasties and, 198, 204, 208; scripturalism, tolerance, and blasphemy/infidelity, 187–88, 190–91; Sovietization and, 253, 256; state/sovereign and ulama, relationship between, 219, 223n26, 231n61, 232; supernatural and, 168
Haran, Mullah Muhammad Isa, 174
al-Harawi, Yaqut, 46–47
Hasan al-Basri, 59n80
Haybat Akhundzada, 139–40
Haydar (amir), 10, 63, 93, 96n109, 107–8, 131, 150, 201, 208n58, 210, 229, 234, 238, 240
Hazini, Abd al-Sattar, 193–94, 195
Hazrat-i Dawlatshah, Mawlana, 83
Heavenly Stone (Kok-Tash), 210–11
Herat, 33n70, 46n14, 48, 79
high Persianate intellectuals. *See* Islamic scholars of Central Asia
Hinduism, 35, 107
Hisar, 53, 77, 77n13, 82, 208
Hisari, Mirza Baba ibn Damulla Safar Muhammad, 31–32, 146
Hisari, Muhammad, 110n51, 131, 182, 183, 184–85
Hobsbawm, Eric, 71n131
Hodgson, Marshall, 27n41
homoeroticism, romance, and sexual panic, 162, 163, 171, 182–87
humanism, 110n50
Humphreys, R. Stephen, 130n11
Husayn ibn Ali, 191, 201
Husayn Tore, 210

Ibn Arabi, 37n87
Ibn Balkhi, *Fars-nama,* 24–25
Ibn Battuta, 48n29
Ibn Bayza Khatlani, 206–7, 214
Ibn Isfandiyar, 24n27
Ibn Khaldun, 8
Ibn Sina (Avicenna), 150n107
Ibrahim, Mulla, 189
Idris (Abrahamic prophet), 60–61n90
imams, scholars as, 142, 149
Imla, Eshan, 63–64, 178–79, 205
Inayatallah Khwaja, 149, 207–8

India: biographical dictionary genre in, 148n95; Dars-i Nizami curriculum, 112, 113; as "little Persianate sphere," 91–95. *See also specific towns within India*
Irnazar, Hazrat Akhund Mulla, 239
Isa Makhdum, 173, 175
Iskander Wali-nima, 227–28
Islam: culture of Turko-Persian cosmopolis and, 22–27, 35–37; post-Soviet resurgence or revival, 255–56; scripturalism, tolerance, and blasphemy/infidelity, 187, 188, 190–91, 194; secular versus sacred, concept of, 23, 24, 26n43, 220–21; Sovietization and, 251–54
Islamic history, high Persianate intellectuals in, 128–30, 248
Islamic law. *See* Sharia
Islamic scholars of Central Asia, 1–17; authority and knowledge base, relationship between, 197, 216–17; chronological scope, 1, 7, 13n34; as coherent social group, 243–47; contradictions and tensions of, 161–95 (*see also* contradictory cultural impulses); culture of, 18–41 (*see also* culture of Turko-Persian cosmopolis); dynasties of, 196–217 (*see also* dynasties of Islamic scholars); as efflorescence before eclipse, 247, 248; geographic centering on Bukhara, 1, 3–7, *5* (*see also* Bukhara); geopolitical backdrop, 7–11; historiographical landscape, 12–14; interdependence of Turkic nobility and, 7–8, 196–97, 199, 208, 213, 216–17, 246–47; as polymaths, 1, 14, 127, 128, 159–60 (*see also* eclectic intellectual range of ulama); source materials for, 14–16; Sovietization of, 242, 248–56; state/sovereign authority and, 218–42 (*see also* state/sovereign and ulama); structure of argument, 16–17; Turkic nobility and, 7–8, 98–126 (*see also* Turkic nobility)
Isma'il Samani, mausoleum of, Bukhara, 63

Jadids (reformist Muslims): after Bolshevik Revolution, 251–52; Bukhara and, 65n107, 71, 89; contradictory cultural impulses and, 161, 171, 174n62, 191n145; culture of cosmopolis and, 33; eclecticism of ulama knowledge and, 160; education of, 110n50, 113n64; Ottoman empire, interest in, 89; state/sovereign and ulama, relationship between, 219, 241
jafr (lettrism), 152–55. *See also* magic and the occult
Jahangir Majnun Irani, 90–91n84, 123–26, 151–52
Jami, 33n70
Jardine, Lisa, 110n50
Jews and Judaism, 35–39, 179n87, 181
jihad, rhetoric of, 229
jinn (genies), 147n93, 163, 165–70, 187, 253
Jizakh, 6, 77n13
Job (Abrahamic prophet), tomb of, Bukhara, 59–61, *61*, *62*, *63*
Jowzjan, 105
Jumanazar, 120n101
jung (scholar's notebooks), 15, 158–59, 169n35, 188n133, 226–28, 231–36, 237n80, 237n82, 245. *See also fatwa* texts
Juwayni, 43n3

Kabul. *See* Afghanistan
Kamp, Marianne, 250
Kant, Immanuel, 21
Karamatallah ibn Sabir-jan ibn Mirza Umid, 237–38
Karamustafa, Ahmet, 138n51
Karbala, 191, 199, 201
Kashgar, 4n4, 86–88, 96, 116n80
al-Kashgari, Mahmud, 33n71, 166n17
al-Kashgari, Muhyi al-Din bin Sabir, 87–88
Kaykawus, *Qabus-nama*, 24–25n28
Kazakhs, 6
Kazan, 71n133, 73, 85, 86, 96
Keller, Shoshanna, 248n3
Keneges, 29, 33, 97n110, 105n28, 209–10
Kerenskii, O., 50, 52n48
Khalid, Adeeb, 43n3, 219n8, 251–52n16
Khalifa Husayn, 134, 135
Khalifa Muhammad, 227–28
khanazir (goiter), 150
Khazeni, Arash, 214n86
Khiva, 6, 9, 10, 12, 44n7, 49n34, 50, 82–85, 96, 229–30
Khizr (mythological prophet), 63
Khoqand: Bukhara, as network center, 80–82, 84, 88n67, 96; Bukhara, mythologization of, 44n7, 50; distilleries in, 179n87; geopolitical backdrop, 6, 9, 10, 12; Ming dynasty in, 174n60; scholarly dynasties and, 202, 208n58, 211, 214n87; state/sovereign and ulama, relationship between, 227, 228nn44–45, 229; Turkic nobility and, 105

Khorezm: Bukhara, as network center, 75, 82–86; Bukhara, compared, 244; Bukhara, mythologization of, 45n14, 47; embassies in, 136n44; geopolitical backdrop, 3n3, 6, 7, 10; Khiva, war with, 229–30; oral traditional collected at shrines of, 250n9; public faces of ulama in, 142n68; state / sovereign and ulama, relationship between, 229–30, 232n62
Khotan, 66, 87, 112n59, 115
Khotani, Hajji Abdallah, 87
Khuday-berdi, 118, 119, 120–21
Khujand, 45, 81n29, 251n12
Khulm, 77–78, 93, 214n85
Khumuli, Juma-quli, 31–33, 38, 40, 173–74, 178, 192–93, 210n65, 239n87, 240
Khunji, Fazlallah ibn Ruzbihan, *Suluk al-muluk,* 223–26, 231, 232, 233
al-Khuqandi, Abd al-Isa, 80n25
Khurasan, 3n3, 6, 7, 9, 10n22, 57, 76–86, 105, 120, 140, 143n73, 178, 213, 246
khwaja, concept of, 134–35n35
Khwaja Ahrar, 227
Khwaja Ubaysallah Ahrar, 136
Kılıç-Schubel, Nurten, 39n96
knowledge base and authority of scholars, relationship between, 197, 216–17
Kok-Tash (Heavenly Stone), 210–11
Kokaltash madrasa, Bukhara, 52, 119
Kotkin, Stephen, 40n98
Kubrawiyya, 193n157
Kügelgen, Anke von, 199n13
Kuhistan, 6, 11, 53, 79n22, 81–86, 93, 95, 246
Kuhn, Alexander L., 99–100, 110n49, 114, 144
Kulab, 137, 172, 206–7, 213–16
Kunduz, 10n22, 76
Kuti Wali-khan Urguti, Hazrat Eshan, 133–34, 135

Lab-i Hawz, Bukhara, 104
Lahore, 64, 75, 76, 92, 95
Laknawi, Abd al-Hayy, 87
Lal, Mohan, 172
Langar Ata, 58n74
Lapidus, Ira, 129
Latypov, Alisher B., 176n73
law. *See* Sharia
legitimacy paradigm, 54
lettrism *(jafr),* 152–55
Levi, Scott, 107n33
Levinson, Sanford, 22n19
lineages, scholarly. *See* dynasties of Islamic scholars
Lucknow, 87n60, 92, 95
Lykoshin, N. S., 152–53, 154–56

maddahs, 122, 123–26, 151, 157, 175
madrasas. *See* education
Maev, N. A., 42, 183
magic and the occult: everyday supernatural, belief in, 162, 165–70; scholars as occultists, 153–58; Soviet suppression of, 255
Mahbubi family, 58–60
Mahdi Khwaja Biy, 102n17
Mahmud ibn Wali, 69
Mahmud Taj al-Shari'a, 58n76
Majma al-arqam, 143, 144n79
Malwana Kasani, 136
Mamluk Turkic literature, 31n56
Manghits: Bukhara, mythologization of, 48, 50–54, 55, 61–64, 72; geopolitics of, 9–10, 12; Iranian military personnel, reliance of, 90n81; scholarly dynasties and, 197, 198n9, 202n29, 206, 208; sovereign/ state and ulama, relationship between, 231; Soviet takeover and, 245; as Uzbeks, 105n28. *See also specific Manghit rulers*
al-Mansur (caliph), 218
Mardawij ibn Ziyar, 24
Marghinani, *al-Hidaya,* 114–15, 168, 182
Margilan, 81
Marjani, Shihab al-Din, 80n25, 84n48, 85n52
Mary (mother of Jesus), 192–93
Mashhad, 172, 199–200
Mashrab, 116n83
Masjid-i Kalan, Bukhara, 134
Maymana, 10n22, 76, 77n11, 105, 120, 139
mazalim, 231
McChesney, Robert, 90, 100n10, 200n15
medicine, practice of, 149–53
Mehrabadi, Mitra, 24n27
merchants and tradesmen, 98–99, 106–9
Merv, 9, 45, 46, 58n77, 90, 104–5, 181
Mir-i Arab, Bukhara, 49, 52, 119, 252, 253
Mir Malik, 140
Mir Siddiq Tore "Hishmat," Sayyid, 103–4
Mirza Baba Hisari, 136n44
Mirza Shah (Fa'iz), 108–9
Mirza Umid, 198, 199n14, 204n36
mirzas (clerks and scribes), 107, 141, 144–45, 149
Mizrab Biy ibn Rahib Biy, 78–79
moneylending at interest, 107n33

Mongol conquests and Mongol empire, 21n13, 47–48, 100, 220–21, 226
Morrison, Alexander, 102n16
mudarris (instructor), 78, 83, 107, 108, 120, 134, 141–43, 145, 149
muezzin, scholars as, 142
muftis (writers of legal opinions), 102, 107, 122, 134, 139, 141–43, 149, 169, 232, 233
Mughal empire, 7, 38n93, 72, 79, 88, 112
Muhammad al-Mubarak Lahuri, 113
Muhammad Ali (ruler of Khoqand), 227–28
Muhammad Alim Khwaja, 207
Muhammad Amin Hakim, 91n90, 151, 155
Muhammad Baqa Khwaja, 208n57
Muhammad Burhan "Qani," 139
Muhammad Hakim Khan, 198n9; *Muntakhab al-tawarikh,* 202, 203, 211n70
Muhammad Hisari, 15n47
Muhammad ibn Dawud, 47, 70
Muhammad Ibrahim of Khotan, 87, 116n80
Muhammad Ma'sum, 94
Muhammad Mutribi Samarqandi, 90n83
Muhammad Nasir, 58, 60, 63, 65
Muhammad Parsa Khwaja-i Salam, 89, 136, 208
Muhammad (Prophet): Bukhara's associations with, 56–57, 60n86, 64; *jinns* and, 168, 170
Muhammad Sharif, *Taj al-tawarikh,* 201–2, 203
Muhammad Sharif ibn Ata'allah Khwaja, 113, 121–22, 134–35, 253
Muhammad Siddiq, 205
Muhammad Tahir, 83
Muhammad Tahir Khwarazmi, 135–36
Muhammad Taqi (Mirza Muhammad Tihrani "Taqi Haft Qalam"), 90
Muhammad Yaqub Bukhari, 202n29
Muhibballah Bihari, *Sullam al-ulum,* 113
Muhtaram, Hajji Ni'matallah, 106–7, 133–35, 137, 141–44, 147, 149
muhtasibs (public morality enforcers), 107, 141–45, 149, 185–86, 189–90, 205–6, 214, 216, 224, 236
Mu'in al-Fuqara, *Risala-i Mulla-zada,* 43n3, 55, 57–60, 62, 63n97, 65, 69, 192
Mukhtar Makhdum "Afzah," 174–75
Mulla-zada, 80n23
Muminov, I. M., 219n5
al-Muqaddasi, Muhammad, 47n26
musallas (cooked wine), 181–82
Musayyab Bukhari, 204n37
Mutribi, 91n87
Muzaffar (amir), 53, 77, 101, 103, 134, 142, 149–50, 205, 207–8, 214

Nadir Shah Afshar: Eshan Imla debating Sunni-Shi'a split with, 178; fall of (1747), 1, 7, 8–9, 96; Hadi Khwaja and conversion to Sunnism, 198–204, 208; invasions of, 245; scholars, importance of support of, 217
Najaf, 105, 199, 200–202, 204n37, 205n38, 206
Naqshbandiyya-Mujaddidiyya, 83, 89n74, 92–95, 113n65, 132n22, 134n32, 135–37, 139–40, 193, 199, 205, 227
Narshakhi, *Tarikh-i Bukhara,* 46, 55, 56, 59, 65–69
Nasafi, Sayyidayi, 70
Nasir al-Din Tusi, 223
Nasrallah (amir), 10, 52, 96–97n110, 101, 136, 146, 150, 183n110, 210–11, 215, 227–28, 237–38
Navoi, Alisher, 26n37, 29n48, 31, 31n59, 33n70, 116n83, 124
Nawha, Muhammad Salih, 175, 180
Mulla Nazar, 186
Nazrallah ibn Mulla Mahmud, 144
Nestorians, 150–51
Ngom, Fallou, 26n36
Nimrod (Abrahamic figure), 69
Niyaz Ali Diwan-begi, 105
Nizam al-Din Husayni, 204, 209, 215
Nizami, Alexander Romance, 12, 68
Noah (Abrahamic figure), 69
nobility. *See* Turkic nobility
Novetzke, Christian, 169n37
Nur Muhammad Kulabi, 93, 137
Nur (poet and *mudarris*), 82n77
al-Nuri, Muhyi al-Din, 59n83

Obolensky, Dimitri, 21n10, 22n15
the occult. *See* magic and the occult
opium use, 163, 170–77
Orenburg Spiritual Assembly, 11
Ostroumov, N., 81n28
Ottoman empire: Ataturk and, 248; Bukhara and, 50, 74, 88–90, 95, 96; culture of cosmopolis and, 23; education in, 110n48, 111n53, 112, 116n82; geopolitics of, 7; Hanafi school of jurisprudence in, 188; as "little Persianate sphere," 88–90, 95, 96; Nadir Shah and, 200; ulama as branch of military elite in, 231n59
Ozbek Khan, 136n40

Pari, Muhammad Rajab Hisari, 147–48
pari (supernatural beings), 165–70. *See also* jinn
patricians, non-scholarly. *See* Turkic nobility
Persianate sphere: Bukhara, as "little Persianate sphere," 74, 75; epic literature of, 64–70; "little Persianate spheres" beyond orbit of Bukhara, 88–95; outer ring of "little Persianate sphere" of Bukhara, 82–88; Sovietization banishing Persianate aspect of Central Asian culture, 254–55. *See also* culture of Turko-Persian cosmopolis
physicians, 149–53
piesakhovka ("Jewish vodka"), 181–82
Pirmast, 6
poets, scholars as, 145–49, 214
political power. *See* state/sovereign and ulama; Turkic nobility
Pollock, Sheldon, 20–21, 22nn15–17, 23n20, 26, 30n54, 254n26
population of Central Asia, 4n4

Qadiriyya, 137, 158
Qajar Iran, 7, 10, 88, 89–91, 95–96, 141n67, 231, 234n72
qalandars (mendicant sufis), 108, 138–40, 157
al-Qarabaghi, Yusuf, 113
Qarakol, 78, 144, 216
Qaratigini, Mulla Muhammad Mir, 93
Qari Azim Bukhari Amlah, 144
Qari Mir Muhsin, 118
Qarshi, 6, 9, 45n12, 94n101, 150, 172, 207, 210, 212n79
Qasim, Muhammad, 87n61
Qasim Zhinda Makhdum, 139
Qatawan, 57
al-Qazani, Hamid Muhammad, 85
Qazi Abd al-Wahid Sadr Sarir Balkhi, 87n63
Qazi Abu Zayd Dabusi, 57
Qazi-Khwaja, Jami, 81
Qazi Mir Sayyid Qamar, 156
qazis (Islamic judges), 11, 37, 81, 92, 107, 111, 114, 122, 138, 141–43, 149, 158, 231–33, 236
al-Qazwini, Zakariya, 46n21
Qizilbash, 200, 201
Qom, 76, 91
al-Quduri, *al-Mukhtasar,* 171
al-Qursawi (Kursavi), Nasr al-Din, 147n91
Qutayba, 62–63, 64n95

Rafeq, Abdul-Karim, 91n86
Rahim Biy Manghit, 9, 198n9
Rahim Khan, 63n99, 202n29, 204–5n38, 215
Rahmatallah ibn Ata'allah Khwaja, 111n53, 152–53, 166–68, 205–6, 207
ra'is (public morality enforcer), 143, 144
Rampur, 95
Ranger, Terence, 71n131
Raz Muhammad Qandahari, 94–95
Rempel', L. I., 176
Risala-i Mulla-zada. See Mu'in al-Fuqara
Roberts, Flora, 251n12
Robinson, Francis, 197n3
Roman Empire, 221n18
romance, homoeroticism, and sexual panic, 162, 163, 171, 182–87
Rowson, Everett, 184n115, 185n117
Rudaki, 28
Rumi, *Masnawi,* 116n82, 123
Russia: Bolshevik Revolution (1919), 7, 17, 88n67, 212, 241–42, 248; Bukhara, subjugation of (1868), 11n26, 48, 52, 88, 206–7, 245; culture of Turko-Persian cosmopolis and, 19–20; geopolitics of region and, 6, 7, 10–12; historiographical landscape and, 13; on opium addiction, 171, 172, 173n52, 174, 175–76; Samarqand, subjugation of (1868), 6, 102; Sovietization, 242, 248, 249, 251, 254, 256; state/sovereign and ulama, effect on relationship between, 227, 241–42; Turkic nobility, effects on, 11, 241–42; on wine consumption in Central Asia, 180
Ruzi-quli Qalandar, 180

Sabir-jan, 207, 238
Sa'dallah (son of Muhammad Tahir), 83
Sa'di, 23, 124
Sadiq-jan "Kufri" "Kuydarakhti," 149
Sadr, Qazi Abd al-Wahid, 87
Sadr al-Din Khatlani, 214, 215
Safar-nama-i Hadi Khwaja, 202–3
Safavids, 79, 91n85, 111n53, 112, 177n77, 200, 201n25, 202, 221n15
Salih ibn Muhammad Qandahari Qa'ini, 152n113
Salman Samarqandi, 209, 211
Samanids, 46, 47, 65
Samarqand: Abd al-Hayy Khwaja, scholarly lineage of, 208–13; Bukhara, as network center, and, 76, 77, 80, 82, 83, 86, 94–95; Bukhara, mythologization of, 45–48, 50, 53, 57, 58n74, 59n79, 66, 67n112,

68n121, 69; geopolitical backdrop, 6, 10, 11; madrasas in, 1909 Russian report on, 110n49, 111n53, 112, 114n70; opium dens in, 175n64; Russian subjugation of (1868), 6, 102; Turkic nobility and, 100, 102, 110n49, 111n53, 112, 114n70
Samarqandi, Mutribi, 56n65
Saqi Muhammad Balkhi Sanchariki, 148–49, 214–15
Sartori, Paolo, 84n45, 241n94, 250nn8–9, 251–52n16
Sasanian culture and empire, 28–29, 37, 222–23n20, 223n22
Sayyid Alim Khwaja "Hatif," 113
Sayyid Ata, 135–36
Sayyid Khwaja Ruzybaev, 88
Sayyid Makhdum Bukhari "Nazmi," 175
Sayyid Qamar, 227, 228, 235
scholasticism, 110n50
Schuyler, Eugene, 186
Schwarz, Florian, 48n29
scripturalism, tolerance, and blasphemy/infidelity, 161, 162n3, 187–93
secular versus sacred, concept of, 23, 24, 26n43, 27n43, 220–21
self-fashioning, concept of, 164–65n10
sexual panic, homoeroticism, and romance, 162, 163, 171, 182–87
Imam Sha'bi, 57
Shah Ahmad Sa'id Faruqi, 137
Shah-Murad (amir), 9, 54n56, 63, 90, 93, 104–5, 204, 209–10, 234–35
Shah-nama. See Ferdowsi
Shahrisabz: Bukhara and, 45–46, 53, 58n74, 76, 84, 97n110; contradictory cultural impulses and, 181, 183; eclecticism of scholarly knowledge and, 143n71; geopolitics of, 6, 11; scholarly dynasties and, 208, 210, 212; state/sovereign and ulama, relationship between, 227, 229, 239; Turkic nobility and, 104, 105
Shams al-Din Damullam, 87n61
Shams al-Din Habiballah Janan-i Janan, 94
Sharafat Oy, 169
Shar'i, Abd al-Azim, 124, 125, 151–52
Sharia: *fiqh* texts, 156n133, 168, 188n133; government, conceptualization of, 222–26; intoxicating substances, relationship towards, 171–72, 179; scripturalism, tolerance, and blasphemy/infidelity, 161, 162n3, 187–93; study of law in madrasas, 111–12, 114–15. *See also* Hanafi school of jurisprudence
al-Shaybani, Muhammad ibn al-Hasan, 60
Sheba, Queen of (Bilqis), 192–93
Shibani Khan, 229n51
Shibanids, 7, 44, 48, 120
Shihab al-Din Marjani, 129, 147n91
Shihab al-Din Suhrawardi, 160
Shi'ism: Eshan Imla debating Sunni-Shi'a split with Nadir Shah, 178; Hadi Khwaja and conversion of Nadir Shah to Sunnism from, 198–204, 208; *jafr* in, 154n122; Ottoman empire, Nadir Shah's negotiations with, 200; in Qajar Iran and Bukhara, 90–91
al-Shirwani, Abdallah al-Daghestani, 86
shrines: Bukhara, relics, tombs, and shrines in, 48n28, 57–64, *61*, *62*; Khorezm, oral traditional collected at shrines of, 250n9; pilgrimages to, 191–92
Siraj al-Din, 154
Sirhindi, Ahmad, 93, 94, 137
Sogdiana and Sogdian culture, 13, 28, 31n56, 45nn12–13, 46, 65n105, 69, 70n128, 117n86, 166n17, 197n2
Sovietization of ulama, 242, 248–56
Spiritual Administration of the Muslims of Central Asia and Kazakhstan (SADUM), 253n23
Stalinabad/Dushanbe, 82n33, 255
state/sovereign and ulama, 218–42; ideal Islamic state versus *realpolitik,* 222–26; Islamic authority of prince, 224–25, 231–34; moral distance/independence of ulama from temporal power, 218–20, 222n20, 223, 226, 234–40; paradoxical nature of relationship, 218–22, 240–41; quietist interpretation of, 219–20; Russian conquests affecting, 227, 241–42; secular/religious contrast, not to be regarded as, 220–21; sufis and sufism, 230, 239; Turkic nobility and, 226–30, 237, 241–42
street preachers, 98–99
Subhan-quli Khan, 31n58, 214
Subtelny, Maria, 67n116, 71n133
Sufi Khwaja, 239–40
sufis and sufism, 130–41; in Bijapur, 129, 131n17; after Bolshevik revolution and Sovietization, 251, 252, 253, 255; concept of, 132n23; forty days in, 108n38; hagiographies of, 14–15; historiography of, 12; lodges of, in Bukhara, 49, 52; outer ring of "little Persianate sphere" of Bukhara and, 91–93, 95; *qalandars* (mendicant

sufis and sufism *(continued)*
sufis), 108, 138–40, 157; Safavids and, 91n85; shrine pilgrimages, 191–92; as social group, 2, 16; spiritual lineages in, 135–38; state / sovereign and ulama, relationship between, 230, 239; Sunni / Shi'a split and, 91; *tariqas* or brotherhoods, 130, 132–33, 135–37 (*see also specific tariqas*); *tasawwuf,* 130; training in / study of sufism, 79n21, 80n23, 83, 117–18; as ulama pursuit, 132–34; ulama-sufi binary, 130–32; viewed as alternative to extremism, 161; wine culture and, 178; *zikr* debate, 131
Sukhareva, O. A., 4n4
Sultan Khwaja Ahrari "Ada," 96–97n110
suluk (spiritual wayfaring), 130, 132, 133n25. *See also* sufis and sufism
Sunni: Eshan Imla debating Sunni-Shi'a split with Nadir Shah Afshar, 178; Hadi Khwaja and conversion of Nadir Shah to Sunnism, 198–204, 208; sufi communities in Central Asia oriented toward, 91

tabibs, 149–53
Taftazani, 111n53
Taj al-Din Balkhi "Aslam," 215
Tajikistan, 6, 14, 31n59, 81, 100, 249, 253n23, 254, 256
Tamerlane (Timur), 6, 61, 65n107
Tamkin, Abd al-Rahman, 60–61n90, 155
tanistry, 103
al-Tarazi, Mubashar, 251, 253
Tarim Basin, 6–7
tasawwuf (mystical philosophy), 130–31, 132–33. *See also* sufis and sufism
Tash Muhammad, 118
Tashkent, 4n4, 6, 10, 11, 60, 102, 116, 146, 154, 251, 252
Tashqurgani, Shah Abd al-Wahid, 93
Tatar language and literary culture, 85, 117n85, 147, 205n42
Tatar scholars, 80n25, 129, 171n41
Tatar students in Bukhara, 36n84, 49n36, 84, 85, 86, 95, 116
Tatarstan, 95–96, 148
tazkira, 14
Thum, Rian, 44–45n10
Timur Khan Bajuri, 94
Timur Shah, 9
Timur (Tamerlane), 6, 61, 65n107
Timurids, 6, 8, 29n48, 48, 57, 62n94, 144n80, 221n15, 227n43
Tirmizi, Mawlana Aman, 83
tradesmen and merchants, 98–99, 106–9
Turkestan: Bukhara, as network center, 81, 84n44, 86–88; Bukhara, mythologization of, 52n48, 53n52, 65, 66n110, 67n112, 68, 71; fanaticism attributed to mullahs of, 164; geopolitics of, 10–12; *muhtasibs* abolished in, 143; opium, wine, and revelry in, 171, 172n50, 186; scholarly dynasties in, 215; shrine pilgrimages in, 191; state / sovereign and ulama, relationship between, 11, 171n57, 219, 241, 242; Turkic nobility in, 102n16; ulama as judges in, 11, 174n57
Turkey. *See* Ottoman empire
Turkic nobility, 98–126; amir, proximity to, 101–2, 103; civil administrators, 99–103; dynasties of scholars and fortunes of, 196–97, 199, 208, 216–17; ethnicity, lineage, and identity, 29–34, 99, 100–101, 221n17; interdependence of scholarly elite and, 7–8, 196–97, 199, 208, 213, 216–17, 246–47; *maddahs,* 123–26; madrasa knowledge system and, 109–22, 126; merchants and tradesmen, status of, 98–99, 106–9; military elite, 98–99, 100, 196–98, 221; Russian conquests, effects of, 11, 241–42; scholars, nobles becoming, 103–6; state / sovereign and ulama, relationship between, 226–30, 237, 241–42; terms for, 8n12; ulama, commonalities with / differences from, 98–99, 102, 126, 221
Turkmen, 6, 33, 82–83n37, 90, 198n10
Turko-Persia, 8, 31n35

Ubaydallah Sadr al-Shari'a, 58n76
Ubaydallah (younger brother of Nasrallah Khan), 237, 238
udaychi, 101–2, 122
ulama. *See* Islamic scholars of Central Asia
ulamologies, 129
Ulugh Beg, 6
Umar (caliph), 63
Umar Khan, 96nn109–10, 141n67, 174n60, 183n110, 210–11
umara. See Turkic nobility
Umayyad caliphs, 28, 223n22, 231
Umayyad Mosque, Damascus, 62–63
Uratepa, 100n8, 174, 209
Urgench, 6n10, 82n37
Urgut, 76, 183n107
Usman A'lam Akhund, 87n61

Usman Beg Katib, 139
Usta Mirza, 189
Uthman (caliph), 63n97
Uyghur, 31n56, 33–34n73, 65, 87n65
Uzbekistan, 1, 14, 58, 248n3, 249, 250, 254n28, 256
Uzbeks and Uzbek, 29–30, 33, 34, 80, 81, 99, 100n9, 105, 226, 254

Vaissière, Étienne de la, 46n16
Venuti, Lawrence, 38n94
vernacular, concept of, 26, 84n45

Wabkand, 6
Wagoner, Phillip B., 23n23, 24n24
Wahhabism, 191
Wahshi, 139
waqfs (endowments), 50, 53, 54n56, 61, 78–79, 109n47, 134, 159, 162n3, 236–37, 249
Wazih, 107, 141–44, 149, 174, 181
Welsford, Thomas, 33n66
Wennberg, Franz, 60–61n90, 143n77
Whitmarsh, Tim, 221n18
Williams, Alan, 25n32
wine, spirits, and revelry, 161, 163, 175, 177–82, 186–87
women: Ata'allah Khwaja, wife of, and *jinn,* 165–67; co-educational primary schooling, 121–22; extramarital heterosexuality and, 185–86; female ulama in Central Asia, 39n96, 122; gender-ambiguous figure of the Beloved, 182–83; as prophets, 192–93; shrine visitation forbidden to, 192

Xinjiang, 75, 86, 88, 96
Xuanzang, 45–46

Yahya Khwaja, 83n37
Ya'kub Beg, 7
Yamaq Dad-khwah, 101
Yari, Abd al-Rahim Tarabi, 142
Yarkand, 86, 140
Yasawiyya, 132n22, 135
yasawul-i mahram, 101, 102
Yusuf, Mirza Muhammad, 182
Yuz, 100, 209

Zabiha, 35–40
al-Zamakhshari, 56n65
Zaman, Muhammad Qasim, 219n8
Zayir, Damulla Hasan, 81n29
Ziad, Waleed, 94n104
Ziya, Sadr-i: scholarly lineage of, 198, 203, 206, 207, 214–15, 216; *Tazkirat al-khattatin,* 148–49; *Zikr-i awa'il-i Bukhara,* 56–57, 59–60, 62, 65–69, 131
Ziya al-Din, 144, 146, 182
Zoroastrianism, 24–25, 35, 65, 68n121, 166n17
Zubaydallah, 237, 238
Zutshi, Chitralekha, 69n126